Food Chains

Hagley Perspectives on Business and Culture

Series Editors: Roger Horowitz, Philip Scranton, Susan Strasser

A complete list of books in the series is available from the publisher.

Food Chains

From Farmyard to Shopping Cart

Edited by Warren Belasco and
Roger Horowitz

PENN

University of Pennsylvania Press

Philadelphia

Published by
University of Pennsylvania Press
Philadelphia, Pennsylvania 19104-4112

Printed in the United States of America on acid-free paper

10 9 8 7 6 5 4 3 2 1

Library of Congress Cataloging-in-Publication Data
Food chains : from farmyard to shopping cart / edited by Warren Belasco and Roger Horowitz.
    p. cm. — (Hagley perspectives on business and culture)
    Includes bibliographical references and index.
    ISBN 978-0-8122-4128-0 (alk. paper)
    1. Food industry and trade. 2. Food supply. 3. Food consumption. 4. Food—Marketing. 5. Consumers' preferences. I. Belasco, Warren James. II. Horowitz, Roger. III. Title: From farmyard to shopping cart. IV. Series.
HD9000.5.F5938   2009
381'.41—dc22   2008021671

Contents

Chapter 1
Making Food Chains: The Book
Roger Horowitz

I begin my food-history classes by drawing a simple line on the blackboard with the word "farm" at one end and the word "dinner" at the other. Then I ask the students to explain some of the steps that are necessary for food to move from one end to the other. Within a few minutes the simple line is a complex tree bristling with stages such as "processing," "trucking," "scientific research," "retailing," and so on. When it starts to get too hard to read the board—which does not take long—I stop, to make the point of how complicated it is to bring food to our tables.

Many students in my classes come with prior interest in food; often spirited discussions break out about the merits (and demerits) of particular Food Network chefs. Some are looking for careers in nutrition, others work in restaurants, and a few even cook themselves. Yet most have little knowledge of the complex chain of firms and social practices that are necessary to make our provisioning system work, and they want to learn more.

A somewhat equivalent gap exists in the growing food-studies field. Among the steady outpouring of books much is written on the culinary and cultural dimensions of food and food consumption practices, along with an astonishing proliferation of books that combine recipes with eating philosophies. Studies that consider provisioning are growing in number but remain small in proportion. Yet there is considerable interest in histories of food that engage with larger patterns of social development, especially how we get the food that we eat.

These insights informed the discussions between Phil Scranton, Susan Strasser, Warren Belasco, and me as we started planning a conference on food history at the Hagley Museum and Library, in Wilmington, Delaware, in the fall of 2006. As the nation's leading business history library, Hagley has considerable resources for the study of food that we wanted to bring attention to scholars in the field. We hold one or two conferences on varying subjects each year; we felt it was time to do another one on food. A 1999 conference, "Food

Nations," had been a big success and was the foundation for a highly success-ful book in our Hagley Perspectives on Business and Culture book series. While "Food Nations" dealt with—as the name implies—food, identity, and social practice, we titled the 2006 conference "Food Chains" as we wanted it to focus on the provisioning systems that supply our world with food. We defined "pro-visioning" in the call for papers as "the complex institutional arrangements necessary for food to move from farm to the dinner table." To complement the conference's impact, we issued a guide to research materials at Hagley that can be used to study food history.

This volume includes all the essays presented at the conference plus two so-licited specifically for this publication. All are original, not previously pub-lished. The book's structure emulates that of food chains, starting with animals from which food comes, moving to the processing necessary to turn natural products into palatable items, and concluding with the process of sales through which consumers obtain their meals. Some chapters hone in on one item each—pigs, chickens, crabs, ice, ice cream, or shopping carts—to show its role in provisioning systems. Other essays look at industry segments—foods processed in imperial nations, dog food, or Mexican food—to elaborate on their internally complex "chains" of acquisition, manufacturing, and distribu-tion. A few consider places—kitchens or retail stores—where consumers make the decisions over what to buy and what to prepare for their families.

The opening "Overview" section contextualizes the volume's content through two synthetic essays. Warren Belasco surveys current literature in the food-studies field and suggests the contribution of taking food chains as an or-ganizing principle to understand food in our society. Shane Hamilton looks closely at theoretical work by historians and social scientists employing commodity-chain analysis. He assesses the value of taking a comprehensive approach to identify actors, technologies, forms of knowledge, and forms of capital in-volved in transforming a raw material into a consumable good.

The section "Animals" follows with essays that discuss pigs, chicken, and crabs. The authors all consider how the nature of consumer demand and food distribution influences the use, and at times the very character, of these animals.

J. L. Anderson charts how farmers and agricultural colleges changed the form of the American pig following World War II in order to satisfy changing consumer demand. He argues that these efforts revealed tension about health and diet within postwar society that was sufficiently powerful to fuel a massive effort to remake a species. As incomes rose and concerns about fat content in-creased, firms, farmers, and other actors in the industry (such as the federal government) altered the hog from an animal intended to supply fat to a "lean" version whose principal purpose was to provide meat.

Andrew Godley and Bridget Williams show how poultry became the most popular type of meat consumed in the United Kingdom after 1960. In contrast to the United States (where the USDA was so influential), the modern poultry industry emerged in the first thirty years after World War II in Britain because of the deliberate investments by a select group of leading food retailers, who needed to economize on the costs of meat distribution as they pioneered self-service stores. The widespread distribution of cheap chicken led to its mass adoption throughout the country.

Kelly Feltault sees the expansion of the imported crabmeat industry as emerging from the development of global supply chains for American seafood restaurants. She emphasizes that scarcity of Chesapeake Bay crabmeat was not a factor in the efforts of large seafood firms to expand production in Thailand. The adoption of domestic quality standards known as HACCP regulations facilitated production and importation of Asian crabmeat into the American restaurant market. Expansion of the crab industry also intersected with Thailand's export-oriented development strategy.

All food has to move from producers to consumers in a market economy, a complex process that requires processing—in complex ways—of raw ingredients in which transportation, processing, and preservation are critical. The chapters in the "Processing" section consider such transitions, both the transformation of the foods that can take place and the complex matrix of production needs and consumer preferences that influence the firms engaged in such activities.

Richard Wilk considers how extended food chains create settings where the cultural significance of products can change as they are moved from place to place. He argues that the transformations that goods go through as they move along industrial commodity chains are just as significant as the conversion of cultural property into commodities such as "tribal" art, music, and traditional medicine. Wilk illustrates his argument by showing how raw foodstuffs from nineteenth-century colonized nations were transformed in substance and meaning when they were moved through trade networks, especially when goods were processed and packaged in imperial nations such as Britain to create genteel "civilized" food.

Jonathan Rees explores the unique character of ice in the late nineteenth-century United States, as it was both part of the food provisioning system and food itself. He adeptly shows that not all ice was the same. Natural ice, cut from lakes and rivers, varied considerably in quality. It could be a factor in food preservation when packed into railroad cars or grocers' freezers, as well as a consumer good when sold for use in home iceboxes or drinks. Rees shows how consumer concerns about the purity of the ice that came in contact with food bedeviled the natural ice industry.

Katherine C. Grier uncovers the roots of the American pet-food business that currently attracts annual expenditures of $18 billion. Curiously, it was a product that nobody really needed; certainly dogs and cats did not demand it. Grier identifies the development of pet food, then, in the way it met human needs in the American provisioning system. Pet food absorbed surpluses among producers of human food, and the decline of urban kitchens as sites for processing of raw materials left fewer table scraps for pets to eat. Pet food succeeded as it satisfied the needs of humans at several places along the provisioning axis.

Jenny Leigh Smith tells a fascinating story of how Joseph Stalin and his successors put the resources of the Soviet state behind the development of a national system of ice cream production and distribution. Soviet citizens could easily purchase ice cream from local vendors, unlike the many obstacles they encountered when buying other kinds of food or consumer goods. Smith sees two main factors explaining this curious paradox. First, the Soviet government wanted to create a cheap luxury product for citizens to counteract the social problems it faced with so much material scarcity. Second, it was easier for the command economy to distribute a frozen good such as ice cream than the more perishable ingredients that composed it, especially milk.

Jeffrey M. Pilcher unravels how Mexican food spread internationally. He focuses on the development of an infrastructure necessary to supply Mexican ingredients to restaurants and home cooks throughout the world. Globalizing Mexican food required basic structural transformations in the traditional labor-intensive nature of this cuisine. To supply such food profitably demanded considerable economies of scale, thereby hindering the competitive efforts of Mexican firms whose advantage lay in local knowledge and advantaging large American-based companies. As a result, Pilcher contends, Mexican food that has been globalized has been in its Americanized form.

Food exists to be consumed, so the next section considers the selling of food to men, women, and children for them to eat. The emergence of particular retail food stores and restaurants depended on changes in the production and distribution of products as well as patterns of consumer demand. We fittingly close this section—and the book—with a chapter on the shopping cart, so necessary for consumers to take their purchases from stores, leaving all other stages of the food chain behind.

Lisa C. Tolbert explains the attraction of self-service retail stores among white women in the early twentieth-century South by focusing on the Piggly Wiggly chain. Southern white women often preferred to call in their orders to stores as there were many challenges to respectability in public retail space. Tolbert shows how grocers strategically used the concept of self-service to transform the cultural message of the southern grocery store and food shopping. Piggly Wiggly created store interiors and advertising campaigns that successfully recast the cultural role of the grocery store as an emblem of modernity and food shopping as an appropriate activity for white southern ladies.

Patrick Hyder Patterson details the transformation of food retailing in Eastern Europe following World War II. He shows that by 1975 relatively prosperous Communist countries such as Hungary and Yugoslavia had markedly improved food production and distribution methods. At the retail end of the food chain, modern self-serve grocery stores paralleled the Western focus on consumer-oriented and well-stocked food emporiums. They were, however, state-owned stores wedded to a discourse of "socialist commerce." Nonetheless they shared much of the theory, styles, and practices of privately owned Western supermarkets—and were able to deliver abundant food to their customers.

Katherine Leonard Turner identifies the choices facing working-class families in the late nineteenth and early twentieth centuries between cooking food and obtaining ready-to-eat food. Kitchen appliances, home sizes, and availability of space to grow food or harbor animals varied widely from city to city and influenced the calculations of housekeepers regarding whether to prepare or buy food for consumption by their families. Especially in the case of baker's bread she shows that locally prepared food did not entirely replace home cooking but provided an important supplement, thereby altering the nature of food preparation in the working-class home.

Catherine Grandclément sketches the technological and mythical processes of creating the supermarket shopping cart. Self-serve food stores needed a reliable means to prevent the weight of goods from determining how much shoppers would purchase to bring home. Yet the development of the proper vehicle was complex as it had to satisfy the customer and also address the needs of the retailer. Grandclément also shows that the traditional "creation myth" of the shopping cart elevated one inventor (Sylvan Goldman) above other claimants, when in fact the invention process was marked by simultaneous innovations all intended to meet the same shopping challenges.

We hope that readers will leave this volume with a richer understanding of the complex arrangements that bring food to our tables. Making this book also required complex relationships, and many thanks go to the Hagley Museum and Library staff, especially Carol Lockman, for their role in organizing the 2006 "Food Chains" conference. Commentators at that conference, including Shane Hamilton, Tracey Deutsch, Phil Scranton, Warren Belasco, and me, commenced the process of turning papers into chapters. Editor Robert Lockhart at the University of Pennsylvania Press expertly brought the book through the editorial review and subsequent manuscript preparation process. It is for me always a pleasure to play a role throughout the complex chain between imagining a book and seeing it finally appear in print.

Part I
Overview

Chapter 2
How Much Depends on Dinner?

Warren Belasco

The science-fiction writer Robert Heinlein is credited with popularizing the saying "There ain't no such thing as a free lunch" in his 1966 novel, *The Moon Is a Harsh Mistress*. Or maybe credit should go to Barry Commoner, whose fourth "Law of Ecology" (1971) said about the same thing, albeit more grammatically.[1] Either way, the context was the late 1960s, when Americans were beginning to confront the environmental costs of their consumer economy. However, the "no free lunch" axiom dates at least as far back as the nineteenth century, when American saloons offered complimentary food as a way to lure workers who either paid for their meals by buying drinks (with all the added social costs of drunkenness) or were "bounced" as "free-lunch fiends" and "loafers."[2] Going back much further to mythical times, the principle applies even to our primordial meals. Think about this much-quoted passage from Lord Byron's epic poem "Don Juan" (1823), which directly links "dinner" and "sinner":

> All human history attests
> That happiness for man—
> The hungry sinner—
> Since Eve ate apples,
> Much depends on dinner!

So how much depends on dinner? Well, in Genesis at least, quite a lot—both before that primordial snack and afterward in the fateful consequences. As for the events upstream leading to the bite of the forbidden fruit, we might start with the six days of heavy lifting that it took God to establish the orchard. Then, in probing Eve's decision, we can cite motivations that often drive culinary experimentation—curiosity, boredom, hubris, ambition, sexual frustration, serpentine salesmanship, and so on. For the sad downstream aftereffects of Eve eating apples, Genesis suggests shame, pain, sweat, difficult childbirth, spousal abuse, the brutalization of animals, along with assorted bruised heals, dust, thorns, and thistles—the primal ecological and economic catastrophe.

In the classical Greek version of the "no free lunch" principle, Prometheus pities shivering, starving humanity and steals fire from his less compassionate boss, Zeus. Humans learn to cook meat and to forge metal; with that technological breakthrough, they proceed to conquer the earth. However, in punishment for his hubris, Prometheus is chained to a rock, where he is doomed to have his liver eaten daily by an eagle. In a rather literalist interpretation of the story, the vegetarian poet Percy Bysshe Shelley (1813) speculated that Prometheus's "vitals were devoured by the vulture of disease." Adding in the ecological costs of feeding grass and grains to animals, Shelley went on to blast the meat eater who would "destroy his constitution by devouring an acre at a meal. . . . The quantity of nutritious vegetable matter, consumed in fattening the carcass of an ox, would afford ten times the sustenance . . . if gathered immediately from the bosom of the earth." Such feed-conversion calculations were already a familiar part of vegetarian analysis a full two hundred years before Frances Moore Lappe's *Diet for a Small Planet* (1971), which educated many baby boomers about the external costs of a meat-based diet.[3]

The reality-based wisdom of "no free lunch" may well be universal, as it is possible to find stories of Promethean innovation (cooking) and punishment (the ravaged liver) in many cultures. For example, in some Native American versions, the people (humanity) steal fire to cook and to warm themselves; but with their new technological edge come dire consequences, including forest fires, rain, and mosquitoes. In one Polynesian tale the mischievous superhero Maui (Prometheus's Pacific counterpart) steals cooking fire from the underworld, but as he escapes to the surface the angry flames follow him, producing the first volcano. Claude Fischler detects more than a residue of such mythical thinking in an analysis of the recent European panic over bovine spongiform encephalopathy (BSE)—thought to be exacerbated by the thoroughly modern practice of feeding animal residues to animals. "The mad cow epidemic is perceived as punishment for some human misbehavior that caused it in the first place by attracting some sort of a sanction, the most common description of this behavior being the conversion of herbivores into carnivores or even into cannibals."[4]

Connoisseurs of catastrophic thought might also relish this compelling reminder of eating's unforeseen consequences from *The Road to Survival*, a 1948 jeremiad by William Vogt, an ornithologist turned environment crusader: "We are paying for the foolishness of yesterday while we shape our own tomorrow. Today's white bread may force a break in the levees and flood New Orleans next spring. This year's wheat from Australia's eroding slopes may flare into a Japanese war three decades hence. . . . We must develop our sense of time and think of the availability of beefsteaks not only for this Saturday but for the Saturdays of our old age, and of our children."[5] Taking such a long view of the future obviously entails taking a long view of the past—that chain of events that brought food to our tables. Eden's pomaceous food chain was blessedly short, a localvore's delight: God–tree–Eve. Thinking about what it takes to assemble dinner nowadays, however, it is a miracle that anyone ever gets fed. Multiply this by billions of meals a day and you have more miracles than any one religion can handle. Yet, this extraordinary food chain is taken for granted, and has been for many years, thanks in part to the efforts of the corporate deities who supply our modern, genetically enhanced apples so quietly, out of sight, mind, and sensibility.

The global supermarket has been open for business for quite a long time. In 1919 the geographer J. Russell Smith marveled at the dependence of a typical Massachusetts consumer on distant sources:

The man of today starts his breakfast with an orange from California or Florida, or a banana from Central America, or an apple from Oregon, Virginia, or New York. He takes a shredded wheat biscuit made in Niagara Falls with Dakota wheat. He sugars it with the extract of Cuban cane. He puts Wisconsin butter on bread baked of Minneapolis wheat flour mixed with Illinois corn flour. He has a potato. In June it comes from Virginia, in July from New Jersey, in November from New York, Maine, or Michigan. If he indulges in meat, it is a lamb chop from a frisky little beast born on the high plains near the Rocky Mountains, and fattened in an Illinois feed lot before going up to Chicago to be inspected, slaughtered, and refrigerated. He warms and wakes himself up with a cup of coffee from Brazil (called Mocha perhaps) or tea from Ceylon or Japan, or cocoa from Ecuador or the coast of Guinea.[6]

Smith actually welcomed such dependence, for as a consummate free-trader, he believed that international exchanges would strengthen human bonds. However, while liberal economists have idolized world trade, critics have decried the "delocalization" that can be found wherever, in pursuit of more food, one people invade, colonize, or otherwise dominate another.[7] Making offers that could not be refused, to paraphrase *The Godfather*'s Don Corleone, imperialists muscled tasty options for Western consumers. As one British economist boasted in 1865: "The plains of North America and Russia are our cornfields, Chicago and Odessa our granaries; Canada and the Baltic our timber forests; Australia contains our sheep farms, and in South America are our herds of oxen; the Chinese grow tea for us, and our coffee, sugar, and spice plantations are all in the Indies."[8] The use of the royal "our" was deliberate, for in the terms of trade set by these "empires of food," the benefits flowed to the metropolitan centers in Europe, while the human costs stayed outsourced.[9] This moral distance between consumers and the nasty factors of food production especially angered the crop geneticist Edward East, whose book *Mankind at the Crossroads*—a warning about overpopulation and overconsumption—was the talk of the nation in 1924. East wrote: "Today one sits down to breakfast, spreads out a napkin of Irish linen, opens the meal with a banana from Central America, follows with a cereal of Minnesota sweetened with the product of

Cuban cane, and ends with a Montana lamb chop and a cup of Brazilian coffee. Our daily life is a trip around the world, yet the wonder of it gives us not a single thrill. We are oblivious."[10]

Of course, this obliviousness goes back way before 1924. A 1701 report on one of the earliest multinational food conglomerates, the East India Company, observed, "We taste the spices of Arabia yet never feel the scorching sun which brings them forth." The global food chain was already quite extensive by 1701—to the point that affluent English consumers could be indifferent to the costs of sweetening their tea and peppering their sausage. Such costs extended far beyond the skin burnt by the "scorching sun" of exotic foreign lands ("Arabia"). Historians of the spice trade can tally up an impressive bill, including the conquest of continents, the enslavement of nations, nasty warfare among the Eurasian powers that controlled the business, and burgeoning opportunities for pirates. Adding up the blood shed to stock our larders with coveted aromatics, Andrew Dalby concludes, "spices are truly a dangerous taste."[11]

An excellent primer in such perils can be found in the environmental educator David Orr's essay "Costs of the U.S. Food System," which starts with this pivotal quote from Thoreau's *Walden* (1854): "The cost of a thing is the amount of what I will call life which is required to be exchanged for it, immediately or in the long run." Pursuing Thoreau's search for an honest reckoning of the consumer's obligations to those who supply him, Orr differentiates "costs" from "prices." Prices are what we pay at the checkout counter, and they are just the start when it comes to the accounting; "costs," he writes, include "1) things of value that cannot be measured in numbers; 2) things that *could* be measured but that we choose to ignore; and 3) the loss of things that we did not know to be important until they were gone."[12] Economists do mention such "externalities," though they sometimes dismiss these costs as issues of subjective morality, and thus external to the things economists like to talk about, especially prices.

A more expansive cost-accounting has gained much traction in recent years, as witnessed in the rise of the sustainable food movement, the Sierra Club's "True Cost of Food" campaign, lively debates about "ecological footprints" and "food miles," and the popular success of books such as Eric Schlosser's *Fast Food Nation* and Michael Pollan's *Omnivore's Dilemma*, the latter the focus of a full term of campuswide events at the University of California, Davis, whose agriculture and food science programs have played no small part in the development of the corporate food chain. That "everything is connected to everything else"—Barry Commoner's first "law of ecology"—is now a respectable tenet of "responsible consumption," as well as of "green" food production and marketing. For example, the Whole Foods corporate Web site features a "Declaration of Interdependence" explicitly linking "environmental stewardship" with the welfare of "stakeholders," which include customers, local neighbors, "team members" (employees), "business associates" (suppliers), and, of course, investors.[13]

Can we push the analysis a little further? We may know that everything is connected, but do we know how those connections actually work, or how they got so connected in the first place? That is where this book comes in.

Before getting to these case studies on how we came to be so interdependent, distanced, and oblivious, it might be useful to ponder our title, "food chains." What does this mean anyway? Even a brief survey of the dictionary reveals that the term "food chain" is richer than we might have thought—but also very vague.

First, there is the scientific meaning, which actually does not get us very far. An introductory biology Web site suggests that "in a food chain energy is passed from one link to another," from sun to plant to animal. In each transfer along the chain, some of the energy is lost, so that by the time you get to the fourth one—say, the human who ate the chicken who ate the bug who ate the leaf—the energy is pretty much dissipated. Hence: "Most food chains have no more than four or five links." In addition, since we generally cannot rely on just one chain to provide all the food we need, we depend on many such chains, which constitute *a food web*.[14]

However, even the notion of a web may not help much in understanding the complex transnational provisioning systems we are discussing here. For one thing, humankind has figured out numerous ingenious ways to supplement the solar power lost along the biological food chain with other energy supplies, mostly fossilized and nonrenewable. Indeed, as every reader of *Diet for a Small Planet* already knows, we spend far more energy greasing our chains, so to speak, than we ultimately derive from the McNugget at the end. So biology alone does not help us much—except to nag us with disturbing questions such as what happens when the fossil fuels run out or when the corn plants become too compromised by climate change to convert solar energy to human food?

Even if the food chain concept has limited scientific relevance here, it does serve us well as a metaphor—a useful conceptual tool for trying to understand the scope and implications of how we get our dinner. Indeed, as a metaphor, the assorted meanings of "chain" offer quite a decent template for studying food systems. For example, most obviously, there are *chain stores* and *restaurants*—elaborate institutional arrangements designed to maximize convenience, economies of scale, and profits while minimizing interactions, competition, and consumer consciousness. Along these lines, the thesaurus lists syndicates, cartels, combines, conglomerates, and trusts as worthy synonyms for chains.

For labor and business studies, there are chains as in bondage—the steely shackles that bind farmers to bugs and weather, workers to bosses, manufacturers to consumers. Closely related are *chain gangs* and *chains of command*. Studying these chains means examining the many orders, obligations, and restraints that move food from field to fork.

For students of sociological distinction, status, and stratification, there are the chains in fences: tools and institutions that divide insiders and outsiders, the privileged and the disposed. Such chain-link fences determine who gets dinner and who does not. Here we might consider issues of class, food security, and obesity.

For ecologists, there are *chain reactions*: the downstream, domino effects of seemingly innocuous actions, such as the piece of toast in Minneapolis that breaks the levees in New Orleans. Peering upstream, there are *genetic chains*, the tiny strands that archive the results of the millions of breeding experiments that produced the tasty ingredients in today's dinner.

For psychologists of consumption, there are *chain smokers*: people addicted to repetitive, compulsive, potentially self-destructive behavior. Along the same lines, there is Aretha Franklin's *chain of fools*—people who get hooked by the cruel seducers but who vow to break the links one day and move on. Chains can bind us, but as Franklin notes, they also have weak links.

For moralists such as Oberlin's David Orr or David Brower, the late environmental activist, there is our unsustainably speculative "*chain letter economy*, in which we pick up early handsome dividends and our children find their mailboxes empty."[15] To what extent is the current food system an elaborate Ponzi scheme, a speculative bubble or pyramid in which, for the sake of low prices and high fat, we are squandering our children's inheritance?

Pondering how we became so entangled in these chains inevitably leads to thoughts about the future. Consider two very different scenarios.

One future, obviously favored by the mainstream food industry, is a continued expansion and rationalization of corporate food chains or webs or nets—the global supermarket supported by industrial agriculture, biotechnology, cheap fossil fuels, hypermarketing, neocolonial politics, and government subsidies. This system has served those in more affluent countries pretty well so far, to the extent that we are indeed fed quite marvelously. Some scenarios do sound suitably miraculous, as in the following predictions from the techno-utopian book *2025*, written ten years ago by the staff of the Washington-based futurist consulting firm Coates and Jarrett.

In *2025* the people in privileged World 1 (us) enjoy "unprecedented choice." True, few people actually cook, as the "tunable microwave," "automated pantry," and "robot chef" do most kitchen drudgery, but menus vary enormously. "In the past five years [2020–25], we have seen the popularity of rainforest fruits, vegetable stews, Hausa shakes (milk and papaya or mango), and for the adventurous, spit-grilled iguana imported from Costa Rica and Mexico." Popular "walkaway foods" include tropical fruit sticks, hydroponic banana pears, and "Andean spiced dumplings." In a "typical food day" for a U.S. family in 2025, Mom, age thirty-seven, enjoys a "well-cooked and tasty" microwaved "California-style lunch" on her supersonic flight to London and that evening dines on a ploughman's platter from the pub down the street from her hotel. Dad, thirty-nine, a surgeon, grabs a multivitamin fruitshake from a machine for breakfast, lunches on a McDonald's chicken sandwich (from a fully automated Model H-13 unit), and dines with his children at a Taste of America theme restaurant, where his Polynesian-style meal consists of parrot-fish (fed Milwaukee brewery wastes in underground tanks), roasted taro, and coconut milk. His son, eleven, has Fruit Rockets cereal and pizza sticks earlier in the day and at dinner opts for "rainforest food," including tapir cutlet with cassava. His daughter, eight, selects waffles with passion fruit syrup for break-fast and Austrian food for dinner. Grandma, age seventy, prepares a blueberry muffin in her Cuisintech for breakfast, lunches on angelfish over salad greens at the senior center, and chooses open-ocean tuna, Inuit-style, with tundra greens for dinner. The Taste of America unit uses "robotic assistance and frozen and vacuum-packaged prepared entrees" and just six employees to serve over 312 different entrees.[16] What is especially ingenious about this ver-sion is that, even as high-tech as it sounds, it also attempts to address and co-opt our nostalgia for the more traditional, ethnic-sounding foods—the "slow" foods of the much shorter biological food chain, yet without the austerity and inconvenience.

This leads to an opposing future scenario, the relocalized, energy-conserving provisioning system of the biological food chain. This is not so much the utopian peasant commissary envisioned by Slow Food and Alice Waters, but rather the nightmare, devolutionary future of much recent dystopian fiction—the scary worlds of Octavia Butler, Starhawk, and T. C. Boyle,[17] in which the fossil fuels have run out, the earth is much hotter, the soil is blowing away, the forests are gone, the spring is truly silent, central institutions have broken down, the rich wall themselves off in new turreted communities, and it is pretty much everyone else for himself. In Coates and Jarrett's *2025*, this is the future for World 3, the "Malthusian" section of the world, mostly Africa, that would "strike a hard line of endless, endemic famine"—only for Butler and company it extends to California, Colorado, and Delaware as well.

To return to that 1701 quote about the East India Company, in this future we no longer will have our multinationals to provide the spices of Arabia, and yet we will be feeling the scorching sun nevertheless. To be sure, this is an ex-treme and can be averted, but only if we keep toting up the "true costs" of our meals—Thoreau's amount of life exchanged in the long run. And that is why we are here.

Chapter 3
Analyzing Commodity Chains: Linkages or Restraints?

Shane Hamilton

"Eating," writes the modern-day agrarian intellectual Wendell Berry, "is an agricultural act." An eloquent defender of the ecological and social benefits of small-scale farming, Berry is disturbed by the distancing of food consumers from farm producers in industrialized agriculture. Food, according to Berry, has become "pretty much an abstract idea—something [urban consumers] do not know or imagine—until it appears on the grocery shelf or on the table."[1] The increasing distance from farm to fork and the complexity of the industrial food chain have led to what the writer Michael Pollan, following the sociologist Claude Fischler, labels the "omnivore's dilemma."[2] In a world in which affluent consumers can eat almost anything at all—whether it be Chilean grapes in North America in midwinter or grass-fed beef served in a Manhattan steakhouse—we are confronted with a constant sense of unease about what exactly we are eating, where it came from, and what the implications of our diet choices are. Fears of contamination—from "mad cow" disease to organic spinach tainted with *E. coli*—only heighten the urgency of these questions. The fact that Pollan's book has spent more than two years on the *New York Times* best-seller list to date indicates that quite a few modern consumers want to know more about what happens to their food before it appears on the grocery shelf.

If eating is an agricultural act, however, it is also an act of intensive commodification in modern societies dependent on industrialized agriculture for their foodstuffs. A supermarket consumer's choice of what to eat is articulated through a vast chain of individuals and organizations woven together by technological networks—from farmers to processors to scientific researchers to wholesalers to retailers to government regulators to truck drivers to supermarket employees to consumers, and so on. The chains through which raw agricultural products become saleable foods are built upon economic structures and technological systems, but they are continually shaped and reshaped by business and political decisions and by shifting cultural patterns of diet, agrarian ideology, environmental concern, and scientific knowledge. Eating, then, is an act of extraordinary consequence—not only for agriculture but also for entire edifices of modern capitalism.

Although such issues have only recently gained much attention in the popular press, they have been carefully studied for quite some time by scholars. Since the early 1980s sociologists, anthropologists, and geographers have produced a substantial body of literature examining the nature of commodity chains in modern food systems. Commodity chains analysis—the subject of this literature review—seeks to identify and illuminate the individuals, institutions, technologies, forms of knowledge, and forms of capital involved in transforming raw agricultural products into consumable foods. All of the essays in the present volume are either explicitly or implicitly in conversation with this literature, and yet much of the work remains unknown or unfamiliar to scholars in historical food studies. In the pages that follow, then, I offer an introductory (and by no means comprehensive) review of the genesis, advantages, and disadvantages of commodity chains analysis. As a rough guide to a complex and dynamic field, this essay aims especially to reach historians and other scholars interested in interdisciplinary approaches to food through the lenses of political economy of agriculture, science and technology, and globalization.

The rural sociologist William H. Friedland generally receives credit for establishing commodity systems analysis. After writing extensively on mechanized tomato and iceberg-lettuce harvesting, Friedland conceived of commodity systems analysis as a means of invigorating rural sociology.[3] By the early 1980s, according to Friedland, rural sociologists were so focused on issues of rural identity that they had become estranged from their original interest in the material and social worlds of agricultural producers.[4] Rectifying the oversight, Friedland argued, required sociologists to pay careful attention to the commodity systems that structured rural peoples' lives and livelihoods. These systems, according to Friedland, were composed of five interlinked components: production practices in modern agriculture, grower organizations, labor supply and labor practices, scientific research in agriculture, and marketing and distribution beyond the farm gate. Taking such a systemic, empirical approach to the study of food production and consumption, Friedland hoped, would boost the relevancy of rural sociology in an era of rapidly declining rural populations. By the mid-1990s Friedland's call to arms was effectively answered, as important articles and books on commodity systems and food chains appeared.[5]

Revivification of the political economy of agriculture was one immediate advantage of the commodity systems approach. Sociologists, anthropologists, and geographers brought new insights to the century-old "agrarian question" that had bedeviled Friedrich Engels, Karl Marx, Karl Kautsky, and Vladimir Lenin. In its original guise, the "agrarian question" dealt with an essential theoretical question: would industrial capitalism subsume the rural peasantry, or would the reactionary politics of small farmers attached to landownership present obstacles to the awaited socialist revolution? With the emergence of new approaches to political economy in the 1980s, the "agrarian question" could be reframed to encompass farmers' political and economic place within a much broader conception of industrial capitalism.[6] Studying agriculture systemically—from labor practices on the farm to marketing practices in and beyond the supermarket—cleared the path for fresh approaches to the power relations embedded in rural societies. Rather than rehash arguments about the peasant's relationship to industrialization and the proletariat, students of political economy began to probe the relations of farmers large and small to workers, manufacturers, bankers, processors, distributors, marketers, consumers, the state, and the environment—all within highly industrialized capitalist economies.[7]

The possibilities of commodity systems analysis appealed to more than just rural sociologists. Within geography, for instance, Margaret FitzSimmons relied on commodity systems concepts to initiate a discussion of the differences and similarities between industrial agriculture and industrial manufacturing. The anthropologist Sidney Mintz and the economic geographers Brian Page and Richard Walker, among others, have extended this analysis to argue that, rather than forming a barrier to the development of industrial capitalism, agriculture and food production have historically been prime drivers of industrialization.[8] On the other hand, the consumption theorist Ben Fine sparked controversy with a 1994 article declaring that agriculture and industry are inherently distinct, as the production and consumption of food involve a "crucial significance of organic factors" at either end of the commodity chain; farming is based on the manipulation of organic matter, and food tends to spoil, so biology presents insurmountable barriers to full industrial commodification of the food chain. Rather than debate the similarities of agriculture with industry, Fine declares, scholars should focus on the role of consumption in shaping the political economy of food. Rather than use the phrase "commodity systems," Fine suggests that scholars use his own terminology, "systems of provisioning." Most controversially, Fine "decisively rejects" the commodity systems approach for focusing on the production end of the food chain, since, according to Fine, what happens on the farm is dictated by business and consumption decisions "further, possibly much further, along the food chain."[9] Theoretical and empirical approaches to the political economy of agriculture have, in short, moved far beyond the "agrarian question" of the late nineteenth century; no longer do we assume that rural farmers will either be subsumed or swept aside by capitalist development. The "agrarian question" has been replaced, as the sociologist Philip McMichael has put it, by " 'food' and 'green' questions."[10] As modern consumers legitimately become more aware and more concerned about how their foods are produced and delivered, the food systems approach offers opportunities for agricultural historians to deepen their analyses and broaden the appeal of their work.[11]

By reframing the "agrarian question" as a matter not so much of peasants and proletarians as one of consumer foodways and agricultural landscapes, commodity chains analysis furthermore helps to shed light on the role of science and technology in the political economy of agriculture. A cornerstone of the commodity systems approach is understanding how new machines and systematic forms of knowledge shape the relationships between farm producers, agribusiness firms, government and educational institutions, consumers, and the natural world. In demanding that farmers turn away from traditional practices tied to local ecological and market conditions and toward modern technoscientific agriculture, agencies from the U.S. Department of Agriculture to the Rockefeller Foundation to Archer Daniels Midland have reconstructed the lives and landscapes of rural peoples across the globe—as historians, geographers, political scientists, sociologists, and anthropologists have recently shown in important works.[12] Transforming chickens from cage-free, cricket-eating egg layers into meat-producing, cellophane-ready biomachines required half a century's worth of technological innovation and scientific research.[13] Frozen foods, bananas, beef, and—disquietingly—even *organic* produce, arrive in consumers' refrigerators only after passing through vast systems of complex machinery deployed by engineers, scientists, and business owners to deliver "fresh" produce and meat over thousands of miles.[14] Biotechnologies promise to allow farmers to grow tomatoes with infinite shelf lives or to boost corn production with less pesticide spraying or to, in the horrific vision of the antibiotech activist Jeremy Rifkin, "raise" tubes of pure chicken breast in laboratories without the annoyance of unprofitable feathers, legs, and wings.[15] As of this writing, the industrial chicken continues to have feathers (albeit all-white and easy to remove), legs (albeit short and barely strong enough to support the bird's meaty breast), and wings (albeit clipped). Nonetheless, scientific researchers at land-grant universities and at processing-firm laboratories have begun to transform the genetic materials of modern food chains in ways that, as European consumer activists have declared, bring to mind the frightful experiments of Dr. Frankenstein.[16]

Given the salience of science and technology in the modern food chain, some scholars have reworked commodity systems analysis in order to understand what they call "food networks." Mainly based in European universities, these scholars deploy the terminology and methodology of actor-network theory (ANT), first developed within science and technology studies as a way to "follow scientists and engineers through society."[17] Among the most important concepts developed by actor-network theorists is the idea that nonhuman lifeforms as well as inanimate technological artifacts can, and do, shape human social relationships and forms of knowledge.[18] Within food studies, this means that even the lowly rapeseed must be treated as a partner—however unequal in power or intentionality with scientists, farmers, and processors—in the construction of a profitable global industry. If, in the lingo of ANT, the rapeseed cannot be successfully "enrolled" by a "mobilized" technoscientific network as a knowable, harvestable, and saleable commodity, then commodification will fail.[19] At the heart of actor-network analysis, then, is a critique of the functionalist and deterministic assumptions that often drive sociological commodity chains approaches. In a food network, as opposed to a commodity chain, neither technology, science, nor capital has all-powerful "logics" that prevent resistance or reconfigurations of the network by human and nonhuman actors. Plant pathogens such as Panama disease, as the anthropologist John Soluri has recently shown, have had the power to restructure one of history's most powerful food networks—that of El Pulpo, "the Octopus," aka the United Fruit Company. The devastating effects of Panama disease on monocropped Gros Michel bananas—the only variety of banana that United Fruit found profitable in a North American consumer market—drove the company to develop a strategy of shifting cultivation in the early twentieth century as it abandoned once-profitable plantations, constantly moving capital and banana trees throughout the Caribbean and Latin America in search of pathogen-free "virgin soils." Science, technology, and capital certainly played important roles in the production and distribution of Chiquita bananas, but so did *Fungus oxysporum*, the fungus that causes Panama disease.[20] Using the terminology "network" rather than "chain" may not be crucial to understanding the interrelationships of science, technology, and nature in food systems, but it certainly opens a window onto a multiplicity of powerful social agents—human or otherwise.

Whether labeled as commodity systems, systems of provisioning, or food networks, then, the conglomerations of people, organisms, institutions, and machines that transform farm goods into marketable foods have enriched scholarly studies of political economy and of science, technology, and the environment. Perhaps the most fruitful result of commodity chains studies, however, has been their contribution to theories and analyses of globalization. According to demographic researchers at the University of Georgia and North Carolina State University, the world's population has, as of May 2007, become more urban than rural for the first time in human history.[21] Rather than spelling the doom of agriculture or the annihilation of rural space, the culmination of this long-term trend only serves to highlight the fraught but essential relationships between urban consumers and rural producers—particularly in terms of food supplies. "Globalization" is often understood in popular parlance to be synonymous with instantaneous worldwide telecommunication and containerized shipping of outerwear and stereos produced in Bangladesh or Taiwan for American consumers. Food-studies scholars, however, have stressed the fundamental role that agriculture and food distribution have played and continue to play in the modern world economy. Reframing the "agrarian question" as a food question, these scholars have shown, allows us to understand the complexity of relationships between rural and urban peoples in a global economy in which the work of a small-scale farmer in the Punjab mirrors the work of an autoworker in Detroit, and where manufacturing workers are increasingly located in the "periphery" of nonurban areas of industrialized countries and in new manufacturing districts in less developed countries.

Global commodity chains analysis—an indirect offshoot of commodity systems analysis—has been at the forefront of recent contributions to globalization literature. As defined by Terence K. Hopkins and Immanuel Wallerstein, a commodity chain is "a network of labor and production processes whose end result is a finished commodity."[22] From such a seemingly simple proposition has flowed a tremendous outpouring of studies that implicitly or explicitly critique older theories of globalization, particularly world-systems theory and dependency theory. Tracing how the links of commodity chains are formed—where and by whom a raw commodity is processed or manufactured, how it makes its way to buyers located elsewhere, how firms react to worker and consumer demands in making choices about where to manufacture goods and what to produce—provides insights into global production, work, and consumption patterns that might otherwise evade the scholar reliant on trade data and policy analyses alone. Whereas world-systems theory and dependency theory sought to explain the persistence of patterns of unequal distribution of resources among nations in the industrialized, urbanized "core" and agricultural, rural "periphery" of world trade, commodity chains analysis seeks to understand how patterns of inequality have been constructed not only between but also within nations in a global economy. Rather than assume a stark divide between the industrial core and the agricultural periphery, commodity chains analysts study nodes or sites of intensive capital accumulation that may or may not correspond to the political boundaries of specific nation-states. Commodity chains analysts tend to focus on a "post-Fordist" global economy characterized by a dissolution of government-erected barriers to "free trade," along with the proliferation of transnational corporations willing to build factories and employ workers almost anywhere in the world. In this post-Fordist world, commodity chains analysts declare, the divide between industrial and rural, core and periphery no longer holds much relevance. Less developed countries are increasingly likely to host the sites of capital-intensive production, while industrialized countries such as the United States are among the leading exporters of agricultural commodities.[23]

Not all global commodity chains analysts focus on food or agriculture; the concept has been applied to such diverse products as athletic footwear, auto parts, and cocaine. Some of the most important concepts, however, have been contributed by scholars interested in how traditionally rural economies have been integrated into the circuits of global capital. Among the intellectual threads that have been woven into global commodity chains analysis is what was called in the early 1990s the "new political economy of agriculture." Its practitioners declared that a fundamental marker of the rise of a post-Fordist world economy since the 1970s was a "global crisis of agriculture," underscored by the collapse of family farms in industrialized nations and the unmooring of agricultural export-based economies in less developed nations.[24] The sociologist Harriet Friedmann, for instance, explored what she called a post–World War II international "food regime," in which the global crisis of agriculture since the early 1970s was the product of efforts by powerful nation-states—particularly the United States—to systematically undermine the self-sufficiency of competitive agricultural producers in less developed countries.[25] While some global commodity chains analysts continue to see agricultural trade and food aid policies as central to the global restructuring of agriculture, however, others have directed their attention away from the nation-state and toward nongovernmental firms and institutions operating within the global economy. According to these scholars, not only has the production of agricultural commodities become globalized, but also the *markets* for everything from kiwifruit to Thai eggplants to winter squash have gone global. In such a world the power of transnational agro-food corporations such as Archer-Daniels Midland, Monsanto, and Wal-Mart has begun to outpace the power of even the most industrialized and urbanized nation-states, inspiring a shift of scholarly analyses toward the firms rather than the countries involved in the construction of global commodity chains. Successful firms tend to be those capable of shifting production and distribution in rapid response to changing patterns of regulation, labor and farmer demands, and shifting consumer desires, thereby contributing significantly to the chaotic and uneven economic geography of contemporary global capitalism.[26]

Analyzing global commodity chains promises more than new theoretical insights into the political economy of global food production and consumption, particularly when issues of culture are worked into the mix. Every scholar interested in food is familiar with Anthelme Brillat-Savarin's oft-quoted line from *The Physiology of Taste* (1825): "Tell me what you eat and I will tell you what you are." For anthropologists, that dictum has long been a cornerstone of ethnographic studies of taboos, eating rituals, and gift-exchange networks in nonindustrial societies, though in recent years anthropologists and cultural geographers have made significant forays into industrialized food cultures. Sidney Mintz's 1985 book *Sweetness and Power* remains a classic text for its connection of British "sweet tooth" culture to the rise of plantation sugar production in the Caribbean and to industrial manufacturing in Britain. More recent studies have probed the question of just how "American" a McDonald's in Beijing or Taiwan is—with rather surprising findings for those who would facilely assume that if you have seen one McDonald's you have seen them all.[27]

When analyzed at the level of a global commodity chain, questions about food culture are reframed not simply as "Americanization" versus maintenance of traditional foodways, but as a matter of cross-cultural standardization versus multicultural hybridization. Supermarkets and fast-food chains around the world offer different products and different shopping experiences tuned to local demographic and cultural considerations; one rarely finds low-fat microwave popcorn in a British supermarket, for instance, while French "McDoos" offer wine as well as soda with the metric-sized "Le Royale" burger. Yet, as Susanne Freidberg's masterful study of French and English green bean provisioning networks attests, European consumers have developed high standards of food quality and safety that transcend national boundaries and regional identities. Even if the French prefer to buy long, uncut beans in outdoor produce markets while the British buy fat, trimmed beans in supermarkets, both cultures have developed exacting standards that reach all the way back to the African farmlands where those beans are raised. All along the food chains between African farmers and European consumers differences in language, gender roles, historical patterns of colonization and decolonization, institutional structures, and race relations inflect and shape consumers' expectations for the final product. Still, the final product in both cases is a highly standardized, mass-produced, and mass-consumed green bean.[28] In short, "globalization" need not portend the erasure of distinctive cultures under the onslaught of transnational food distribution networks; instead, culture continues and will continue to be an important factor in shaping those networks.

So far we have seen some advantages of the commodity chains approach for probing issues in political economy, pushing science and technology studies further afield, and reframing discussions of globalization. However, as with any theoretical or methodological approach—even one as diverse as this— some large grains of salt must be taken with the intellectual feast. First, historians of agriculture are likely to note that much of what is proposed to be "new" about commodity systems analysis or of the "new political economy of agriculture" was actually introduced a half-century ago, when Harvard Business School professor John H. Davis coined the term "agribusiness." The neologism, which Davis introduced in October 1955 to signify that modern agriculture had become "inseparable from the business firms which manufacture production supplies and which market farm products,"[29] explicitly challenged scholars and policy makers to recognize that farm producers and food consumers were woven together in tightly interlocked chains. Agribusiness, according to Davis, was composed not only of farmers and fertilizer manufacturers but also of webs of government regulation, technological and scientific research, labor patterns, business behavior, and distribution and marketing networks. Although the term was quickly taken up by both supporters and critics of industrialized agriculture to denote "large-scale mechanized farming," Davis believed that the word "agribusiness" would have an intellectual and political impact quite comparable to that expected for the "commodity systems approach" outlined several decades later by William H. Friedland—namely, to reorient the study of agriculture to include what happened beyond the farm gate as well as in the farm field. Because the word was quickly subsumed within American political debates over the "death of the family farm" in the 1950s and 1960s, however, the "agribusiness approach" never gained the intellectual heft that it might have. Commodity systems analysis, then, was not really a new concept in the 1980s, although the politicization of the term "agribusiness" made new terminology necessary.[30]

More problematic for commodity chains scholars is the lack of coherence within the field. William H. Friedland's original conception of commodity systems analysis proposed exactly five areas of research relevant to agricultural commodity chains: production practices, grower organization, labor markets, scientific research, and marketing. Other scholars soon added components such as consumption and the environment to the list, while the sociologist Lawrence Busch has proposed no fewer than eleven rules for commodity systems analysis. Given the length and complexity of the modern food chain, one could easily propose many more.[31] When commodity chains are redefined as "agro-food networks," the possibilities for sites of analysis become nearly infinite. Determining the relevant sites or nodes or links in the commodity chain or network can be mind-bending when there are literally hundreds or thousands of firms spread across dozens of countries involved in producing, processing, and marketing any given food product. Which sites of production and consumption are most relevant? How far up, down, forward, or backward should the chain extend—from a food processor to a supermarket shelf, from farmer to consumer, from a microbe in a farm field to a microbe in a landfill? Such questions are of obvious importance but can be debated by scholars ad infinitum if not ad nauseam. As the geographers Peter Jackson, Neil Ward, and Polly Russell note, the concept of a "commodity chain" has taken on so many differing meanings and has been used by such a diverse set of academics that it verges on what the sociologist Andrew Sayer has called a "chaotic conception" capable of being redefined at will.[32] Still, given the possibilities of the commodity chains approach, such issues should spark only more research and conversation rather than outright dismissal.

Perhaps most troubling of all, at least for historians, is the tendency of commodity chains analysts to build teleological assumptions into their theoretical and methodological frameworks. Considering that much of the commodity chains approach is built on a rejection of the economic determinism of world-systems theory, this is a matter of great concern. References to the "logic" of global capitalism abound within the literature; there is "a certain structural logic in liberalization" of trade laws and labor patterns, according to some scholars, while according to others, "globalization, like early capitalism, is simply a process whose time has come."[33] Ontologically, it is difficult if not impossible to swallow the proposition that capitalism of any stripe exists as an entity unto itself with its own internal logic, rather than as an abstraction produced by the contingencies of social interaction and the analyses of theoreticians. Politically, those who wish to see food-processing employees and farmers earn decent livings, or to have food chains built on ecologically sustainable agriculture, or to minimize the power of monopoly capital in food processing should be troubled by the teleological assumption that food is produced by the "logic" of the market. Empirically, the presumption of a "logic" of capitalism fails to explain certain salient features of modern food networks. If food chains are the product of a unitary "logic" of capitalism, for instance, one would be hard-pressed to understand why fresh beef is sold primarily in unbranded plastic packages while nearly all fresh chicken packages carry prominent brand names, or why Vermont dairy farmers continue to cling to an "outmoded" form of small-scale dairy farming while Californians construct ever-larger industrial dairy feedlots, or why Iowans located on some of the most fertile soils in the world have become almost wholly dependent on imported sources of food. The reasons, as it turns out, are historically complex and contingent upon ecological conditions, differences in regulatory structures, changing business and labor patterns, and cultural values.[34]

Because food is so deeply saturated with layers of cultural meaning, no amount of "logic" will ever satisfactorily explain the workings of any food chain, past or present. A teleological approach to food chains can too easily fail to take into account resistance, adaptation, local exceptions to the rule, and alternative historical tracks. Fortunately, the essays in this volume attest to the fruit that continues to be borne by historical studies informed not only by theory but also by careful empirical research that accounts for contingencies, complexities, and subtleties. To riff once again on Wendell Berry, the essays in this collection aim to show that food is much more than an "abstract idea," and yet we can nonetheless hope that larger generalizations about the commodification of food emerge from studying what happens in the space between farm and fork.

Part II
Animals

Chapter 4
Lard to Lean: Making the Meat-Type Hog in Post–World War II America

J. L. Anderson

In July 2006 *USA Today* reported that pork was the "other 'lite' meat," a play on the late 1980s National Pork Producers Council campaign that promoted pork as "the other white meat." United States Department of Agriculture (USDA) researchers announced that the pork tenderloin of 2006 was leaner than skinless chicken breast. Earlier generations knew pork as a flavorful but fatty meat, characterized by intramuscular fat and a layer of fat around each cut. The new development, however, was proof that pork was a healthy diet choice, although many pork aficionados argued that modern pork was easy to overcook and lacked flavor due to its low fat content or high acidity.[1]

Why and how did this transformation occur? Farmers, producer groups, scientists, meatpackers, and extension professionals collaborated to change the hog in an effort to keep pork on America's tables. Roger Horowitz demonstrated that in the first half of the twentieth century meat processors standardized hams and bacon to make them more appealing while Americans increasingly rejected salted and pickled cuts in favor of fresh cuts. However, fresh cuts were still fatty, the products of what were known as lard-type hogs: valued more for lard than they were for meat. After World War II, however, there was less demand for this kind of animal as vegetable oils replaced lard and Americans increased their consumption of beef and chicken meat but not pork. The meat industry successfully transformed the hog into a meat-type animal in an attempt to remain competitive; ironically, these efforts failed in their ultimate objective of increasing pork consumption.

The effort to change the fat hog into a lean animal, in terms of both morphology (shape) and the living tissue itself, is a transformation that Edmund Russell labeled "macrobiotechnology." Russell explained that as humans have shaped organisms to meet human needs, we have done so at two levels, as whole organisms (macrobiotechnology) and at the cellular level (microbiotechnology).

The macrobiotechnology of lean hogs reveals tension about health and diet in American society and shows the collaborative nature of agribusiness in the postwar world. The ultimate failure of this effort to stimulate greater pork consumption also indicates the limited capacity of such transformations to influence consumer behavior.[2]

Humans have in fact remade the hog several times to meet the needs of changing societies since its domestication approximately ten thousand years ago. The ability of hogs to store energy as fat made them attractive candidates for domestication and a valuable food source around the world. For most of American history, omnivorous hogs fed themselves for much of the year, feasting on mast, grass, foliage, insects, and any other available food supply until fall. These thrifty hogs were known by various names, including razorbacks, prairie sharks, and land pikes due to the prominent bristles along their spines that stood up when the animals were agitated. After the harvest, farmers rounded up hogs into enclosures, where they fed them grain (often corn), household waste (known as slop), and farm by-products (including skimmed milk). During the nineteenth century, improvement-minded farmers with regular corn surpluses imported new varieties of hogs from England and developed distinct types of animals, bred to a set of standard shape, size, color and markings, and other attributes such as rate of maturity. The breeds established during the nineteenth century, including the Chester White, Hampshire, Poland China, Berkshire, and numerous others, became popular on American farms.[3]

In the early twentieth century, governments in the United States and Europe added their power to efforts to transform hog production. Danish researchers were among the first to use scientific techniques to test hogs for rate of gain and efficiency in converting feed to body mass. They selected for breeding stock that displayed those traits and then developed the Danish Landrace breed, characterized by a long body and a high lean-to-body mass ratio. In 1936–37 the USDA and thirteen state experiment stations collaborated to establish the Regional Swine Breeding Laboratory in Ames, Iowa. In spite of this research there was little change in hog breeding since most farmers focused on surviving the Great Depression and meeting production goals during World War II.

Attention by pork packers and hog farmers to improving breeds spread following World War II. They were worried by clear indications that American consumers were leaving them behind as per capita beef consumption rose while pork held steady. In 1953 average per capita beef consumption surpassed that of pork, when each American consumed an average of 77.6 pounds of beef and 63.5 pounds of pork. By the end of the decade annual per capita beef consumption exceeded eighty pounds while pork remained in the sixties. Even more alarming to those in the pork business was the trend in poultry consumption, which reached 35.2 pounds in 1959.[4]

Pork's lack of appeal was tied to major transformations in American life. Although the urban population grew faster than the rural population throughout the twentieth century, after 1940 there was a massive population shift from the country to the city. During the 1950s the number of rural households fell by approximately one-third compared to the number in 1940. Urban people consumed twice as much beef as country people and less pork than the rural population. The grim truth for hog farmers was that Americans were willing to purchase pork, but urban consumers ate more beef and chicken. With rising incomes in the postwar period, a growing segment of the population could afford beefsteak and chicken, long considered status or special-occasion foods. For a generation that confronted postwar prosperity after enduring the privation of the Great Depression and meat rationing during World War II, beef was "what's for dinner" and chicken became common fare.[5]

The challenge for the pork industry included more than competing with a rise in beef and poultry consumption. The problem also lay in the *kind* of pork that farmers raised. Fatty meat fell out of favor due to the changing character of the consumer market. An Iowa State College agricultural economist linked the preference for lean meat with the growth in white collar employment. As long as physical labor was a central part of the workplace, fattier meat was acceptable. In one study researchers placed lean pork chops next to fatty chops in grocers' cases. When the price was the same for both, shoppers selected the lean items over the fat items ten to one. Appearance was pivotal to sales in postwar America, since supermarkets with self-service meat counters sold a growing portion of America's meat to suburban dwellers. Bernard Ebbing, farm service director of Rath Packing Company, located in Waterloo, Iowa, explained, "Meat today has to sell itself on its own merits. Quality and eye appeal are of the utmost importance." In the 1960s Spartan Stores, a Michigan grocery chain, displayed a large sign in the meat department claiming to have "The Leanest Pork in Town," appealing to consumers' desire for lean pork and simultaneously fueling that desire.[6]

The demand for lard declined at the same time that consumers shifted toward leaner cuts of meat. Animal fats such as lard and tallow became less important after the war because of new substitutes that could take their place in food. Availability of alternative sources of edible oils expanded after the war as the U.S. government provided price incentives to farmers to grow more soybeans, peanuts, flax, and cotton for oil. The use of soybeans for oilseeds rather than as a forage crop was a major change for farmers and demonstrated the soybean's potential as a food product to processors. Soybean acreage surged to over ten million acres in 1943, representing a 248 percent increase over 1939 and far outstripping the acreage of peanuts and flax raised for oil.[7]

The demand for lard, once a major source of farm and packer profits, experienced a rapid decline. In 1949 Russell Plager of John Morrell Company observed that the price of lard in the early twentieth century was higher than that of pork and continued to be a high-priced commodity up to 1940. During the war years, however, the price of lard fell below the price of live hogs. Not surprisingly, industry representatives argued that it was time to raise hogs with less fat and more meat. The U.S. government agreed. In 1952 the federal Office of Price Stabilization ruled that pork packers violated government regulations by selling pork with too much fat. Even so, it was uncertain if farmers would respond to this market pressure to preserve or gain market share.[8]

Pork packers led the effort to transform hogs. In 1946 the Hormel Company revived the National Barrow Show, which had suspended operations during wartime. The show was an effort to reward producers who minimized fat and maximized lean. Hormel hosted the show in Austin, Minnesota, in collaboration with the Austin Chamber of Commerce, the Austin Public Schools, and the Mower County Agricultural Society. The first year of the show producers from thirteen states attended. Each entry was slaughtered at the Hormel packing plant in Austin during the show and scored according to the percentage of weight in the various cuts. The top-scoring hog was comprised of 49.7 percent in lean meat cuts and 21.3 percent in fat, while the lowest-scoring hog was 44 percent lean and 23.6 percent fat. The difference of almost 6 percent would have rewarded the top producer a premium of $2.95 per pound—a nice sum for a two-hundred-pound hog. The results at the 1950 show confirmed the results of 1949, with the leanest hogs valued the highest.[9]

The Ohio Pork Improvement Program was the first cooperative effort among different segments of the pork industry to change the nature of hogs and hog production. Commenced in 1948, it was a collaborative venture of the Ohio State University Swine Evaluation Station, the university's meat laboratory, the Ohio Agricultural Extension Service, and the Agricultural Experiment Station. The goal was to facilitate the breeding of a meat-type hog, defined by four characteristics. First, at least 51.75 percent of the chilled carcass weight of the meat-type hog should consist of lean cuts with high-quality (low-fat) loin, ham, and shoulder. Second, meat hogs should gain 100 pounds from no more than 340 pounds of feed after weaning, and third, they should reach a live weight of 200 pounds in 180 days or less. Fourth, meat-type sows should raise at least eight pigs per litter.[10]

W. H. Bruner, an Ohio State University Extension specialist in animal science, argued that hog farmers needed to raise meat-type animals if they were to remain competitive with beef and poultry producers. In 1952 Bruner reassured farmers and breeders who feared that raising meat-type animals would be a more costly endeavor than raising traditional fat hogs. Tests from the first few years of operation at the Ohio station proved that raising meat animals was actually less expensive than raising lardy ones. The longer farmers fed hogs beyond 225 pounds, the more fat they produced and the more feed they required. Researchers at Beltsville, Maryland, and Ames, Iowa, showed that the cost of raising 3,600 pounds of hogs at different market weights was powerful evidence for the advantage in raising lighter, meatier animals. Producing sixteen hogs of 225 pounds each (3,600 pounds of live weight) required 14,796 pounds of feed, while it took 16,560 pounds of feed to have twelve hogs reach 300 pounds apiece (also 3,600 pounds). The difference between raising heavier hogs and raising lighter animals amounted to almost a ton of feed, a significant production expense. Furthermore, heavy hogs yielded more lard and fattier meat. As Rath's Bernard Ebbing noted, the expenses of developing meat animals were negligible compared to the costs of standing still. "We can afford the meat-type hog," he concluded; "he is our salvation."[11]

Swine breed organizations and livestock shows defined the characteristics of meat-type animals for various breeds and rewarded those who met those requirements. In 1954 the National Swine Record Association invited representatives from Ohio State and Purdue Universities along with Bernard Ebbing of Rath Packing Company, Carroll Plager of Hormel, and Wilber Plager of the Iowa Swine Producers' Association to help develop certification standards for meat-type animals based on the Ohio Pork Improvement Program. The breed associations responded quickly. The 1954–55 edition of the *Iowa Swine Breeders Directory* featured advertisements that proclaimed the strides each group had made in developing new standards. The Hampshire Swine Registry was the first breed organization to develop certification criteria, while the Poland China Record Association maintained that its breed was already a "meat type" with a high percentage of carcass weight as lean cuts. In 1955 Michigan State University issued specifications for the Michigan Certified Meat-type hog and the Michigan Commercial Meat-type hog, designations that hogs of any breed could attain. The National Barrow Show and the International Livestock Show implemented hog-carcass contests to judge and reward producers of meat-type animals. In 1955 the National Duroc Congress, the trade show of the Duroc breed association, convened a committee of packers, extension livestock specialists, and farmers to develop standards for meat animals within the Duroc breed.[12]

Defining the meat-type animal did not answer the question of how to achieve results, which was more than a matter of simply marketing lighter-weight hogs. Hogs (like humans) are what they eat, which means that diet plays a large part in influencing pork quality. For many farmers of the mid-twentieth century, finishing hogs before marketing meant providing as much corn as the hogs could eat, supplemented by farm by-products such as skimmed milk. Experts argued that forage crops should play a larger role in hog diet, with a corresponding reduction in the role of corn in the finishing ration by as much as 50 percent. Proponents of forage feeding argued that forage crops provided hogs with all the nutrients they needed without the fattening qualities of grains. Researchers at the University of Georgia conducted feeding trials that showed it cost less per one hundred pounds of pork to use clover pasture rather than dry-lot grain feeding. University of Illinois Agricultural Experiment

Station scientists reduced the amount of feed and concluded that lower caloric intake lowered the fat composition of the carcass, even though it slowed rate of gain.[13]

Breeding was also a concern. As plant breeders demonstrated in the early twentieth century, it was possible to inbreed parent stock and cross those inbred lines, producing superplants known as hybrids. The USDA began an inbreeding program in the 1930s at the Regional Swine Breeding Laboratory, where researchers developed inbred lines within the leading hog breeds. Inbred lines would preserve particularly desirable traits such as leanness or litter size and when crossed would yield animals with several of those desirable characteristics. By 1943 the USDA had developed forty inbred lines of breeding stock, but research-station hogs comprised a minuscule portion of the total number of breeding animals compared to those on farms. To achieve results in the consumer marketplace it was necessary to improve breeding stock on farms, not just at labs and state experiment stations.[14]

Swine testing stations were important facilities in helping producers raise meat-type animals since they provided producers with hard facts about their herds. Land-grant colleges and universities took up the work of swine testing, establishing swine testing stations throughout the country. Ohio State University established the first swine testing station, and in 1955 Iowa State College and the Iowa Swine Producers Association collaborated to open a boar-testing station in Ames. Five stations eventually operated in Iowa, with funding from Consumers Cooperative Association (CCA) of Kansas City for stations at Ida Grove, Eagle Grove, and Lisbon. Midland Cooperative of Minneapolis provided funds for the station at New Hampton. Minnesota established a station in 1957 with financial support from Hormel, which leased a barn to the station for one dollar per year. The Missouri legislature appropriated sixty thousand dollars to establish a testing station and service in 1958, Kansas opened a station at Manhattan in 1959, and CCA established Nebraska stations at Wahoo in 1960 and Clarkson in 1961.[15]

Procedures at the testing stations varied, but the goal was to provide farmers with information about their herds so they could make decisions about developing or obtaining promising breeding stock and culling herds. Depending on the station, farmers could send a group of four or five barrows (castrated males), or boars with twelve or more nipples from litters of eight or more pigs from gilts (first-time mothers), or nine or more from sows. Each boar ranged in weight from thirty to fifty pounds at admittance. Station employees vaccinated and wormed the animals and, over the next few weeks, fed each group a standard ration. Station staff collected data on each animal within the group, recording the amount of feed consumed, rate of gain, and the amount of back fat on each animal. At the conclusion of the test farmers paid their feed bill and received valuable information about how their animals performed in relation to other animals at the station. Stations conducted twice-yearly sales of

Figure 4.1. Inside the sale ring at the Lisbon, Iowa, swine-testing station boar sale. Farmland Industries Records, Morse Department of Special Collections, Hale Library, Kansas State University. Used with permission.

tested boars for those who wished to sell breeding stock. (See Figure 4.1.) Buyers viewed performance records to determine which animals would fit their breeding programs.[16]

The spread of swine testing was limited in the years before 1952, however, because there was no good way to assess the quality of the carcass, fat content in particular, on a live animal. It was relatively easy to determine the amount of feed consumed and changes in weight, but studying internal properties such as loin eye size, intramuscular fat, and back fat could be done only on carcasses. Promising breeding stock, therefore, would be killed, just like undesirable animals, and thus could not serve as foundation stock for "new and improved" meat-type herds. Compared to plant breeding, genetic manipulation in animals was a much more time-consuming process and more expensive in terms of initial investment and the costs of feed, shelter, and care, since the life cycle of animals is considerably longer than that of most crop plants.

Researchers struggled to find a way to test the internal characteristics of hogs without killing them. One promising trait for study was back fat. The amount of back fat on an animal corresponded to loin eye size and intramuscular fat. A thinner layer of back fat had positive correlations with large loin eye and low intramuscular fat. At Purdue University the animal husbandry expert F. N. Andrews and the physicist R. M. Whaley developed what they called the "lean meter" for testing live animals. The lean meter measured electro-conductivity of fat and lean tissue. It was a gun-styled device with a needle to record electro-conductivity at different depths. In 1954 studies of hogs tested immediately before and after slaughter indicated that estimated back-fat thickness based on lean meter tests closely matched the actual levels.[17]

No one, however, managed to develop a tool that did a more accurate job with less expense than Lanoy N. Hazel. Hazel, an Iowa State College animal scientist, developed a tool called the "back fat probe" in 1952. The back fat probe was simply a thin metal ruler that could be inserted in an incision made with a scalpel in a hog's back. One person held the hog in place by using a snare in its upper mandible, immobilizing the hog. A second tester made the incision and inserted the probe. The probe would slide through the fat with relative ease until it reached a layer of connecting tissue, indicating that the muscle had been reached. The tester could then simply read the ruler to determine back fat depth. Three measurements along the hog's back provided an accurate assessment: above the first rib, the last rib, and the last lumbar vertebra. The Ames station and the many other stations around the country measured carcass quality in this manner on live animals. (See Figure 4.2.) Boars that tested with desirable traits would literally "make the cut" and survive as breeding stock, while boars with less desirable traits would be castrated and sold for slaughter. Hazel's back fat probe, a ten-cent tool, was the technological fix that accelerated the pace of carcass assessment.[18]

Pork packers were in a key position to lead the educational campaign about meat-type hogs. Each of the major packers had field representatives who worked with county extension directors, vocational agriculture teachers, farmers, and producer groups to spread the message about what the packers wanted. In addition to Hormel's Carroll Plager and Rath's Ebbing, John Morrell and Company hired Russell Plager (Carroll and Wilber's brother) and another field man. Oscar Mayer employed two Iowa field representatives, including one former county extension director and farm broadcaster. Wilson and Company hired four field men.[19]

With this staff in place, the meat industry sustained an aggressive campaign

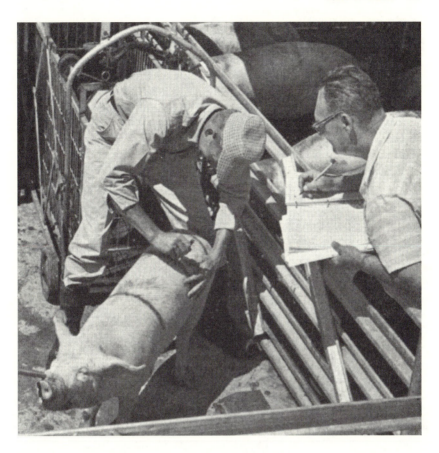

Figure 4.2. Iowa swine-testing station employees probing a pig and recording back-fat measurements. From "Iowa's Swine Testing Stations and the Pork Producer," Iowa State University Cooperative Extension, *Pamphlet 291* (June 1962). Special Collections Department, Iowa State University Library. Used with permission.

in the 1950s to encourage farmers to transform their herds from lard hogs to meat hogs. The Iowa Swine Producers Association (ISPA) hosted the American Meat Institute's annual meeting in the spring of 1953, and there meatpacking representatives from across the country discussed meat-type hogs. Wilber Plager, field secretary for the ISPA, predicted that the meeting would be remembered "as the beginning of the avalanche towards meat-type hogs." In 1954 Rath's Bernard Ebbing developed a set of slides that showed the "Outside and Inside" of a meat-type hog, featuring cross sections of both. Wilber Plager informed Ebbing that he sold or gave 280 sets to the Universities of Wisconsin and Nebraska, Kansas State, and North Carolina State, as well as county agents, farmers, feed dealers around the country, and stockyard managers in Ohio, Texas, and Tennessee. W. A. Coon, general manager of Armour and Company's Spokane, Washington, meatpacking facility, told hog farmers that the "long term popularity of pork . . . can be maintained only by producing a leaner type of animal." In 1957 Hormel collaborated with the Fort Dodge, Iowa, Chamber of Commerce and the Iowa State Cooperative Extension Service to establish the Fort Dodge Market Hog Show, headed by one of Hormel's hog buyers.[20]

Industry-produced films also carried the message to farmers about the merits of lean-hog production. Chicago's Union Stock Yards and Transit Company financed a twenty-nine-minute film, "Leaner Hogs and Longer Profits," for distribution to farm clubs, county extension directors, and community groups. The film reinforced the history of changing diet preferences and the housewife's role in selecting meats from refrigerated cases. The bulk of the film focused on an Illinois farm family's collaboration with the University of Illinois Extension Service and the county extension director to conduct a breeding program for profitable meat hogs.[21]

It was one matter to assess carcass quality at a testing station and to promote meat-type animals, but it was another problem altogether for farmers to understand how to raise a meat type or to know one when they saw it. It was not, as J. F. Lasley, a University of Missouri swine specialist, pointed out, a "long, rangy, [and] half starved" pig. As one Iowa farmer observed in 1953, "Sometimes you can mistake a poor-doing lard hog for a real meat hog. Result is you breed for poor-doing hogs. And you get hogs that don't gain fast."[22]

Farmers who were eager to reap the rewards of the marketplace by producing lean swine had to undertake careful breeding and testing programs. Gesley Knickerbocker of Iowa began experimenting with a meat-type boar from Iowa State College. By the late 1950s his hogs were some of the meatiest on the market and displayed some of the fastest growth rates in the business. From 1949 to 1955 Dean Snyder of Illinois kept accurate production records on each litter farrowed on his farm. He slaughtered two pigs from each litter to determine their meatiness. In 1954 he raised hogs with an average of 1.4 inches of back fat and loin eye of 4.68 inches, which was far less back fat and significantly larger loin eye size than national averages. Encouraged, Snyder held his own sale, which attracted buyers from fifteen states.[23]

Hog buyers rewarded farmers such as Knickerbocker and Snyder by paying premiums. In the spring of 1955 forty-two of Snyder's Hampshire hogs from certified meat-type litters averaged almost $288 apiece, compared to the sale of forty-three noncertified Hampshire hogs, which averaged $90 apiece. Hormel's Carroll Plager explained that farmers who had their animals carcass-graded at the plant generally earned about eighty cents more per hundredweight than those who did not. A farmer from northwest Iowa reported that he received twenty-five to forty cents premium for meat-type animals. He explained, "That's not as much as it should be, but I'm satisfied that it pays to raise meat hogs anyway."[24]

Farmers adopted a range of strategies to improve their herds. The president of the Cedar County, Iowa, Cooperative Swine Improvement Association stated that he selected for meat animals by eye but acknowledged that "backfat probing spots the real meat type." In 1958 a farmer from northwest Iowa reported satisfaction with tested boars in terms of litter size, rate of gain, and meatiness. Claude Messner of Caney, Kansas, built a six-pen testing station on his farm in 1960 and constructed a fifty-pen station in 1970 to realize the gains associated with selling meat-type boars. Wiley Blair of north Florida did not purchase test-station boars but tested the offspring of his new breeding stock and sold a boar if his progeny were not satisfactory.[25]

By 1970 hog farmers were on their way to transforming U.S. herds. Two veteran Iowa State University livestock extension specialists recalled that by the 1960s it was common "to see a backfat probe protruding from the overall top pocket of a farmer, alongside the always-present stub pencil or pen, and seed corn notebook." The 180-pound hog carcass that yielded 35 pounds of lard in the early 1950s yielded only 20 pounds of lard by the mid-1970s. During those two decades breeders changed the ham and loin proportion of the carcass from 32 percent to 44 percent. Carcass measurements of show hogs reflected changes in herds across the country. From 1973 to 1977 carcass length increased from 30.7 inches to 31.1 inches, back fat decreased from 1.22 inches to 1.19, and loin eye size increased from 4.69 square inches to 5.05. In 1972 a Wisconsin farmer set a ham-loin record of 51.24 percent of total carcass weight at the northeast Iowa testing station. A generation of lean boars was now available to sire lean offspring for American tables.[26]

The pork industry faced problems, however. Despite the initiatives of innovative pork farmers, many other farmers resisted the transition to the meat-type hog. Even more troubling, per capita pork consumption lagged. In 1969 David Topel, associate professor of animal science at Iowa State University, noted that the average market hog went to slaughter with 1.7 inches of back fat, while meat-type animals were characterized by less than 1.0 inch of back-fat thickness. In 1972 an Oscar Mayer executive expressed concern that "the demand for pork has not kept pace with beef." Studies conducted in 1977 and 1985 indicated a declining demand for pork among adults. The percentage of women ages nineteen to fifty who consumed pork fell from 24.0 percent to 20.5 percent, while the percentage of male consumers in the same age group declined from 28.2 percent to 25.3 percent.[27]

Those who consumed pork found that the new pork, a success from the production standpoint, posed problems in the kitchen. With little intramuscular fat and less fat surrounding each cut, the meat was easier to overcook. The industry recognized the problem in the 1960s, as researchers determined that instead of cooking pork loin to an internal temperature of 185 degrees Fahrenheit, cooking it to 170 degrees preserved moisture, making it juicier and more desirable. In 1971 Ralston Purina published a new cookbook, *American Heirloom Pork Cookbook*, to "let the housewife know how delicious the new pork tastes." As advertisers claimed, "the average housewife didn't know much about the new pork . . . she was using the old cooking temperatures and had few tempting recipes to encourage her to serve pork to her family." The cookbook provided consumers with new information about cooking pork as well as modern preparations for the high-value cuts such as the loin. Gertrude Kable, Checkerboard Kitchens manager, explained, "Pork as a type of meat and the preparation of the various cuts of pork are changing more than any [other] type of meat," and she urged consumers not "to be left behind in pork fashions." Authors reminded readers of the scientific and cultural emphasis on issues of overweight and stated that the modern hog was a lean animal: "[t]he new pork is now on the market . . . [and] has just about replaced the heavier product."[28]

New information about cooking temperatures for lean pork had difficulties countering long-established consumer anxieties concerning trichinosis, the illness caused by the Trichinella spiralis, or trichina worm. In the 1960s Iowa State University researchers discovered that this parasite was killed by cooking pork to an internal temperature of 140 degrees Fahrenheit, considerably lower than the traditional wisdom of 185 degrees. Pork cooked to 185 degrees was often gray and dry, but those very qualities were reassuring to those who saw pink pork cooked to 140 degrees as an invitation to trichinosis.

Changing consumer attitudes about the link between new cooking temperatures and trichinosis was a difficult task. The Iowa Porkettes, the women's auxiliary of the Iowa Pork Producers, organized in 1964 to promote pork consumption and marketing and challenged those who continued to spread the old ideas. In 1975 Porkette Joyce Oberman wrote to the General Foods Company about a recipe printed on Grape Nuts boxes that recommended baking thin pork chops for forty to fifty minutes in a 400 degree Fahrenheit oven. When Oberman pointed out that 140 degrees was an adequate internal temperature for pork, the company representative responded by stating that cooking pork "to an internal temperature of 170 degrees" was necessary to kill trichina worms and that the company proscribed the higher temperature "to protect both ourselves and our consumers." Oberman replied that customers who followed the cooking instructions on the Grape Nuts box would be left with "hard and tough" chops. "It is cooking instructions like these," she continued, "that give pork a bad reputation. Unless it tastes good when it gets to the table consumers won't want to eat it or serve it again." Oberman suggested that the company's home economist try the recipe with thicker chops in a 350 degree oven instead.[29]

New pork cooked at lower temperatures was not always an appealing choice, however. It was sometimes pale, soft, and watery (also known as pale, soft, exudative, or PSE). In addition to losses from shrinkage due to high moisture content, the lack of color in PSE meat in a grocer's meat case was a detriment to sales. Consumers found that PSE meat changed cooking rates and affected taste and texture. In the 1960s consumers and meat experts such as Oklahoma State University animal science professor Irvin T. Omtvedt complained that PSE pork was a side effect of the relentless breeding for leanness.[30]

The pressure on hog farmers and the pork industry increased in the 1960s and 1970s as poultry consumption grew in response to health concerns. While most Americans of the postwar period ate what they could afford or what they wanted, there was a growing sense of urgency about health as medical researchers discovered links between health hazards and a diet high in fats and cholesterol. In the 1950s a minority of Americans surveyed indicated an interest in weight loss, but concerns about weight became much more pronounced in the 1960s and 1970s. Dieting or reducing, a women's concern since the 1920s, became a men's issue as well during this period. As Harvey Levenstein has observed, for a man "to lunch on a poached fish and/or a salad and reach for a Diet Coke after a workout connoted a healthy concern for one's well-being." It was now manly to drink "lite" beer. A USDA survey conducted in 1979–80 that showed that 28 percent of those who made dietary changes did so because of concerns about fat intake, while 43 percent of those who made changes did so to lose weight. Jogging, fad diets, and admonitions by physicians to give up or reduce consumption of eggs, butter, and red meat became part of the national scene and alerted the industry that it had not convinced consumers that pork was a healthy choice.[31]

Engaged in a struggle to win the hearts and minds of consumers, hog farmers challenged negative portrayals of pork and pork by-products. They protested when television advertisers promoted vegetable shortening by making unfavorable comparisons to lard. The editor of *National Hog Farmer* claimed, "Just an occasional exposure to TV will give you the full impact of the attack on 'greasy' animal fats, with the blow quite naturally hitting on lard." Advertisements from 1966 for Crisco and Snowdrift shortening products reinforced the negative associations. In the Crisco advertisement, a woman was surprised to learn that the brand she planned to purchase contained animal fat. "Isn't there some way I can be sure I'm not getting animal fat?" she inquired. Crisco, the advertisers claimed, allowed users to consume fried foods that did not taste greasy. Snowdrift was "greaseless shortening" that contained no animal fat, which meant "no animal fat in your pie crust, cakes and cookies" as well as greaseless chicken, shrimp, and French fries. *National Hog Farmer* encouraged readers to write to these companies and urge them to sell their products "on their own merits" rather than through comparisons to lard. The changing landscape of fats in American culture dogged pork.[32]

The industry strove to improve promotion and marketing efforts as consumers clung to perceptions of pork as a fatty and unhealthy meat. A promotional film developed by Iowa State University and the Iowa Agricultural Marketing Association told the story of "New Pork" in a format suitable for television broadcast. Pork producers positioned pork chops the same way beef producers had capitalized on the New York strip by developing the "Husker Chop" in 1966. This was an attempt to provide restaurants with a prestigious alternative to steaks. The Nebraska Swine Council and University of Nebraska Extension swine specialists recognized that pork was not a popular menu item and that the chop could be an attractive option for increasing demand. Ten years later the situation was largely unchanged. In 1976 Iowa producers introduced the "Iowa Chop," claiming that "a tasty, juicy chop" had not "previously been available on restaurant menus." Wilson Food Corporation developed Butcher's Trim Brand pork in 1978 to emphasize the leanness of its pork.[33]

In 1980 the editor of *Hog Farm Management* proclaimed, "Pork needs a new image," advising producers to develop favorable images and associations for pork. The most important consumer concerns, according to the editor, were cost and nutrition. A 1977 Nebraska consumer study showed that 37 percent of consumers agreed with this statement: "pork would be a good meat except for the fat." In spite of the remarkable gains in making a lean hog, pork producers, packers, and researchers had not managed to reverse the problem of negative perceptions of pork.[34]

Pork producers turned to marketing to solve their image problems. The journalist Dan Murphy in 1966 wrote a series of articles in *National Hog Farmer* titled "Blueprint for Decision," in which he described some of the obstacles to changing negative perceptions of pork and stagnant consumption even after years of efforts to do so. He called for a voluntary check-off program in which producers would contribute a portion of the proceeds from each hog they sold to a fund for research, consumer education, and marketing. Iowa farmer Bernard Collins responded with a contribution and a rallying cry to producers: "We need a national promotion and education arm financed by the producers of many states." On January 1, 1968, the voluntary check-off program called "Nickels for Profit" began with funds divided between the National Livestock and Meat Board, the state and county producer groups, and the National Pork Producers Council (NPPC). By the end of the first year approximately 8.0 million hogs, or 10 percent of all market hogs, had been included in the program, with Iowa producers accounting for 2.3 million hogs. Just three years later Iowa's number increased to over 8.0 million animals. In 1976 hog farmers voted to increase the check-off to ten cents per head of market hogs. These funds served as the basis for an expanded research program and future promotional efforts.[35]

Pork-industry leaders hoped that the fast-food industry, with its success based on beef, could be opened to pork. University of Nebraska researchers attempted to utilize undesirable cuts to make "fabricated" or "restructured" pork. Roger Mandingo, associate professor of animal science, explained how this kind of convenience food would add value to pork. "Most people would be extremely unhappy if they were served a heart or tongue on a plate," he observed. "But flaked into a restructured product it loses its identity. Such products as tripe, heart, and scalded stomachs are high in protein, completely edible, wholesome, and nutritious, and most are already used in sausage without objection." Pork patties could be shaped into any form and marketed in restaurants or for airlines, solving a secondary problem of irregular portion size of cuts such as pork chops. In 1981 McDonald's introduced a boneless pork sandwich of chunked and formed meat called the McRib, developed in part through check-off funds from the NPPC. It was not as popular as the McNugget, introduced in 1983, would be, even though both products were composed of unmarketable parts of the animal (skin and dark meat in the McNugget). The McNugget, however, benefited from positive consumer associations with chicken, even though it had none of the "healthy" attributes people associated with poultry.[36]

The meat-industry alchemy of turning low-value meat into gold was a side effort to the most important task of selling the loins, chops, and hams, which comprised the larger portion of the hog carcass. These cuts of meat most needed an "image" makeover. In 1982 the NPPC prepared to reach out to consumers and communicate the idea that pork was lean and healthy meat. The theme that emerged from discussions with hog farmers and consumer tests in shopping malls was "America, you're leaning on Pork." Advertisements featured a svelte woman with a tailor's measuring tape cinched around her waist and a pork chop with a tailor's tape cinched around the middle of the chop. This campaign reduced the number of those who did not use pork, although the extent to which Americans increased the frequency of pork consumption was unclear.[37]

Encouraged, the NPPC attempted to dramatically reposition pork in the marketplace. The Omaha, Nebraska, firm of Bozell Jacobs pitched a marketing campaign to the NPPC that labeled pork as "the other white meat," trading on popular perceptions of chicken as leaner meat. As NPPC president Orville K. Sweet recalled, "At the end of the presentation the lights came on and found some of us in a state of shock. The lingering question," he observed, "was how pork producers would react to a slogan identifying pork with chicken when for many years they had spent their check off dollars selling pork as a red meat." Wary of making an untrue claim about pork as a white meat, NPPC staff members tried to determine if pork really was a red meat after all. Researchers at Texas A&M University provided the answer the NPPC hoped to hear when they concluded that myoglobin, the substance in meat that determines color, is present in approximately the same levels in pork as it is in fish and chicken, while it is present in higher levels in beef and mutton. Bozell

Jacobs and the NPPC not only gave pork a makeover but also redefined it for consumers.[38]

The NPPC rolled out the campaign in January 1987 at a New York City press conference. With editors from *Woman's Day, Better Homes & Gardens,* and *Health* magazine and other media present, NPPC leaders and their new spokesperson, former Olympic skater Peggy Fleming, announced that pork was the other white meat. NPPC spent approximately nine million dollars on this campaign during its first year. Over the course of that year millions of Americans were exposed to the campaign. Reader surveys of restaurant-industry magazines indicated that subscribers read the other-white-meat advertisements more than any other ads. Consumer recall in target market cities was as high as 72 percent, with "unaided associations of pork as a white meat" up 163 percent since the beginning of the campaign.[39]

By the 1990s members of the pork industry achieved the goal they had set in the 1950s: the creation of a meat-type hog. (See Figure 4.3.) Virtually all hogs that went to market were meat-type animals. The amount of fat per carcass and the degree of intramuscular fat were low compared to those of the typical hog of 1970, which was already a changed animal from that of the mid-1950s. Producers, packers, scientists, taxpayers, and commodity organizations invested millions of dollars required to modify the species and to market new pork to consumers who preferred leaner meat.

The meat hog, however, failed to solve the fundamental problem of the pork business. Per capita consumption remained stagnant in part due to the continued appeal of other meat and in part because low-fat pork was not always a satisfactory taste experience. The lean hog may have prevented further declines in American pork consumption, but industry insiders suggested that the new pork lacked appeal for a portion of America's consumers. As one of the manager's of the Ames Swine Testing Station reflected in 1995, "It makes you wonder how far the industry will go before we decide we've gone too far." In 2006 the journalist Nathanael Johnson discovered a consensus among meat-packers and researchers that they had indeed "gone too far" in the quest for lean meat.[40]

The evidence was the rising demand for what became known as "heritage" pork, a euphemism for fatty meat. In California during the 1990s the entrepreneur Bill Niman found that urban restaurateurs and affluent consumers paid premium prices for pork that had more marbling, not less. Niman began pork production in earnest in 1995, insisting on free-range, antibiotic- and hormone-free techniques. Niman Ranch–brand farmers produced 120 hogs per week in 1997 and less than ten years later produced over 3,000 per week. To fill his contracts, Niman turned to Corn Belt farmers where he found Iowa producers who were dissatisfied with the high capital requirements of modern industrial methods and willing to change production strategies to receive a premium price ranging from 20 to 30 percent higher than that for regular hogs. Georgia

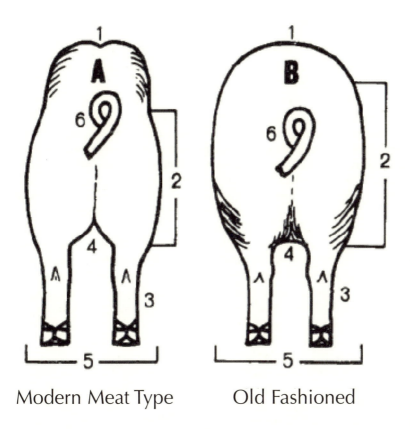

Modern Meat Type   Old Fashioned

Figure 4.3. Changes in hog morphology during the postwar period as depicted in a guide to livestock judging. Roger Hunsley, "Livestock Judging and Evaluation," AS-388, Cooperative Extension Service, Purdue University, Lafayette, Indiana. Used with author's permission.

hog farmers responded by raising more Berkshire hogs, a breed that is traditionally fattier than other breeds. Leading chefs from both coasts turned to fattier pork for more flavorful food.[41]

American consumers' preference for lean meat set in motion a chain of events that led to the transformation of the lard-type hog into the meat-type hog. Scientists, farmers, livestock-industry leaders, and extension personnel all played a part in remaking the hog into an industrial animal. The trait that allowed the hog to survive periods of food scarcity was its ability to store fat. This characteristic made the hog an attractive and popular domesticated animal for thousands of years throughout much of the world, as long as farmers, processors, and consumers prized meat and fat. However, in just fifty years hogs became different animals. The overwhelming majority of today's hogs are lean, meat animals. There is no real choice for most middle- and working-class consumers who want something different. As Nathanael Johnson has noted, consumers "can select only from what the industry chooses to give them," and the industry pursued a lean course.[42]

Ironies abound in the lard to lean story. Per capita pork consumption remained stagnant, with one notable exception. Bacon, one of the fattiest cuts, surged as a commodity in the 1990s. Fast-food chains, the largest purchasers of meats in the United States, raced to lace sandwiches with bacon. The pork industry worked tirelessly to develop meat animals, convinced farmers to raise them, and promoted consumption of lean pork, but consumers continued to view pork as just one of the meat options for their tables, and often a lesser one. Furthermore, as hogs became leaner, Americans became more obese. All of this occurred at a time when the amount of fat from meat sources in America's diet dropped precipitously, as indicated by an American Meat Institute study. By the time the "other white meat" campaign began in 1987, fat from fresh beef and pork accounted for 26 percent less of Americans' total dietary fat than it did in 1977. Animals that arrived at packing plants were leaner, while packers and retailers trimmed more fat from fresh cuts than they did in 1977. In what must be an especially distasteful irony for hog producers, chicken, the white meat Americans perceived as a healthy diet alternative, is increasingly served in fat-laden forms. As Stephen Striffler notes in *Chicken*, the processed convenience forms of chicken that became popular were much higher in fat than traditional preparations. Compounding the problem was the fact that a growing portion of American consumers rejected the ultralean pork and rewarded the slightly fatter and higher priced Niman Ranch product. The final irony is that the pork industry succeeded in their objective to remake the hog but failed to meet their principal objective in convincing Americans to eat more pork.[43]

Chapter 5
The Chicken, the Factory Farm, and the Supermarket: The Emergence of the Modern Poultry Industry in Britain

Andrew C. Godley and Bridget Williams

"Rationing and price control of feeding stuffs ends on August 1st," declared the lead article of the British trade journal *Poultry Farmer* on March 14, 1953. A revolution in modern British agriculture was to follow, with the poultry industry utterly transformed through intensive rearing and factory farming. The resulting cheap chicken meat led to a revolution in the British diet. In 1950 British households consumed only around 1 million chickens. But by the mid-1960s, like many other things in the country, meat-eating habits were transformed. Over 150 million chickens were sold for consumption in 1965, and over 200 million by 1967. If the postwar decades of the 1950s and 1960s saw a transformation in British society, its revolutionaries sustained themselves with mouthfuls of roast chicken.

This chapter describes how the modern poultry industry emerged in Britain principally through initiatives from food retailers. It is this that distinguishes the British case from parallel developments in the United States, where there was also a great expansion in poultry production and consumption. As in the United States, entrepreneurial poultry farmers collaborated with pharmaceutical and animal-feeds companies and with food retailers and refrigeration-unit manufacturers, and together they conducted a wholly novel experiment in the organization of agriculture. However, at the forefront of the emergence of modern poultry farming in the United States was the active and interventionist hand of government through the U.S. Department of Agriculture (USDA). In Britain the role of innovator and coordinator fell to a small group of entrepreneurial poultry farmers and a handful of highly innovative food retailers, with one, J. Sainsbury, leading the way.

The American Origins of the Broiler Chicken Industry

Chicken meat had long been eaten throughout most of the world, but never as a staple. In the 1920s chicken was code for an enticing luxury in America, with Herbert Hoover's 1928 electoral slogan "A chicken in every pot" victoriously aimed at aspirational voters at the end of the Roaring Twenties. It was there that the transition from occasional luxury to everyday staple occurred first.

Initially only one section of America's heterogeneous population saw chicken as a staple, America's Jews. New York City, with almost three-quarters of America's first- and second-generation immigrant Jews, was the largest Jewish city in the world. It represented the largest and most concentrated urban demand for chicken meat anywhere in the early twentieth century.[1]

Kashruth restrictions on slaughtering methods meant that Jewish demand was for live chickens, and from the mid-1920s these were increasingly reared in the Delmarva peninsula, between the Chesapeake Bay and the Atlantic Ocean.[2] While chicken production there in the 1930s grew, the industry remained small overall. It was not until Jewish demand could be met with pre-slaughtered chickens that the scale of chicken production was transformed, with the first processing stations opening in Delmarva in the late 1930s and early 1940s. Production capacity then mushroomed, so prices fell and producers began targeting the Gentile market. The long-standing preference for the American method of dry frying, or broiling, gave the emerging industry its name.[3] A massive increase in demand followed, first during the war and then especially afterward. Per capita consumption of chicken in the United States increased from five pounds in 1945 to over twenty-eight pounds in 1961. The American broiler-chicken industry emerged as the first modern agribusiness.[4]

Despite its parochial ethnic origins in serving the specialist needs of the Jewish community, the industry's transformation was no accident. In the 1920s chemists at the University of Wisconsin realized that supplementing chicken feed with synthetic vitamin D enabled poultry flocks to be better managed and the laying season to be extended.[5] This coincided with a USDA initiative (in conjunction with its Cooperative Extension Service, attached to the land-grant colleges) to encourage those farmers badly hit by disease in the 1920s to switch to broilers.[6] Research at the land-grant colleges further focused on mineral and vitamin feed supplements to boost growth, although the next chemical breakthroughs came from the leading pharmaceutical companies such as Merck.[7] By the early 1950s U.S. feedstuffs producers were supplementing their maize, soybean, and feather meal high-energy feed with a melee of vitamins, coccidiostats, and antibiotics, with the result that poultry growth rates jumped.[8]

Some breeds of chicken grew more quickly than others. Poultry farmers rapidly converged on one strain, the White Cornish stock developed by Charles Vantress, which grew from 12 percent to 76 percent of the Delmarva commercial broiler population from 1953 to 1957, for instance.[9] As the conditions for the mass production of chicken meat were increasingly ripe, Americans increasingly ate a single, standardized chicken product. Within a decade—from the late 1940s to the late 1950s—the American broiler-chicken industry had expanded enormously and begun to move away from its Delmarva peninsula heartland, with former tobacco and cotton farmers elsewhere turning to poultry production. Arkansas quickly developed into a major center of production. However, such rapid growth in the industry led to overproduction, falling prices, and industry reorganization. Poultry farmers with anything less than deep pockets were forced to withdraw or to become contract farmers working for the big feedstuffs companies (such as Ralston Purina), hatcheries (such as Perdue in the Delmarva peninsula) that integrated forward into chicken rearing, or the distributors (such as Tyson), that integrated backward from trucking in Arkansas.[10] During the 1950s, in other words, American poultry farming was evolving into a major industry that applied the latest technology in production, processing, and distribution.

Innovation and Growth in British Poultry Farming

British poultry farming began the 1950s far, far behind the U.S. industry in techniques, efficiency, and scale, partly, as the *Poultry Farmer* headline indicated, because of restrictive government practices. Yet—unusually for British industry— the poultry sector rapidly caught up with and even overtook American practice in the second half of the 1950s, to a large extent because the different institutional structure in British poultry farming encouraged better coordination between the principal parties during the industry's formative years.[11]

Before the war Britain's poultry flock of fifty million or so was reared for egg production.[12] Eggs had become a staple in the British diet before 1914, most obviously in their derivative form in cakes and biscuits, confectionery, and drinks, but some were eaten fresh.[13] Most were imported from Ireland, Denmark, France, and Austria as well as Poland, Russia, and Egypt. Frozen and dried eggs came increasingly from as far afield as China.[14] However, the British poultry population expanded during the 1930s as demand for fresh eggs grew. The flocks were small, typically only around two hundred to four hundred birds each, and were fed farmyard scraps. The eggs were collected by any one of Britain's 616 approved local packing stations, where they were boxed up and sent on.[15] It was a seasonal activity, with hens laying in the lighter summer months, and so could only ever be a sideline to the main farm business. Egg laying was mostly managed by the farmers' wives, with its significance deprecated as merely their "pocket money" activity.[16]

Significant or not, an egg-producing industry needed chickens, for a hen's productive life lasted around two years; and while there were some small commercial hatcheries, most egg-laying flocks reproduced themselves. This inevitably led to the production of surplus cockerel chicks all around the country.

It was these young cockerel chicks (males) that supplied the early demand for small "roasters." The older "spent," or redundant, layers were mostly only fit for the pot.[17] Apart from some imports from chicken farms in Hungary, Lithuania, and Russia, the chicken supplied to British households in the 1940s was overwhelmingly a by-product of these egg-laying flocks.[18] They were mostly sold in local markets or through small, independent egg and poultry retailers. However, demand was growing in the 1940s and 1950s. For one thing, chicken was left off the postwar British rationing system, and so a genuine market emerged. A few regional grocery chains that had sold poultry before the war also involved themselves in the poultry trade. Some went on to become instrumental in its transition.

The Coordination Problem and the Development of the British Poultry Industry

The early entrepreneurial poultry farmers were attempting to introduce techniques already developed in the United States. Whether it was increasing flock size in ever larger sheds, augmenting feed with ever more sophisticated supplements, or improved processing methods, knowledge flowed eastward across the Atlantic.[19] However, the British environment was different from that of the United States in two critical ways.

First, the role of government differed. The U.S. Department of Agriculture had long established its preference for direct intervention into the U.S. agricultural sector. With successive British governments embarking on a path of economic planning and control after the war, agricultural activities in Britain were also severely impinged by regulation. The more entrepreneurial of the poultry farmers became intensely frustrated at official restrictions on their growing businesses. Under the 1950 Diseases of Animals Act, Vantress chickens could not be imported, for example, ensuring that British chicken farmers were less productive than their American counterparts. To compound matters, official attempts to improve the domestic broiler stock were too slow. Entrepreneurs resorted to smuggling in fertilized Cornish Rock eggs from the United States. Antony Fisher, the founder of the leading producer Buxted Chickens, brought two dozen back in his hand luggage disguised as Easter eggs. An additional impact of the act was to bar imports of cheap American chicken meat, and so to offer protection to the infant British poultry industry.[20] This encapsulates the difference in the two governments' approaches to intervention. The USDA took responsibility for reorganizing the U.S. agricultural sector, commissioning research and disseminating information on new feed innovations, farming practices, and on how the industry should be structured. The British government had no truck with such prescriptive practices. Rather its philosophy was to control the market (through veterinary regulation, price controls, or import restrictions) but otherwise not intrude on actual farming practices.

Second, British food retailing, poultry retailing in particular, was seemingly far more concentrated than that of the United States, enabling a few leading retailers to exert more control over the emerging industry than was the case in the United States. This needs some explanation, for while there were many thousands of small, independent poultry stores in Britain in the 1930s, the trade "disappeared" during the war.[21] By the early 1950s only a dozen or so chains dominated the reemerging trade. The Unilever subsidiary MacFisheries and the regional grocer J. Sainsbury were the most important by far.[22] With the continued uncertainty over import restrictions in the postwar years and the expected growth in consumer demand for chicken, these leading retailers wanted to encourage greater quantity and better quality from domestic suppliers. Sainsbury's had already invested in its British supply lines with a long-standing trading relationship with Lloyd Maunder, a meat supplier based in Tiverton, Devon, and had even established its own poultry farm and processing plants in East Anglia. Sainsbury wanted to extend such collaborative supply arrangements to other leading poultry producers.[23]

It was not that American food retailers ignored chicken producers. Horowitz mentions the East Coast retailer A&P as one that was involved with the Delmarva producers, for example.[24] However, the leading retailers in Britain were able to exercise far more influence over their supply lines because they handled proportionately a much greater share of the total poultry trade. Sainsbury's, the market leader, reckoned that it had around 15 percent of the total market. With far more stores than Sainsbury's, MacFisheries could not have been far behind. Add in several of the other strong regional grocers, and the nascent poultry industry was dominated by perhaps fewer than a dozen retailers.[25]

Retailers were therefore able to exert far more control over the industry than retailers in the United States were, and it was these retailers, not the Ministry of Agriculture (the British equivalent of the USDA), who pressed British poultry farmers to follow American methods, exploit economies of scale, and so drive down the price of chicken. The net result was that British retailers not only possessed more market power than their American counterparts but also did not have to compete with an assertive state agency in efforts to restructure and coordinate poultry production. They nevertheless shared a similar goal to the USDA, wanting to create a mass market for chicken. In Britain this proved problematic, for despite its privileged position off the meat ration, chicken in Britain was firmly identified as a luxury in the mid-1950s, and it came with a price to match.

Self-Service-Inspired Retailer Intervention in British Poultry Production

The consensus view in the early 1950s was that chicken remained too expensive in Britain to compete effectively with alternative meats. The price had to fall before a significant market could emerge. Retailers took the initiative and introduced the principal pricing innovations in the early years of the industry's development. Most obviously they insisted on smaller birds that cost less to rear so that they could be priced more attractively. Price was far more important than size, as Max Justice, Sainsbury's manager of the Poultry, Game, and Rabbit Department, explained in his keynote speech to the inaugural broiler-industry conference in October 1955. He said that a "very substantial market for broilers can be developed if it is possible continuously to offer a bird of about 3lb cleaned, plucked weight for 10s ($1.40) retail."[26]

Retailers then began to reduce their range of offerings to just three grades of chicken: small chickens (very young birds at 1 pound to 1.5 pounds weight), roasters (up to 3 pounds and selling at the ten-shilling price point), and "the heavier" boilers.[27] "Standardization is long overdue," claimed *Poultry Farmer* in late 1954, "and until we have got some common basis on which to compare one bird with another, the whole business of buying table poultry is quite a hazard." Retailers pressed for far more uniformity, especially in the popular 3-pound category.[28]

As retailers began to influence both the size and permitted rearing costs, pressure was increasingly brought to bear on the palatability and presentation of the chicken meat. Alan Sainsbury (executive director and chairman of the family firm) insisted on buying white-fleshed birds, claiming that (and in contrast to prevailing tastes in the U.S.) "yellow-fleshed birds are not popular" with consumers. "Put yellow and white-fleshed birds side by side and you can be sure the yellow will be left to the last." Sainsbury also became active in breed selection, collaborating with commercial hatcheries and sponsoring the competitions in the first official broiler tests in 1959.[29] Retailers also dropped the word "broiler." It had been imported from the United States along with the industry, but British cooking habits did not include broiling. The term merely confused British shoppers; it was too close to the word "boiler," the lower-quality fowls.[30]

These few retailers were so interventionist because they were at the forefront of adopting the self-service format during these years, and none more so than Sainsbury. From the second half of the 1950s onward, Sainsbury was aggressively moving away from the traditional counter-service format and incorporating a self-service format with greater shelf and refrigerator space than its peers. Before the war Sainsbury had sold a huge variety of poultry and game in large quantities, and senior management wanted to continue with this trade. However, the new format could no longer tolerate such a range and variety of products. Increased standardization from suppliers was now paramount, prompting the retailer to become far more instrumental in managing the supply chain.

Sainsbury was already active in communicating novel farming techniques to the company's suppliers. Sainsbury's Max Justice told John Maunder (who had taken on the poultry business in the family firm) of advanced U.S. techniques in 1956, for instance, a conversation that ultimately precipitated a total transformation of rearing methods in Devon.[31] However, the introduction of self-service was to take the rate of retailer-led change in the organization of the industry to a new level.

Self-service was, of course, another American invention being introduced somewhat haphazardly and experimentally into the United Kingdom by several pioneers.[32] It was understood partly to be a solution to the growing difficulty in recruiting skilled labor for the grocer's traditional counter-service functions. Self-service's real benefit, however, was the format's impact on the productivity of scarce retail space. Sales per square foot could potentially increase, as backroom-preparation and storage space was converted into selling space. For most of the early experiments with the self-service format this meant following more or less exactly the American model of restricting the number of lines available in supermarkets to nonperishable packaged goods.[33]

Unlike Tesco, Fine Fare, and other self-service pioneers, Sainsbury was already committed to perishables, especially poultry. However, poultry presented something of a dilemma for a nascent self-service operator. It required both specific skills for preparation (drawing and trussing) and refrigerated storage space. Poultry was, in fact, so difficult to handle that butchers did not sell it, preferring instead to concentrate on red meats, which required less cold storage and could withstand more robust handling than poultry.[34] Harold Temperton, director of the National Institute of Poultry Husbandry at Harper Adams agricultural college, castigated butchers' conventional approach to poultry: "Undoubtedly the good work of the poultry farmer was frequently spoiled by crude methods of dressing, evisceration and presentation of many butchers."[35]

Poultry was, in fact, an ideal product for a labor-intensive, high-service quality retail format such as Sainsbury's traditional counter-service operation. But Sainsbury had committed itself to pursue expansion in self-service. It was because, uniquely among British food retailers, the company wanted both to continue serving its large existing market for poultry and to incorporate more self-service features in its stores, that it became the driving force behind the transformation of intensive rearing and factory processing of poultry in Britain. As Giles Emerson summarizes in his recent history of the company, "Sainsbury's was once again pioneers [sic] . . . [in the] product innovation stimulated by self service . . . the introduction of 'ready-to-cook' frozen chickens."[36]

Figure 5.1. Fresh chickens displayed in the window of one of Sainsbury's traditional counter-service stores. Copyright of the Sainsbury Archive, Museum in Docklands.

Frozen chickens sold in self-service supermarkets differed in one crucial respect from their forebears sold in the traditional counter-service stores. Without either the space for preparation or even the skills among branch staff, evisceration had to take place at the packing station rather than in the store. This was to have enormous implications for the processing side of the industry because chicken meat deteriorated rapidly after evisceration unless it was kept under refrigerated conditions.

Even before adding evisceration to processing operations, pressure from retailers had begun to transform Britain's packing stations. The retailers' demand for standardization of chicken sizes in the mid-1950s had a dramatic impact on the most labor-intensive elements of the poultry industry, slaughtering and processing. Standardizing bird sizes encouraged introduction of specialized machinery and allowed "packing stations [to] . . . get busy on the conveyor belt system and process at low cost."[37]

Packing stations that wanted to supply supermarkets with eviscerated chicken from the late 1950s onward had to go further and completely refigure their production methods in order to address the greater perishability of eviscerated chicken. They especially had to make substantial new investment in refrigeration and hygiene. For companies such as Buxted, able to make the additional investment, the gains were soon apparent. Writing his annual survey in *Poultry Farmer and Packer*, Tony Pendry, Buxted's managing director (and Antony Fisher's right-hand man), emphasised that "1959 has seen the opening of two or three very large broiler packing stations." Over half of the entire trade now went through just four processing stations.[38] One of those large packing stations was Buxted's new Aldershot "poultry factory," "with 80 people turning 30,000 pre-packed and frozen oven-ready birds a week" and planning to reach a throughput of 150,000 birds a week by 1961. With its conveyor-driven, automated processing system and quick-freezing plant in four enormous blast tunnels capable of freezing 1,800 birds an hour, semiautomatic packaging machinery, and shrink-wrapping, this new factory cost £250,000. It was probably the most advanced processing plant in the world, seemingly ahead of practice in the U.S. poultry industry.[39] The company was appealing for producers capable of producing batches of no fewer than 5,000 birds at a time. It was a far cry from traditional poultry farming and those flocks of 200 to 400 birds.[40]

The self-service imperative for off-site evisceration inevitably led to increased capital intensity, specifically in refrigeration, and not just in processing stations. All the way along the supply chain from slaughtering to sale, eviscerated poultry needed to be kept cold. "The temperature . . . must be reduced quickly to below zero Fahrenheit and held at this until a few hours before the bird is put into the oven. This means some formidable problems for distribution and the expense of such distribution must be charged to the product. Much so-called quick frozen poultry is badly trussed, low frozen and just pushed into a cellulose film bag, and after a few days' handling the bag bursts and the bird then begins to develop freezer burn, which means the flavour is lost," explained *Poultry Farmer* in 1958.[41]

The demand for refrigeration units in trucks and vans grew, with Imperial Chemical Industries emerging as the country's leading supplier.[42] The need for refrigeration at the point of sale of course became paramount, and so an unintended consequence of the self-service format's imperative need to push nondisplay activities up the supply chain was to give those retailers with large existing investments in expensive refrigeration units a strong competitive advantage in selling chicken.[43] Indeed, even among the supermarket pioneers only Sainsbury's, MacFisheries, and the much smaller Waitrose had made the necessary investments. By the mid-1950s Sainsbury typically installed up to two dozen refrigerators in each of its new self-service stores. Its chief electrical engineer reported, "Some idea of the load required at Lewisham can be given by the fact that it is practically double that required by the Lewisham Gaumont Cinema and had our building not been well advanced, the [electricity] supply company would have insisted on the construction of a sub-station to take this load." MacFisheries was also rolling out refrigeration-intensive, self-service format stores across the north of England.[44]

Figure 5.2. Fresh meat and frozen chicken in one of Sainsbury's self-service stores. Copyright of the Sainsbury Archive, Museum in Docklands.

Other grocers, even those developing self-service formats, such as the Allied Suppliers group (the Unilever subsidiary incorporating the Liptons, Home and Colonial, and other brands), the Co-operative Retail Service (CRS), Fine Fare, and Tesco, lay far behind the leaders in refrigeration capacity, preferring instead in their self-service experiments to follow the U.S. self-service archetype more exactly and focus on building up sales of nonperishables.[45] Of course the U.S. self-service model was also changing, and by the late 1950s chicken was increasingly distributed via self-service stores. In 1959 Denby Wilkinson claimed that "help-yourself stores handle 60%" of American poultry output. However, the chicken retailed in the United States differed crucially from the British product, distributed chilled not frozen and wrapped by the retailers in their central warehouses, not at the packing stations. By 1960 the British and American consumers were buying different products, with important consequences for the two industry structures.[46]

Retailer as Industry Coordinator

The net effects of continual innovation in the British poultry industry in the ten years after the decontrol of feedstuffs were a technological revolution in intensive rearing methods among farmers, the adoption of factory processing at packing stations, and the creation of a market for a slightly different product than that in the United States—the frozen chicken. These retailer-led influences were to have a dramatic impact on the speed with which the poultry industry developed in Britain and the organizational structure it adopted. The reduction in the size of the bird from 4.5–5 to 3 pounds reduced the growing cycle from twelve to ten weeks (and with later improvements in feedstuffs to nine weeks), meaning that farmers were able to move from three harvests per year to four and then to five. The productivity of farm space rocketed.[47]

However, it was the remarkable increase in the capital intensity in processing that forced the leading firms to invest heavily or lose out. Processors increasingly contracted out chicken rearing. Despite such precipitate change in firms such as Buxted Chickens and Lloyd Maunder, investments followed a careful sequence of discussion and agreement with the leading retailers.

While retailers were eager to consult with producers on product quality and price, they were quickly dragged into the industry's reorganization because of one important consequence of the drive to expand rearing. As the economies of scale began to be exploited and flock sizes rose from the hundreds to the thousands, retailers became increasingly agitated over fluctuations in supply. In the United States as the industry spread, it was plagued by periods of glut before falling prices subsequently led to producers exiting and so to undersupply. Such volatility hampered the industry's ability to market the product.[48] However, the much smaller number of retailers in Britain exerted far more control over the supply chain there than was possible in the United States and so could coordinate production cycles. They needed to because they depended on "regularity in supplies, . . . steady prices to the consumer . . . [and] consistency in quality," claimed Sainsbury's Max Justice in his keynote to the inaugural broiler conference.[49]

However, volatility in supply was difficult to eradicate because of the increase in batch size as chicken flocks grew. With the early producers rearing a flock of, say, one thousand or more chickens over a ten- to twelve-week season, the aim was to slaughter and distribute the entire flock of chickens as soon as they reached the target weight. The costs of two or three additional days of feeding could eliminate the farmers' profit margin. As flock sizes increased into the tens of thousands, the risks multiplied. Therefore, the leading growers began to contract directly with supermarket retailers in advance of the chickens even hatching, in order to reduce the risk of too many flocks being brought to market simultaneously.[50] In 1958, according to *Poultry Farmer and Packer*, "the chief development . . . has been the rise of the 'group system,' " whereby farmers had fixed contracts with packing stations, which in turn had fixed contracts with retailers, enabling the market to be coordinated.[51]

Leading retailers, in particular Sainsbury, precipitated the development of the contract-raising system. Alan Sainsbury had been very involved in the wartime controls of food production and distribution, which revolved around the zoning of supply, eliminating competition, but enforcing cooperative behavior. The company sought to adapt wartime practices for the fully competitive markets of the mid-1950s. John Maunder recalled being summoned to Max Justice's office in London in 1956 along with a few other pioneer poultry processors. They were told by the Sainsbury representative, "we're going to organise the country into sectors. And Maunder, you can have the West Country, and Antony Fisher you can have the South-east. . . . And we just sat there and took this as our marching orders. We were basically told, and 'Go home and organise it.' We had nothing more than that to go on. We literally had to go back and organise it."[52] Maunder, Buxted, and the others then recruited farmers to supply them, and they in turn then had the processors as guaranteed outlets. It was not straightforward, but the "group system" spread.

John Maunder later recollected that "you had to go out and literally persuade farmers to invest in chicken houses, at a time when it was a relatively unknown and unproven thing. It gathered momentum, of course, in a matter of a strikingly short period of time—only a couple of years. Farmers talked amongst themselves and we virtually had to do very little selling of the idea because it was an attractive commercial proposition at that time. In those early stages it was very novel. And to get a farmer to actually understand the fact that he had to put these day-old chicks in when we wanted them put in, because it had to be on a programmed output."[53]

The system guaranteed revenues to its privileged insiders, which in turn facilitated their commitment to a high level of capital expenditure in what were still quite small firms. Buxted worked closely with Sainsbury's as it embarked on its major expansion of processing facilities, for example. Perhaps unsurprisingly, "Sainsbury's became by far their biggest and best customer."[54] The lead suppliers collaborated among themselves, facing little incentive to compete once inside the Sainsbury "sector system," sharing knowledge about how to obtain the best supplies.[55] It was a system that constrained competitive forces and so indeed privileged insiders, but at the enormous benefit of increasing the returns to investment in new facilities in what was inevitably a highly volatile trade.[56] It was a form of collaboration that echoed contemporaneous developments in the United States but which remained significantly different. In the United States it was farmers and feed companies, prompted by the USDA, that integrated forward. Retailers, and initially processors, were omitted from the standard integrated U.S. poultry business. Processors indeed continued to buy their meat at auctions until recently, prompting incredulity from their British colleagues.[57]

In Britain as the scale of rearing and processing increased, and as the quality or product was increasingly assured, so did incentives to firms to incorporate multiple stages of poultry production. A few processors with close relationships to the dominant retailers initiated this process. By the early 1960s the leading processors had integrated backward beyond rearing and into commercial hatcheries, and they then developed close ties with feedstuffs producers. Buxted, for instance, sold a 10 percent block of shares to Spillers (a leading British feed manufacturer) in October 1961. After its flotation in 1963, a controlling stake was subsequently, in February 1964, acquired by Nitrovit, the Yorkshire-based feedstuffs company, which also then sought to create a wholly integrated business, "from a day old chick to the shop counter."[58]

In 1963, after only ten years of development, Geoffrey Sykes was able to characterize the British poultry industry as being composed of a handful of large, fully integrated units, where minimum efficient scale of output was five million broilers per annum. "From the stage of hatching-egg production to processing, the cost of this chain of enterprises exceeds £1½ million. The organisation behind the achievement of putting a chicken weighing 2½ lb ready-to-cook in the shops at 7/6d to 10/-."[59]

Well before then, by the end of 1958, the British poultry industry was claiming to have reached the American industry at the technological frontier of poultry production, in terms of both the rate of growth and the efficiency of processing.[60] Maunder and his fellow integrated processors would "all . . . make fairly regular trips to the States. The realization that we all came to was that in fact the only benefit that they [the U.S. producers] brought to this whole scene was the genetic benefit. We rapidly overtook them in almost every other sphere, and we would go there and we would say 'Yes, very interesting, but. . . .' In most areas they were behind us. . . . So we were always interested in what they were doing, but if we were interested in anything at all, it was the genetic progress that they were making with the stock."[61]

The growth in the poultry industry in the decade or so after the decontrol of feedstuffs was truly impressive. Total commercial broiler-chicken production grew from a near insignificant 1 million in 1950 to 5 million by 1953, or perhaps one-eighth of the egg-laying population. After the summer of 1953 growth was truly remarkable, the table-poultry population rising to 10 million shortly after 1956, 100 million by 1961, and well over 150 million by 1965–66. By 1967 the total number of birds produced for table poultry in Britain was 202 million, compared to only 52 million egg-layers.[62] This explosive growth in the size of the chicken industry was associated with a no less dramatic concentration: by 1963, 90 percent of the entire chicken production was "in the hands of only one thousand growers," each either owned by or contracting with only a few dozen processors.[63] At the top of the industry were Sainsbury's and MacFisheries in retailing and Buxted and Lloyd Maunder in production and processing. Together these firms had captured around one-third of the total market during the late 1950s and early 1960s, albeit at different stages.[64]

Such concentration had yielded tremendous gains in efficiency, which allowed the price to fall.[65] In 1954 Sainsbury's stores were selling their roasters for four shillings per pound or more, which for a four-pound bird placed a chicken firmly in the luxury price category.[66] Hall and Clark show how chicken prices fell by 30 percent from 1955 to 1965, while pork and lamb prices rose by between 20 and 30 percent and beef prices rose by over 40 percent over the same period.[67] As prices fell, demand for chicken soared. British meat consumption overall was broadly static after 1953. The share going to poultry rose from only 1 percent in 1955 to 10 percent by 1965. Once the idea of chicken consumption gained credence with the British public, they switched to poultry in ever greater numbers. Poultry consumption represented almost a quarter of all British meat consumption by 1990.[68]

Conclusion

Within ten years after the *Poultry Farmer* heralded the decontrol of feedstuffs, the British poultry industry had been transformed from an agricultural backwater into one of the most dynamic sectors of the British economy. In 1964 Buxted was processing over five hundred thousand birds *per week* at its three processing plants.[69] This transformation was dependent on a series of critical innovations: in poultry breed selection and reproduction techniques at commercial hatcheries; in nutrition, growth management, and disease control, especially through exploiting developments in pharmaceutical technologies; in the accommodation of ever larger flocks, including their feeding, ventilating, and control of their behavior; in their slaughtering and processing, with the enormous investments in refrigeration throughout the distribution channels, and the ever more widespread use of antibiotics; in retailing, with the emergence of supermarkets and the self-service format prompting so many of these changes in the supply chain; and in cooking, with families by the million taking first to roasting chickens with greater regularity and then frying, baking, and grilling in their experimentation with new culinary tastes.

Yet all of these innovations originated in the United States, where all of the advantages of scale and access to investment finance in the 1950s lay. Even self-service techniques originated there and were widely adopted by retailers of chicken. Despite this, British producers were able to catch up and even, in many areas, overtake the American producers by the mid-1960s. To a large extent this was because the institutional structure of the British industry differed significantly from that in the United States.

The coordinating role played by a few leading food retailers enabled efficiency levels to rise quickly in the British industry. Sainsbury was committed to introducing self-service techniques into its chain of stores from the late 1950s while still retaining the company's traditional commitment to poultry. It was only after realizing the possibilities that arose from introducing American methods in processing that Sainsbury's then organized the industry by allocating regional sectors to its privileged suppliers, who then had to ensure that supplies came from their local farmers. This "group system" echoed wartime practice, and yet it was superbly successful in peacetime competitive markets because it allowed the British industry to avoid the volatility associated with the

U.S. model. The lack of coordination there meant that the market for chicken initially oscillated between periods of glut and periods of scarcity before consolidation occurred. In Britain the market was created for frozen, not fresh, chicken, so perishability was reduced. Coordination around this frozen chicken enabled the creation of a stable market early. Revenues then became far more predictable, prompting higher rates of investment in advanced mechanization and, with the guaranteed sales, high rates of utilization across all new capital equipment from the outset. This provided an institutional structure that enabled scarce investment to be used efficiently and so encouraged rapid growth.

The British model was based on collaborative relationships along the supply chain instigated and controlled by retailers. This was absent in the United States. The American preference for "arm's-length" contracts even to the 1980s bemused John Maunder. In a sector where quality assurance was of paramount importance in guaranteeing product quality to the consumers, the British model was to opt for the organization closest to consumers, the leading retailers, to be the principal coordinator. The American model largely left such coordination to the relevant government department and the firms with the deepest pockets and therefore best able to survive the industry's periodic downturns and drive consolidation through. In Britain, instead of the proactive role of the USDA, the government was essentially broadly protectionist but uninterested in pursuing any interventionist policies that might have helped to encourage modernization of poultry production. Indeed, their protectionist measures hindered innovation in the closely related egg sector, permitting archaic production and distribution methods to continue unchallenged.

The British model eventually changed and became somewhat less integrated, although food retailers still carry far more influence there today than their counterparts in the United States do. The significance of the remarkable British poultry industry experiment was to have important repercussions for the country's leading food retailers for many years afterward. Of all the supermarket pioneers, Sainsbury's emerged as the market leader in the early 1960s and increased its dominance during the 1980s by learning how to innovate using strongly collaborative relationships with its supply chain.

Chapter 6
Trading Quality, Producing Value: Crabmeat, HACCP, and Global Seafood Trade

Kelly Feltault

As I entered the company's lobby, I was drawn to a brochure that announced "The Story of Crab: the Maryland Crab Cake." The brochure featured an image of a succulent, golden crab cake made from the cultural food icon of the Chesapeake Bay region—*Callinectes sapidus*, or the blue crab. However, I was not in Maryland or even in America. I was in Bangkok at Pakfoods Incorporated, a Thai-owned multinational seafood corporation, waiting to meet with company executives. The crab cake on their brochure was made from a different species of swimming crab, *Portunus pelagicus*, harvested from the Gulf of Thailand. Pakfoods ships these to large chain restaurants in the United States, where crab cakes are one of the most popular menu items, part of a trend in growing seafood consumption. Between 1980 and 2005 America's per capita seafood consumption increased 14 percent over the previous seven decades, but over 70 percent of this seafood was imported.[1]

Crabmeat was not initially an imported product. U.S. harvest levels of blue crabs rose 57 percent between 1970 and 1990 when Chesapeake crabmeat companies experienced a boom period through high-volume sales to expanding restaurant and grocery chains.[2] However, in 1992 one of their largest customers, the restaurant chain Phillips Seafood, began importing crabmeat from its new plants in Southeast Asia. In Thailand companies such as Pakfoods converted their shrimp factories to crabmeat facilities, which became the latest high-value seafood export supporting the country's economic development strategy. Between 1995 and 1999 the amount of imported crabmeat increased 550 percent, and Chesapeake companies began losing customers.[3] Then in 1995 the crab stock in the Chesapeake showed signs of collapse.

This story may appear as a tragedy of the commons: consumers' desire for a healthier, low-fat diet led to overfishing in the United States, resulting in increased seafood imports from developing countries. However, my research suggests that restaurants' increased competition for crabs was the initial reason for offshore production. Back in the boardroom of Pakfoods, executives told me that they were better able to control the natural resource through quality control because "the process became standardized here in Thailand, the fishery— the crab—was standardized, to regulate quality."[4] This statement suggests that global seafood networks trade quality distinctions that shape supply and demand, as well as environmental change.

The tragedy-of-the-commons argument does not connect environmental change and resource capture to the restructuring of the food service industry in the 1980s, nor does it explain how or why seafood companies create global seafood commodity networks. The search for new seafood products combined with mergers and expansions of regional seafood restaurants restructured purchasing toward high volumes from single suppliers. This reshaped the quality demands on seafood suppliers and required an element of control over the network starting with the natural resource. The seafood industry gained control over natural resources through a new global seafood safety inspection system, the Hazard Analysis and Critical Control Points (HACCP). This science-based auditing system facilitated the creation and maintenance of global seafood networks and created environmental and social change.

In this chapter I unravel how and why transnational crabmeat networks were constructed and sustained based on quality distinctions, and how these networks operate within neoliberal globalization and development policies. I argue that HACCP formalized a scientific definition of quality, remaking the seafood industry in the image of pathogens and hazards—risks to be controlled— through the production of knowledge and value systems that facilitated the control of the natural resource and reshaped its value. However, despite the status of HACCP as a global regulatory standard intended to harmonize trade, it is not homogenous and instead operates as a heterogeneous global governance system producing uneven outcomes through differentiated products, production sites, environments, and workers.

Globalizing Networks and Nature

Since the 1980s development agencies such as the World Bank have encouraged developing countries to specialize their food production toward high-value foods (HVF) as a way to increase export earnings and foreign direct investment.[5] Seafood has been a cornerstone of this export-oriented industrialization, and developing countries account for half of all exported seafood products in the world.[6] As a result, fish have been the most heavily traded international food commodity for the last twenty-five years, and capture (wild-caught) fisheries remain the dominant form of harvesting.[7] However, this development strategy required foods and states to compete on quality traits across transnational boundaries. By the 1990s regulations governing global food trade expanded beyond trade tariffs to encompass food-quality and safety standards.[8] Most of these regulations, such as HACCP, were auditing schemes in which the state validates the procedures and practices of companies, emphasizing procedural values while allowing companies to police themselves.[9] This reregulation at the national and international levels embodied the values of neoliberal globalization of economic efficiency and privatization. The question, however, is what makes food safe or good?

Food quality and safety are hybrids of social constructions and physical realities assembled from food production methods, scientific knowledge, the biophysical characteristics of the raw materials, and the cultural value of the food. This makes safety and quality political and cultural negotiations, not only in defining quality but also in providing quality assurance.[10] Measuring quality assurance and then certifying quality and safety raise questions of trust and credibility, demanding measurable standards and constant monitoring.[11] Global food-quality and safety governance systems are therefore about regulating social and environmental relationships embodied in the rules, procedures, codes, tests, and evidence for measuring and monitoring quality.[12]

Actors in global seafood networks use the body of knowledge generated by quality standards to create relational power binding actors in the network, while the legitimation and adoption of quality standards form a structural power relationship between the industry and actors outside the network.[13] Ultimately quality and safety standards arrange products, people, and places into classes with distinct values.[14] This creates "a geography of quality" in which different states are constructed socially, politically, and environmentally as constituting specific levels of production quality.[15] This leads to regionally differentiated value production and uneven development, as states and other institutions come to develop, adopt, and enforce quality standards, as well as the values and relationships embodied in them.[16]

As one of the last wild-caught foods, seafood presents a unique opportunity to analyze these relationships.[17] Seafood companies will tell you that quality starts with the raw material, but fish present a daunting set of variables with over five hundred edible species harvested in a diversity of habitats, depths, and distances from shore. To harvest crabs, Chesapeake fishermen go out early in the morning in small, motorized boats and return in the afternoon to processing factories, where they sell their crabs through long-standing personal relationships or family ties. Seafood is an extremely perishable food item, producing enzymatic reactions that immediately start the decomposition process upon harvest. For this reason, crabs must be alive when sold to processors and must be cooked immediately and then cooled under refrigeration. Once cooled, crabs are distributed to tables, where women use sharp knives to open the crabs and pick the meat out by hand, packing it into plastic cans. The cans are then weighed, sealed, and put on ice.

Different types of fish have specific textures, protein structures, tastes, and color traits that shape production practices, quality standards, and the cultural value of the food.[18] U.S. consumers have preferred fresh crabmeat, but like all fresh fish, crabmeat will last seven to ten days if kept cold, while freezing depends on the ability of the fish to hold its shape, texture, and taste—and not all do. Fresh crabmeat demands immediate sales and distribution networks, and the perishability limits the geographic distribution.

Marine water quality presents another variable, as fish absorb toxins and pollution from the marine environment, introducing environmental contaminants. In the United States seafood never came under a national, mandatory inspection system. Instead, each state produced its own seafood sanitation regulations, which conflicted with those of other states. In addition, each plant maintained its own modifications to production practices, making each factory a stand-alone unit.[19] The results have been a highly fragmented industry and multiple standards of quality. These biophysical, cultural, and political elements present challenges for defining global quality standards because definitions must start with the natural resources, requiring transnational seafood networks to gain control of local environments.[20]

In the next sections, I outline the Chesapeake quality assemblage followed by the quality definitions produced by crab restaurants in the Chesapeake who became crabmeat importers. I follow this with a discussion of HACCP and the science of quality that it established in relation to global seafood trade. Then I describe the reorganization of production and value in Thailand. Throughout the essay, I frame these processes through the trade case filed by U.S. crabmeat packers with the U.S. International Trade Commission (USITC) and conclude with their decision that solidified companies' definitions of quality and structural power.

Chesapeake Quality

In business since 1890, the J. M. Clayton Company claims the title of oldest crabmeat packer in the world. As fourth-generation owners and managers, Jack, Bill, and Joe Brooks have witnessed great changes in the industry, including the boom period in the late 1980s. They explain that as Phillips Seafood restaurants expanded into a regional chain featuring Maryland crab cakes, new customers began selling crab cakes and everyone needed high volumes of crabmeat. "Then I remember 1997 being the year that things started really getting hard to sell and we started to see more imported crabmeat coming in from places like Thailand," explained Jack.[21] Bill showed me their sales records for 1993–97 and the list of customers they lost—high-volume restaurant chains and retail customers. Between 1995 and 1999 imported crabmeat increased from 3.2 million pounds to 20.9 million pounds and market share for the domestic crabmeat industry dropped from 60 percent to 30 percent.[22] In 1999 J. M. Clayton and other domestic crabmeat packers filed suit with the USITC seeking trade relief under Section 201 of the U.S. trade law.

Section 201 investigates whether imported commodities pose a substantial threat to the domestic industry.[23] The key to establishing the case for threat rests in determining whether the domestic commodity is "like or directly competitive with the imported article."[24] According to U.S. trade law, "like" is defined as substantially identical in inherent or intrinsic characteristics, while "directly competitive" is defined as substitutable.[25] This required importers and domestic producers to make distinctions about their products based on their material and semiotic aspects. The testimony reveals two definitions of quality. First, domestic conventions focused on taste connected to the species of crab, grading standards, and historical and cultural factors that geared the industry toward producing fresh crabmeat. Second, importers' quality conventions built on the grading standards of the domestic industry in order to conform to cultural notions of crab cakes but claimed to meet the demands of retailers and restaurateurs through "consistent grading," long shelf-life from pasteurization, no shell fragments, stable supply and prices, high-volume production, and a stricter adherence to HACCP than domestic packers. As a result, definitions of quality assembled from production processes, sociopolitical relationships, and science became the primary focus of the case.

Maryland has influenced domestic quality criteria since 1910 when Frederick Jewett invented grading standards. As the owner of Coulbourne and Jewett Seafood Packing Company, Mr. Jewett sought to expand the company's market by adding value and differentiating its product based on the flavor of the different cuts of meat.[26] Until this time, crabmeat companies mixed all of the meat into one container, but lump meat is very mild while claw meat has a "fishy" flavor. Mr. Jewett divided the carapace of the blue crab into sections and cuts of meat: lump from the back of the crab near the swimming fin; special from the middle sections of the body; backfin as a mix of broken lump and special; regular as a mix of special and leg meat; and claw.[27]

This grading system also allowed Coulbourne and Jewett to restructure their pricing, positioning lump meat as the premium and most expensive grade and claw as the cheapest. The grading system worked. By 1935 the company shipped thirty-five hundred one-pound cans of graded crabmeat to Acme grocery stores in Baltimore every Sunday and eighteen hundred to the grocer's warehouse in Philadelphia, becoming the only company to pack one million pounds of crabmeat five years in a row.[28] Other packers adopted the system, creating a hierarchy of tastes and prices with lump meat at the top. The hier-

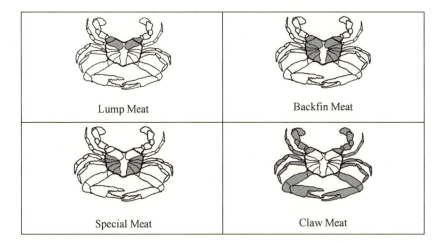

Figure 6.1. Grades of crabmeat shown in shaded sections. Courtesy of Phillips Foods, Inc.

archy continues today, but these standards were never formalized, and packing houses have created their own versions of the lower grades according to the packer's personal preferences or special requests of buyers.

In the 1950s certain grades of crabmeat became associated with specific dishes when microbiological contamination produced new state sanitation regulations that altered production methods and eliminated the removal of shell fragments. In 1951 Byrd Incorporated, a packinghouse in Maryland, perfected a method of pasteurizing crabmeat. In the pasteurization process, fresh crabmeat is canned and then heated in a water bath to at least 185 degrees internal temperature for three minutes, cooled, and then held in cold storage at 38 degrees.[29] This extends the shelf life from ten days to eighteen months. Initially the industry viewed pasteurization as a way to manage the fluctuating crab harvests and stabilize the supply of crabmeat through inventory. The method would also allow for long-distance shipping and thus expand the market. However, pasteurization also eliminates bacteria, and the invention occurred as state health departments began testing food for microbes.

Crabmeat is cooked first and then handpicked and packed, making it a ready-to-eat product and a high-risk food for microbial contamination. In 1952 Pennsylvania health officials found E. coli in one-third of the crabmeat sampled and threatened an embargo.[30] Pennsylvania was the largest outlet for Maryland processors, and this began a three-year debate on sanitation and inspection regulations coupled with increased research on pasteurization. In 1954 the University of Maryland created a seafood laboratory to provide sanitation extension services to crab packers and research to improve the pasteurization process.[31] The lab issued industrywide guidelines, but each state health department created its own regulations for pasteurization, mirroring the existing structure for seafood safety regulation. In 1955 and 1957 Maryland issued new crabmeat processing regulations aimed at controlling the risks of contamination at the picking stage. Prior to 1955 crab pickers were allowed to "pick through" crabmeat to remove the shell fragments as part of quality control, but after 1955 this quality check stopped. The law required crab pickers to pick crabmeat directly into the can and then seal it, leaving high levels of shell pieces in cheaper grades of meat. This standard applied to pasteurized crabmeat too, even though the pasteurization process eliminated bacteria introduced during the shell-removal process. As a result, restaurants began purchasing lump and backfin to make crab cakes because they contained fewer shell fragments, while cheaper grades went to grocery stores and frozen food manufacturers, such as Mrs. Paul's.[32] Because of its association with sanitation problems, "picking through" crabmeat became a sign of low quality and was heavily resisted by Maryland officials and packinghouses into the twenty-first century. As a result, grading and shell fragments remained quality-control problems for domestic packers.

Despite guidelines and marketing efforts, pasteurized crabmeat never gained acceptance in the frozen-food era of the 1950s and 1960s. First, shoppers and packers felt that pasteurization removed some of the sweet flavor of crabmeat, making the mild lump meat rather bland. Second, in the early stages many packers used the pasteurization process to pack meat that was on the verge of spoiling, and shoppers and retailers began to associate pasteurization with low-quality crabmeat.[33] By the 1960s restaurants still wanted fresh crabmeat, not pasteurized, and industry reports emphasized the need to improve the pasteurization process in order to expand the market. However, states and the industry made no effort to address the cost barriers of equipment and cold storage. Instead, packers used pasteurization to "put their money on ice" or can surplus crabmeat in the fall for sale during the winter when crab harvests and quality were low.[34]

Because of the fluctuating supply, retailers and restaurants sourced from several processors, which required finding packinghouses with similar concepts of quality. Reports on the crabmeat industry from 1964 and 1983 lament that companies still had not cooperated to solve industrywide quality-control problems such as "uniformity of product [or] product specifications," and by the boom period of the 1980s 70 percent of the crabmeat still went to market as fresh.[35] This assemblage of quality standards presented challenges to the changing restaurant and retail industry of the Reagan era. The quality assemblage of the 1980s and 1990s emphasized few shell fragments, long shelf life, stable supply, consistent grading, and traceability of ingredients to support the corporate kitchen and its new purchasing structures.

Restaurant-Quality Crab Cakes

Prior to the 1990s only a few crab cake products had appeared on the national market, resembling what Chesapeake packers and importers called "hockey pucks"—machine-formed patties using cheaper grades of crabmeat augmented with breading and minced fish.[36] In contrast, Chesapeake restaurants used backfin and jumbo lump to make hand-formed crab cakes containing little filler. These "restaurant quality" crab cakes transformed the industry as they moved from a regional to a national menu item, producing a new set of quality standards tied to changes in the restaurant industry, especially purchasing practices. These changes meant increased pressure on the natural resource as restaurants searched for the least available, most expensive grade of crabmeat—lump meat.

Distributors, trade journals, crabmeat importers, and even the domestic packers point to Phillips Seafood restaurants as the driver in transforming the Maryland crab cake into a national commodity. Phillips began as a family-run crab packer on Hoopers Island, Maryland, in 1914, much like J. M. Clayton. However, in 1956 the family opened a small restaurant in the sleepy seaside resort of Ocean City, Maryland, selling crab cakes and steamed crabs to the growing number of tourists. Phillips opened three more restaurants in Ocean City throughout the 1970s as the beach became Maryland's largest tourist destination and the Chesapeake became a recreational destination. The company continued to expand in the 1980s as part of urban renewal and waterfront development projects in Baltimore and Washington, opening 350-seat restaurants in both locations.[37] By 1985 Phillips restaurants served an average of 25,000 people a day and the company's Baltimore restaurant was the fifth-largest restaurant in sales in the country. Crabmeat amounted to 65 percent of total restaurant sales, mostly as crab cakes on the all-you-can-eat buffet.[38]

The expansion of the restaurants and their reliance on crabmeat presented

Figure 6.2. "Hockey puck" crab cake (*left*) and "restaurant quality" crab cake (*right*). Photo by Kelly Feltault (*left*) and courtesy of Chef Greg Johnson, Chez Foushee Richmond, Virginia (*right*).

a new set of challenges for the domestic industry and the natural resource on which it relied. Phillips used fresh domestic crabmeat because of its taste, but its perishability required high customer turnover to keep the product from spoiling before diners consumed it.[39] High turnover translated to high-volume purchases from Chesapeake processors, even in the winter months, producing several results. First, the variety of quality standards between packinghouses meant that Phillips relied on a select number of packers but now needed pasteurized crabmeat from these plants on the Chesapeake and in other states. However, they could not get enough crabmeat because so few packers had pasteurization facilities due to costs for equipment and cold storage space to hold inventory for such a historically unpopular product. Phillips tried to substitute Dungeness crab, but the taste, texture, and grading were not the same, so the meat did not produce "Maryland" crab cakes.[40] As a result, Phillips frequently removed crab from the menu from January to March starting in the mid-1980s.[41] Second, shell fragments, once a sign of sanitation and quality, were now a large cost to kitchens, which employed full-time staff to pick through thousands of pounds of crabmeat each day.[42] Third, Phillips's high-volume sales meant increased crab harvests for the Chesapeake, which had reached its maximum sustainable yield in the late 1960s.[43] As the catch per unit effort by fishermen jumped, Maryland responded with increased harvesting regulations. Maryland crabmeat processors relied more heavily on crabs from Louisiana and North Carolina.

As Phillips and the popularity of crab cakes grew, other restaurants and manufacturers began offering crab cakes, creating new competition for crabmeat and crabs. For example, during the early 1980s M&I Seafood began producing value-added crab cakes for sale in wholesale clubs such as Costco, and in 1992 McDonald's began selling a McCrab Cake sandwich produced by Seawatch International, a Chesapeake manufacturer. Project manager Norman Whittington recalled that "regional McDonald's stores were serving crab cake sandwiches using all domestic meat. This amounted to 4% of the chain's sales for the region so it was incredibly popular."[44] By the early 1990s local seafood restaurants from Boston and Texas expanded into regional chains much like Phillips, adding crab cakes made of lump meat to their menus, and M&I Seafood began selling crab cakes on the cable network Quality, Value, Convenience (QVC).[45] As new competitors attempted to make "restaurant quality" crab cakes, they faced the same quality concerns, and competition for the crabs intensified while many states increased their conservation regulations.

Changes in purchasing structures compounded these issues during the 1990s. As restaurants began to expand regionally, they consolidated purchasing, while grocery retailers began to merge and consolidate operations, and national distributors such as Sysco ventured into seafood sales.[46] Overall, the goal was to gain control of the supply chain through economies of scale, centralized purchasing, and traceability of products.[47] Phillips consolidated purchasing under Lloyd Byrd, who sought to buy from one supplier, as he did with farmed foods such as chicken and shrimp. However, purchasing crabmeat required daily telephone calls to processors and seafood distributors to see who had crabs. Although the domestic industry responded with increased production of pasteurized crabmeat even in the summer, the fragmented structure of the industry, including state regulations, prevented it from meeting other standards such as high volumes of lump and backfin, consistent grading standards, and shell-free crabmeat.

In 1989 Steve Phillips and Lloyd Byrd traveled to the Philippines and Thailand with their shrimp distributor and saw *Portunus pelagicus*, the blue swimming crab, for the first time. A cousin of the U.S. blue crab, the *Portunus* crab has the same taste, texture, and body structure as a blue crab, meaning that it would conform to the same picking and grading methods as those used in the United States—they were restaurant quality. In 1990 Lloyd became director of international operations for Phillips Foods, opening the company's first overseas processing factory in the Philippines. Between 1992 and 1999 Phillips opened plants in Thailand, Indonesia, China, and Latin America and began selling crabmeat to other restaurants. Phillips Foods invested millions of dollars in marketing programs directed at chefs and restaurant owners (their target consumers), and with incentives and subsidies from Maryland they opened a factory in Baltimore to manufacture frozen crab cakes.[48] Meanwhile, Seawatch International and M&I began sourcing crabmeat from Asia, and Lloyd Byrd left Phillips in 1996 to start Byrd International, which began exporting crabmeat from Thailand and Indonesia the following year. In 1995 pasteurized blue crabmeat emerged as the hot new product at the largest seafood trade show, the Boston Seafood Show, propelling it onto menus at chain restaurants across the country, while larger seafood companies added imported pasteurized crabmeat to their product lines.

Phillips and Byrd were specifically named in the USITC case as the two largest crabmeat producers and importers in the United States. They quickly responded to the suit by creating the Coalition for the Free Trade of Crabmeat, which included retailers, distributors, foreign governments, seafood chain restaurants, trade associations, and foreign packers such as Pakfoods in Thailand. During testimony, Phillips and Byrd argued that their product was of a higher quality because adherence to new global seafood safety standards, HACCP, allowed them to standardize the product according to the current demands of the food industry, consumers, and governments, and expand the market. Representatives from the largest regional grocery store, Super Giant, and America's second-largest food distributor, U.S. Food Service, supported this argument, testifying that they now defined crabmeat quality by "a long shelf life with a constant, reliable supply, and with a low shell content" rather than by taste.[49] The testimony indicated that definitions of quality had shifted toward the science of quality that had emerged in the seafood industry under mandatory HACCP regulations that went into effect in 1995. As the USITC hearing got under way, the newly formed Bi-state Blue Crab Advisory Committee issued a report that the Chesapeake crab population was in crisis; it had lost 70 percent of its female biomass and could no longer reproduce itself. Steve Phillips blamed the scarcity of crabs in the Chesapeake on poor resource management, divorcing the restaurant industry from any role in the collapse of the fishery.[50]

TABLE 1. Time Line of Events

Year	Event
1970–85	Phillips restaurants expand and consolidate purchasing
1977–95	Domestic packers experience a growth period
1984–89	Maryland increases crab harvesting regulations
1988	Phillips announces company cannot get enough crabmeat due to seasonality and competition for the resource
1990	Phillips begins overseas operations
1992	Phillips's first offshore factory opens
	McDonald's debuts its McRib Cake sandwich made with domestic crabmeat
1993	Crab harvesting peaks in the United States
1993	Seawatch sources crabmeat in India
1994	Domestic packers increase production of pasteurized crabmeat
1995	J. M. Clayton sees decline in sales
	Phillips opens first factory in Thailand
	U.S. FDA requires HACCP compliance by 1997 for all seafood processors
	Maryland passes emergency crab harvesting regulations
1996	Byrd International opens factories in Thailand, Indonesia
1997	Phillips opens frozen food factory in Baltimore, producing 200,000 crab cakes a day made from imported crabmeat
1999	Domestic packers file USITC case
2000	Reports indicate Chesapeake crab population has 70 percent decrease in female biomass, not able to reproduce itself; Maryland and Virginia increase harvesting regulations
	A decision is reached in the USITC case
2001	Bi-State Blue Crab Advisory Committee recommends 15 percent reduction in harvests

The Science of Quality

Crabmeat importers testified that pasteurized crabmeat was actually "fresher than fresh" crabmeat because the pasteurization process provided a bacteria-free product.[51] The restructuring of seafood restaurants, along with global sourcing, refocused concerns over food quality from adulteration (adding substances) to food safety (microbes, contaminants).[52] This shift began in the 1950s, but a fear of food-borne pathogens overtook the food industry in the late 1980s culminating in the adoption of the Hazard Analysis and Critical Control Points inspection system (HACCP). However, safe food was just the organizing principle as politics, trade, and science merged to reshape the industry through HACCP, a new set of mandatory regulations intended to harmonize global seafood trade. However, HACCP did not produce homogenization. Companies and governments implemented HACCP differently across national and state regulatory environments, even as it supported neoliberal changes to regulatory systems.

The seafood industry was the first food sector mandated to implement HACCP at national and global scales. Between 1987 and 1992 Congress produced a record number of legislative proposals requiring a national seafood safety inspection system, as public concern over unsafe seafood hit an all-time high.[53] Unlike meat and poultry, seafood did not have a national inspection system, relying instead on states and limited FDA regulation. Media reports on "widespread fish spoilage, bacterial contamination, the oil spill of the Exxon Valdez, and hospital waste washing up on beaches" outlined why seafood presents the most complex food safety issue of any food commodity.[54] Representatives from the National Fisheries Institute (NFI)—a trade association— summed up the problem before Congress: "We do recognize that nature is no longer pristine. Residues of an industrial society are present in the environment and many times in plants and animals. Fish, at the top of the food chain, are particularly susceptible and may carry some chemical residues in their edible flesh."[55] In other words, the consequences of industrial development and modernization produced a specific set of hazards and risks in seafood that needed to be controlled, while consumers needed assurance of seafood's wholesomeness.[56] The marine environment had become a risk.

Because of this, seafood faces what Nestle calls "the two culture problem" of risk assessment—it requires both science-based and value-based approaches.[57] Science-based approaches identify preventable, measurable hazards in order to set standards and make decisions on trade, while value-based approaches consider the cultural value of the food and what makes it "good" or "wholesome."[58] The growing amount of imported seafood arriving from distant environments complicated these concerns. By the 1980s the United States imported approximately 63 percent of the seafood consumed nationally, mostly from developing countries, raising concerns that America was importing environmental hazards and poor food sanitation standards from beyond its borders.[59] In a landmark study on seafood safety, the National Academy of Sciences (NAS) argued that increased imports and consumption of fish required a new food safety system that met the unique environmental and physical properties of seafood.[60] In testimony, representatives of the NAS stated that traditional end-product testing at the factory level "would not significantly reduce current levels of seafood-related illness."[61] The NAS recommended mandatory HACCP inspections, and the FDA and NFI concurred. All agreed that HACCP would create a "stronger national approach to fish inspection and control to ensure both quality of performance and reasonably uniform standards."[62]

HACCP holds "space-age" science-based credentials. In 1959 the National Aeronautical and Space Administration (NASA) contracted the Pillsbury Company to produce food for the emerging space program that would provide 100 percent assurance food products would be free of pathogens, toxins, chemicals, and physical hazards.[63] Pillsbury realized that the current end-product testing and continuous inspection systems would not meet these requirements. Instead, Pillsbury needed to gain control of the supply chain "from farm to table," starting with the raw ingredients. The resulting system, HACCP, focuses more on the processes of production, operating as a preventative system in which food safety is designed into the product and production systems.[64]

Companies create their own HACCP plans based on seven principles: identify hazards in a food processing chain, develop critical control points (CCP) to prevent the hazards, establish limits or standards for each CCP, create monitoring procedures, establish corrective actions to maintain standards, keep records for traceability, and continuously validate and update the HACCP system.[65] State inspectors then audit the HACCP plan through its records, not inspection of the products. HACCP operates as a private-interest regulatory system in which states assume a monitoring role while encouraging companies to police themselves.[66] In this way HACCP fit within neoliberal goals of privatization, economic efficiency, and good governance.

Auditing emphasizes procedural values and the regulation of relationships within the network. For seafood, the first control point is the raw material, extending quality and traceability backward to the marine environment, harvesting vessels, and landing sites. In the United States these locations are not officially under the control of seafood companies or the U.S. FDA, but countries such as Thailand brought fishermen and crabs under corporate and government control.

To gain control of these relationships, processors use HACCP together with fish microbiology to establish rules and conventions regarding limits and standards throughout the commodity network on how to handle raw materials, production processes, time and temperature sequences, the industrial and natural environments, personnel behavior, and work methods. Companies maintain these relationships through HACCP's record-keeping system borrowed from NASA. The system requires traceability of the raw materials down to the production factory, the names of the workers and fishermen, and any other "information that might contribute to the history of the product."[67] Thus, HACCP is a historical process in its own right, one in which the flow charts, time and temperature monitoring charts, lists of employees for each shift, and the signatures of HACCP team leaders represent social relationships and value production in the network. Furthermore, the focus on gaining control of the natural resource created value and redistributed risk as it included and excluded fishermen and processors based on their ability to meet new quality standards, in effect privatizing the fishery.

Despite the demands for HACCP inspection in the United States (and its success with NASA), Congress never passed any of the proposed legislation. Instead, the FDA and NFI collaborated to develop the system, and in 1995 the FDA announced mandatory HACCP compliance for all U.S. seafood companies by 1997. This included imported seafood, which meant requiring developing countries not only to implement HACCP but also to share the risk and higher levels of blame for unsafe seafood. This new relationship with developing countries reflected the changing trade climate of the 1980s and 1990s. Under the liberalized trade regulations of the Uruguay Round of GATT, developed countries, especially the European Community (EC), used health and safety requirements as a way to limit imported food and protect domestic industries—a nontariff barrier to trade (NTB).[68] As a result, the EC announced mandatory HACCP compliance for all seafood imports in 1992, and a year later the Codex Alimentarius adopted HACCP as a global guidance to all countries.[69] The World Trade Organization (WTO) codified this shift toward private interest, regulatory science in 1995 when it adopted sanitary and phytosanitary measures (SPS), which allowed individual governments to ensure safe products for human consumption but specified "that national-level regulations must be based on appropriate science and risk assessment processes and be applied evenly to domestic and imported products."[70] HACCP met these science-based requirements and quickly became the national and global standard to facilitate seafood trade as it reshaped definitions of quality toward industrial and scientific standards.

In the United States, the NFI partnered with government agencies to create model HACCP plans for each seafood commodity, including crabmeat. The model plans and FDA HACCP guidebooks are the standard in seafood factories around the world. However, all HACCP models are adapted for the specific harvesting and production environments, factories, workers, and distribution systems, so no two plans are alike.[71] In addition, HACCP allows for different interpretations of risk assessment, both science- and values-based, evidenced by EU and Japanese regulations that set different limits and standards for the same hazards, but all based on science. Thus, HACCP is inherently a socially and politically negotiated process whereby regulations and individual plans are created within specific multiscalar political, social, and historical contexts that shape the meaning and implementation of the system. As a result, HACCP produces uneven outcomes leading to a "geography of quality" and new systems of value, despite its status as a "harmonization" code. However, it also allows actors in the network to create value, restructure production, and control nature, reshaping social relations in production through its regulations and technology.

Producing Value

Sitting in the boardroom of Pakfoods, the managing director told me that "Globalization is an opportunity for something you think is not worth anything to be worth something someplace else. You can't blame globalization for non-differentiation of products."[72] Phillips Foods, Byrd International, and Pakfoods used HACCP to differentiate their products, adding value by gaining control of the natural resource and its biophysical traits together with the social relationships throughout the commodity network. The Thai state was an integral part of this network, adopting and legitimizing HACCP as a modernist form of development by creating the infrastructure to support the science of quality and the mechanisms to participate in the global seafood market now obsessed with quality control. These relationships articulated nature, science, and production with neoliberal development efforts to transform the value of the crab through quality control, as the Pakfoods executives described in their boardroom.

In 1972 seafood officially became a cornerstone of Thailand's export-oriented industrialization (EOI) strategies when the Third National Development Plan (1972–76) "emphasized fisheries production for export."[73] To support this plan, the Board of Investment (BOI) and the National Economic and Social Development Board (NESDB) began transforming the industry and Thailand's coasts. The NESDB provided economic development aid to cities such as Songkhla for international port facilities, while the BOI designated the southern region of Thailand as a "zone 3" investment area, allowing for additional incentives to companies. These incentives included exemptions from income and import taxes; deductions for electricity, transportation, and water; and a 25 percent deduction for infrastructure installation and construction costs. These applied equally to foreign and Thai-owned companies but encouraged a merger and consolidation period starting in the 1980s for Thai companies.[74] Companies such as Pakfoods bought out smaller seafood processors in zone 3, giving them three subsidiaries in southern Thailand and two in Bangkok.[75] By 1987 seafood exports (especially tuna, shrimp, and squid) held the second-largest growth rate of all industrial products in Thailand and made up the largest agricultural export for the country.[76]

However, Thailand found its new development leader increasingly banned for chemicals and contaminants starting in the late 1980s, as European countries set new food safety laws.[77] By 1993 the U.S. FDA listed imported Thai canned tuna and frozen shrimp as an "automatic detention" item, stating that more than 50 percent did not meet standards for decomposition based on organoleptic testing—smell, taste, texture, color.[78] Thai processors claimed that the agency had no scientific basis for the detentions, but imports of Thai canned tuna fish decreased substantially.[79] Given Thailand's position as the world's seafood supplier, the country was disproportionately affected by nontariff barriers from the EU, Japan, and the United States Adding value through quality standards, especially HACCP, led Thailand's development strategy for seafood throughout the 1990s. Thailand implemented HACCP faster than any other Southeast Asian country, receiving more FDI and other aid as well.[80] The government began working closely with the Thai Frozen Foods Association (TFFA), a trade association comprised of all the leading Thai seafood export companies. As part of this relationship, the TFFA created a joint government-industry team to negotiate trade problems, leading delegations to European countries, the United States, and Codex meetings to address seafood quality and harmonization codes.[81] As a result, the TFFA and the Thai government moved toward streamlined comprehensive quality standards with regulatory authority split between the government and the industry through the association.

First, the government required all seafood companies wishing to export products from Thailand to join the TFFA, which in turn required all members to become HACCP certified.[82] In 1987 the government appointed the Department of Fisheries (DOF) as the lead certification agency, and by 1992 the department had become the lead inspection and licensing agency for approving HACCP plans, inspecting factories for compliance, and conducting chemical, biological, and physical inspections prior to export.[83] Second, the government invested in training factory workers and food scientists for HACCP standards and established laboratories to test all seafood exports. Simultaneously the industry received funding through development projects to upgrade factories, transportation, and storage facilities. In addition, the government established several new agencies to assist companies in creating HACCP plans, including the National Food Institute and the National Agricultural and Food Products Standards Office. By the time Phillips started in 1995, and Byrd in 1996, the Thai government and seafood industry were adopting HACCP principles and legitimizing the science of quality. However, specific crabmeat plans had not been adopted because the product was not a prominent export. U.S. companies took advantage of this growing infrastructure and BOI incentives but also began shaping the standards directly related to crabmeat, and thus the relationships in the network.

Prior to the arrival of Phillips, small-scale fishermen harvested *puumaa* (blue swimming crabs) along Thailand's southern gulf coast, selling them to local female seafood vendors (*maekhaa*) who had village women steam and pick the crabs at home.[84] Afterward *maekhaa* sold the crabmeat either on the local market or to larger female seafood merchants known as *phae*. Women became *phae* by capitalizing their *maekhaa* operations and acquiring waterfront property where they built docks and sorting facilities, attracting more fishermen, including small trawlers. *Phae* sold the crabmeat to companies in Songkhla for cat food or sterilized canned crabmeat (similar to canned tuna), both for export to Europe. Sterilized crabmeat was not graded, and *phae* owners recalled that *puumaa* did not command a high price from Thai seafood canneries.

Phillips set up the company's main factories in Songkhla, which had become one of the most concentrated areas of seafood production in Thailand. The company initially owned its main factories, believing that this would give them better control over the quality and the relationships required to produce value. Phillips used existing *maekhaa* and *phae* networks to obtain crabmeat, but women still picked crabmeat in their village homes. Suppliers drove three to four hours in their trucks to Songkhla carrying crabmeat packed in plastic bags and stacked in industrial insulated food containers full of ice. Phillips's factories then reprocessed the crabmeat, packing it in cans, pasteurizing, and exporting it to the United States on container ships through Singapore.

Despite owning the factories to control quality, *phae* owners disclosed that at first Phillips was not concerned with quality: "when Phillips first came, they bought crabmeat directly from me. I bought crabmeat from fishermen's wives who picked it in their homes. They did that only two years, then Phillips had to change the production process; then Phillips required quality."[85] Early quality problems included ants in the meat and microbiological and organoleptic problems indicative of old crabmeat. Phillips had concentrated on volume, often only accepting backfin and lump grades, and had not extended the hazard analysis back to the harvesting and picking operations beyond the company's main factory.[86]

Only the main factory was HACCP certified; the *phae* were not. However, companies needed to include harvesting and initial processing as critical control points (CCPs) in their hazard analysis. The Thai DOF and Maryland's seafood scientist helped to create new CCPs to control fishermen and *phae*.[87] The first rule: *phae* buy only live crabs from fishermen. By this time Byrd and Pakfoods had started operations and they developed a system of fifty-gallon plastic drums filled with oxygenated water carried by fishermen on their boats to keep the crabs alive. However, the system worked only on small or medium-sized trawlers, and thus small-scale fishermen were classified as producing low-quality crabs. During my fieldwork, suppliers regularly rejected dead crabs during the sorting process, sending them to *maekhaa* to pick for sale on the local market, where they were worth less.

The second rule: *phae* buy only the two largest sizes of crabs, rejecting oth-

Figure 6.3. Crabs in aerated holding tanks onboard Thai fishing boat. Photo by Kelly Feltault.

ers during the sorting process. Thus, larger, live crabs became export quality, while all others became secondary quality for either the domestic or sterilized markets. This particular definition of quality affected the factory production phase, as it provided companies with two new grades of lump meat: super and colossal jumbo lump. These additional grades meant a further differentiation in quality resulting in higher prices for these cuts in the United States but also revalued the dockside price for larger crabs in Thailand. Colossal jumbo lump has only thirty to forty pieces per one-pound can, compared to Chesapeake jumbo lump, which has up to one hundred. The DOF codified these rules and relationships in 2004 through a specific set of product standards for *puumaa*.[88]

The third change involved moving the crab pickers from their homes into miniplants. Phillips's strategy of volume and quality meant creating more *phae* by giving out small loans to *maekhaa* and *phae* to build picking rooms and steaming facilities.[89] Phillips built seventy-five miniplants throughout southern Thailand, transforming *maekhaa* into *phae* and stationing managers inside to control quality. Byrd opted for a different approach, instead loaning money to small fishing villages to build community steaming facilities and transporting their steamed crabs to centralized miniplants for picking that Byrd owned and operated. As a Thai company, Pakfoods had stronger relationships with suppliers developed over decades of sourcing other seafood in southern Thailand. The company's seafood buyer often acted as adviser to fishermen and *phae* on village matters from weddings to fishing technology. These relationships allowed the company to underbid the U.S. companies and buy crabs from suppliers still in debt to Phillips and Byrd.[90]

The combination of loans to suppliers and companies' demands for quality restructured the existing relationships between suppliers, fishermen, and the larger factories. Many of the new *phae* used the loans to increase their fleets and put more "fishermen in their hand" by bringing more fishermen into the fishery. However, "you had to have quality and not everybody did," explained the owner of PhaeWiya. "This created some conflict because they advanced money and gave a very high price for the crabmeat. I could not afford to pay that price, so I lost a lot of my smaller suppliers to Phillips. Then everyone wanted to be a supplier and the price got high and there was strong competition among the suppliers."[91] Nevertheless, the companies still experienced quality problems, leading to additional quality checkpoints inside the main factories and the policy of rejecting crabmeat.[92]

Phillips's main problem stemmed from combining crabmeat from all the *phae* into each can. This violated the traceability requirements of HACCP, as it was impossible to determine which supplier had provided the problem crabmeat in a can. The fourth CCP required companies to separate crabmeat by suppliers, processing them one by one so that one can of crabmeat comes from one supplier. This requires more detailed record keeping in the factory and among the *phae* in order to trace a container of crabmeat to the individual crab picker and fisherman at the *phae*.[93] HACCP team members from each company praise this approach because they can "control the workers," who can now be pinpointed as having packed rejected batches of crabmeat and have their wages reduced.

Other problems focused on organoleptic testing—color, texture, smell, and taste. Byrd and Pakfoods added a fifth CCP to their HACCP plans, specifically for sensory testing based on corporate and cultural standards. However, this meant that companies had to write organoleptic testing into their HACCP plans—the smell, texture, taste, and color of crabmeat needed to be standardized, measurable, and controlled. Additionally, companies had to train people to recognize the standards with their senses. The quality technician for Pakfoods explained, "I train the smellers to find the right smell range, they must be able to do this or they can't be a smeller. We test the smell abilities of the smellers all the time through control smells and if they pick the wrong thing then their smell ability has changed and they must be moved to another job in the factory. But these smell ranges are stated in our HACCP plan, we list these people by name in our HACCP plan."[94] Pakfoods employs seven women to perform sensory tests twelve hours a day on all crabmeat arriving from suppliers. In 2004 the Thai government issued national sensory standards for pro-

Figure 6.4. Quality-control "smellers" testing colossal jumbo lump crabmeat. Photo by Kelly Feltault.

cessing *puumaa* that closely mirrored the companies' HACCP plans and standards. In the fall of 2006 the U.S. FDA ran workshops for sensory testing of crabmeat to determine new standards scheduled for implementation by 2008. Here again, these standards closely mirror existing HACCP plans in Thailand.

HACCP, as enacted in Thailand, has allowed companies to remove the shell fragments at three different points in production. For this sixth CCP, quality technicians at the *phae* or miniplant remove shells from picked meat and pack the crabmeat into Tupperware for delivery to the main factory. At the main factory, women packing crabmeat into cans pick out any remaining shell. Companies then subject special and backfin grades to black-light rooms where women sit at long tables using tweezers to remove the last shell fragments that glow in the dark. Women pack the crabmeat into containers after three stages of shell removal and sensory testing. The cans are sealed and pasteurized to kill bacteria. Prior to export, the DOF and the companies conduct random sampling, not only for sensory tests, but also for chemical and microbiological contamination.

Thailand encourages these steps in HACCP plans, and yet Maryland regulations and historical definitions of sanitation prevented similar changes until 2003, when state laws incorporated HACCP allowances to remove shell fragments. However, domestic packers do not have the same level of control over

Figure 6.5. The black-light room at Pakfoods. Photo by Kelly Feltault.

the raw material and the fishermen, nor did they receive government assistance for factory upgrades or HACCP costs. In contrast, company and state control over relationships and the natural resource has only increased in Thailand. In 1995 the Thai government began training and certifying suppliers and miniplants for HACCP through small medium enterprise (SME) development aid. However, *phae* who had sold to the companies in the early days and had a reputation for low quality find themselves graded on a scale of A, B, or C, with C-grade companies incurring additional quality inspections.

Conclusion: Trading Quality

The first shipment of pasteurized blue swimming crabmeat arrived in Baltimore in July 1992. Phillips had not established retail production facilities, and cases of crabmeat sat in inventory. At this point, Lloyd Byrd recalled, the company decided to change its brand extension strategy to sell crabmeat to local restaurants but encountered the historical prejudice against pasteurized crabmeat and fears of imported products. He said, "I couldn't give it away, could *not* give it away; because it was pasteurized, because it was foreign—people wouldn't even look at it. And then we had an extremely big marketing tool that came along on the 15th of August [1992] and it was called Hurricane

Andrew. And Hurricane Andrew came tearing up the coast and it shut down all the southern [U.S.] plants. Hurricane Andrew put this [pasteurized] meat in peoples hands 'cause there just wasn't any domestic meat."[95]

To overcome U.S. restaurants' and retailers' historical and social identification of pasteurized crabmeat as low quality, Phillips implemented a highly aggressive and innovative marketing campaign that paired the company's retired restaurant chefs with seasoned sales executives—the chefs went directly to other chefs, and the salesmen worked with the distributors. Lloyd explained that "when chefs start asking for your product, distributors start calling you."[96] A discounted pricing scheme for high-volume purchases made the product even more attractive to the food service industry, which began conceptualizing and serving crab cakes as more than summer food.

In their decision, the U.S. International Trade Commission acknowledged that domestic crabmeat and imported crabmeat were "substantially identical" and "directly competitive" and that imports had increased exponentially.[97] The Commission even stated that claims of scarcity of blue crabs were unfounded, as supplies from other states remained stable. Despite these conclusions, the Commission ruled against the domestic crabmeat industry, citing the use of imported, pasteurized crabmeat in value-added products for the food service industry and claiming that this was a new market. The Commission also stated that the domestic industry could not take advantage of this market because it was too regional and traditional and lacked any of the scientific and modernized approaches of the importers even though both domestic and import companies adhered to HACCP.[98] This solidified the science of quality and the structural power of the import companies by identifying the Chesapeake as underdeveloped and Thailand as modern. The result has been the creation of a "geography of quality" for the global crabmeat industry in which Thailand is seen as producing the superior product over all other locations. Additionally, Thailand is now the site for most HACCP lab testing for crabmeat from other Southeast Asian countries, as well as the primary location for producing value-added products, such as Maryland crab cakes.

Part III
Processing

Chapter 7

Anchovy Sauce and Pickled Tripe: Exporting Civilized Food in the Colonial Atlantic World

Richard R. Wilk

Sustainability and Supply Chains

The opening of discussions about the long-term sustainability of present consumption patterns in developed countries has focused some attention on the general characteristics of long-distance supply chains. These chains are important because of the way they shift the environmental impact of production far away from the final location of consumption. In particular, those living in rich countries are often able to consume with little or no regard for the social and environmental costs of production, which may be borne by people in poor countries and regions. To use the language of ecological economics, the "externalities" of production—the costs that are borne by the public, the environment, and governments instead of the producing firm—end up on one side of a border, while corporate profits and benefits to consumers are on the other. While finance and products flow freely through international trade, those who seek redress for the environmental and social costs of their production run into all kinds of legal and political obstacles. These displaced impacts of production have been called an ecological "shadow" or "footprint."[1]

This kind of analysis has mostly been done on the flow of modern industrial commodities and finished consumer products, but it has the potential to be useful in thinking about the historical development of food chains. Long-distance trade in raw and processed foods separates the environmental and social contexts of production, processing, and consumption. Just as importantly, extended food chains create a setting where the cultural meanings attached to food products are segmented, so that products can change their cultural significance as they move from place to place.

Some anthropologists and social historians have adopted the "social life of things" approach advocated by Igor Kopytoff, which tracks objects as they change their social positions and cultural contexts. Generally these transformations consist of movements back and forth across the boundary between gifts and commodities as cultural property is alienated and commoditized and as market goods are reintegrated as inalienable wealth through ritual.[2] However, these authors have not paid equal attention to the transformations of goods that take place along commodity chains, because the objects remain commodities throughout—they may never become anything more than consumer goods that are bought and sold commercially, and consumed prosaically without fanfare or ritual. I argue that this neglect is unwarranted. Instead, the transformations that goods go through as they move along industrial commodity chains are just as mysterious, dramatic, and significant as the conversion of cultural property into commodities that anthropologists have typically studied (usually in the realms of "tribal" art, music, and traditional medicine). My argument will be illustrated by showing how foodstuffs are transformed in substance and meaning as they move through trade networks, focusing particularly on the crucial role of processing and packaging, which alter and recombine both substance *and* meaning.

Shading and Distancing

Another way to think about the role of food processing and packaging is in terms of the flow of information in the commodity chain. Thomas Princen, who works primarily on the environmental impacts of consumption, has recently developed two concepts, *shading* and *distancing*, which point to the important role of trade intermediaries in blocking or altering the information content of goods.[3] Princen's goal is to show how trade can sever the feedback connections between consumption and production, so that signals about environmental or social damage caused by production are blocked from consumers and are not transmitted as price signals. As we will see, food-processing intermediaries play a similar role by shading and distancing the geographic and social origins of raw food materials.

Princen uses the term "shading" to refer to the process of slanting or highlighting certain kinds of information, particularly those that shift attention away from externalized costs. Shading highlights benefits and minimizes costs, sometimes by shifting the costs onto another party or measuring them only in the short term. For example, on the one hand, Chiquita's plantation-produced bananas are cheap, and they contribute export earnings to Honduras, Ecuador, and other Latin American countries that desperately need the foreign exchange. On the other hand, the cheapness of these bananas is driving thousands of small farmers in eastern Caribbean islands such as Dominica out of business, and local government agencies or international donors will have to pay the costs of helping those farmers find new occupations and aiding the

devastated economies of the islands.[4] In addition, in the long term island bananas are sustainably produced using rainfall, hand labor, few chemical inputs,
and long-term soil conservation methods. The low price of plantation bananas
is based on subsidized cheap fuels and chemicals, starvation-level wages for
nonunionized workers, and short-term agricultural practices based on limited
genetic diversity and intensive use of soils, which leads to crop disease and
large-scale abandonment of fields in order to clear new areas of forest.

Shading conceals the illegal or semilegal shady practices of adulteration,
dumping, and evasion of quality regulations by highlighting prominent and
visible advantages. So, for example, Wal-Mart is shading when it trumpets low
prices and latest styles, while the real net benefits of cheap or attractive products are never totaled up. By subcontracting out production, the large firm
evades any responsibility for the illegal activities involved in making what they
sell. The farmworkers who picked the green beans may have been illegally exposed to pesticides and penalized for taking bathroom breaks, but the vendor
has a legal shield.

Shading also obscures the "true" costs of goods under the guise of normal
business practices, technological efficiency, quality standards, and fair commercial competition, which often promote unsustainable practices. According
to Princen, many forms of competition in the marketplace that favor short-
term profits over long-term stability, or domination of markets by a single large
company, inevitably lead to long-term environmental damage and militate
against sustainability.[5]

Princen measures distancing—the separation of consumers from producers—
using four dimensions: geography, culture, bargaining power, and multiple
agencies. The first two are relatively straightforward and refer to the way
information about production is lost with increasing geographic and cultural
distance between producers and consumers.

As an example of geographic distancing, when people buy crabmeat from
a neighborhood packing company, they may well know some of the workers or
managers of the business. If there are water-quality issues in the nearby bay, it
will be reported in the news and widely discussed. An unusually bad smell hov-
ering over the packing building will raise obvious questions. This kind of information is completely lost when you buy a tub of lump crabmeat from
Thailand in a supermarket. Your crab cakes may look and taste the same, and
they may be cheaper, but they have lost information content and have therefore severed a set of ecological connections. Cultural distancing works in a similar way through incomplete or inadequate translation. North Americans, for
example, do not share the cultural reverence for maize common among indigenous people in southern Mexico; they are ill-equipped to appreciate that corn
is more than just another agricultural commodity south of their border. The
tortilla loses some essential ecological meaning and value as it travels north.

Distance also conceals aggregated effects. One jar of salmon caviar from the shelf does little damage to the huge spawning runs of the Pacific coastal rivers of Russia, but thousands of individual purchases together can entirely wipe out salmon from the accessible streams. Because the purchases are spread out over a wide area, no individual sees overconsumption taking place. At a distance it is easy to think that just one small portion of an expensive spice could hardly do harm to the forest where it was gathered.

Distancing caused by imbalances in bargaining power and multiple agency are best understood by the example of the role of wholesalers and buyers of food products in commodity chains. Because producers are scattered and there are often alternate sources of supply, buyers can play them off against one another to keep pressure on prices. For example, a manufacturer of exotic fruit-flavored sodas can buy pineapple concentrate from many companies in countries as diverse as Thailand, Costa Rica, and the Philippines. This is why buyers often seek out and promote new areas of production, driving producers to compete with each other by externalizing their costs and adopting short-term economic strategies. They might, for instance, use slave labor instead of free or overfish their coastal sardines or switch to a cheaper and more toxic insecticide. This in turn pushes the social and environmental costs of production even further upstream where they are less likely to be seen or counted.

According to Princen's model, the more producers there are and the more they are dispersed and separated from one another along a commodity chain, the less accountability there will be. Each time a good changes hands, information is lost and accountability is reduced. By the time a product has been processed, blended, and packaged, its origins may have been completely lost. Food processing in modern industrialized economies is a quintessential demonstration of how these sequential distancing effects can wash products of their origins and turn them into anonymous and interchangeable substances, no more than industrial feedstocks. When I tried to trace the origins of the ingredients in a bottle of Fuze fruit drink, the manufacturer confessed to not knowing the source of the "crystalline fructose sweetener" in any particular batch of bottles; there were several suppliers, and it was difficult to tell where they in turn had bought the corn with which they started.[6]

Distancing in Food Supply Chains

Perhaps the most important form of distancing in the historical growth of long-distance food chains is the deliberate severing of information flow by strategies of *substitution and appropriation* (my terms rather than Princen's). These are completely familiar to those who study the history of branding, which is an art applied by one agent along a supply chain to appropriate the role of originator and source.[7] Substitution and appropriation are forms of relabeling; in *substitution* one source is substituted for another or a series of others. Thus vinegar and mustard from France may be processed in London and then labeled and sold as "English Mustard." *Appropriation* takes place when one particular agent along the supply chain claims credit as the source. In the United States of America early meat packers such as Swift and Cudahy, through their brands and their role as packers, displaced all other information about the origins of processed pork with their own identity carried on labels, stamps, and brands.

Appropriation through branding did not begin as a device for elevating the role of intermediaries. Instead early forms of branding of wine, fish sauce, and olive oil in the Roman Mediterranean or among the busy market towns of tenth-century A.D. China, for example, allowed *manufacturers* to build reputations for consistent quality and therefore to get higher prices for their goods. This required some way to guarantee that the wine in the amphora or the scissors in the package were genuine, so early brands incorporated sealing devices.[8] In early modern Europe branding also emerged in a context where goods traded over long distances were subject to adulteration, counterfeiting, and substitution, and the quality of goods could not be easily assessed by the buyer, a common occurrence with early forms of bulk packaging. Sealed and branded packaging built on long-standing associations of particular places with processed foods of high or at least consistent quality. For example, by the seventeenth century Yorkshire hams, fortified wines shipped from Oporto, Dutch herring and cheese, and dried cod from Newfoundland all established lasting reputations for quality in the long-distance food trade that are still maintained today.[9]

However, the power of such location branding was gradually lost as commodity chains grew in size and complexity. Yorkshire ham gradually became a generic term for a particular style of curing, a fate of many local products as diverse as Cheddar cheese and Tequila. A particular tavern may have become known for the quality of its beer, a retailer for cleanliness and freshness, or an importer for consistent quality, and these names and locations became more reliable indicators than generic points of origin. The first packaged teas in Britain were packaged by the Quaker John Horniman, whose personal reputation (and religious persuasion) served to guarantee quality, a power which he passed on to his descendants.[10]

Gradually agents such as Horniman *appropriated* the role of producers and other companies or individuals further up the food chain, a process easily furthered when the agent is responsible for mixing, processing, and packaging. This can easily be seen in the coffee business, where unblended beans retain their nationality (Kenyan, Colombian, for example), while blends take the name or brand of the processor or roaster. Instant coffee retains no trace of other origins, and the corporate brand (for example, Nescafe, Folgers) becomes a putative source and a totalizing identity. In modern food-processing systems branding is usually a complete block to the flow of information along the food chain, as food processors, packagers, and more recently retailers have appropriated the origins of food products. It is almost impossible to find out the physical origins of the ingredients in many processed food products today. Large food-processing companies are aware that many consumers are dissatisfied with the anonymity of the corporate source, with the idea that their food flows from a faceless entity, so they have gone full circle and reinvented the personalized agents and geographic origins that they have displaced.

Early examples, such as Betty Crocker and Aunt Jemima, built on existing historical meanings, but today the imaginary agents of brands are more likely to be fantasy characters such as elves or celebrity sports stars.[11] It took longer to establish the veracity of imaginary *places* as the symbolic origins of food products. The Jolly Green Giant was invented for Minnesota Foods in 1928 (the company later changed its name to Green Giant Foods), but the giant did not have a home in a fictional valley until the 1950s. In a kind of "populuxe" version of *terroir*, fictional places such as Nature Valley and Wild Ocean now stand in for the geographical sources that still function as marks of quality for elite products such as fine wine and cheese. These attributions skirt the edges of false advertising, as when the giant Miller brewing company (now SABMiller plc based in South Africa), in an effort to compete with artisanal breweries, invented the "Plank Road Brewery" as a fictional source for its premium "small brewery" brands.[12] Corporate folklorists are now employed inventing fanciful histories of the mythological people and places that otherwise-anonymous goods are said to "come from."

Food Chains: Crossroads of Ecology and Cultural Politics

Long-distance commodity chains have important environmental effects in today's global economy, shifting environmental costs away from privileged consumers, to the extent that it takes thousands of hours of research to trace the full life-cycle costs of simple products.[13] As we go back in time, it becomes much harder to trace the connections between consumption and particular environmental impacts and effects, despite the rapid growth of the field of historical ecology.[14] Certainly we can point to specific examples, such as the drastic changes in North American forest ecology caused by the near-elimination of beavers in order to satisfy the demand for fashionable hats in northern Europe or the culling of hundreds of millions of white-tailed deer for their hides at the same time. In the realm of foodstuffs we could argue that the demand for turtle soup as a delicacy in Victorian England contributed to the devastation of coral-reef ecosystems throughout the Caribbean basin.[15] However, there is a legitimate question about whether or not shading, distancing, or branding was a major factor in these dramatic cases. At the time Europeans may not have had a concept of nature or ecology that would allow them to understand the consequences of their actions; or if they knew of those consequences, they may not have placed any value on the lives of inferior people or alien forests and seas. Today it is hard to imagine what it was like to live in an unexplored world of infinite resources; if sealskin could no longer be obtained from the Caribbean because seals there had been wiped out, more seals would be found somewhere else.

The historical growth of shading and distancing in the global food trade dates not to the age of exploration but to the period when European countries were consolidating their overseas empires, and food itself grew to be an important element in the cultural politics of empire. These practices transformed diverse and heterogeneous products from scattered territories and colonies into products of the metropolitan center of the empire, in what people were encouraged to think of as the "home" country. This does not mean that the exotic origins of foods were completely erased. In the British Empire curry, for example, retained an Indian identity and even sometimes a fictive origin in the Indian city of Madras. However, because the condiments were blended, packaged, and branded by a British company based in London, India was effectively shaded and became no more than an exotic backdrop that gave authenticity to a product whose quality and purity were guaranteed by a British agent. The foreign or colonial consumer buying curry powder imported from Britain was partaking in the bounty of empire, but entirely through the agency of the "mother" country. In addition, for expatriates and their descendants, curry powder could become a taste of home, a reminder of British identity, a "memory food" just as potent as potted anchovy paste, mustard, bottled porter, or smoked herring.[16] Later in the nineteenth century, British brands became reminders of home, part of the cultural furniture of empire, mnemonics of quality, and some of these brands, such as Crosse & Blackwell, retain some of that power.[17]

Packaging and Processing Food in the British Atlantic

The path from the leaking casks of salt pork that filled the holds of sixteenth-century British sailing ships to the neat crates and boxes of branded and labeled tins, bottles, and packages carried in the late nineteenth century is long, complex, and hardly direct. Tracing it requires excursions into many fields, and so far no single author has taken on the task. This may be because the histories of consumers, merchants, food processing, import trade, customs, food culture, and packaging have been written separately, instead of tracing the flow of particular goods through the hands of all these actors and institutions.

Here I can do no more than make three linked arguments about why this daunting interdisciplinary task is worth pursuing and how we might go about it. First, tracing the commodity chains of food processing in the Atlantic world is worthwhile simply because of the absolute magnitude of the trade and the crucial role it played in maintaining the prosperity of metropolitan countries, particularly their rural areas, during a time when trade was expanding. The food trade also kept the colonies and newly settled areas both culturally and economically dependent on the home country. Second, I point to two particularly important ways that government and industry articulated with one another in promoting food processing and export industry: explicit trade and taxation policy on one hand, and the interactive co-development of legal measures and standards by government and grading methods by industry. Third, I argue that over time the two most important and consistent long-term trends in the food trade were the following: continuous technological innovation in packaging and labeling; and constant diversification of products, both through new brands and varieties within food categories and through the invention of new categories. In making these arguments I draw mainly on secondary sources limited to the British Empire and its predecessors. For information on labeling, packaging, and branding of goods that were reexported to the colonies, I also use nineteenth-century newspapers from the Caribbean port of Belize, which include numerous listings of cargoes offered for sale and later advertisements from retailers.[18]

Recent work by historical archaeologists has also proved helpful in tracing the variety of packaged foods, beverages, and medicines that were exported from British home ports. The physical evidence of tins, crocks, and glassware reveals a much larger and more complex British food export trade than that attested by documentary evidence. Given the general paucity of material, I have used a broad definition of "food" to include "drug foods" such as coffee and tea, alcoholic beverages and liquors, and the tonics, stimulants, and patent remedies that often had ambiguous qualities.

The Economic Importance of the Food Export Trade

It is difficult to assess just how much prepared and processed food England (and later Great Britain) exported through history and how important it was to the development of the British economy. The quantities of food imports that were reexported in processed, mixed, and repackaged forms were never accurately measured, and most economic historians have tended to view them as relatively unimportant compared to cloth and other manufactured goods. On the other hand, a recent reappraisal by the economic historian Anne McCants suggests that "luxury trades of the early modern period were in fact transformative of the European economy. . . . New evidence will show that global groceries, long thought to be merely exotic, were actually in wide use by the early decades of the eighteenth century."[19]

We do know that food-processing export industries had an early start in England. As early as the late sixteenth century, quantities of processed fish and beer were exported from coastal ports to the Continent.[20] As large-scale imports of exotic food and drug products began in the following century, the reexport trade grew accordingly. At the end of the seventeenth century, two-thirds of the tobacco and 90 percent of the spices (compared to 80 percent of textiles) imported to England were reexported to Europe.[21] However, we do not know how much of this food was processed and packaged in England and how much was simply sold in the same bulk packages in which it was imported. We do know that even in the seventeenth century, large numbers of English glass and pottery retail packages (including prefilled clay pipes) were already showing up in the trash heaps of colonial towns and cities in the New World, as well as in smaller numbers in Asia and Africa. Excavations at Port Royal in Jamaica and other locations in the Caribbean disclosed enormous numbers of bottles, crocks, and other kinds of packaging from England and other northern European ports.[22]

According to Jacob Price, the foreign trade in reexported exotic products (most prominently tea, coffee, sugar, and tobacco) grew in the Atlantic world in the period from 1675 to 1775 because of increasing demand from North American colonies (and the related Africa trade), presumably because these products were significant marks of status and cosmopolitanism.[23] The greatest growth period for reexports from England was apparently the end of the eighteenth century. "Grocery" was the fastest growing reexport category between 1790 and 1800, increasing from 1.2 million pounds sterling to 11.0 million and from 26 to 64 percent of all reexports.[24] The economic importance of exports and reexports of groceries and liquor continued to grow throughout the nineteenth century, although by the end of the century they were far overshadowed in monetary terms by the bulk food imports needed to feed a growing British population on a limited land base.[25]

At times it is hard to separate the economic impacts and roles of food imports and exports from colonies and metropolitan centers in the colonial trade system. Part of the issue here is one of categories. There is a world of difference between a bulk load of grain or chilled beef sides and an equivalent weight of bottled beer, tinned corned beef, bottles of beef extract, and carefully packaged tea biscuits, but they are all categorized as food when import and export figures are aggregated. For a better understanding of the real impact of the colonial food trade, it would often be more useful to categorize processed food as an industrial product and to aggregate it with goods such as books, silverware, crockery, finished clothing, hats, and other kinds of consumer products that were important *positional goods* in the social status system. My own experience assembling a one-hundred-year time series of imports into Belize based on customs records is that this is a tedious and time-consuming enterprise even on a small scale.

Articulations between Government and Industry

Governments and various food-processing industries had different interests in trade policy, which could be pursued quite separately at times, while on other issues they may have been in close accord or in conflict with one another. If my own reading of colonial government in the Caribbean is accurate, there was also a great deal of ignorance, miscommunication, confusion, miscalculation, and unintended consequence, which makes it hard to read intention into policy. For example, colonial officials in Belize who wanted to promote local food production often appeared completely unaware of the way their own customs regulations stifled the colony's farmers.

In the broader sweep of history, it is not clear to what extent British trade policies were important in promoting the reexport trade in processed food. The seventeenth-century Navigation Acts, by excluding foreign merchants and shipping from home and colonial trade, certainly encouraged inbound ships with raw materials to find British outbound cargoes to fill their holds. Due to expansionist diplomacy and economic policies, Britain consolidated its control of the East and West Indian trades and included a large portion of South America as well. The volume of trade was not as important as the direction; customs policies consistently discouraged shipping from one colonial port to another. Instead the vast majority of raw materials went straight to home ports, from whence came return cargoes of finished goods, manufactures, and of course, groceries and liquors.[26]

Quite early on the British government prohibited the import of wines and spirits in small retail-sized packages, as a measure to reduce smuggling. This had the effect of encouraging rapid growth in glass manufacturing and bottling for local retail trade, and these bottled products quickly found their way into outbound cargos.[27] This also demonstrates the constant synergy between production for local markets and export production; goods, packages, and brands that became accepted and well known in the home market followed expatriate officials and military officers to the colonies, where they became established in those markets as well. Even as early as the seventeenth century, the ornate branded tobacco papers used by retailers to wrap small quantities of their own blends were finding their way into colonial trade. Similar printed retail wrappers were used by British merchants throughout the eighteenth century for other retail products such as tea and sago powder.[28]

Rather than overt trade policies, the major factors that affected the rapid growth in the export grocery trade were cheap shipping and easy credit. Raw materials imported to British ports were bulky, even when they were tightly compressed into holds with screw jacks (as was done with cotton and some tobacco). Outbound ships therefore offered extremely low (and sometimes free) shipping rates, which averaged about 2.5 percent of invoice value in the early nineteenth century.[29] Export trade was further facilitated by easy credit terms extended by British wholesalers and merchants, at low rates for periods up to two years.[30] The flow of exports was further smoothed by the development of a system of public and private auctions for bulk goods, the growth of dockyards and associated warehouse districts and transportation facilities, and a

Figure 7.1. Eighteenth-century English and Dutch tobacco paper wrappers. Alex Davis, *Package and Print: The Development of Container and Label Design* (New York: Clarkson N. Potter, 1968), plates 50, 51.

class of brokers and factors who served as intermediaries in both breaking bulk and assembling outbound cargos. Further in the background but equally important were an efficient insurance industry and a legal structure that adjudicated disputes between merchants, shippers, and factors relatively quickly.[31] Surely various arms of government were complicit in these developments, though again it is not clear how much this complicity was reactive, accidental, or even the result of corruption.

The overlapping roles of government and private companies are even more difficult to disentangle in the important arena of grading and standards. Raw and slightly processed materials imported to British ports from America, Asia, and Africa varied widely in their quality, condition, and packaging. One of the key roles played by British ports in the reexport trade was turning this unruly and variable stock into more standardized products, so that overseas merchants and retailers could know what they were buying, predict what would arrive, and effectively compare prices.

The predominately wooden packages used to ship raw materials in sailing ships were notoriously variable in capacity from port to port, with thousands of customary measures and quantities. As early as the seventeenth century, English customs authorities passed laws requiring standardized packaging and

Figure 7.2. Three nineteenth-century American wooden firkins in three sizes; the largest one, on the left, is a butter firkin. Courtesy of Willis Henry Auctions, Marshfield, Massachusetts.

weights for particular indigenous products. A 1673 statute, for example, required butter firkins to weigh eight pounds and hold fifty-six pounds of butter (which at the time was heavily salted for preservation and shipping). This eight-pound firkin later became a standard shipping package and measure for small amounts of many kinds of processed foods, including lard, pickled tripe, herring and salmon, parched barley, and tallow.[32] Similar standards were adopted for other sizes of casks and barrels, so tables could be worked out to show how much weight of each kind of product should be expected in containers of each size. Retail containers became standardized quite early, probably at the initiative of the manufacturers, so that by the beginning of the eighteenth century glass bottles already came in a range of standard capacities, and many were specifically designed to fit in shipping containers to maximize efficiency and minimize breakage.[33]

The customs and excise authorities constantly pushed for greater standardization in both packaging and quality so that the correct amounts of duties could be collected. The containers that goods were imported in were so unstandardized and variable that even using special calipers and gauges could not accurately judge volume and weight. Customs therefore insisted that almost every product imported to the country—even many of those intended for di-

Figure 7.3. Hobnailing tea in a wholesaler's warehouse. Denys Forrest, *Tea for the British: The Social and Economic History of a Famous Trade* (London: Chatton and Windus, 1973), plate 13.

rect reexport—be emptied from its original packages ("breaking bulk"), examined, and then repackaged. Until 1884, for instance, all the tea chests in a "package" had to be emptied out onto a warehouse floor, mixed, and put back in chests (a process called "hobnailing").[34] Special tools were also used to test the quality and consistency of bulk packages, including coring tools to reach the insides of bales and sacks. Because many wooden containers leaked, measuring the remaining quantities inside variable-sized casks, pipes, and puncheons was a task for skilled gaugers.[35]

Processing and mixing products in British ports often had the crucial distancing effect of obscuring the origins of component raw materials. Many times the British merchants did not even know where the lots of spices, sugar, and other products they bought were produced because they were identified only by the names of the ports from which they were shipped. Therefore, they might know only that a cask of fish oil was shipped from New York, not where it was actually rendered. In addition, some goods, such as black and white pepper, sesame, coffee, and tobacco, were loaded loosely in bulk, either filling part of a ship's hold or used as dunnage and packing material to stabilize other cargo, so they could come from various ports. Of course, customs regulations and the intricacies of duties and excise often gave shippers and merchants strong incentives to falsify shipping documents and bills of lading, practices that continue to be common in international commerce.

The tea industry typifies the elaboration of grading standards over time by merchants on their own, without any government regulation or interference. Bulk packages were graded by overseas factors and buyers, but all were carefully reexamined and regraded on arrival in Britain, as part of a system of organized auctions that functioned in some ways as a cartel limiting competition. Nineteenth-century tasters and smellers used twenty-two different marks to indicate qualities such as mustiness, mold, dust, roast, and color. Beyond this, each kind of tea came in numerous grades depending on the size, picking method, and time of picking; hyson tea, for example, came in thirteen different grades. Given all the labor involved in moving and repackaging, it is no wonder that already in 1800 the East India Company's London warehouse employed more than seventeen hundred manual workers.[36]

Continuous Developments through Time

There does not seem to have been, at least through the end of the nineteenth century, any consistent trend in the way government and industry related to one another in the realm of trade regulation, standards, and grading. Judging by the slow changes in customs classifications, authorities often struggled to keep up with rapidly changing commercial practices and consumer tastes for new kinds of goods. Only slowly and unevenly, toward the end of the nineteenth century, did food adulteration and quality become a matter of national, rather than local, regulation.

However, some consistent changes in the Atlantic processed-food industry seem to have proceeded in a single direction, if not at a consistent pace, from at least the late eighteenth century to the present day. All contribute directly to the growing shading of the impacts of production and the distancing of producers from consumers.

One has already been mentioned: that an increasing proportion of exports and reexports were shipped already blended and packaged by retail merchant houses, and smaller percentages went in bulk packaging from wholesalers. This clearly built on the long experience of grocers and other retailers in blending and packaging teas, coffees, and tobaccos, a role intensified by the greater prevalence of adulteration at this time. Distinctive tastes and qualities were also attributed to particular merchants. The formulation of snuff from imported tobacco was an early example of the important role that retailer-manufacturers played in giving a guarantee of quality, and increasingly a sign of status, to highly processed products. Patronage by nobility and expositions that granted medals and awards for quality were part of the same brand status system, which flourished in the Atlantic trade.[37]

Branding depended, in turn, on advances in the technologies of processing,

THE BEST BEER BOTTLED

IN THE EASIEST BOTTLE TO OPEN.

Jeffrey's Lager Beer can now be obtained in bottles fitted with the new hygienic stopper:—

Cases of 4 doz. qts.
"   " 6 " pints.

Tear flap straight down, holding thumb on cap till pressure is released.

This stopper is made of highest grade Alluminum---Ensures absolute cleanliness and freedom from rust round bottle mouth.

A most convenient stopper on a well known product.

Jeffrey's is the only Beer in the Colony with the New Hygienic Stopper.

STEVEN BROS. & CO.,

DISTRIBUTORS OF JEFFREY'S PRODUCTS.

Figure 7.4. Innovations in new packaging technology advertised in Belize newspapers; note the appeal to improved hygiene and health. *Clarion*, August 14, 1907.

filling, packaging, and labeling. Innovative manufactured packaging materials, such as cardboard and tin, that could be standardized tended to replace wood, straw, and wicker. New innovations such as canning were quickly picked up by the export trade, so that in 1817, just a few years after the process was invented, tins of meat were already being shipped to New York.[38] Manufacturing cooperage was at least partially mechanized as early as 1820.[39] Basic forms of machinery for filling and sealing packages developed rapidly through the nineteenth century, and by the 1870s the design and manufacture of food-processing and packaging machinery had become a separate industry. Better printing technologies allowed bright, eye-catching labels that were visual cues to memory, capable of evoking nostalgia and images of real or imagined homes.[40]

Perhaps the most conspicuous trends in the export grocery trade from Europe were the expansion of the number of categories of food and liquor and the increase in the number of brands and varieties within each category. Early food exports tended to fall into a few major categories, with a few grades of each; for instance, salt pork came in four basic grades through most of the nineteenth century. Beer and wine might be shipped with no more identity than their putative cities of origin, as in "London Porter" or "Burgundy wine." While even in the late 1700s a surprising range of exotic grocery products, such as anchovies, cheeses (sometimes cased in lead), pickled walnuts, capers, gherkins, and sugared fruits, were regularly sold in colonial shops, their origins and quality were rarely specified, and they were never branded.

One of the first product categories to proliferate in variety was bottled sauces. These sauces played an important role in colonial cuisines by giving familiar flavors to unfamiliar meats and dishes. They also literally and metaphorically covered the local origins of main courses with a British cultural blanket.[41] Named sauces appeared first in the export trade in the 1780s, and by 1820 well-known brands included Quin's, Sauce Royal, Cherokee, Harvey's, and Burgess' Essence of Anchovies, among others.[42] The variety of sauces broadened to include many kinds of ketchups, soy sauces, chutneys, mushroom sauces, and mustards, some of which included tropical fruits and spices. Jellies and preserves also proliferated, initially in ceramic jars and pots and later in glass containers and tins.

Completely cooked and prepared foods that could be served directly with no preparation were exported from Britain in some quantity even before the advent of tins and sealable glass containers. Vinegared dishes such as pickled "Bristol" tripe and tongues were shipped in the late eighteenth century in wooden firkins or small kegs. Anchovy butter, meat pastes, and jellied meats were packed into interior-glazed ceramic pots, each sealed with a thick layer of suet or other fat. Glass bottles sealed with cork and wax contained barley, cooked peas, tomatoes, and other vegetables, presumably preserved in brine. Dried portable soups made from different meats and vegetables, the

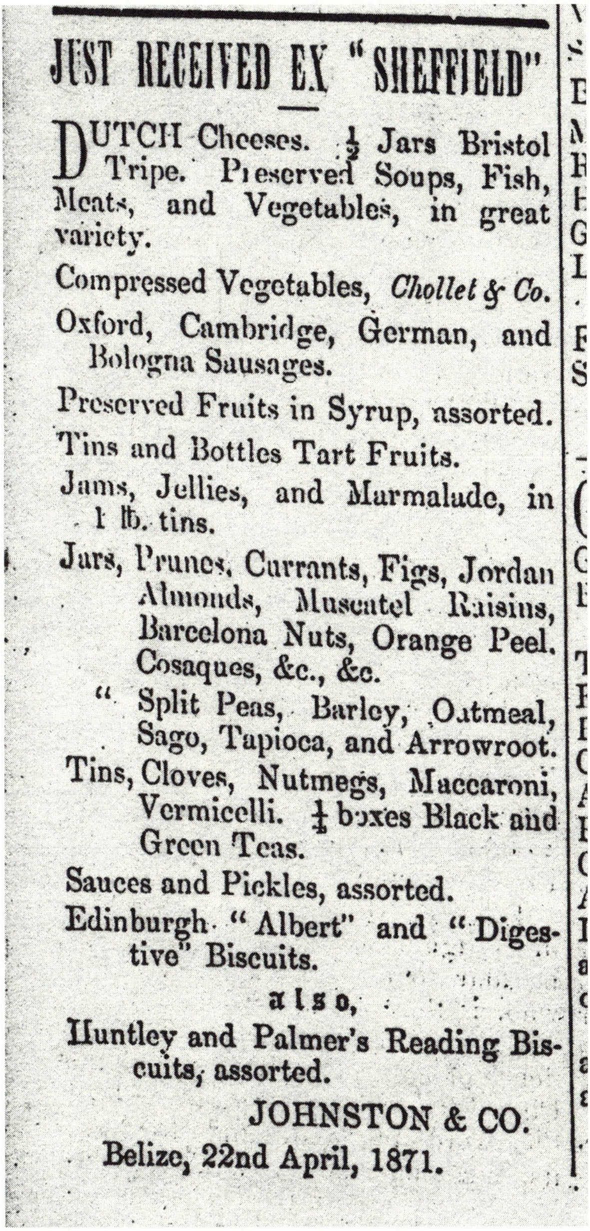

JUST RECEIVED EX "SHEFFIELD"

DUTCH Cheeses. ½ Jars Bristol Tripe. Preserved Soups, Fish, Meats, and Vegetables, in great variety.

Compressed Vegetables, *Chollet & Co.*

Oxford, Cambridge, German, and Bologna Sausages.

Preserved Fruits in Syrup, assorted.

Tins and Bottles Tart Fruits.

Jams, Jellies, and Marmalade, in 1 ℔. tins.

Jars, Prunes, Currants, Figs, Jordan Almonds, Muscatel Raisins, Barcelona Nuts, Orange Peel, Cosaques, &c., &c.

" Split Peas, Barley, Oatmeal, Sago, Tapioca, and Arrowroot.

Tins, Cloves, Nutmegs, Maccaroni, Vermicelli. ¼ boxes Black and Green Teas.

Sauces and Pickles, assorted.

Edinburgh "Albert" and "Digestive" Biscuits.

also,

Huntley and Palmer's Reading Biscuits, assorted.

JOHNSTON & CO.

Belize, 22nd April, 1871.

Figure 7.5. Some of the wide variety of processed imported foods available in the colonies; an advertisement from a Belize City newspaper in 1871 includes sauces as well as branded biscuits. *New Era and British Honduras Chronicle*, April 29, 1871.

antecedents of soup mixes and bouillon cubes, were sold overseas in hand-made tin boxes as early as the 1760s.[43]

As the art of canning progressed through the nineteenth century, the range of these products went far beyond sauces and preserved meats and vegetables to include cooked dishes, real British meals in cans. This was more than "tastes like home"; it really was home food, often the same brands presented in exactly the same packages, including Crosse & Blackwell Scotch haggis, Christmas cakes and puddings, Fortnum and Mason roast pheasant breast, Bovril beef extract, Horlicks malted milk, Colman's mustard, and Guinness Stout.

Ship's biscuit supplied to the navy was one of the earliest industrially processed foods in Britain.[44] It was a staple good for mariners, forts, and other enclave settlements that could not produce their own food, and it was the basic food of land armies in wartime.[45] Even when local staples were produced in the colonies, imported biscuits remained a major import. They quickly mutated into many shapes and styles, occupying market niches from cheap, every-day items to expensive, luxury products that were suitable platforms for caviar and imported cheeses at fine dinners. They were also branded quite early; the earliest branded food I have found in Belize advertisements was "R. S. Murray's Tea Biscuits and Rusks" in 1839. Even today British biscuits have a distinct identity in the global grocery market, and many early brands survive.

The formulas and contents of many sauces were guarded by manufacturers, as were the flavorings and essences used in making liquors and wines. The same secrecy extended to the proliferating number of patent medicines that became an important part of the export trade in the middle of the nineteenth century. While not strictly food products, many of these patent mixtures crossed boundaries when they were consumed as "tonics" for pleasure or when they contained intoxicating drugs and alcohol and were drunk as beverages or flavoring. In each of these cases, the secrecy of the ingredients made it impossible for a buyer to know much about a product's origins beyond the name of the British (or sometimes French or German) individual or company on the label. By granting patent protection for these formulations, governments essentially gave legal protection to the practice of distancing, in this case actually *severing* the flow of information about origins and contents. Perfumes and scents also crossed the boundary into foodstuffs on occasion; ingredients such as rose water or lemon oil could end up in either.

Many products, some of which are today quite obscure, were imported to Britain in large quantities for use in sauces, tonics, medicines and perfumes. Honey was imported from Cuba in eighty-two-gallon tierces, much of it used in preserves, medicines, tonics, and other processed foods, while the rest was repackaged in bottles for reexport to the Continent. China root, harvested from a variety of smilax, was imported from Bombay and China as a flavoring and medicinal tonic, often as a substitute for sarsaparilla. Bdellium (also known as guggul), a resin extracted from a shrub in Iran and India, was an ingredient in perfumes, medicines, and tonics. Gambier was extracted from the leaves of a tropical vine in Malaysia and found its way into medicines and perfumes. Dried chunks of chicory root imported from southern Europe were roasted, ground, and exported around the world packed in twenty-eight- or fifty-six-pound tins as a coffee additive; the root was also sold premixed with coffee.[46] Sarsaparilla vines cut in the forests of British Honduras and Guatemala were dried and shipped off to London, where they were used to flavor beverages and in patent medicines, some of which then found their way back, in processed form, to Central America. Spices such as Cayenne pepper and ginger and large quantities of sugar made the same round-trip voyages.

As food products diversified, so did the size and quality of their packaging and labeling. By the end of the nineteenth century bulk packaging of retail foods was on the way out, and instead individual sealed packages were packed by the dozens in larger wooden boxes with their own designations. Crates were used for ceramic and glass, either empty or filled, often cushioned with straw. Chests, sometimes quite decorative, were used for tea, medicine, olive oils, and other specialty Mediterranean goods. Cases held bottles of pickles, condiments, wine, and alcohol and held anywhere from one to ten dozen bottles. Smaller custom-made wooden boxes of varied sizes held fresh or preserved fruits, noodles, and luxury products such as caviar.[47] The invention of pasteboard and then cardboard revolutionized the packaging industry toward the end of the nineteenth century.

The proliferation of products and ingredients was checked only toward the end of the nineteenth century by the vertical integration and consolidation of many food-processing companies in the home countries. Thomas Lipton was an exemplar of this trend in the early 1890s; he was the first in the tea business to combine the functions that had previously been divided between buyer, importer, broker, wholesaler, blender, and retailer.[48] In the two decades straddling 1900, many other British producers and companies followed Lipton's model of vertical integration, developing the modern concept of branding for entire ranges of related products. Anglo-Swiss, for example, produced a wide range of tinned milk products. Many of the companies that were successful in integrating buying, processing, and retailing are still with us today; Anglo-Swiss became a part of Nestlé in 1905.

Because the large food-processing companies were able to field their own groups of commission agents, who traveled around the world, they were able to set up exclusive distributorships with many scattered retailers. By becoming the "local agents" for major metropolitan food companies, foreign retailers got better credit terms and subsidized advertising in local outlets. In the process, though, they usually had to narrow their stock, squeezing out competing local products and rival European companies. This ultimately had the effect of reducing the total variety of goods in the shops. By the 1920s in Belize, only one British and one American brand of tinned goods were still regularly available, in contrast to earlier profusion, and retailers no longer competed with each other by introducing new processed-food products with any great regularity.

Conclusions

The vertical integration of food processing and retailing, a process begun at the end of the nineteenth century, introduced the modern corporate forms of shading and distancing. This is very much unlike the main forms of environmental distancing envisioned by Princen; according to his assumptions, the more agents a good passes through on the way to the consumer, the more information is lost. Yet vertical integration in the food chain *reduces* the number of corporate agents and may actually narrow it to one if the same company that owns the tea plantation, for example, is also shipping, processing, packaging, and retailing the tea.[49] How can reducing the number of actors in the supply chain actually maintain or even deepen the actual distancing effect?

Princen takes a primarily geographic and economic approach to understanding the flow of information along commodity chains, with a focus on natural and cultural barriers. This seems to me a perfectly valid approach to the colonial food supply chains discussed above. However, the cultural and linguistic processes of appropriation and substitution, primarily through practices of branding and labeling, have become more important in food chains since the late nineteenth century. The mechanism of branding works through the metaphorical substitution of imaginary people and places for the real workers and machines that make food and their real physical locations. The complex identities of products are appropriated by the puppets of the food-processing corporation, animated by the power of marketing and advertising, and legalized by patents, trademarks, and proprietary recipes.

Substitution and blending are also powerful means of washing the identity out of raw materials. To give but one example, Belize produces tens of thousands of tons of frozen orange juice concentrate each year, most of which is sold in the United States. However, only a small number of specialists in the business know this because the high-quality Belizean product is used, along with some Mexican and Arizona concentrate, in blends to improve the flavor of cheap Brazilian concentrate. The quality of Belizean concentrate is rewarded in the corporate (B2B) marketplace with a higher price, but at the cost of its meaning and identity. Belize gets no recognition, no visibility or pride, for the extremely high quality of its highest-value agricultural export. In addition all of this substitution takes place behind the bland corporate face of the food-packaging company that sells frozen orange juice concentrate with no national origin listed.

Yet the power of food processors, and increasingly retailers, in modern food chains also presents an opportunity to reduce the effects of shading and distancing. In the colonial food chains physical distance, poor communications, and the number of agents involved made it virtually impossible to connect consumers to producers. There was no legal accountability anywhere along the chain for the ultimate origins of foodstuffs, and it was often in the best interests of agents to conceal or falsify the sources of their wares.

The vertical integration of food supply today raises many important questions about food purity, risk, and ecological degradation. However, it does provide unprecedented opportunities for eliminating distancing and shading because even if food companies conceal origins from the public through marketing, they do have many of the records and information needed for tracking and tracing. While tortuous multiagent chains can still conceal the ultimate origins of goods such as ivory and drugs from the strictest regulations, with the support of strong public opinion large integrated companies can indeed be forced to divulge their sources of supply. As the ecological and public-health consequences of food supply chains continue to generate controversy, pressure for such regulation may increase.

Chapter 8
What's Left at the Bottom of the Glass: The Quest for Purity and the Development of the American Natural Ice Industry

Jonathan Rees

In the nineteenth-century United States, ice was a unique commodity. It was both part of the food provisioning system and food itself. It had been used for centuries as a food preservation technique at the household level, but only in the early nineteenth century did ice become an item that was bought and sold. At first merchants such as the industry pioneer Frederic Tudor shipped it from New England to tropical climates. While technologically impressive, this feat made little money for the people who accomplished it because only the affluent could afford to buy ice at the necessary price after such costly voyages. Ice remained an expensive luxury until the price came down. The cheaper ice of the late nineteenth century gave rise to a vast expansion in the length of food chains when shippers realized that it could be used to chain foods that had never been chained before and to ship longer distances too. However, the ice that made the delivery of meat, fruit, and vegetables across vast distances possible was not the same ice people popped into their drinks. Market segmentation in ice based on differences in usage and the means of production accompanied increased production and lower prices because of variations in the quality of natural ice and competition from higher-quality, machine-made ice made from purified water once the industry perfected mechanical refrigeration technology around 1890.

In order to understand the ice market's segmentation, imagine that it is the height of summer in 1882. You are hot and decide to have an iced drink. After finishing your cold beverage, you leave the cup or glass, and the ice melts. If the ice you used was natural ice, consumers expected that dirt and other sediment from the water the ice came from would be left behind at the bottom.

"Natural ice contains, always, a certain amount of impurities, gaseous and solid, no matter where it is obtained from," explained a manufacturer of mechanical ice-making equipment in 1899. "These impurities are imprisoned in the ice and released only when the ice is melting."[1] In the early nineteenth century, when the natural ice industry was relatively new, consumers sought clear ice for reasons of taste and convenience. Apparently clear water became comparatively clear ice, which meant that cold drinks tasted less of sediment and that consumers did not have to avoid that sediment as the ice melted. Later in the century, after the advent of mechanical refrigeration, consumers sought clear ice to protect their health from the diseases that natural ice increasingly bore, especially typhoid fever. Ice made through mechanical refrigeration had the advantage of completely eliminating the sediment at the bottom of the glass as well.

This almost century-long consumer-based push for purity in the natural industry led to two kinds of market segmentation. Consumers bought the higher-quality product. Dirtier ice went into railroad cars or grocers' freezers in order to keep other food cold. As the journal *Ice and Refrigeration* protested in 1902, "To entirely prohibit the harvesting of polluted ice, as is so often proposed, would in some places be a hardship, for such ice is as good as any other for the purposes of wholesale refrigeration at points where contacts with foodstuffs is impossible."[2] When machine-made ice became a viable alternative in the 1890s, the market segmented again, with the higher-quality "artificial product" getting dropped into people's drinks and natural ice going for industrial uses and poorer customers irrespective of its quality. The low cost of natural ice allowed the product to keep some consumer market until the advent of the electric refrigerator around 1930. Despite the fact that ice harvesting was practically the epitome of nineteenth-century technology, the industrial market for natural ice continued well after the turn of the twentieth century.

Blue Ice from Green Water

Before 1800 food preservation revolved around drying or salting. If you had a large estate and lived near a source of potable public water, you might build your own small-scale icehouse for personal use. Most people simply dug holes under their houses and placed food there in the hope of getting a few extra days of freshness from their food. If they had access to ice, they used it there in order to get still more time. The first commercial venture involving the cutting of natural ice to bring it to those with no access occurred in 1805 when the Boston businessman Frederic Tudor commissioned a boat to ship 130 tons of ice "harvested" around Boston to Martinique for the local population to put in their drinks. While people in Martinique greeted the venture with enthusiasm, Tudor still lost forty-five hundred dollars on it.[3] It literally took decades for the natural ice industry to become profitable. This explains why Tudor, eventually known as the "Ice King" of New England, continued to trade in different goods such as coal, copper, and coffee. The profits he made in these lines made up for the early losses in the ice trade, particularly as he had to pay for the construction of icehouses in places such as Kingston and Calcutta so that the cargoes would not melt before people bought them.[4] Yet even to have a chance in this line of business, Tudor had to cultivate a taste for ice among the public in the ports he served. Fixed costs such as building icehouses and bribing government officials to gain trading privileges in foreign countries made ice expensive, as were the ads he placed in newspapers to drum up demand for his product. As the steward of his Charleston icehouse explained in 1829, "The inhabitants, therefore, are invited to call for ice in such quantities as shall enable the Proprietor of the House to continue the present price, which cannot be the case, unless ice is used rather as *necessity of life* than as a luxury" (emphasis in original).[5] This would not happen for another fifty years.

Tudor's plan for cultivating that taste was simple. "The plan which I had about this time adopted in my ice-trade was not to act as the monopolist, but to give the ice to the consumer, in all the southern regions, at a low price," he explained in a letter looking back on the start of his business in 1849; "in doing so, I was dealing more justly with the consumer."[6] An 1821 letter to his agent in New Orleans explains exactly how his system worked: "Grog shops are to be considered of first and primary importance in getting the system of cold drinks into vogue. The better and higher kind will come of themselves. In order to effect this, it will be necessary that you hitch upon about 4 grog shops frequented by low people and negroes with whom you will make a confidential bargain to give them their ice for one whole season, provided they will undertake to sell cold at the same price as tepid drinks."[7] His concentration on low-end saloons or taverns is no accident as patrons consuming hard liquor had less chance of seeing or caring about what remained at the bottom of their glasses. Yet even increased demand from this demographic could not counter the fixed costs of establishing the business. Tudor was constantly in debt for most of his career. He made his fortune as much on land speculation from the ice ponds he controlled as he did from selling ice.

Besides the cost of shipping, stiff competition also made it difficult to achieve profitability in the natural ice industry. While fashionable Boston laughed at Tudor's idea of shipping ice to the Caribbean when he first undertook the venture, many other merchants quickly followed him. By 1849 Tudor handled no more than a quarter of the ice leaving Boston.[8] Price competition in this struggle over markets proved impossible because any dealer with a few tons of ice melting on the dock was willing to sell it at the lowest price possible. Therefore, Tudor did his best to differentiate his ice in terms of quality. For example, in 1828 his manager, Nathaniel Wyeth, informed Tudor of a new pond that was "protected by the sun and wind as to be now excellent" (sun and wind produced ice honeycombed with holes that was difficult to ship and unsightly to consumers if they encountered it). As Tudor explained in his diary, "We are obliged to conceal in a degree the character of the good Pond to keep off the enemy."[9] Another innovation that Wyeth and Tudor developed was to skim off the top layer of ice where most of the sediment collected even before harvest. This allowed more clear ice to develop as long as the weather stayed cold.

Tudor also kept up the quality of the ice he sold by starting to cut it on the Kennebec River in Maine. His competition beat him to the Maine ice fields in 1824, but Tudor quickly countered by contracting for ice from local cutters. By 1831 Tudor had invested enough to own operations near Gardiner and other places along the river.[10] The appeal of Maine ice came from the quality of the water there. The Kennebec River originates from underground springs in northern Maine. Before the sawmills came, the quality of the water remained good, and the turbulence of the fast-running river helped keep sediment from accumulating in the ice.[11] Therefore, Kennebec-cut ice was clear and blue. In 1830 Tudor wrote, "Wyeth tells me the ice is so fine that you can see + read a printed paper through a block 42 inches long!"[12] Transparency would, in fact, become a major selling point for natural ice for the rest of the century because it seemed to advertise the purity of the water from which it came. "The quality of Kennebec ice," reported the Maine Bureau of Industrial and Labor Statistics in 1890, "years since established itself as the standard. Its beauties can be seen, 'clear and blue as the sky,' in thousands of ice wagons in southern cities."[13] As early as 1879 the *Ice Trade Journal* reported that Kennebec ice was "the best in the world."[14]

Yet even high-quality natural ice had sediment in it. The deep blue water of Henry David Thoreau's Walden Pond attracted ice cutters during his famous stay on its shores. Some of it came as a result of the packing process. Thoreau, a kind of self-taught expert on water quality, described the natural sediment in Walden Pond's ice: "Like the water, the Walden ice, seen near at hand has a green tint, but at a distance is easily blue and you can easily tell it from the white ice of the river, or the merely greenish ice of some ponds, a quarter of a mile off."[15] That greenish tint came from the organic matter in the water. Thoreau found it beautiful compared to neighboring waters because Walden Pond's sediment was diluted because of its depth. As the *Ice Trade Journal* explained in 1881, "It is in accordance with the experiences of all intelligent dealers, that the depth of the water in any given place has much to do with the color, and often with the other qualities of the ice formed on its surface, and that, as a rule, the deeper the water the better will be the product. It will not make so rapidly, but it will be purer and more transparent."[16] However, "purer" was not the same as completely pure; or, to put it another way, even natural ice made from the best water in ideal conditions still had some sediment in it.

Another source for sediment in even the best natural ice was the manner in which the harvester packed it. As Thoreau wrote near the end of Walden of the ice-harvest process at the pond, "[W]hen they began to tuck the coarse meadow hay into the crevices [to insulate it], and this became covered with rime and icicles, it looked like a venerable moss gown."[17] Hollis Godfrey, in a muckraking article from 1909, further explained the problems with packing methods that originated from the beginning of the industry:

After a few inches of ice have formed, holes are sometimes cut and the water below allowed to flow over the ice sheet. When this freezes it forms what is known as "overflowed ice." Such ice, of course, simply imprisons any impurities which may be lying on the surface, and, freezing solidly above the surface-layer. . . . Few methods could be devised which would more surely imprison undesirable solids than this. The second method is even more troublesome than the first. In mild winters, when the ponds where ice is generally cut do not freeze to a sufficient depth to give a satisfactory cake, narrow sheets are sometimes cut and packed together in such a fashion as to give a doubled cake. Under such circumstances two upper layers with their impurities often come together in the centre of the cake and give out their combined impurities when the ice melts.

From filth produced or preserved in such fashion comes a large part of the mud which fouls your ice compartment [a reference to ice boxes], or leaves a line of black scum in your glass of water.[18]

Of course, sediment had been in natural ice since the beginning of the industry. Only after the advent of machine-made ice did the public have a cleaner alternative. (Machine-made ice could still have dirt on it, but not in it. That filth came from drivers dragging ice in the dirt during the delivery process rather than from the manner in which companies produced it.) These inherent drawbacks of natural ice might explain why consumers did not warm to this commodity until they got used to the muck at the bottom of their glasses. However, fears later in the century about the cleanliness of the water that natural ice came from sent shockwaves through the industry.

Typhoid Fever from Natural Ice

In the late nineteenth century the Schuylkill River, the main source for Philadelphia's drinking water, became famous for its pollution. As early as 1875 a consultant for the city, the chemical engineer Julius W. Adams, reported, "It is needless to multiply evidence to the effect that the water of the Fairmount Pool," the reservoir which the Schuylkill drained into inside city limits, "is, at times, from the amount of refuse, from the slaughterhouses, breweries, and above all, the manufactories at Manayunk, not a proper water for domestic use. This is conceded by all who have examined it."[19] The negative externalities associated with industrialization had begun to affect the food chain, and the effects on water and the ice made from that water were perhaps the easiest of these externalities for the public to see. Smokestacks meant progress, but when chemicals entered their source of drinking water, Philadelphians knew they had a problem. Two chemistry professors named Booth and Garrett thought they could fix this problem:

> That offensive organic matter does enter the Schuylkill is certain, and its presence becomes known to a sensitive organ of smell in the winter. You have suggested this, and the remedy also; i.e. to allow ice to be cut freely in the winter season, so as to expose the water to aeration, and thereby improve the quality of the water. If this were done, we think that every citizen of Philadelphia might be thankful if he could always enjoy as healthful and refreshing a beverage as Fairmount water, cooled in the summer by Fairmount ice.[20]

While the city of Philadelphia had banned the cutting of ice from the Fairmount Pool around this time (presumably for sanitary reasons),[21] natural-ice companies cut thousands of tons of ice from sites further up the Schuylkill and on its tributaries during the late 1870s and early 1880s. Ice firms did not think that this carried any risk because they, as well as many independent experts, incorrectly believed that freezing was self-purifying—in effect, that disease germs trapped in ice froze to death. (In fact, they starve.)

In the winter of 1882–83 the stench from the Schuylkill became so bad that even Philadelphians long accustomed to polluted water took notice. That year the city described the water in the Eighth Ward as "having a disagreeable smell, an acid burning taste, and an oily feeling when used for washing purposes." People living in Philadelphia in the summer of 1882 might have seen woolen and cotton fabrics float by; large amounts regularly appeared in the water north of Vine Street, the part of the city closest to the river from which this polluted ice would have come.[22] The city's water department suggested that the ice needed aeration—to be cut open so that the impurities could waft away. The largest ice company in Philadelphia, the Knickerbocker, performed this service free of charge, reporting later:

> [A] number of blocks of ice were taken out of the river at points where the water was deemed to be the most objectionable, and being carefully protected from the dust allowed to melt. The product was examined and drank, and found to be entirely free from sediment and any kind of offensive odor, and to the taste perfectly sweet and pure, thus confirming the theory which many sensational writers affect to dispute, namely, that crystalization is a self-purifying process, which, under ordinarily favorable conditions, eliminates all foreign matter from the water.[23]

While the Knickerbocker Ice Company may have thought that ice from the Schuylkill was safe for human consumption, it is easy to show that many Philadelphians did not agree.

Evidence from Knickerbocker's Philadelphia ice cards from these years indicates the extent to which consumers rejected the local product. Ice companies distributed these cards to display in windows on days when customers wanted ice delivered to their homes. They included not just a company logo but also price information for that year as well as information about the product. Figure 1 is a composite of three ice cards issued by the Knickerbocker Ice Company in Philadelphia. The top card, from summer 1882, before the river became unbearable, includes no language about the origins of the ice. The second card, from summer 1883, has the words "We furnish PURE EASTERN ICE ONLY" stamped on it, suggesting that the company came to realize how the market had changed in just the last season after the printing of the cards but before they were distributed that spring. "Eastern ice" might be a euphemism for ice from Maine, but the important point was that Knickerbocker's ice did not come from the Schuylkill. By 1884 the words "PURE IMPORTED ICE" were printed on the cards in bold. The similarity of the cards in every other respect across this time frame only underscores the significance of this change. This large, stable natural-ice supplier had to adapt or die.

As water pollution grew worse not just in Philadelphia but also elsewhere in America, consumers concerned about the safety of ice made with tainted water demanded cleaner sources. Around Chicago, for example, ice dealers moved from local sources to the Fox River up in Wisconsin as it was still pure.[24] In most instances the water they fled from was not nearly as bad as water in Philadelphia was. It must have been obvious, on aesthetic reasons alone, to avoid ice from water that stank or had wool floating in it. However, over the course of the 1880s consumers had become increasingly concerned about ice contaminated with pathogens they could not see. Despite assurances by the natural-ice industry that ice purified itself through freezing, customers began to recognize that ice from tainted water bore a safety risk. Of all the water-borne diseases of the late nineteenth century, the one most associated with ice production was typhoid fever.

Typhoid fever has been a scourge to humankind for centuries. It is caused by a microorganism that attacks the intestinal tract. This microorganism is carried by human feces and spread through poor sanitation, and its initial symptoms include fever, dehydration, diarrhea, abdominal pain, chills, headache, cough, weakness, and sore throat. Because of the similarity of these symptoms to those of many other diseases and because it takes from five to twenty-one days for symptoms to appear, typhoid fever is often misdiagnosed even today. (Red-spot rashes are a giveaway as to typhoid infection, but the spots appear only in 30 percent of cases.) In the days before antibiotics, fatality rates from typhoid fever were about 30 percent.[25] As late as 1911 a government scientist reported that "450,000 persons are incapacitated and about 35,000 are killed by typhoid fever each year."[26] Undoubtedly many more were stricken by the disease without authorities recognizing it.

While the relationship between lack of sanitation and typhoid fever had long been suspected, it could not be proved until the German bacteriologist Karl Eberth first established a direct connection between feces and this disease

Figure 8.1. Ice company trade cards, 1880s. Courtesy of Hagley Museum and Library.

when he discovered the typhoid fever bacillus in 1880.[27] However, at this juncture, when the germ theory of disease was still in its infancy, there remained many doubters. It was particularly difficult for scientists to find typhoid bacilli in a sample of drinking water. Therefore, many scientists still doubted the connection between typhoid and poor water quality (let alone ice) because these microbes were not found in water until years later.[28] Unfortunately, even a tiny quantity of typhoid microbes could do enormous damage. Some people could be carriers of the disease without showing symptoms (think of "Typhoid Mary" Mallon, a cook by trade). Yet, if the waste of even one such individual made it into the water supply, it had the potential to infect thousands of people.

Using the newest technologies, scientists who tested ice samples in the 1880s and 1890s concluded that there was a risk of contracting typhoid (as well as other waterborne diseases) through the consumption of ice. "That ice does not purify itself in impure water is a well known fact," concluded *Scientific American* in 1887.[29] Dr. William Blackwood, writing in an 1893 medical bulletin, explained, "Most folks think that ice 'purifies' itself in freezing by some mysterious process, but how it does this they can't say." On the contrary, argued Blackwood, "It is very well known that many germs which are inimical to health are not killed by even long continued cold, even if the temperature is carried far below zero. Among these, it is said that the bacillus of typhoid fever is highly resistant to freezing."[30] A 1902 outbreak at a mental hospital in upstate New York that could be directly traced to ice rather than water did much to cement this conclusion in the minds of scientists, government officials, and the general public.[31] The next year the *New York Times* editorialized, "Probably no bacteriological fact is better established than that much of the ice of commerce is dangerously impure. The assumption that water purifies itself in freezing was long ago shown to have but a limited basis in truth. The individual crystals are likely to be purer than the mother liquid from which they are formed; but ice is a mass of crystals in which may be entangled all kinds of impurities." This article came in the midst of a flurry of scare reporting in the New York press about the dangers of natural ice cut from the Hudson River, which New Yorkers still consumed by the ton every summer. "We have entered upon the icewater season," wrote the *Times*, "and perhaps the best thing to do is to give thanks that this particular sin is not as summarily or invariably punished as, theoretically, it should be."[32]

Confronted with repeated charges that its product could carry diseases such as typhoid, the natural-ice industry and then industry-friendly scientists began to make the same argument that the Knickerbocker Ice Company did back in 1883. They claimed that water "self-purifies" as it freezes. As the aptly named Professor Thomas M. Drown wrote in 1893, "Freezing of water is ordinarily a process of purification, that is to say, the ice is usually purer than the water that is frozen."[33] At first the industry's most important trade journal, *Ice and*

Refrigeration, acknowledged that bacteria can survive freezing, but it significantly downplayed the risk involved. According to the editor, "For as all men who walk the streets on a dry day are liable to inhale the infected dust of the dessicated [*sic*] sputtum [*sic*] of the consumptive who spits upon the street, nevertheless the actual number so poisoned compared with the whole number of inhabitants is comparatively small; so, too, are the numbers who are actually poisoned by bacteria in ice."[34] By the middle of the 1910s, despite mounting evidence that ice could carry disease germs, the industry took a much harder line, arguing that "Natural ice has never been shown to be the cause of any disease and epidemiologists no longer consider it even a *possible* source of epidemics."[35] Luckily for consumers, they never accepted the conclusions of scientific experts as filtered through industry trade journals. In fact, when given a viable alternative to natural ice, they voted with their pocketbooks and abandoned natural ice largely due to precisely such safety concerns.

In part because of these health concerns and in part because of other advantages, machine-made ice increasingly challenged natural ice for business in the markets where the two products met head-to-head during the late nineteenth century. This new product came about after 1877, when the German scientist Carl von Linde perfected a commercially viable ammonia compression refrigerating machine powered by steam that could be used to produce ice any time of the year.[36] He quickly sold the patent to the Fred C. Wolf Company in Chicago, which began manufacturing them in the United States. Wolf soon faced countless imitators producing similar devices.[37] They were manufactured by a small number of producers and sold to small businessmen who began to sell machine-made ice to household consumers for the first time.[38] Many companies used this technology to produce "artificial" ice. This machine-made ice, produced near the point of consumption, soon competed against natural ice in both price and quality (since producers purified the water they used to make it). Mechanical refrigeration offered a steady supply of regularly shaped ice. (Regularly shaped ice was important for storing and transporting it. The less its surfaces were exposed to air, the slower it would melt.) Furthermore, this ice had none of the sediment that would accumulate in the bottom of a glass when natural ice melted. After the failure of the Hudson River ice crop led to a boom in the building of mechanical ice machines, there was a viable ice-manufacturing industry in the United States by 1890. Many firms riding this wave subsequently competed directly against natural ice in many markets, especially in the South, where natural ice was obviously rarer and therefore more expensive. This competition helped split the ice industry in two ways.

Market Segmentation by Use

Considering the eventual widespread recognition that ice could carry disease, it is worth examining why the American natural-ice industry survived for so long. The most important reason that the natural-ice industry fought off competition from superior machine-made ice was market segmentation. Cheap, dirty, natural ice had a large market among industrial and small business customers who did not care whether it was dirty because it did not touch their products. For example, even though its cards suggest that the Knickerbocker Ice Company no longer sold Schuylkill ice to its customers in 1884, the company still sold eighty-four thousand tons from that river that year.[39] Where did it go? Brewers, the first large consumers of ice in the United States, used natural ice to chill metal vats of wort and barrels of beer after brewing.[40] Their ice never touched the beer. The same was true for grocers' freezers and in taverns. Commercial freezers of this day had separate compartments for the meat or produce displayed in them and the ice used to keep them cold specifically to avoid the possibility of contamination (see Figure 8.2). Likewise, beer in barrels behind bars would be protected from contamination.

However, when considering the role of natural ice in food chains, railway cars constituted by far its most important use. Mary Yeager has described the various efforts to perfect the railway refrigerator car in the 1860s and 1870s.[41] The most successful of these cars were built by Gustavus Swift in the late 1870s in order to save his company the expense of shipping entire cattle from the Midwest to East Coast butchers for slaughter. By 1883 Swift had set up icing stations along his northern rail route to make sure that his cars had enough natural ice in them to keep his perishable cargoes cold even at the end of their long journey.[42] Soon producers were giving the same treatment to fruits and vegetables. By 1896 the California produce trade required 150,000 tons of natural ice gathered from the Sierra Nevada mountains in order to keep its cars cold.[43] By 1905 thirty thousand ice railway cars a year left California for points east. A real refrigerated railway car (as opposed to one that depended on ice in any fashion) was not perfected until the 1950s.[44] All of this industrial ice (in railroad cars, freezers, and so forth) formed a vital link in many different food chains but no longer constituted food itself.

This use of a product unfit for human consumption in a food chain raised health concerns because it was so easy to cheat by substituting tainted ice for the more-expensive article intended for human consumption. This prospect raised the specter of government regulation to prevent cheating. "While natural ice, properly isolated, is entirely suitable for use in cold storage warehouses and under similar conditions," wrote *Scientific American* in 1914, "there is no doubt but much that is now sold to the public is not fit for human consumption, and the time is not far off when official recognition of this fact will be made by authorities charged with the supervision of pure foods."[45] That offi-

Figure 8.2. By having a separate ice compartment (on top in this model), butchers, grocers, and other merchants could use dirty ice to chill their wares because the sediment trapped in the ice would not contaminate the food once it melted. *The Excelsior Refrigerator* (Baltimore: C. H. Roloson & Co., n.d.). Courtesy of Hagley Museum and Library, Wilmington, Delaware.

cial recognition never came in most municipalities. Consumers had to act for their own protection, which they did by expressing a growing distaste for natural ice. For example, one manufacturer of mechanical ice equipment reported, "In 1894, we built a machine for a natural ice company, we found this machine running during the winter when this company had a crew of men on the river harvesting natural ice. We questioned them as to why they were running the machine when ice was so abundant. Their reply was that ice made with our machine was so far superior to natural ice that many of their customers would have no other."[46] In those locales where mechanical and natural ice competed directly against each other in the market for private consumers, the former invariably replaced the latter. "[T]he family trade will want the manufactured article as the quality is so far superior [to that of the natural ice]," explained a local ice firm in 1899.[47] Yet the replacement of natural ice with machine-made ice took time because there were not enough ice plants (particularly in the north) in order to satisfy the public's ballooning demand for the product. In 1911, for example, especially hot weather in May (rather than a warm winter) meant that demand so far outstripped supply that New York dealers were forced to buy ice from other dealers at inflated prices from as far as three hundred miles away.[48]

Understanding ice prices can be difficult because the markets in the 1880s and 1890s were entirely local. Since the early seaboard ice trade from New England to the South was entirely shut down by the introduction of the mechanical ice machine, natural ice prices fluctuated wildly during this era depending on the weather in a particular area the previous winter. One of the appeals of purchasing a mechanical ice machine for businesses was that it would produce a steady supply of ice no matter what the temperature had been the previous winter. Nevertheless, there were not enough ice manufacturers in America to satisfy demand through at least World War I. Perhaps they did not want to make the capital investment in machinery when natural ice was so much cheaper than the machine-made article. Even the growth of ice manufacturing operations run off the residual energy from electric power plants around 1910 was not enough to satisfy the public's rapidly increasing demand for ice. The failure of machine-made ice to quench demand, particularly in summers after warm winters when supply was low, is another reason that the consumer market for natural ice persisted despite health concerns for the product.

Anecdotal evidence concerning the relative prices of the natural and machine-made products suggests both the failure of the machine-made ice producers to satisfy demand and the extent of the money consumers could save if they did not mind organic matter at the bottom of their drinks. For example, a representative of the Passaic Ice Company in New Jersey complained in 1899, "About 75,000 tons have been harvested this winter, about twice as much as last winter. If prices will not be cut too much by big outside companies the prices may be kept at $1.50 to $2 per ton, that is $1 less than last season. It is hard for artificial ice companies to compete with such prices."[49] In 1908 the treasurer of a cold storage and ice-making plant in a New England city wrote the journal *Ice*:

Over a year ago we built a large cold storage plant in this city, also an ice making plant in connection therewith, and have been making and selling artificial ice. This is the first artificial ice that has ever been sold in this city, and it is new to our people. It has been believed that we cannot compete with the natural ice which is so abundant in New England. However, we have had a successful summer, devoting our attention almost entirely to the family trade and serving from twelve to fifteen hundred customers. This artificial ice has been sold to the family trade *at thirty cents per hundred while the price of the natural ice has been twenty-five cents*. We found some difficulty in making the people believe that the artificial ice is so superior to the natural ice in purity and healthfulness as to command a higher price. [emphasis added][50]

The poor quality of ice sold to industrial users is also reflected in the price. For example, in Anderson, Indiana, in 1893 natural-ice dealers sold industrial customers ice at two dollars per ton and domestic customers ice at six dollars per ton.[51] This price difference allowed natural ice to gain a niche with the poor, or perhaps just those poorly informed on the risks of consuming polluted ice.

However, at some point during the early twentieth century, the price of machine-made ice came down low enough so that regular employees could afford it. The movement of natural ice from consumer good to exclusive industrial good was probably complete by the advent of the household refrigerator around 1930. Nevertheless, natural ice persisted and even thrived for industrial usage decades after its domestic market disappeared. "The day is long past when an ice dealer could count on every household as a potential customer," reported the *Bangor Daily News* in January 1953. "Still, the total tonnage of ice being sold today is far greater than 50 years ago, long before the invention of the mechanical refrigerator." Much of that Maine ice was machine-made by then, but "[t]he old methods of ice harvesting on rivers is still used to some extent especially in the northern part of the state."[52] With quality completely irrelevant, this nineteenth-century technology still had a toehold in the food chains of the twentieth century.

Market Segmentation by Means of Production

Faced with fierce competition from machine-made ice, the natural-ice industry played up its strengths and played down its vulnerabilities. Perhaps the only ace that natural-ice makers held in their hands was the widespread notion that natural ice was better than the machine-made product because it was "natural" and therefore "pure," even if it came from polluted water. For this reason, machine-made ice dealers did much to tout a quality that seemed to give them an upper hand with the public in this competition over perception: transparency. As one equipment manufacturer explained in the company's catalog, "In the beginning of the industry of ice-making, many manufacturers were satisfied with producing an article regardless of quality. Therefore no special pains were taken to make transparent ice, but by and by the demands for a better product were made."[53] Notice the association of transparency with "a better product." The opaque part of machine-made ice was just air. Nevertheless, these ice manufacturers went to great pains to eliminate this harmless part of their product (usually by agitating the water before freezing) in order to satisfy customer demand and compete better against natural ice. They often touted it in ads that showed various people or objects behind blocks of transparent ice (see Figure 8.3).

While this kind of marketing worked well during the days when consumers were primarily concerned about natural ice on aesthetic grounds or because of an aversion to sediment in their glasses, this strategy did not work against these newer health concerns because typhoid microbes were invisible. Dirty ice could come from clear water. The *New York Times* explained the public's dilemma well in 1903, "Clear ice from pure water is not a source of danger to the public health. No doubt all of that made from distilled water, and much of that from the deep ponds of Maine, is free from impurities. The difficulty, however, is that no one can know what his iceman is giving him or whether it is the same one day as another."[54] Moving from natural to machine-made ice constituted the logical solution to this problem. In a twist that seems ironic in light of modern concerns about industrial food chains, "natural" ice carried a health risk while "artificial" ice did not. Natural ice even compared badly to machine-made ice on the aesthetic front. "I see a great number of wagons having hygienic ice, perfect in shape, perfect in appearance; in all ways pleasing to the eye," complained the New York natural-ice dealer H. W. Bahrenburg in 1908, "whereas, on the other hand, I find the natural ice, more particularly referring to the Hudson River ice, in all kinds of shapes; ice twelve inches thick, having three inches of sap on it; ice with corners broken out; turtle backs; any old thing; and it is the same old story—any old thing is good enough, as long as we get it in the home."[55] With such problems, natural-ice companies faced the prospect of having their entire consumer market disappear.

As a response to this problem, by the 1890s natural-ice manufacturers began to tout the point of origin for their ice as a way of signaling the purity of their products to consumers. In a way, this resembled the manner by which corn or cattle would be graded. The industry wanted to train consumers to look for its label as a sign of quality and an assurance that its product would never be contaminated. While there was no graduated scale of quality as there was for other commodities, the natural-ice producers shared the goal of wanting to make consumers believe that all ice was not the same. Their message to consumers was, in effect, not just that natural ice was better than machine-made ice but that some natural ice was better than others because it came from better water. This process is easiest to see in the ads from the trade press placed by ice wholesalers. "Pure Spring Water Ice from Ballston Lake," began an ad from the Ballston Spa Ice Company of Ballston Spa, New York, "Retails at 10 cents per 100lbs. above any other ice," presumably because of its superior quality, "No sewage."[56] Abraham Rich printed his location in Gardiner, Maine,

Figure 8.3. Manufacturers of machine-made ice often used photographs of people or things placed behind their ice in order to demonstrate to potential consumers the supposed purity of their ice. Here a Delaware ice manufacturer, Lea Pusey, is pictured behind the ice that his firm, the Diamond Ice Company, sold. Photograph c. 1884–86. Courtesy of Hagley Museum and Library, Wilmington, Delaware.

near the top of his banner ad in the August 1896 issue of *Ice Trade Journal*. "Heavy thick ICE (cut of 1895), of superior quality," it explained, since older ice could keep more than one year in Maine, though its quality suffered over time.[57] A Chicago firm that cut ice from Lake Geneva in Wisconsin went so far as to publish the results of a chemical analysis of the water in its ice as part of its marketing efforts.[58]

This kind of point-of-origin advertising became increasingly important as news about the safety of natural ice grew increasingly worse. "There has been much printed in the newspapers recently about the foulness of the Passaic River, and the many cases of typhoid which have resulted from the use of the water in Newark," reported the journal *Cold Storage* in 1899. "The water is so foul that the [ice-cutting] rights of the Simmons family are worthless, they say."[59] Yet judging from a complaint about the low price of ice in Newark in the same article, the Simmons family probably cut anyway. This kind of behavior was a threat to the entire consumer sector of the natural-ice industry, which explains why despite earlier industry claims that water purified itself through freezing, one natural-ice dealer from New Jersey recommended that any firm whose competitors cut from polluted sources be turned in to authorities.[60] While the industry had once derided efforts by local governments to regulate its product, dealers of quality natural ice now welcomed these same efforts in the same way that respectable meatpackers supported the Pure Food and Drug Act of 1905. A government seal of approval offered the prospect of consumers buying their product without fear of adverse health effects.

Naturally, while its competition struggled, machine-made ice companies increasingly used health concerns directed at *all* natural ice as a marketing tool. "Your physician will tell you that a great deal of sickness is caused by drinking impure water," wrote one ice company in an ad from 1909. "Impure ice contaminates not only water alone, but all the food with which it comes in contact."[61] By this stage ice boxes had become an important household use for ice. As these were literally boxes with ice in the back, the possibility of dirty water touching the food in these containers was very real. As a columnist writing for the *New York Tribune* explained in 1922, "Much of the Natural Ice used in a box contains foreign matter that accumulates in the drain pipe or corners of the chamber and is liable to result in disagreeable odors or prove a source of contamination."[62] Therefore, the larger the consumer market a firm had, the more likely it was to handle exclusively manufactured ice. "We do not handle lake ice," explained an ad from a firm that sold only machine-made ice. "The character of the lake ice which has been found in my own ice chest has been bad," explained one of seven physicians whose testimonials appeared in the ad, "and a menace to the health of the community."[63] Point-of-origin marketing essentially said, "You may have read about health scares related to pollution in some waters, but that doesn't apply to the pristine body where we cut our ice." While natural ice remained a viable industry for a long period after the turn of the twentieth century, it did so despite losing enormous ground in the consumer market rather than because its marketing succeeded. The continuing market for the product in the industrial sector made this possible.

Conclusion

On the consumer front, ice went from being a luxury in the United States to being a necessity in the last decades of the nineteenth century. For that to happen, the market had to separate itself into industrial and household users and a new source of cheap, high-quality ice from machines had to emerge. The stuff in natural ice besides water formed the basis of both these splits. At first, users simply preferred to avoid organic matter left at the bottom of their glasses, but later the quality of the water that formed their ice became a major health concern. As the price of machine-made ice dropped over time, those household users gradually abandoned the natural article. While commercial ice customers needed ice only to keep their products cold during production or when moving through the long food chains that developed in the United States during this period, household consumers were much more discerning. The quality of ice used in food chains was largely irrelevant to industrial consumers and invisible to the consumers who ate the food packed in that ice, so as long as ice remained a cheap and convenient way of chilling perishable goods, it continued to have a market. Considering the drawbacks of natural ice, its persistence seems remarkable. However, the long history of ice as a cooling method came about more as an effect of low production costs and convenience that will never go away. Consumers might no longer tolerate sediment in the bottom of their glasses, but industrial food chains to this day care only about the cold.

Chapter 9
Provisioning Man's Best Friend: The Early Years of the American Pet Food Industry, 1870–1942

Katherine C. Grier

For food-history scholars, "food" typically means what human beings eat, and yet over 60 percent of American households also shelter tens of millions of other eaters: pet animals. According to the American Pet Products Manufacturers Association, we spent $16 billion on commercial pet food in 2007, mostly to feed cats and dogs.[1] The story of this particular food chain has been unexamined, however. This chapter focuses on the development of dog food, particularly canned dog food prior to the 1942 ban on the use of cans for the mobilization for World War II. The emphasis here is a discussion of just what went into those cans. As with many other aspects of the pet industry in the first half of the twentieth century, evidence for the production, sale, and use of commercial cat and dog food is scattered widely, challenging to compile, and tricky to interpret. This is because the pet food industry was built on scores, perhaps hundreds, of small producers, many of whom served local or regional markets. Even when the large Chicago packers and the major animal-feed millers got into the business, pet food was a relatively small part of their product lines for several decades, although it was one more way to wring value out of the inevitable inefficiencies of processing on a large scale.[2] The relative invisibility of pet food also reflects the fact that this is also a story about animal bodies, parts or whole, that people will not or cannot eat. Except for periodic flurries of regulatory activity, people did not want to think about what was in those cans and what it suggested about industrial meat production. (As I prepared this essay for publication, the public outcry over contaminated ingredients imported from China for use in pet food was already dying down; people were having a difficult time critiquing a problematic processed food when it has become such a fundamental part of their shopping and food preparation habits.)

What did American dogs eat before their owners were able to pick up cans and paper bags of prepared food at their local supermarkets? The quality of dogs' diets depended on the characteristics of the households they occupied. Dogs were beneficiaries of each household's supply of food scraps. Except in the largest cities, housewives oversaw the processing of a wide array of raw materials for family meals; in the case of meat, they often handled animal parts with which almost no modern consumers are familiar, such as hearts or calf heads and feet. Thrifty cooks knew how to use these parts, and what the family absolutely could not or would not eat went to the animals that were part of the household, along with leftover starches and vegetables. Fond dog owners cooked up "dog stews" or simply scraped all plates into the dogs' dishes and added other kitchen refuse such as bones. If a family was prosperous, so was the family dog. In families of more limited means, dogs were not as well fed, and since even the larger cities tolerated wandering dogs, these animals fended for themselves in the streets and gutters. Both owned and ownerless dogs were still part of the ecology of the towns and cities where large numbers of animals lived and worked, and where municipal services were limited at best.[3] (I leave the exact components of their diets to your imagination.)

To a large extent, commercial dog food was, and is, the packaged industrial food scrap that supplanted table scraps, especially once meat packers got into the business. This statement must be qualified somewhat because in the early years of dog food manufacturing, some operations were in the business of creating "health food" for dogs. Big packers eventually appealed to consumers on the basis of dog health, but dog health food companies were often in the business of making whole-grain-based health foods for people too, and their ingredients reflected that.

The dog food industry originated in Victorian England in the 1860s with a company named Spratt's Patent Limited. James Spratt, an American businessman visiting England, apparently saw stray dogs eating discarded hardtack on the London docks and decided to package similar biscuits for sale to kennel owners. Around the time of Spratt's eureka moment, the British military establishment was engaged in experiments to create better battle rations for its troops in response to conditions during the Crimean War, when malnutrition had been epidemic. These trials included "meat biscuits," which I surmise were made with beef meal and extract.[4] At present I do not know whether Spratt was aware of these efforts, but he probably used a recipe very much like it. An expensive but convenient alternative to home cooking, the resulting "dog cakes" were a product directed to sportsmen, who needed a convenient food for hunting dogs in the field, and dog fanciers.

The company's decision to undertake manufacturing in the United States coincided with the appearance of the organized dog fancy here, and Spratt's directed its marketing efforts to this small but growing elite. The firm centered its efforts on dog shows, including the 1876 Centennial Exposition, providing free food to get exhibitors into the Spratt's habit. Recognizing that it had to create a new habit to build demand, Spratt's was also a relentless advertiser, anticipating the marketing strategies of canned dog food packers by fifty years. It bought the entire front cover of the first issue of the American Kennel Club's official journal in January 1889 to trumpet its identity as "Contractor to the leading American and European Kennel Clubs" and its "Special Appointment" to that notorious dog lover Queen Victoria. Spratt's even provided free blank AKC pedigree-registration forms; the flip side of the sheet was a full-page ad for its products.[5]

Spratt's most famous product was its Celebrated Patent Meat "Fibrine" Dog Cakes, which included "Beetroot." These large, square, and undoubtedly high-fiber biscuits were meant to be broken up and moistened for feeding, although the company noted that forcing the animal to gnaw whole ones would have the effect of stimulating its digestive juices, just as health breads for people were intended to do. In fact, the company's explanation of the problems of the overcivilized diet of the family dog and the consequent benefits of Fibrine Dog Cakes used rhetoric that echoed the era's discourse on health food for humans: the biscuits were a "plain, wholesome diet" that would "obviate constipation, which is almost natural in the domestic dog, and the cause of more disease than anything else."[6]

Spratt's also pioneered specialization in dog foods, anticipating the "life stages" approach used by modern marketers by nearly one hundred years. By the 1890s the company offered the basic Patent Meat "Fibrine" Vegetable Dog Cakes, Patent Charcoal Dog Cakes for sour canine stomachs, Greyhound Cakes, Oatmeal and Plain Round Dog Cakes (for use as a supplement where fresh meat was part of the training diet of greyhounds and hunting packs), Pet Dog Cakes ("especially valuable for pets kept in the city"), and Patent Cod Liver Oil Old Dog Cakes ("invaluable for delicate or old dogs and those recovering from a sickness"). Puppies were served "Puppy Cakes," "Pepsinated Puppy Meal" (intended for weaning, "Bad doers," and dogs with weak digestions), Bone Meal, and a powdered bitches' milk substitute. Later Spratt's advertisements even addressed a debate among breeders whether "purebred" animals, like purebred (read "white") people, were less likely to be able to breed successfully because of over-refinement; the company's strengthening Malt and Cod Liver Oil Dog Cakes were "excellent as a safeguard against sterility." From the beginning Spratt's also pushed brand recognition; every Fibrine Dog Cake was stamped with the phrase "Spratts Patent" and an "X."

Spratt's Patent, Limited, had the dog food market in America pretty much to itself for several decades, which suggests that the customer base was small. Even Sears, Roebuck and Company experimented with offering Spratts in its 1897 catalog.[7] By the end of the nineteenth century, however, a few other businesses undertook the manufacturing of dry dog food, adapting their biscuit-baking technologies for a new class of consumers. This packaged dog food was marketed as health food, reflecting the turn-of-the-century interest in diet reform. Some companies developed dog food lines as a sideline to grain milling for human consumption. Old Grist Mill Dog and Puppy Bread was introduced around 1905 by Potter and Wrightington, a Massachusetts company that specialized in "Hygienic Health Foods for family use." The company mixed its special whole-grain flour with beef, bone meal, rice, and vegetables and baked the dough into "cakes" and a special "Boston Terrier Biscuit."[8] A few companies also introduced dog health food as an outgrowth of the expanding business of veterinary patent medicines. By around 1900 the A. C. Daniels Company of Boston, one of the most successful manufacturers of veterinary patent medicines, began to offer its own brand of "medicated dog bread" as an aid for convalescent or chronically ill pets.

By the 1910s another, more successful path for making dry dog food developed, associated with livestock feed manufacturing. The most famous, although not the pioneering, example of this business model is the Ralston Purina Company, which first added dog food to its product line in 1926. The product was sold only through licensed Purina livestock-feed dealers and may have been the first dog food to penetrate rural markets. The Purina™ Dog Chow® that became America's most popular dry dog food was added to the line only in 1957, after six years of formulating and marketing experiments made with the intention of cracking an already established market in grocery stores.[9]

The other path for dog food manufacture, canning, appeared first during the 1910s. Canning meat for human consumption actually began in the mid-1840s; however, the economics of making metal cans prevented their use for animal food until the early 1900s, and technical problems associated with canning meat continued to affect the industry well into the 1930s. The Kennel Food Supply Company of Fairfield, Connecticut, seems to have been the first dog food canner. Advertising to breeders in the *American Kennel Gazette* in 1916, the company promoted "Canned Meat" in two-and-a-half-pound cans, packed in cases of ten, twenty, and forty.[10]

The first large-scale dog food canning operation serving a national market seems to have been Chappel Brothers, Inc., a company based in Rockford, Illinois, eighty miles north and west of Chicago. In 1934 P. M. Chappel offered his account of the origins of canned dog food packing during the hearings for the National Industrial Recovery Administration's (NIRA) Code of Fair Practices and Competition organized by the dog food industry: "I have been dubbed, as the boys, say, the father of the canned dog food industry. . . . In 1919, being interested in dogs, I decided that a canned dog food would go over big. I set about then with the assistance of Dr. Hoskins, Dean of the New York State Medical College, to work out a dog food. We spent upwards of three years doing that, spent in the neighborhood of $60,000 in working it out. . . . In 1923 we were ready to go with it." Chappel recalled having trouble selling either pet store owners or grocers on his dog food, called Ken-L-Ration, until he met a well-to-do man in Detroit who imported German shepherd dogs and was worried about their diets. After his enthusiastic report on the canned food, Chappel was able to convince Detroit pet stores to take the product, and he built a market from there.[11] By 1928 Chappel Brothers had added Kit-E-Ration to its line; a dried food for dogs followed shortly thereafter.

Chappel Brothers does not appear in the 1922 *Packer's Encyclopedia*, the business directory of the meat industry, as a packer, renderer, or wholesale provisioner. In Chappel's case the absence is because the company seems to have been exclusively a horse slaughtering operation. Horse slaughter is a shadowy part of the story of meat in America. Killing and cutting up broken-down or unwanted horses was an unpleasant but necessary part of the horse world. In nineteenth-century cities horse bodies went for rendering. Their hides, hooves, and bone were useful for various products. Some horse meat probably found its way into the market as cheap meat for human consumption and some for cats and dogs, following an old English practice; most of the meat, blood, and organs were turned into fertilizer. By the 1890s a handful of businesses began to can horse meat with the intention of exporting it to Europe, a practice that increased during and after World War I. Efforts to get Americans to eat the meat were doomed to failure, however.[12]

Chappel Brothers, which apparently first packed horse meat for export, capitalized on the dramatic decline in the number of working horses beginning in the 1920s, as per Chappel's own time line above. Leroy Judson Daniels, an Iowa farmer and horse trader whose memoir was published in 1987, recalled that he was recruited during the Depression by three men who "wanted me to buy old horses for the Clapper (*sic*) Brothers of Rockford, Illinois, a killing plant." Desperate to earn money for his family, Daniels took out contracts to provide "killer" horses (horses purchased for slaughter) at ten dollars a head. While some of the meat may have been exported for human consumption, most of the animals Daniels shipped were killed for pet food.[13] By 1934, however, Chappel Brothers' dog food business was so large that the company had to tap another source for horses, the wild populations in the western states. Testimony at the NIRA Code hearing reported that P. M. Chappel "raises his horses on the range, and then, in certain times of the year, they are corralled, and they are shipped to Rockford, Illinois, and they are slaughtered." In fact, the horses were the feral animals called mustangs. Their grazing put them in direct competition with beef-cattle ranchers, who were only too happy to dispose of as many as could be herded together and sold for hard cash. The carcasses at Chappel's slaughterhouse underwent inspection by the Bureau of Animal Industry, and the butchered meat was prepared for shipment overseas or canned for use as pet food. Chappel's was one of four horse-slaughtering operations that canned their own brands of dog food; other dog food companies purchased horse meat for canning.[14] The Hugo Strauss Packing Company of Brooklyn was another slaughtering operation; it offered Purity dog food composed of "Solid Cooked Horse Meat," and Laddie Boy Kennel Ration, a mixture of horse meat, cereals, and cod liver oil, the latter a universal tonic used for dosing both children and dogs.

The fact that horse slaughter was the heart of the early canned dog food business was probably one reason for the relative slowness with which meat packers embraced canned dog food as part of the repertoire of sidelines that they already relied on for profitability. It also explains why finding early discussions of technical matters in dog food canning is a challenge. Canned pet food lay largely outside the meat industry as it defined itself and as it was defined by the compilers of agricultural statistics. Pet food was considered part of the "prepared feeds" industry, in which the largest volume of products was based on milled grains, alfalfa, soy meals, and flours and used for livestock. The 1937 U.S. Census of Manufactures provided what seems to have been the first federal assessment of pet food production that separated it from the general data on feeds and distinguished wet- and dry-food production. That year canned dog and cat food "outside the meat industry" but not having grain as a "principal ingredient" totaled 237,792,250 pounds with a value of $10,740,642; "other" foods for cats and dogs (probably dry foods that contained meat or blood meal or "feed tankage") weighed in at over 114 million pounds with a value of $6,703,872.[15] Thus, canned dog food was an expanding market in the 1930s, the heart of the Depression, when one would assume that homemade dog stews were the best alternative for families on tight budgets. Why did this happen?

Meat packers' introduction of canned dog food lines represented creative thinking about the use of marginal or outright inedible meat "by-products" by canning plants if not by the packers themselves. In the meat industry, by-products are defined as all the parts of an animal body other than the fresh meat sold for human consumption, and they fall into two categories, "edible" and "inedible."[16] In 1927 Rudolph Clemen, the assistant director of Armour's Livestock Bureau, published an entire book on the subject. He explained that the modern packing industry was in tune with other American businesses in its quest to reduce its waste stream and extract value in the process. By-products generally had become "such a source of revenue that in many cases the by-products have proved more profitable per pound than the main product."[17] Requirements for successful development of agricultural by-products manufacture generally depended on several factors: the recognition of "actual or potential markets"; the ongoing adaptation of industrial processing techniques to agricultural products, resulting in a steady supply of the waste "gathered in one place or capable of being collected at sufficiently low cost"; and the ability to store unprocessed by-products until they could be used, in either dried, liquid, or frozen form.[18]

Slaughter and butchering presented particularly nasty and voluminous waste problems in industrial settings. Clemen pointed out that only 55.6 percent of a steer by weight was meat, which left a lot of material to be recycled in other ways, to say nothing about animals that were unfit for human consumption.[19] In the old days, city butchers had passed off some of the waste of their work by shoveling offal (the organs) into the street, where it was consumed by urban scavengers: pigs, dogs, cats, crows, and, of course, insects. Blood simply ran away in gutters; hides, hair, hooves, and green bones were given or sold cheaply to nearby small-scale renderers and tanners, who produced glue, horn and bone for buttons, tanned hides, fats for soap, and other products. Some materials seem to have been composted and used as fertilizer, anticipating the eventual ties of the commercial fertilizer business to packinghouses. At the time, rural or small-town home and neighborhood butchers were still probably the most efficient users of the organs, tongues, and other pieces that resulted from disassembling animals. These meats were prepared in a variety of ways, sometimes as cuts in their own right (beef hearts, for example, were stuffed and baked) or minced into sausage or other dishes. Whatever was left could be fed to family pigs and chickens—or cooked and served to the family dogs and cats.

At first, large-scale meat packers simply replicated these relationships, supplying some raw materials to the small businesses that clustered around them and disposing of the rest. By the 1890s and perhaps earlier, however, packers began to process by-products for sale, collecting bones, blood, cracklings (meat scrap), and tankage, which consisted of a meal cooked from the trimmings that hit the packinghouse floor along with the bodies of condemned animals and offal. Packers generally dried but sometimes ground these materials and then sold them to fertilizer plants. As early as 1901 land grant universities published studies promoting the use of "digester tankage animal protein" for fattening livestock; soon "feed tankage" was sold by packers for use in raising hogs and chickens.[20] By the 1920s almost all "high-grade" tankage and 75 percent of the blood collected during slaughter and butchering went into the production of animal feeds. With their high protein content—from about 20 percent for raw bone meal to 60 percent for high-grade tankage—by-products created animal feeds that could be used to increase rate of weight gain for supplementing or "finishing" livestock. By then companies also recognized that there was a special market for particularly high-grade tankage: Clemen reported that a form of cracklings "free from bone . . . makes a good dog feed and dog biscuit ingredient."[21]

A second category of by-products was "edible." Packers called these "specialties," and the parts included "beef- , sheep- , and calf-head meats, sweetbreads, tongues, weasand meat [genitalia], hearts and livers, beef spleen (melts), tripe, kidneys, and ox tails." Packers prepared specialties for fresh shipment, froze them for export, and transferred them to their own sausage, canning, and curing departments. Clemen described canning operations as "a necessary and important adjunct to any large meat-packing establishment" and reported that smaller plants often disposed of specialties to separate canning operations located nearby. At least some of these operations became the smaller dog food plants whose stories are proving so difficult to trace; it is probable that these small canners packed both dog and people foods on the same lines. By the 1920s packers' canning departments increasingly absorbed the "difficult marketing problem in fresh meat by-products": "the supply usually exceeds the demand."[22] Beef trimmings were the most important ingredients for canned meats, which were regarded as foods for working-class consumers. Some items, such as the canned tongue that was popular as a luncheon meat in Great Britain, were sold mostly overseas.

Clemen's book on by-products does not mention dog food as part of his discussion of the economics of canning in the meat industry, but the utility of pet food to meat packers is already evident there: canning made good sense generally, and the principal products of canning for human consumption were items for which the fresh market was probably in decline. Tongues, hearts, and other organs may have been nutritious (something that progressive-era home economists reiterated repeatedly in their discussion of wholesome food for families of modest means), but outside of ethnic and rural consumers, fewer and fewer people seem to have been willing to cook or eat them, except perhaps as part of the mysterious content of sausages. A 1941 report in the *Consumers' Research Bulletin* reported that "dog food provided a ready outlet for meat scraps and various organ meats . . . (some of which human consumers should eat for better health, but as a rule reject)."[23] One category of animal turned over for slaughter, the elderly dairy cow, was even explicitly called "canner." While the demand for canned meat for human consumption in general needs further research, by the mid-1930s canning capacity was in place in scores of packing firms. They received further encouragement to take up canning when the federal government let large contracts to supply canned meat as part of relief efforts. Thus, packers were actively engaged in solving problems associated with canning, from technical issues to marketing in grocery stores. In fact, as the 1930s progressed and especially after 1935, the *National Provisioner*, the weekly periodical of the meat industry, devoted an increasing number of pages to improving both canning methods and marketing for canned meats.

Despite this, the *National Provisioner* neglected canned dog food in its discussion of canning until it expanded coverage of "allied lines" as packers struggled to restore profitability as the Depression deepened. In April 1934 the paper reported that products already sold in meat markets, such as cheese, oleomargarine, and eggs, were particularly compatible with existing distribution systems; it also mentioned dog food in its list of profitable sidelines.[24] In November of that year, the *Provisioner* published directions on canning dog food at the request of a reader, noting that the product was processed "the same as canned beef."[25]

The big Chicago packers turned to canning dog food in the early 1930s as part of their continuing vertical integration, but there is an interesting story to be told on the scores of smaller canning companies. These companies, little studied in histories of the canning or the meat industries, pioneered canned dog food and continued to thrive until the pet food industry underwent consolidation in the 1950s and 1960s. The 1934 Census of Manufactures reported that there were 1,160 meat-packing operations that slaughtered around eighty million animals; 561 of these packers were in California, Illinois, Indiana, Ohio, Pennsylvania, and New York.[26] In all likelihood, many dog-food-packing locations were neglected in this count because they were not engaged in slaughter.

It is important to recognize that even as the meat industry grew more concentrated in the early twentieth century, slaughter still took place in many communities as old, unproductive, or unwanted animals were converted into meat or the raw materials for products from glue to soap. It was not difficult for the slaughterhouses or small contractors located near local stockyards to can meat and by-products that people could not—or would not—eat for the delectation of dogs. As horse meat became harder to come by and demand for canned dog food continued to increase, packinghouse meat by-products became the most important sources of protein for dog food, although companies were creative about what they canned. Various meat from other domestic ruminants and from such wild species as whales, salmon, and reindeer from Alaska all found their way into dog food. In 1933, for example, three million pounds of whale meat frozen by the California Whaling Company was used in canned pet foods.[27]

When the State of Minnesota Department of Agriculture did an analysis of the composition of commercial dog foods in 1941, it tested 125 different canned and 75 different dry foods available for sale in that state alone.[28] After World War II another factor supporting this proliferation may have been the increased volume of meat that was handled by independent processors and jobbers, as the packers reduced the number of "branch houses" they supported by 35 percent. This meant more meat handled by "breakers," "boners," and "peddlers," who had one-quarter of the red-meat trade by the end of World War II. "Boners" were processors who specialized in provided boneless meat, mostly of lower quality, for further processing by bulk users, including canners of both human and pet food.[29] The Rival Dog Food Company of Chicago, for example, never actually slaughtered an animal; rather, it contracted for meat, probably "canner" quality beef. In the late 1930s Rival built a modern canning plant, which it was able to turn over to war-rations processing in 1941 and then back to dog food manufacture in 1945.[30]

By 1933 the *New York Times* reported that dog food brought $80 to $90 million in business and "has not suffered from the general business slump but has actually made substantial gains in both dollar and unit volume in the last three years." In 1934 Charles Wesley Dunn, the general counsel for the National Dog Food Manufacturers Association (DFMA), a new trade group created to respond to the National Industrial Recovery Act, testified that "something like 85 per cent" of the business he represented lay in canned food.[31] At the time DFMA stated that there were already 105 dog food manufacturing businesses in the country; only 25 were represented by sponsors of the proposed code for canned dog food.

While the trade was already beginning to be dominated by a small group of larger companies, it was still the "Wild West" of meat packing. In the volume of the hearings that I have been able to retrieve from the National Archives (two of the three were missing at the time of this writing), one of the most heated discussions had to do with the problem of determining what was called the "nutritive value" of canned dog food and the problems created by the absence of standards. J. R. Manning of the U.S. Bureau of Fisheries reported "considerable exploitation of the consumer" as "many kinds of decomposed materials, unfit for either human or animal nutrition have in times past entered such products. In some cases where the wholesome quality of the raw materials is acceptable, quite often these raw materials have little or no nutritional value. According to our information, chemists have found almost every conceivable variety or combination of materials in these products. Garbage and inert materials have sometimes found their way into the finished products." While Manning praised the majority of manufacturers, he argued for "the absolute necessity for the establishment and applications of standards and marketing grades in the industry." R. H. Kerr, representing the Bureau of Animal Industry (BAI), reported that canned dog food he had examined contained as little as 5 percent protein and that it was made with "organs and parts that yield incomplete proteins of low biological value."[32] Among the companies represented in the hearings, the obvious preference was for voluntary standards. Some companies present requested more federal inspection of the meat they used, at least partly as a marketing strategy, but the representative of the BAI responded that the agency did not have the personnel to extend inspection to pet food.

Expanding packer interest in entering the dog food business is also suggested by increased coverage in the *National Provisioner*. In 1935 the paper responded to a request for recipes, including variations for dog food flavored with fish and cheese, by "an Eastern packer who is considering making this product." Pointing out that recipes varied considerably "depending on quantities and class of materials available," the editors revealed that sausage departments and dog food operations shared the same pool of raw materials: "few packers with sausage departments have enough meat products available to supply all their protein requirements in dog food manufacture. They either purchase them from other packers, therefore, or supplement meat with a vegetable protein— soya bean meal, for example—to bring protein content to point desired."[33]

The 1934 NIRA hearings exposed a debate inside the industry about the nutritional quality of canned dog food; this went public on April 28, 1936, thanks to a floor speech by Republican senator Lester J. Dickinson, a candidate for his party's nomination to run against Franklin Delano Roosevelt. The senator charged that "human beings, under the 'planned scarcity' of the New Deal annually are consuming 100 million pounds of dog food—food unfit even for dogs to eat." Dickinson quoted the code hearings of 1934 on dog food, reporting that only fifteen of the two hundred plants manufacturing dog food were "under regular inspection" by the government. "It comes from two sources—carrion, made from dead animals, or else from diseased lungs, livers and fibrous tissues which make up the refuse from slaughter houses. . . . On the farm and around the stockyards it is known as tankage. Before this bonanza in dog foods it was used exclusively for fertilizer, and that is all it actually is fit for."[34] The rumor that canned dog food was eaten by people had been around a while, and it may have reflected the marginal quality of some canned meats offered for human consumers. In the 1934 NIRA hearings, a brief discussion about whether people ever ate canned dog food had taken place; whether this was one source of the senator's information is unknown. An industry representative had acknowledged that "there has been some use, some incidental use, of canned dog food for human consumption; Dr. Manning from the Bureau of Fisheries mentioned 'unconfirmed, unofficial' reports of canned dog food consumption in West Virginia and 'by the negroes of the south.' "[35]

Senator Dickinson's speech immediately inspired a brief flurry of activity from both the industry and the federal government. One of the reasons that dog food companies had gotten into trouble was their own sales practices. Some brand labels described the contents as being "government inspected," a statement that did not necessarily mean that the cuts therein were parts that people typically ate or wanted to eat but that consumers were unlikely to question. Interviewed for the *National Provisioner*, Meyer Katz, president of the Rival Packing Company, defended the practice by arguing that "there is no reason for humans to eat dog food since many more suitable foods are cheaper" and that "the product is labeled 'fit for human consumption' to prove to the dog owner that it is pure." The head of Wilson & Co.'s dog food division helpfully pointed out that dog food was sold mostly in "well-to-do areas," implying that few poor people were even able to purchase the cans in the stores they frequented.[36]

The next week the Bureau of Animal Industry revised regulations relating to animal feed, forbidding manufacturers from printing the federal inspection stamp or legend on their packages. However, canners who already operated under federal inspection—typically the large packers—were allowed to note that their products were prepared under sanitary conditions supervised by BAI employees.[37] This was not enough; the very next week legislation was proposed increasing regulation for pet food sold or transported in interstate commerce and empowering the secretary of agriculture to create new regulations for "any meat food product in can, pot, tin or other receptacle, if made from fish, cattle, swine, goats or other animal for consumption by dogs, etc." Federal meat inspection regulations had been extended to dog food, or at least to dog food that crossed state lines. Dickinson's charges that poverty-stricken people were using canned meat intended for dogs as their source of animal protein set this regulatory process in motion.[38]

The next year the Institute of Meat Packers appointed Dr. James W. Kellogg, formerly the chief chemist of the Pennsylvania Department of Agriculture's Bureau of Foods and Chemistry, to head its recently established Dog Food Division.[39] Its work was several years behind the makers of dry food, however. General Mills may have been the first company to pay for nutritional research on its own dog food. Brochures directed to consumers noted that "Gold Medal Dog Food is the result of specialized nutritional research with *dogs* since 1929 in the kennels at Larro Research Farm—internationally known as one of the world's leading institutions devoted to the study of animal nutrition." The Larro tests involved 1,195 purebred dogs in its first decade.[40] Albers Brothers Milling Company tested its Friskies brand on both white rats and dogs beginning in 1932 and made sure that the public knew about it.[41] Of course, P. M. Chappel, the energetic horse-meat packer and maker of Ken-L-Ration, claimed that Chappel Brothers was the first company to actually do research on the nutritional needs of dogs. (As we have seen, P. M. Chappel testified that he had sponsored research before producing Ken-L-Ration for sale.) The company may indeed have been the first to research the nutritional contents of canned dog food. By the early 1930s the company had established the Chappel Laboratory for Canine Nutritional Research at its home base in Rockford, Illinois. A mimeographed copy of a report titled "The Generation Test as Applied to Canned Dog Foods," published in 1935 by the lab, survives in Harvard's Baker Library: "With only a limited amount of regulations in its manufacture, a large number of canned dog foods are now being manufactured with no consideration as to the food requirements of the dog. This situation has become critical and at the present time steps should be taken to remedy conditions as they now exist. . . . This report gives some of the work which has been done and which is responsible for what is known as 'The Chappel Standard of Biological Value for Canned Dog Foods.'" The Standard required that food "permit growth and successful reproduction and lactation through three generations of animals, with continued reproduction and lactation within each generation." Documenting studies done in 1931 or 1932 with "the standard albino rat" and acknowledging that the findings were only indicative, Chappel's report noted that most of the dog foods tested did not support the healthy reproduction of its rodent subjects.

By 1937 the American Veterinary Medical Association and its affiliate the American Animal Hospital Association, which served the growing number of practices in small-animal care, announced that they would study the nutritional content of dog food. Bob Becker, who wrote a weekly column on pet dogs for the *Chicago Daily Tribune*, reported, "it means that men who know and have reputations in their field are going to test the scores of foods now flooding the market to find which are honestly made and will nourish a dog, and those that are so cheaply made that they provide little if any nourishment."[42] Becker quoted extensively from an article published in the American Kennel Club's monthly magazine, describing a new dilemma for dog owners, an abundance of choice in canned foods with little assurance of nutritional quality:

When [buyers] get to a store, they find a price range on one pound cans of dog food from two for a quarter down to five cents; yes, even to five cans for 23 cents and six for a quarter. Personal calls on fifty grocery stores in the trading area adjacent to New York City this spring disclosed 57 brands of dog food and 2,500 cans out of a weekly total of 9,400 retailing at 6 cents or less. . . . Purchasers might well ask themselves how a manufacturer could put all the food value needed for adequate nourishment into a can at 5 cents. Especially can he ask this question if he knew that it costs more than 5 cents to deliver a can to the retailer's store without any allowance for retailer's profit and without any food in the can.[43]

Early analysis of the chemical contents of canned dog food supported Becker's concerns. One chemist found that his sample of twenty-three commercial canned foods contained as little as 4.67 percent crude protein.[44]

Well into the 1940s, however, dog food formulas seem to have been based on the availability of various ingredients and a general sense of the efficacy of a mixture of grains and meat, along with a few added ingredients such as brewer's yeast, cod liver oil, and tomato pulp, rather than a strict set of nutritional standards. A 1941 report on canned dog food published in *Consumers' Research Bulletin* pointed out that while dog owners relied on the canner "for the character and adequacy of nutritional content," feeding a dog exclusively on canned dog food still had the possibility of "unhappy results." *Consumers' Research Bulletin* consulting chemists evaluated nine brands of canned food, both national and regional, including several of the most heavily advertised (Chappel Brothers Ken-L-Ration, Swift & Co.'s Red Heart, and Rival Packing Company's Rival) and gave none a grade higher than "B." The report concluded that canned food "should be kept on the emergency shelf for an occasional feeding when there just isn't another thing in the house."[45] In 1943 the same periodical pointed out that federal regulation of dog food was inadequate even though it was inside the scope of the Pure Food and Drugs Act and the responsibilities of the Food and Drug Administration: "It is understood that no money is being spent by the F. & D. Admin. on the control of the quality of dog food."[46]

Two small notebooks documenting recipes for canned dog food survive from the Rival Dog Food Company, apparently compiled by an engineer named Rogers for the use of Meyer Katz, the president of the company. One handwritten notebook documents experiments with formulas for Rival dog food, about which more in a moment. The typed notebook contains recipes that were in use "at the different periods during the three years previous to the war. The various changes were due to scarcity and price of the different products at the time and still hold to quality." Six formulas follow. A typical example, Formula #4, reads: "15 lbs. Beef Hearts, 15 lbs. Beef kidneys, 40 lbs. Beef udders, 50 lbs. Beef melts (spleen), 10 lbs. Beef lungs; 20 lbs. hog liver, 16 lbs. Rolled oats, 36 lbs. cracked Barley, 32 lbs. Cracked Wheat, 33 lbs. Soya grits, 15 lbs. Soya flour, 315 lbs. Water."

Rogers's handwritten notebook offers a behind-the-scenes peek at factory experimentation with dog food formulas, along with statistics on batch sizes, the number of runs one factory could support in a day, and cost estimates for production between 1946 and 1948. One set of notes dated July 28, 1946, documents the batch-cooking process; each batch resulted in about 290 gallons of dog food ready for canning, and a day's run was estimated for 420 batches feeding three packing lines for eight hours. At this time, when meat was still in short supply and the recipes relied on meat meal and liver to provide the animal protein in a mixture predominantly consisting of "soya," wheat, and barley, Rival relied on making "stock" from bones to provide the liquid for each batch ("about 28000 bones @ 6 to 1"), probably to provide extra protein, fat, and taste from the marrow. The notebook is silent on this point, but the spent bones may have been dried out and sent off for further processing by another by-products operation. With the cost of the ingredients per dozen cans at 20.8 cents, supplies and labor adding 22 cents, and a charge of 4 percent overhead (1.8 cents), the cost per dozen cans at wholesale was 44.6 cents. To test the palatability of the recipe, Rogers noted that he fed it to his dog Fritz, who liked it, but that his other tester, "Bill Cavanaugh (*sic*) dog did not," probably because the meat-meal scent and flavor were too strong.

By January 23, 1948, Rival was able to return to a formula and two-step process of stock making followed by cooking that made extensive use of organ meats purchased from packers. Rogers's notes list the following as the "Present Formula": "50# Livers, 30# Kidneys Cooked in 2000# Water at from 200 to 210 Deg. For 1/2 hour if fresh and one hour if frozen. Above makes stock and meat is then ground and used in formula. Formula: 15# Lungs, 5#Melts, 8# Cooked Meat, 15# Meat Meal, 5# Bone Meal, 10# Suet, 50#S. (soy) Grits, 40# S. (soy) Meal, 10#Wheat Germ, 25# Ckd. Wheat, 400# Stock, 6oz. Onion Pdr.," yielding 583 pounds of dog food in each batch. Notice the absence of nutritional supplements and preservatives in this recipe. Assuming that Rival represented standard operating practice at the time—and Rival was a popular product with wide distribution—canned dog food was a much simpler product than are even the inexpensive brands on store shelves today.

While it took decades for dog food, wet or dry, to become an established part of the middle-class grocery list, by the 1930s its availability, relatively decreased cost, and convenience meant that even the short-lived dog-food scandal of 1936 did not affect growing demand. Consumers' beliefs about the needs of dogs were also changing, mediated by the dog food makers' growing use of experts, their limited support of research, and the insistent voices of dog food marketing campaigns. By the advent of World War II, *Consumers' Research Bulletin* reported that around 20 percent of American dogs lived on commercial dog food in all its forms, and the industry volume for 1941 was reported as 650 million pounds.[47] The market for canned dog food was interrupted by mobilization, however. In 1942 the War Production Board forbid the use of cans for the purpose, and other restrictions and shortages made animal protein harder to get.

While the market for canned pet food was interrupted by World War II, the packers' capacity for canning increased dramatically. Swift & Co., for example, expanded its canning capacity from under two million pounds per week to eight million at the same time that it converted its Pard dog food into a dehydrated meal.[48] Other dog food companies experimented with frozen dog food, "particularly after it was discovered that the dehydrated foods did not find favor with their canine customers." Limited access to refrigeration technology and the higher price of frozen dog food limited that product's success. The biggest problem facing dog food buyers, however, may have been the federal limits placed on the amount of animal protein in pet food in January 1943. Pet food could contain only 8 percent animal protein and 24 percent protein overall; the proteins freed up were redirected to livestock feed.[49] Drawing on new research in canine nutrition, groups such as the American Humane Association urged pet owners who were regular dog food users to purchase one of the only two dry foods that met association standards (Friskies from Albers Milling Company and Gro-Pup, produced by the cereal maker Kellogg Company) or to return to home cooking, which the majority of dog owners still did anyway.[50]

When the war ended, the use of canned dog food increased in the late 1940s, as it had in the early 1930s. A combination of excess canning capacity and changing meat-processing practices meant that less scrap meat went out to supermarkets; thus there was, again, an abundance of meat by-products available for dog food. Postwar consumer prosperity, and the era's interest in a particular vision of modern family life, led to increased consumption of packaged meat, which meant fewer scraps to feed family dogs, and convenience foods of all kinds, including pet foods. In 1954 American Can Company, the giant packaging conglomerate, released a report on the market for cat and dog food that was picked up by the *New York Times* in its April 18 edition. The reporter opened his story with the assertion, "Gastronomically, Fido and Kitty never heretofore have had it so good. They are eating food that for tastiness and nutritive value match and, in some cases, even surpass the victuals consumed by their owners." American Can figured that in 1953 three-quarters of

all dog owners had spent $200 million on packaged foods for their pets, includ-
ing 1.5 billion cans. Further, the market was expanding rapidly; this number
was "about double the 1947 volume."[51] At the time of the report, commercial
dog food had been sold in the United States for eight decades, and yet its popularity seemed to surprise the author somewhat. It was still an invisible product, at least to people who did not own dogs. Old practices survived, however.
The reporter invited readers deploring "all this fuss over mere animals" to
"take some heart" from the fact that most dog-food-purchasing families still
followed the "time-honored practice" of feeding table scraps to their pets.

Chapter 10
Empire of Ice Cream: How Life Became Sweeter in the Postwar Soviet Union

Jenny Leigh Smith

The Ice Cream Line

Standing in line in the Soviet Union was often a draining experience. Long queues were a fact of life for purchasing almost every Soviet good or service imaginable. Since much of the Soviet economy was based on a general rule of scarcity where demand was expected to outstrip supply as a matter of course, lines meant competition, sacrifice, and endurance for prospective consumers. By regularly waiting in queues for everyday necessities citizens surrendered time out of their private lives and publicly demonstrated their dependence on a state authority that meted out "just enough" and no more of staple items.[1] Even so, in the postwar period lines for a few products transcended this sacrificial limbo of socialist consumerism. These were the queues for newly available everyday luxuries such as ice cream, chocolate bars, and cognac: indulgences to which Soviet citizens became entitled in the postwar era by mandate of the same regime that forced them to stand in line for staples such as bread, milk, eggs, and sugar. These small treats were meant to nourish the spirit as well as the body. In the words of one dairy-industry specialist in 1961, "ice cream is beloved by all, and because of this it should become a mass-produced food product, included in the menus at breakfast, lunch and dinner."[2]

Soviet food technologists, not necessarily famous for having their finger on the pulse of popular cultural trends, may have been close to the truth when they posited that ice cream was a food "beloved by all." While the queuing of consumers in ice cream lines still demonstrated civilian reliance on the government as a provisioning authority, supplying a luxury good such as ice cream held a different social and political significance for consumers than furnishing essential staples did. The particular social and technological history of ice cream's production, distribution, and consumption sheds light on the contribution of modernist foodways to a uniquely socialist form of twentieth-century public culture.

It is not unexpected that ice cream, with associations of summer, childhood, dessert, and public recreation, should be a happy memory for citizens of the former Soviet Union. What is surprising is that ice cream was not just a beloved commodity but also a plentiful one during the Cold War, an era better known for food shortages and bread queues than abundant dessert. Technical problems as well as nutritional priorities prevented the Soviet Union from provisioning ice cream to every citizen at breakfast, lunch, and dinner, but as early as the 1950s ice cream, once a rare province of the aristocracy, had become a ubiquitous and affordable product in every major city across the Soviet Union.[3]

In a country that never succeeded in producing a reliable, year-round supply of fresh dairy products and where refined sugar was available only sporadically, high-quality ice cream made of precisely these ingredients became a cheap and consistently available treat soon after the end of World War II. How did ice cream attain such an important place in the planning agendas of Soviet food distributors? Why did an ephemeral luxury product such as ice cream take precedence over staples such as sugar and milk in the Soviet Union's push to rationally distribute food to its citizens? Even more remarkable, Soviet ice cream was a high-tech and high-quality product in a country where many experiments with new domestic technologies are stories of plagiarization, deficiency, and fiasco. What made the ice cream line, stretching not just from vendor to consumer but also back to producers, food industry planners, packers, and transportation authorities, succeed so brilliantly?

The Kitchen Convergence

A part of the answer to the question Why ice cream? begins with the year 1932, when Moscow's Municipal Cooler #2 installed an ice cream plant and processed its first twenty tons of ice cream. While ice creams and fruit sorbets were popular summer treats among Russian upper classes during imperial times, the newly empowered Soviet regime that led the country after the 1917 Russian Revolution introduced ice cream to the masses. The rapidly expanding Moscow plant manufactured seventeen thousand tons of ice cream per annum by the end of 1936.[4] While popular in the country's new capital city, ice cream's distribution was initially limited by a lack of freezers and refrigerated transportation, difficulties that would eventually plague national distribution as well.

Ice cream was also limited by an unrealistic socialist vision of food provisioning popular in the 1930s. Socialist food planners initially believed that ice cream should be produced primarily for consumption in communal settings:

worker cafeterias, school lunchrooms, and the like. This was consistent with a 1930s push to discourage private family meals in favor of public dining experiences, which in turn was part of a larger movement to create public spaces of ritual and sociality that would replace and improve upon the isolated and potentially bourgeois private home setting.[5] To this end, the first ice cream produced by the Soviet Union was packaged in large cartons and tubs meant for institutional rather than private distribution. While a small percentage of Cooler #2's output was individually wrapped bars and cones, a paucity of packaging materials, an inability to fully automate the processes of production and packaging, and ideological objections to so-called "personal" ice cream limited the output and therefore consumption of individually wrapped cones and bars during this early history of Soviet ice cream.

Food rations and wartime mobilization placed the ice cream industry as well as most of the dairy industry on hold during World War II. After the war all food supplies but especially dairy were in a state of crisis because the war had decimated the farm animal population. The Soviet Union lost over half of its collectively owned horses, draft cattle, and pigs and a third of its milk cows in the war.[6] Most numerous among bovid casualties were the purebred, high-producing dairy cattle that had lived in the European parts of the Soviet Union occupied by German forces during the war. The cows that survived, in addition to being genetically less inclined to productivity than their purebred counterparts, had also endured malnutrition, stress, and the effects of disorganized postwar agricultural management. As a result, the quality and quantity of dairy cows and dairy products suffered for years.

In response to agricultural scarcity, the Soviet government continued to ration food until the end of 1947. Especially closely rationed were meat, eggs, and dairy products. While all these products could be purchased under the table from private producers, the state was not in a position to effectively procure and distribute its collective holdings of animal-sourced agricultural products in an equitable and orderly way until years after the war. Rationing ended in December 1947, but scarcity in practice lingered on for years, and animal by-products were consistently harder for private citizens to obtain than staples such as bread and vegetable produce. Fresh milk in particular was hard to come by outside of the summer season when cows lactated most abundantly.

Food industries acquired a new primacy in the late 1940s because of a shift in state policy toward pleasing the individual consumer. While the Soviet Union had always struggled to feed its citizens, the agriculture and food sectors had been of secondary importance because they were so-called "light" industries during a time when the Soviet Union advanced its socialist ideal of industrialization through mammoth, performative, great works projects. While the Soviet Union embarked on a large-scale and ill-fated project of farm collectivization in the early 1930s, much of the food production and distribution infrastructure remained in an unimproved condition until after World War II.

The food policy changes that were implemented, such as the movement to herd citizens toward cafeterias and away from home kitchens, met with only modest success.

The aftermath of World War II steered Soviet policy away from the "cafeteria consumer" of the prewar period and toward a recognition and acceptance of the more private "kitchen consumer." The leader most closely associated with this newly fashioned kitchen consumer is Nikita Khrushchev, who led the country after Stalin's death in 1953. However, the new policies that pushed ice cream and the other small luxuries were enacted as early as 1948. After the suffering and sacrifices of World War II, access to consumer goods such as furniture, kitchen appliances, bicycles, chocolate bars, nylon stockings, and ice cream was meant to quell potential unrest and restore public faith in socialism.[7]

In the process of introducing such products, Soviet planners also modified their message about what citizens could expect in the future; Stalin's often-repeated 1936 promise that the future would be "more joyful" still held true, but as of 1946 the future would also be sweeter and more comfortable. This vision of anticipatory socialism became one in which conveniences and luxuries helped prove the success of the socialist model. Where once even the most banal middle-class possessions—a rubber plant, a jazz album—were suspect bourgeoisie entrapments, in this new postwar empire of ice cream, modest affectations of plenty were tolerated and even promoted by the state. Khrushchev mocked the extravagance of American kitchen appliances during the 1959 "Kitchen Debate" at the American Exposition in Moscow ("Don't you have a machine that puts food into the mouth and pushes it down?" he asked Nixon as he walked past the dishwasher), but by the 1950s the Soviet Union had largely abandoned its vision of a citizenry dependent on cafeterias and other outlets of public nutrition.[8] The state was instead focused on bringing identifiably socialist foods, appliances, recipes, and consumption patterns into the hearts and homes of its citizens.

Provisioning: A Context

While ice cream may have fit well into the Soviet Union's newly envisioned kitchen culture, producing the stuff was clearly not going to be an easy project to carry out. Regardless of ideology and ambitious five-year plans, sugar, milk, and cream were all in short supply well into the 1950s. How did the state make ice cream available to its citizens if these basic ingredients were not? The first answer to this question requires an understanding of how socialist food collection networks differed from their capitalist counterparts. While it was difficult for private consumers to access scarce food, it was much easier for the state to do so. A second part of the answer lies in the realm of food distribution and processing technologies. Many processed foods (although initially not ice cream) had advantages of distribution over fresh products because they were more shelf-stable and could stand up better to the abuses of shipping and the uncertainties of socialist boom-bust production cycles. It was both easier and ideologically more desirable for the Soviet food industry to create processed foods than it was to distribute high-quality fresh ingredients. While purveying a delicate frozen product such as ice cream was initially a challenge for the uncertainties of socialist food planners, refrigerator technologies eventually contributed to the success of the distribution of even this most needful of commodities.

Consistent ice cream production depended on regular supplies of two principal ingredients, sugar and milk, that often were not available directly to consumers. Sugar scarcities reflected a vicious circle common to many Soviet consumer products: there was an unpredictable supply, which led to scarcity, so when it was available consumers hoarded what they could get, which led to shortages. State agencies, aware of hoarding practices, did everything in their power to regulate how much sugar private citizens could obtain, but they had limited influence over the consumer sugar market.[9] Sugar also was expensive to make and buy. Unlike Britain or the United States, the Soviet Union did not hold tropical, sugar-producing colonies or territories, and thus its costs of trade in the product were considerably higher than those of these two countries. The climate of the U.S.S.R. was ideal for sugar beets but not sugarcane, and of the two products, beets yielded a less-sweet product that was more costly to refine. Technological advancements in the 1960s and 1970s lowered the cost of beet sugar production and raised its quality, but in the immediate postwar period sugar was scarce and expensive, and the Soviet Union imported the bulk of its supplies from Southeast Asia and Cuba.[10]

While sugar was rare and costly for both state industries and private consumers, the Soviet state had the power to requisition it for industrial use. After repeated attempts to make sugar available in stores year-round, distributing agents seemingly gave up on the year-round policy. Instead the Ministry of Food Provisioning released refined sugar for purchase by private citizens only a few times a year, most notably during the fruit-canning season and over the New Year's and Easter holidays. This may have been an exasperated if rational response by the ministry to hoarding behavior, but regardless of the motivation, this policy ensured that sugar was available year-round for industrial food production while private citizens could obtain it only occasionally. Instead of making sugar a staple ingredient for home kitchens, the Ministry of Food Provisioning upped its production of sweetened processed foods, including boiled candies, chocolate, condensed milk, and of course ice cream. As planners saw it, the Soviet sweet tooth could be better sated by these industrially manufactured goods than by the raw ingredients.

Milk, and in consistent supply, was the second essential ingredient for Soviet ice cream. Its distribution was hampered by a lack of refrigeration capacity.

Chilled bulk tanks were scarce in the Soviet Union until the 1970s, and trucks with refrigeration technologies were never common.[11] However, this lack of technological infrastructure affected collection and distribution patterns unevenly. Cows gave most of their milk in the summer, when it most needed cooling. Partially because of the centrally planned nature of the dairy industry, most dairy processing plants were situated in urban areas, far from the cows that furnished their raw materials. In spite of the obstacles posed by poor refrigeration technologies, the Soviet Union did a good job of collecting milk from its farms. Milk stored on farms was cooled in covered, pit-style tanks down to ground temperature and held a few days until it was collected and transported to large plants in nearby towns.

While Soviet food professionals were skilled agents of collection, limited refrigeration capacity meant that they were not so handy at redistributing processed dairy products outside of urban areas. While dairy processing plants located within the city gathered milk from all over the region, the reverse milkshed—how far processed dairy products traveled back out again—varied by product. A diagram of this process in the Kharkov district of Eastern Ukraine demonstrates just how variable this redistribution network was.[12] The most fragile product, bottled fresh milk, did not travel far out of the city, and its distribution closely followed the main train tracks that ran through the Oblast. The *smetana*, or sour cream zone, stretched further out, several dozen kilometers past every train stop, presumably limited principally by how far light trucks were willing to travel to pick up fresh shipments. It seems likely that other cultured products such as yogurt, kefir, and *tvorog*, a farmer's cheese, followed a pattern of distribution close to that of sour cream. Most durable of the processed dairy products was butter, which was shipped out from Kharkov to all regions of the Oblast. The illustration does not indicate where ice cream fit into this reallocation of milk, but given the lack of refrigeration on cars and trains well into the 1960s, it seems safe to conclude that ice cream was principally available to urban residents and that mass ice cream distribution to rural areas was not common in the time period this essay considers.

Perhaps because fresh milk and other perishable dairy items were so hard to ship, the Soviet Union produced a great deal of condensed milk and dehydrated milk, cream, and whey. The Ministry of Food Distribution invested much of its research and development budget in the dairy industry to further advance these technologies and to expand the distribution of these far more durable dairy goods, effectively sidestepping the need for a well-oiled refrigerated distribution infrastructure. Powdered milk was far more widely available on grocery store shelves than fresh milk was well into the 1970s, and it was also much cheaper to buy. Because of their stable shelf-life as well as their year-round availability, dehydrated products and condensed milk also became important ingredients in the ice cream industry.

Sugar, milk, and milk by-products were a constant provisioning challenge for the Soviet state because they took so much extra energy and effort for the country to produce. While sweet and fatty foods were generally in short supply in the postwar period, the state worked hard to increase access to these small tastes of luxury. In the late 1950s Khrushchev's food ministers not only prioritized domestic kitchen consumers over the masses dining at worker cafeterias but also privileged the production of animal products and sugar to the exclusion of more so-called practical staples such as grains and root crops. An increased production of cold-hardy cereals and tubers might have maximized the caloric productivity of the Soviet Union, but instead of focusing on the quantity of staples, food and agriculture officials focused on increasing the quality base of the nation's food supply: its sweetness and its richness. In the postwar Soviet Union the state wagered that its political legitimacy and social stability would derive at least in part from access it could provide for its citizens to everyday luxuries such as ice cream.

Cold Machines

While this turn toward private tastes depended in part on a shift in agricultural policy, it was just as dependent on new and better food-processing technologies for both factories and homes. Ice cream was especially dependent on the new and unruly technology of industrial refrigeration for its success. Throughout its history the Soviet Union had relied more on mimicry than invention, and many of its early twentieth-century food-processing technologies were derived from American or German precursors. The dehydration technologies that turned fresh milk into powder packets, for example, came from American World War II–era equipment developed to help supply soldiers with lightweight, high-quality foods that could survive long-distance journeys and harsh field conditions. Soviet experts were famous for reverse-engineering major technological innovations such as the combine harvester, the airplane, and the Soviet Union's most popular make of car, the Lada (patterned after the Fiat).[13] For the most part, food technologists were content to do the same with new advances in food technology and techniques of dehydration, and canning and packaging were closely imitated from Western inventors, if not copied outright.

Contrary to this general pattern, refrigeration technology in the Soviet Union has a history of homegrown Soviet innovation. Sometimes this innovation was misguided—one short-lived experiment, for example, proposed creating and storing massive icicles near train tracks in the winter to cool railroad cars in summer—but often the Soviet Union's research and development into cold technology displayed an impressive range of creativity and adaptability, two traits not often associated with Soviet engineering.[14]

The expansion of dry-ice manufacturing, another Soviet by-product of World War II, was crucial to the development of the ice cream industry; indeed, the standard view of Soviet ice cream technologists as they explained the history of the industry was that the two industries coevolved from the World War II era on. While a few dry-ice factories had existed before the war, dry ice became a practical solution for chilling industrial meat lockers and other municipal coolers during and after the war, since even at these centralized locations freezers were expensive to operate, noisy enough to elicit complaints from workers, and prone to breaking down.[15] The vagaries of war also disrupted central power supplies, and most lockers and municipal freezers that depended on electric compressors were not equipped to handle a blackout for more than a few hours without major losses. Municipal coolers initially constructed dry-ice factories as a stopgap measure to supply dry ice for on-site refrigeration in times of electrical uncertainty and also to use dry ice as a desiccating and cooling agent for the coolers, which tended to overheat and produce large amounts of condensation.[16] Even after municipal infrastructures became more reliable in the postwar period, freezer motors would overheat, burn out, and need repairs, and dry ice remained a cheap and reliable way to guard against factory meltdowns.

While dry-ice factories had existed on-site at many municipal freezers since World War II, dry ice remained on-site at these facilities for almost a decade after the war. The role that dry ice would play in uncoupling Soviet frozen foods from unreliable Soviet freezers went unrealized for a full decade. Not until 1955 did dry-ice facilities receive positive attention from state planners trying to increase the reliability and productivity of municipal freezers, and from this time forward Soviet food technologists began to think of dry ice as a substance with possibilities. While the Ministry of Railways experimented with dry-ice-cooled railway cars, a technology that had been popular in the late nineteenth-century United States, irregular shipping schedules and the distance between dry-ice factories and rail stations frustrated efforts to reproduce the American model.

Ironically, it was through a low-tech and nonmechanized form of distribution that dry ice's potential to further a socialist form of consumerism was fully realized. By the late 1950s freezers with dry-ice facilities had also acquired a fleet of insulated pushcarts that were chilled with dry ice. It is not clear which ministry or department ordered the manufacture of these carts, but in the later postwar period they rapidly became a common part of the delivery fleet associated with meat- and milk-processing plants. Almost as soon as manually operated pushcarts appeared on Soviet city streets, they were used not simply as retail delivery vehicles (although this was one purpose they served) but also dealt in direct sales. Municipal coolers hired vendors to push the carts around the streets during the day. These vendors, often older women, were required to wear lab coats and white head kerchiefs and follow a strict culture of hygiene and sanitation. During the 1960s this "pushcart lady" became an identifiable labor category in Soviet society.

This kind of direct sale from manufacturers (in this case the municipal coolers) to consumers was almost unheard of in the Soviet Union before the rise of the ice cream trade. For even the simplest of staple items—bread, for example—there was an orderly if cumbersome chain of production with at least three links between processor and consumer. A central bakery baked the bread, a distribution network of carts and trucks dispersed bread to small shops across the city, and a personal sales transaction (more often than not the time-consuming bread line) completed the chain. Direct sales from processor to consumer were associated with graft or gray areas of private trade. Transcending the standard, albeit inefficient mode of goods distribution was the province of those who were either above the law or willing to ignore it. For municipal coolers to employ a cadre of hygienically robed pushcart operators to take to the streets as representatives of the coolers themselves was a serendipitous marketing maneuver made possible by the unfettered nature of dry ice. Convenient, public, and directly associated with a large, well-funded municipal industry (those coolers that were poorly funded did not make ice cream), ice cream was a popular product possibly not just because it was delicious to eat but also because, unlike almost every other good in Soviet consumer society, it was pleasurable to buy.

Ice cream sold from pushcarts was most often intended for immediate public consumption rather than home use. While the Soviet Union made "family" sizes of ice cream that could have fit in home freezers, the home freezer was one domestic appliance that Soviet technologists could not get quite right. Because of both cost and a technology lag, the Soviet Union was slow to switch from ammonia-cooled refrigerators to those that ran on Freon, the cooling technology that had become standard in the United States and other Western countries in the 1940s. Soviet ammonia refrigerators and fridge-freezer combination boxes were plagued with a host of problems: they were loud when turned on or off; their freezers did not get food much below the freezing point; water had a tendency to condense on the outside, hastening corrosion of their casings; and the temperature sensors did not always work. A review of the performance of home refrigerators and freezers in 1960 noted that "every third or fourth freezer has a serious thermostat defect."[17] The most common defect was a hyperactive relay contact, which led to frequent and messy defrosting events.

Perhaps because there were still kinks in the technology, home refrigerator-freezer combination units were in limited supply (and they were quite expensive), and refrigerator units sans freezer boxes became the norm for the first-time refrigerator buyer. Until 1960 the most commonly sold refrigerator model was the Okean or Ocean, which—aptly named—did not freeze.[18] Thus, when Soviet citizens lined up to buy ice cream from insulated, dry-ice-chilled pushcarts, their most common purchases were individually wrapped cones, popsicles, cups, or sandwiches, which were intended to be eaten on the spot. Family ice cream packages rated a distant fifth place in units of sale for the mid-1950s.

The Soviet Union's home freezer technology may have left something to be desired, but its research and development teams built state-of-the-art industrial ice cream manufacturing equipment. Inspiring this research was a fascination common to many food technology agendas of the postwar period: creating completely processed foods that no human hand touched from start to finish. While Soviet food planners often mentioned the desirable hygienic properties of such processing as well as the labor-saving aspect of freeing people from assembly-line work, the driving force behind much of this preoccupation with total automation was a technocratic fascination with the potential machines offered for perfect control and infallible order. In the words of one 1960s-era Russian-language journal: "(in the future) the principal ice cream varieties, sandwiches, cones and Eskimos, will be manufactured by continuous, mechanized process, equipped with modern control and measuring instruments."[19]

The invention of the Eskimo-Generator in 1959 brought the Soviet Union ice cream industry closer to its ideal of total automation. As its name implies, the Eskimo-Generator made chocolate-covered popsicles, commonly known as Eskimo pies in North America (a trademarked brand name held by Russell Stover until 1999) or as simply Eskimo in the Soviet Union, which did not recognize international trademarks. The Eskimo-Generator was a swirling stainless machine tub with numerous levers and small paddles protruding from the sides, and it assembled an Eskimo popsicle from its various components (vanilla ice cream, chocolate sauce, popsicle sticks, foil wrapping) at a rate faster than any human work squad could. While the Soviet Union had earlier perfected semiautomated ice cream bars and cones that required only minimal human handling, the Eskimo was the first fully automated ice cream bar, and because of this, as much as because of its appeal or economical manufacture, it became one of the leading products of the Soviet ice cream industry.

The Eskimo-Generator and the potential of full automation helped the state prioritize some kinds of personal ice cream above others. While confections such as ice-cream-filled cakes and ice cream cones were popular among consumers, in 1961 dairy planners despaired because these products were still only *polufabrikaty*, or half-automated. A cadre of human workers known as *master-shpritsovchikii* (master injectors) was in charge of filling tubes and waffle cones with soft-serve ice cream before they were refrozen for shipping. While these workers were highly trained, half-automated production lines were clearly less desirable to Soviet planners than fully automated ones such as the Eskimo line. Hence much of the technological research into ice cream production in the decade of the 1960s went into developing fully automated ice cream manufacturing processes for personal ice cream products (mostly bars and cones) that did not yet have them.[20] The industry steadily added new technology during the postwar period, and by 1970 one ice cream trade journal estimated that the ice cream industry was 80 percent fully automated.[21]

Flavors and Fat

While ice cream styles may have been dictated by the ideal of total automation, Soviet ice cream offered consumers a surprising variety of flavor options in a society that often advocated limiting or eliminating consumer choice. The list of ice cream flavors available in 1976 is long and includes standards such as chocolate; sweet cream; and strawberry as well as cultural specialties such as "Springtime," flavored with birch sap and honey; "Mixed Berry," a sorbetlike emulsion of currants, raspberries, and gooseberries (which varied by season); and "Northern," which featured toasted Siberian pine nuts. There were also regional specialties: Moscow-style ice cream resembled an eggy French vanilla, whereas the Iaroslav-style was tangy and fluffy, more like a soft-serve frozen yogurt.[22]

While usually made from high-quality ingredients with a minimum of stabilizers and additives, ice cream was not immune from the Soviet state's occasionally misguided ambitions of social improvement, and a line of vegetable-enriched ice creams was introduced in the 1950s. Heralded as a way to get children to eat more beets, carrots, and tomatoes and given romantic, euphemistic names such as "Golden Autumn," vegetable ice cream did not really catch on, and these flavors were not produced in great quantities after the early 1960s.[23]

Adding vegetable pulp to ice cream was an extreme way of establishing the health benefits of eating ice cream; typically promoters simply extolled the virtues of regular ice cream's fattening qualities. To Soviet publicists, ice cream in the postwar period was a healthy food because of—and not in spite of—its high fat and sugar content. The same 1961 publication that advocated serving ice cream at breakfast, lunch, and dinner also professed that "ice cream is one of the most healthy and delicious food products . . . both ice milk and ice cream contain fat, protein, carbohydrates mineral salts, and vitamins. The Calorie content of regular ice cream averages 1450 Calories per kilogram, for high-fat ice cream 1950, *plombir* 2400, and fruit sherbet 1230–1430. It is higher in calories than milk, non-fat *tvorog* (a farmer's cheese), eggs, meat and many other products." The fattening qualities that made ice cream a healthy food in an economy of scarcity with limited access to fat and calories were the same features that have turned ice cream into an unhealthy luxury food in countries such as the United States, whose citizens chronically overconsume fat, sugar, dairy products, and other sweets.

If high-calorie products were the definition of health food in the Soviet postwar period, then Soviet consumers tried to eat as healthily as possible. In spite of the plethora of choices available to consumers, most ice cream purchasers had just one of two favorites: crème brûlée, flavored with caramelized condensed milk; or *plombir*, a whipped, 15 percent fat delicacy with the unappetizing English translation of "putty" or "sealant."[24] It is hardly a coincidence that the two most popular ice creams were, respectively, the sweetest and richest varieties on the market. If ice cream was a showcase of Soviet state requisitioning savvy, it was also one of the few truly decadent outlets of mass consumption, and Soviet consumers responded to this decadence with gusto, consistently choosing ice creams that were highest in fat and calories.

Retail Therapy

Advertising in the Soviet Union served different purposes than those of advertising in capitalist countries, where private firms compete with one another for customers. While advertising was still intended to persuade Soviet citizens to spend their hard-earned money on ice cream, the subordinate messages of socialist advertising campaigns were very different from those of their capitalist counterparts. Rather than advertising goods that consumers were supposed to buy, as in Western nations, Soviet ads displayed the kinds of goods that the producers felt were the most useful to produce.

The state had what effectively amounted to a monopoly on large-scale ice cream production, and while this might have led to the elimination of advertising, it in fact simply worked to steer Soviet advertising culture in different directions than those pursued by capitalist marketers. Two separate ministries within the government were in charge of producing and purveying ice cream: the Ministry of Meat and Milk Industry and the Ministry of Refrigerated Goods. Nationally business was more or less evenly split between them, and in 1970 the two organizations each accounted for about half of annual production.[25] Unlike in a capitalist model of production, the two ministries did not compete with each other, and each made nearly identical products. While their circles of distribution overlapped, one or the other ministry tended to be the primary ice cream purveyor for a particular region. It is interesting to note that the two ministries employed slightly different technologies in ice cream production, with the Ministry of Refrigerated Goods primarily making ice cream in plants without freezers and then storing it in warehouses chilled by dry ice, while the Ministry of Meat and Milk produced the bulk of its ice cream in factories that possessed large-scale ammonia- (or later Freon-) based coolers.[26]

Competition between the two ice cream production authorities was a moot point, but there were still good reasons to advertise the products. Socialist ads educated; they informed citizens about the newest products that were available in stores and on the street. Unlike their counterparts in capitalist countries, socialist ads also gave accurate price information. Since food prices were set nationally, most food products, ice cream included, cost the same in all parts of the Soviet Union. More often than not, however, posters and ads in the Soviet

Union advertised products that were available in theory but not in practice: nylons, fresh juice, and caviar might look present and affordable in the world of the Soviet poster advertisement, but looks could be deceiving, and ads often offered an image of a potential world of plenty that was just around the corner. In anticipating this future, the state used ads as a medium through which it could boast about its technological prowess in provisioning the country before this success had been proven through experience.

While false advertising was commonplace, ice cream was the exception to the rule: it was a regularly advertised product that was also reliably available. Even so, an important purpose of Soviet ice cream ads was not simply to promote ice cream but also to inform citizens about new methods of ice cream manufacturing. Ads from the later 1950s display the newly perfected and fully automated "Eskimo" bar front and center, sidelining more common but less technologically sublime ice cream varieties.

The widespread availability of ice cream in the postwar period gave the Soviet state a flagship product that showed off several triumphs in its new network of socialist food production. Ice cream, previously a rare and seasonal product, was now available year-round, a fact that indicated the success of developing freezer technology and the efficiency of the frozen foods distribution system. This success was in step with a general notion of widely distributed, egalitarian mechanization that was supposed to set the Soviet Union apart from both its capitalist and preindustrial counterparts. Soviet ice cream was also made out of high-quality ingredients, which signaled a major accomplishment for a food industry that had previously tried to improve mass distribution by lowering the quality of basic staples. In an era of milk sausage, tinned organ meats, and margarine that never melted, Soviet ice cream was an authentically high-quality homegrown product that Soviet producers and consumers alike could take pride in as an example of technological success.

Even though its quality standards were high, postwar ice cream was an inexpensive treat, and it was this economic accessibility that helped to make life a little sweeter for a diverse group of Soviet urban citizens. Since ice cream was priced at just a few kopeks per package, buying it on the street was an act of consumerism in which even children could participate and everyone could enjoy. In a country with little to purchase recreationally, ice cream was affordable to all. The act of obtaining ice cream was a public, social event, and the Eskimos and other hygienically manufactured, hermetically wrapped, sweet frozen concoctions were eaten on the spot in the areas where they were purchased from dry-ice chilled pushcarts: parks, playgrounds, busy street underpasses, and the courtyards of large apartment houses. Catering to the individual eater by providing single servings of ice cream, the Soviet state created at least one outlet of socialist dining that regularly occurred in public. In the midst of a kitchen revolution in which the state paid more attention to individual desires, in ice cream it inadvertently created a product that, by virtue of its cold ephemerality, had to be eaten out of doors, in the company of other urbanites.

Conclusion: Sweet Power

The pathways of production, processing, distribution, and consumption of ice cream in the postwar era made life sweeter in the Soviet Union, but they were also unique, creative responses to a challenging food situation. Soviet agricultural authorities' priorities worked to increase the production of higher-input "luxury" meat and milk products as well as sugar at a time when a back-to-basics approach to agricultural sustainability might have been more rational. The state correctly banked on the idea that the social and political impact of making a few food luxuries available would do more to persuade a generation of war-weary Soviet citizens of the legitimacy of the postwar regime than a focus on virtuous cereals and root crops might.

In processing and distribution technologies the Soviet Union made its own way in the world of modernist ice cream production. Ice cream was created in large, centralized, multipurpose municipal freezers but distributed by small, hand-operated pushcarts that were successful because they used reliable, low-tech dry ice to chill their products rather than uncertain and centralized ammonia and Freon refrigerator technologies. A Soviet obsession with mechanization helped to inspire all sorts of ice cream making and packaging machines, most importantly the Eskimo-Generator. The development of fully automated machines that wrapped single-serving bars, cones, and popsicles helped push the ice cream market in the direction of personal ice cream and away from the family- and community-sized ice cream tubs that the state's socialist food-policy makers had embraced during the prewar period.

Soviet consumers, ice cream lovers all (at least in the eyes of the state) were perhaps the most predictable link in the ice cream chain. Eager for ever sweeter and fattier new tastes and grateful for purchasing opportunities that allowed them to avoid interminable lines and inferior products, consumers flocked to pushcarts for ice cream in both winter and summer, surpassing the per capita ice cream consumption statistics for every country but the United States by the early 1970s. Eating ice cream in the streets and parks of Soviet cities alongside friends, neighbors, and family members became a uniquely Soviet public ritual—one that is remembered today with nostalgia and pride. Ice cream's status as a social and public commodity transcended its identity as a dessert. Ice cream became more than dessert; it was also a way for Soviet consumers to participate in a pleasurable and socially rewarding public rite.

The Soviet Union was not the only place in the world where ice cream became a symbolic centerpiece of centralized food distribution. Portugal under the populist leader Antonio Salazar and India during the reign of Indira Gandhi were two other bold twentieth-century experiments in socialist modernity in which state-sponsored ice cream trades thrived. Nor has this trend completely faded. In Havana during 2007, under the strictest dairy and meat rationing the Cuban nation had seen in its fifty-year history, a *frozzen*, or prepacked cone of vanilla ice cream, was available in almost every small town for just a single peso—approximately four cents. Just what is it about ice cream that appeals to the populist sentiment of authoritarian states?

Perhaps a part of the answer lies in Juvenal's pessimistic second-century observation that latter-day Roman citizens hoped for only "bread and circuses," abandoning the political freedom and democratic power their predecessors had held dear during the early Roman Empire in favor of food subsidies and mass spectacles. Ice cream's sugar-coated popularity also conforms to some of the more cynical observations that the food anthropologist Sidney Mintz has made about the powerful and destructive role sugar played during the Industrial Revolution across the British Empire; our modernist love affair with sweet foods is damaging to our bodies and was initially built on the labor exploitation of slaves. In the industrial age the biological and social cost of producing sugar, costs that once limited its production, have now helped to create a complex and profitable infrastructure of exploitative labor and agricultural practices. Even as sweet foods become commonplace on the tables of working-class peoples around the world, their once-rare status persists as a cultural touchstone for developing and developed societies alike. Sugar remains an ingredient of desire that industrial societies are inspired to overconsume in spite of the environmental and social costs that the production of sweetness accrues.

However, while ice cream potentially signals political complacency and a socially corrosive sweet tooth, the rise of modernist ice cream also gestures toward a society that prioritizes free will and mass pleasure. While ice cream was never used as a tool for democratic revolution in the Soviet Union, the historical meaning of ice cream in socialist countries, crafted as it was by ideology, accessibility, and a celebration of public culture, may well have planted the seeds for ice cream revolutions yet to be. An early example of the revolutionary potential of ice cream occurred in Minsk, the capital city of Belarus, one of the world's most oppressive, formerly Soviet authoritarian nations. The city has retained most governmental structures from its period as a Soviet republic, and it had the honor of hosting the world's first prodemocracy ice cream flash mob in May 2006.[27]

The ice cream mob was a seemingly spontaneous public demonstration organized via Internet message boards and cell phone text messages in which hundreds of young people gathered at the same time in the same place for the express purpose of eating ice cream. President Aleksander Lukashenka, an unabashed Soviet nostalgic with a penchant for civil oppression, had made most forms of public demonstration illegal, and absurdist or not, the Minsk ice cream mob was no exception. Several rebel ice cream eaters were carted off by the police, although they were all released after booking. While the event was initially planned as an apolitical gathering, Lukashenka's oppressive police force turned the ice cream mob into a small but poignant public protest event.

Flash mobs, beloved by theorists of new forms of social protest, represent a new and dynamic ideal in creative social protest. While flash mobs sometimes convene for overt political reasons, they also come together just for fun (the world's largest flash mob to date was an "iPod Rave" at Paddington Station). Some of the most intriguing flash mobs are events that combine these aspects of spontaneous celebration and political assertiveness. A few weeks after the Minsk ice cream debacle a smiling mob convened in the same central square, and people stood together waiting to be arrested simply for smiling at one another.

In the case of the Minsk ice cream mob, it was not ice cream's evocative sweetness that allowed it to become such a powerful symbol in the face of mass arrests. Rather it was ice cream's banal and public character that made it an effective weapon of protest against oppression. After all, in Soviet (and now post-Soviet) spaces ice cream was supposed to be eaten out of doors, en masse. In the contemporary United States sweet, fattening foods such as ice cream are more than just dessert; they are also overt political and contentious symbols of the current diabetes and obesity epidemics. Socialist (and now postsocialist) ice cream, though just as sweet, fattening, and delicious as the richest pint of Ben and Jerry's finest, holds a very different contemporary social meaning. The inherently socialist and public nature with which eating ice cream on the street with a group of other people is associated historically in countries that have been influenced by communism and socialism is precisely what endowed the ice cream mob in Minsk with its meaning.

Soviet food planners, advocating a massive increase in the output of ice cream in the years of scarcity and reconstruction that followed World War II, most likely never imagined that mass-produced dairy confections might have permanent and symbolic effects on the society they were trying to provision. While it is notoriously difficult to guess the intentions of historical figures, most especially when they are Soviet bureaucrats, archival sources indicate a surprising attention to consumer preferences as the Soviet ice cream turn was planned and carried out. While ideology and a fascination with mechanization structured parts of the Soviet ice cream industry, a strong consumer preference for high-fat and very sweet styles of ice cream also dictated production lines. Soviet ice cream, as a unique, delicious, high-tech product produced during a time in which most Soviet foods were none of these things, sheds new light on the standard story of what everyday Soviet citizens ate and why they did so.

Chapter 11
Eating Mexican in a Global Age: The Politics and Production of Ethnic Food

Jeffrey M. Pilcher

As late as the 1960s tacos, quesadillas, and mole poblano were largely unknown outside of Mexico and its former territories in the southwestern United States. Now you can buy Mexican food in restaurants ranging from Barrow, Alaska, to Sydney, Australia, and from Addis Ababa, Ethiopia, to Ulan Bator, Mongolia. Thanks to packaged taco kits, eating Mexican is possible virtually anywhere in the world; NASA even launches tortillas into space to feed astronauts onboard the international space station.[1] This sudden proliferation resulted from a confluence of economic factors—new food processing and distribution technologies—and cultural politics—the emergence of tacos as a fashionable sector in the food service industry. While observers of globalization have devoted increasing attention to the international relations of power that determine whose culture is packaged and marketed around the world, an equally relevant question is, Who does the globalizing? North American entrepreneurs have taken the lead in marketing Mexican food, and Tex-Mex stereotypes have become widely entrenched as a result. Even NASA's tortillas are made of wheat flour—generic "wraps" of indeterminate ethnicity—rather than the Mexican preference of maize.

Technological efficiency and the availability of ingredients help to explain this disparity; after all, nobody would carry a Mexican tortilla factory with corn mills and conveyor belts to the Mongolian steppe, much less into outer space. Such basic considerations suggest the usefulness of approaching culinary globalization from a commodity chain analysis, with its comprehensive perspective on production, distribution, and consumption. The commodity at the heart of Mexican cuisine, maize, has undergone historical changes at each stage of the supply chain. A versatile and productive grain, it traveled the world in the early modern era, offering peasants from West Africa to East Asia a new and dependable source of subsistence. However, Native American women did not come along to teach local cooks the intricate skills of tortilla making; only after the mechanization of tortilla production in the twentieth century did Mexican food become available beyond the ethnic community. For such outsiders, the Tex-Mex taco shell was not obviously inferior to fresh corn tortillas. Thus, at each historical juncture farming patterns, cooking methods, and consumer tastes shaped the fate of the Native American plant.

As these cultural considerations indicate, the process of ethnic formation is crucial for understanding globalization. Foods have long been central to ethnic identity, both by building up affiliations within a group through the commensality of shared meals and by marking the differences between groups in a particularly visceral fashion by definitions of the edible and inedible. This role of policing boundaries is central to Frederik Barth's concept of ethnic groups as political constructs rather than primordial organisms. Recently, however, mass media and corporate marketing have begun to challenge more immediate forms of social contact in the construction of group identities, particularly on a global scale. Under such circumstances, commercial expedience has taken precedence over individual tastes, leading to the homogenization of cuisines and the loss of subtle local variants.[2] Another constant factor in the transformations of globalization has been the basic human desire to domesticate the foreign and fit it within familiar cultural patterns. In the early modern era, the inability to make bread from maize because of the lack of gluten led Europeans to dismiss it as inferior to their own staple, wheat bread. By the same token, cultures without an existing tolerance for spicy foods tend to adopt watered-down versions of Mexican cuisine—that, or they jump madly into the macho world of the jalapeño-eating contest, which is just as alien to Mexican sensibilities.

Such examples of appropriation, whether by corporate food formulators or creative cooks, have raised concerns among philosophers and social critics about cultural property rights. Already in the 1930s, as Anne Goldman has observed, New Mexico women such as Cleofas Jaramillo and Fabiola Cabeza de Vaca were inspired to write cookbooks in order to refute the distorted image of their food appearing as recipes in mainstream women's magazines.[3] Corporate advertising has been an even more blatant source of ethnic defamation, in campaigns ranging from the Frito Bandito to the Taco Bell dog. Moreover, Uma Narayan and Lisa Heldke have questioned the colonial power relations inherent even in individual acts of consumption.[4] Yet Meredith Abarca has rightly warned against trying to define or claim authenticity for a cuisine because recipes are constantly changing as people experiment in the kitchen. The working-class Mexican and Mexican American women she spoke with were uninterested in notions of authenticity and dismissed the concept as meaningful only to posers with no other claim to authority.[5]

This essay surveys the historical evolution of Mexican cuisine, first within the boundaries of Greater Mexico, as Américo Paredes called the cultural region encompassing Mexico and its former territories in the southwestern United States, and then around the world. The first section describes the blending of Native American and European foods within Mexico proper, while the second examines how one regional variant, the frontier foods of the north, changed as a result of contact with the United States. Next, following the travels of Tex-Mex food around the world shows the further fragmentation of Mexican dishes as they became localized into diverse cultures. The final section discusses Mexicans' attempts to reclaim the global image of their cuisine from Mexican American stereotypes. From these multiple possible identities, the conclusion tries to answer the seemingly simple question, What is Mexican food?

Mexican Cuisine

The regional cuisines of Mexico emerged from colonial encounters between Native American and European cooking traditions. The first such blends were created by Indian women in the service of Spanish conquistadors and priests; dishes such as mole poblano, a deep brown sauce combining the fire of New World chiles with the fragrance of Old World spices, laid the foundations for a mestizo, or mixed, cuisine. Nevertheless, throughout the colonial period corn tortillas and wheat bread remained the cultural symbols and economic sustenance of two largely separate societies. Juridical distinctions between Indians and Spaniards were finally abolished with independence in 1821, but discrimination against native culture remained pervasive. Wealthy Mexicans savored the cosmopolitanism of French restaurants while denouncing the subsistence crop maize as the root of indigenous backwardness. Twentieth-century technology later commodified women's kitchen work, particularly the arduous task of making tortillas, at the same time that revolutionary governments hailed the mixed-race mestizo as a unique Mexican national identity. Racial and class stereotypes, however, had already set enduring patterns for future globalization.

A combination of climate and settlement patterns shaped the regional character of Mexican cuisine. The Native American diet was a largely vegetarian but nutritionally balanced complex of maize, beans, and squash, combined with chiles and other produce and game. The Spanish conquistadors had little interest in these foods and sought to implant their own familiar Mediterranean cuisine, especially wheat bread, olive oil, and wine. In the southern provinces of Oaxaca and Yucatán, heavily populated before the conquest and with little mineral wealth, the indigenous people preserved their cuisine largely intact while adding some European foods, especially meat. By contrast, the central highlands, including Mexico City, had large urban markets for European produce, although native beans and chiles were eaten by all levels of society. In general, the social hierarchy of foods depended on their association with European or indigenous society.[6]

Although social status and taste preferences helped shape the emerging Mexican cuisine, economic conditions also had a significant role. Maize, a hardy and productive staple that grew well in all climates, provided farmers with relatively low incomes because of the lack of Spanish demand. By contrast, wheat was a risky commercial crop, low yielding, susceptible to disease, and requiring expensive plows, mills, and ovens. However, the subsistence advantage of corn came at the price of hard labor for women, who spent hours every morning grinding the grain on volcanic stone metates into masa (dough), then patting it out by hand into round tortillas and cooking them briefly on an earthenware griddle—all before men went out to work in the fields. Festivals multiplied the workload, for in addition to preparing masa into tortillas and tamales, they also labored over the metates grinding chiles for mole.[7]

As Mexico began to industrialize in the late nineteenth century, the social connotations of foods acquired new significance. The elite shifted their cultural affiliations from Spain to France, importing chefs and champagne to celebrate their sophistication, although this did not stop them from buying enchiladas from street vendors at night. Even while indulging themselves on the sly, they came to view popular cuisine as a positive menace to the nation. Using the newly developed science of nutrition, Mexican leaders attributed Indian backwardness to the supposed inadequacy of maize-based diets. Worse still, they believed that malnourished plebeians would slake their hunger with pulque, an alcohol made of fermented agave juice, thus contributing to widespread drunkenness. The solution was to wean the lower classes from the subsistence crop maize and get them to eat the more fashionable, and commercial, wheat. Although based on spurious science, this "tortilla discourse" correctly recognized maize as the root of village life, and thus a potential barrier to national integration.[8]

The dream of modernization was ultimately achieved not through the replacement of corn but rather through its commodification. Mexican inventors mechanized the complex skills of the tortilla maker in three distinct stages at roughly fifty-year intervals. In the early twentieth century forged steel mills first took over the arduous task of hand-grinding maize at the metates, which not only freed women to enter the commercial economy but also required outside earnings to pay the milling fee. About 1950 mechanical engineers perfected the technology for automatically pressing out and cooking tortillas, but the industry never achieved economies of scale because of the Mexican preference for completely fresh tortillas. For decades small factories operated on street corners throughout Mexico, with customers lined up before every meal. Eventually the invention of dehydrated tortilla flour (masa harina) allowed vertical integration by a company called Maseca. Although connoisseurs dismissed the resulting tortillas as dry and tasteless, with government support the company gained a firm hold on Mexican corn markets by the end of the century.[9]

The association of indigenous food and drink with the lower classes, particularly Native Americans, and the elite preference for the imported status through European haute cuisine helped to shape the future globalization of Mexican cuisine. Moreover, the taste for freshly made tortillas limited the staple to communities with significant demand, even after production was mechanized in the twentieth century. Yet even in the colonial period, alternative versions of Mexican cuisine were developing in what eventually became the southwestern United States.

Mexican American Cuisine

Although purists often dismiss Tex-Mex as a shallow imitation of the original, Mexican American foods began as simply another regional variant, *norteño*, within the diverse geography of Greater Mexico. After the U.S. invasion of 1847, these foods became ethnic markers of a subjugated people, feminizing Mexican Americans through the images of chili "queens" and "hot tamales." Nevertheless, Anglo businessmen appreciated the potential profits from manufacturing chili powder, and even as they packaged Mexican foods for mainstream audiences, Mexican American cooks learned to use new ingredients made available by the food-processing industry. Thus, ethnic cuisine evolved through the interaction of community members seeking legitimacy from the broader society and corporations eager for new product lines and markets. By the 1950s, when chili had lost its ethnic identity, tacos were discovered as a new and exotic dish, sparking another wave of competition between ethnic restaurateurs and nascent fast-food chains such as Taco Bell.

Silver mining and frontier defense prompted the settlement of New Spain's northern territories including California, New Mexico, and Texas, as well as Sonora, Chihuahua, and Nuevo León. With few native inhabitants, the region acquired a strong European cultural imprint, although Tlaxcalan settlers from central Mexico added mestizo flavor to the mix. Wheat flourished in irrigated fields, but without expensive mills and ovens, it was often ground on metates and cooked as tortillas. On one hand, great herds of livestock grazed the plains, allowing *norteños* to eat a more carnivorous diet, and particularly more beef, than Mexicans farther south. On the other hand, the arid environment offered less variety in vegetables, herbs, and chiles, limiting the potential for baroque sauces. Chili con carne, for example, may have contained more meat than a mole from central Mexico, but it was made with a single fiery pepper native to the region, the chiltepin, along with wild oregano and cumin, which still remain the distinctive flavors of Tex-Mex cooking.[10]

When the United States acquired the Southwest through the Treaty of Guadalupe Hidalgo (1848), foods inspired many of the stereotypes that Anglo newcomers used to justify subjugating the inhabitants. Subhuman images of Mexicans appeared in the complaints of laborers that they could not compete with peons subsisting on tortillas and beans as well as in the notion that buzzards refused to eat the bodies of Mexicans "because of the peppery condition of the flesh."[11] However, as the frontier faded in the late nineteenth century, Mexican foods became a tourist attraction for those seeking to experience the "Wild West." No journey to San Antonio was complete without visiting, in addition to the Alamo, the street vendors called chili "queens" in order to taste their "savory compounds, swimming in fiery pepper, which biteth like a serpent."[12] Food came to symbolize the sexuality of Mexican women, hot and alluring, yet also dangerous and polluting, an association supported by city council restrictions limiting vendors to the plazas around the red-light district. Likewise in Los Angeles, tamale pushcarts set up shop outside of taverns, and the predominantly male vendors gained a reputation for drunkenness and petty criminality.[13] The lower-class image of Mexican American food received ironic confirmation from Mexican elites who fled across the border during the revolution of 1910. After a period of exile in San Antonio, Texas, the linguist Francisco J. Santamaria denounced chili con carne as a "detestable food with false Mexican title that is sold in the United States of the North."[14]

Plebeian associations did not diminish the taste of nonethnics for Mexican food or their desire to profit from it. African Americans quickly learned the art of making tamales and carried them east to the Mississippi delta, while African, Anglo, and Asian Americans competed with Mexicans for the pushcart tamale trade in California. By the 1890s some Texas businessmen, notably D. C. Pendery and William Gebhardt, had begun selling commercial chili powder; one of these early promoters may well have financed the San Antonio chili stand at the 1893 Columbian Exposition in Chicago. Inspired by this tourist attraction, chili parlors were soon operating throughout the Midwest, and Chicago meat packers discovered canned chili and tamales as a profitable outlet for scraps of meat off the cutting-room floor. Not all business ventures came from outside the ethnic community. E. C. Ortega, of Ventura, California, founded the Pioneer Green Chile Company in 1899, canning mild Anaheim chiles for predominantly Anglo consumers. Although advertisements for Mexican food invoked ethnic stereotypes, generally they downplayed the exoticism—and the heat. Gebhardt's published a cookbook assuring customers: "Anybody can make all the latest Mexican dishes."[15]

Restaurants were another meeting ground between ethnic and mainstream tastes. Small-time establishments in Mexican communities often appealed to outsiders, whether Bohemian diners seeking a cultural experience or simply working folks hungry for a cheap and tasty meal. Many hamburger and barbecue joints acquired a Mexican flavor when Anglo managers encouraged ethnic employees to add their own foods to the menu. Otis Farnsworth's The Original of San Antonio sought to make Mexican cuisine respectable by presenting enchiladas and tamales on fine china with pristine napkins and silverware. Although small restaurants have a high mortality rate, a few Mexican restaurants still survive from the 1920s and 1930s thanks largely to customers outside the ethnic community. Such institutions include El Cholo and La Golondrina of Los Angeles as well as the El Chico chain, which began as a Depression-era tamale stand in Texas. Even beyond Greater Mexico, Juvencio Maldonado ran a successful restaurant called Xochitl near Times Square in New York for decades beginning in the 1930s.[16]

These cultural encounters also brought new ingredients and technology into Mexican American home cooking, whether in response to assimilationist pressures of nutritionists and home economists or simply from an innate desire to ease domestic burdens. The historian Vicki Ruiz has examined the innovative strategies that ethnic women used to mediate between the demands of Mexican family traditions and U.S. citizenship and consumer culture. The food-processing industry, for example, allowed cooks to supplement family diets with more eggs, dairy, and fresh produce, including iceberg lettuce and canned green chiles. Thus, many of the distinctive elements of Mexican American cooking—generous servings of cheddar cheese, shredded lettuce, tomato, and ground beef—were simply adaptations to foods available in the United States. Ethnic cooks and businessmen devised their own technical innovations as well. The San Antonio corn miller Bartolo Martínez began making dehydrated tortilla flour in 1908, decades before Maseca. In the 1940s the home economist Fabiola Cabeza de Vaca published a cookbook recipe for making tacos by prefrying the tortillas in the characteristic "U" shape of a taco shell before adding the filling, a method unheard of in Mexico. In 1947 the restaurateur Juvencio Maldonado filed a patent application for an industrial tortilla fryer for making taco shells.[17]

These distinctively Mexican American tacos became the next big trend, which helped launch Mexican cuisine to national attention in the postwar era. Fifty years of canned chili con carne and tamales had stripped away any sense of novelty or authenticity from earlier versions of the ethnic food. Moreover, the fried taco shell offered newcomers a relatively easy introduction to that peculiarly Mexican performance of eating with a tortilla. One guidebook explained: "The Mexican's dexterity with the tortilla is as amusing to watch as the Italian's business-like disposal of spaghetti and the chop sticks of the Oriental."[18] One of the earliest taco restaurants in Los Angeles, called simply the Taco House, operating by 1946, inspired countless imitators. A hamburger and hot dog stand operator from San Bernardino named Glen Bell joined the competition in 1951 by devising a taco fryer—unaware that Maldonado had beaten him to the patent office—and modifying his chili-dog sauce to use as salsa. Contrary to theories of "McDonaldization," the success of Taco Bell and rival chains owed less to technological improvements than to aggressive franchising campaigns that brought Mexican fast food to segregated neighborhoods, first in California and eventually around the country.[19]

A new generation of industrial food processors introduced taco shells and other newly popular Mexican foods to the growing supermarket trade. Some of these stories are already well known, such as those of Elmer Doolin, who claimed to have purchased the formula for Frito chips from the San Antonio miller Bartolo Martínez, or Dave Pace, the future picante-sauce king. Midcentury businesses also included Ashley Food Products and the Powell family's Mountain Pass Canning Company, later renamed Old El Paso, as well as Louis Strumberg's Patio Foods of San Antonio. Yet other entrepreneurs came from the Mexican community, such as Pedro Guerrero of Rosarita, who started out selling fresh tamales in Phoenix and later manufactured frozen entrees for a predominantly Anglo market. Housewives wishing to serve an exotic Mexican dinner in the late 1950s had two options: canned or frozen. The former might mean assembling enchiladas from canned tortillas and sauce, accompanied by canned beans and Spanish rice, while a frozen taco dinner or combination plate went straight into the oven. Taco kits complete with shells, sauce packets, and salsa followed a decade later. Unappealing perhaps to sophisticated palates, such dinners nevertheless offered a welcome break from Jell-O salad in the Midwest.[20]

Thus, the taco evolved gradually from a Mexican regional dish to a market segment of the U.S. food industry. The lower-class associations of the taco remained clear even as it went from being a familiar street food to an exotic ethnic taste. Nevertheless, the change may well have symbolized the process of citizenship for some Mexican Americans in the 1920s and 1930s, as the taco acquired new ingredients, including hamburger, cheese, lettuce, and for some, a wheat tortilla instead of corn. The commodification of labor was also vital for this transformation, beginning with the time-saving step of frying the tortillas separately and culminating with Taco Bell, where ingredients are delivered from central commissaries and assembled with caulking guns. The industrial process distanced food both from the source of production and from its origins in the ethnic community. By the 1960s, when making tacos no longer required fresh corn tortillas, frozen dinners and shell-and-salsa kits could be shipped around the country or the world.

Global Tex-Mex

For centuries Mexicans have carried food abroad to satisfy their taste for spicy dishes while on diplomatic missions, religious pilgrimages, or in political exile. Because the national cuisine had a lower-class image and the lower classes rarely traveled outside Greater Mexico, there were few opportunities to sample such foods. However, when Mexican American food manufacturers began to distribute their products beyond the Southwest, they did not stop at the national borders. With the postwar spread of tourism and military bases, expatriate North Americans alone provided a significant market, and once foreigners also began to acquire a taste for tacos, the potential growth was unlimited. In the 1960s and 1970s aspiring restaurateurs needed considerable ingenuity to obtain ingredients across oceans or to improvise with local produce. By the turn of the millennium European, Australian, and Asian demand for Mexican food had created a commercial infrastructure capable of supplying a wide range of products to professionals and home cooks. Mexican food, already transformed by its encounters with Anglo culture, continued to evolve to fit ever more diverse consumer tastes. In the 1990s Tex-Mex became widely fashionable in its own right, making the Mexican label even less meaningful on a global level.

The United States military became one of the earliest international promoters of Mexican food, giving an entirely new dimension to the concept of cultural imperialism. Although Coca-Cola was the leading brand to emerge from World War II, thanks to government-subsidized bottling plants near all battle zones, cans of chili con carne were equally pervasive if less well advertised. The humorist Art Buchwald was not completely exaggerating when he imagined the principality of Lovlost, where the "gastronomic regional specialties" included "Heinz pork and beans, Hormel's Spam, and Mother O'Hara's chili con carne. Most of it was left over from the war when the American army had a food supply depot just outside the capital."[21] More ephemeral—and memorable—were the improvised creations of Mexican and Mexican American servicemen, who supplemented standard-issue rations with chile pepper care packages. Don Dedera recalled: "Wherever the Arizona [National] Guard goes, it takes a pack of Mañanaland spices. In the Pacific in World War II, the Bushmasters ate C-rations tacos. During the Berlin crisis, they invented wiener-schnitzel tamales."[22] Cold War containment policies regularized the presence of U.S. troops in Europe and Asia, creating a steady demand for spicy foods; for example, "in 1965 a West German store chain, Karstadt, opened a special department handling 'genuine Texas foods,' in the vicinity of American military bases."[23]

Nevertheless, building restaurant supply chains from the ground up could be difficult for pioneers, as Tom Estes discovered in founding the Pacífico Café, Europe's oldest Mexican restaurant. During his first trip abroad in 1964, this California gym teacher saw a vision of his future in the sweet smoky coffee shops of Amsterdam. Unfortunately, to get a visa to stay, he needed to be self-employed, and so he returned to his old job. Inspiration struck while he was driving a Volkswagen camper down the Inter-American Highway to Panama. Abandoning plans to see the canal, he toured the countryside instead, collecting recipe ideas and curios for a Mexican restaurant. In Mazatlán the family of a former student put him in touch with an executive of the Pacífico Brewery, who filled the old camper with discarded promotional materials.

Estes finally made it back to Amsterdam in 1970, although it took another six years to open the restaurant. With a meager initial capital of fifteen thousand dollars, he could afford a place only in the red-light district. Twenty-five years later the Pacífico was still there, across the street from the Leather Rubber Twisted Gear shop.

Given his limited budget, Estes improvised supply chains for his restaurant. The biggest problem was obtaining fresh tortillas, and he imported masa harina directly from the Valley Grain Company of Madeira, California, using a Rotterdam grain agent to clear customs. After mixing the dough, he used an old, hand-cranked tortilla roller with oval blade, still common in rural Mexico, and then cooked them on two used domestic stoves purchased at a flea market and fitted with sheet metal plates as griddles. Like a Mexican peasant woman, Estes started work early in the morning to make the tortillas and spread them out around the kitchen to cool without turning moldy. His first chef, Dennis Real, another former student, arrived later in the day to prepare menu items such as chili Colorado and tacos California using family recipes. Estes had to re-create these provisioning networks when he opened new outlets in London in 1982 and Paris in 1984. At first he supplied the restaurant chain through informal means, smuggling tortillas on the channel ferry from Holland to England in a hippie "Magic Bus."[24]

Tortillas were the most labor-intensive task for restaurants, as they were for rural women, but unlike the latter, expatriate cooks had to travel farther than the backyard for other ingredients. Arizona native Earlene Ridge recalled the difficulty of assembling a Mexican meal while living in Paris in the early 1980s. The Sonoran wheat flour tortillas of her youth could be made by hand using French wheat. For fresh green chile peppers similar to jalapeños she made a pilgrimage to Algerian markets in the *banlieu*, picking up pinto beans and cumin along the way. A combination of grated Cantal and Edam provided an acceptable substitute for longhorn cheese, and hamburger meat, tomatoes, and limes were also readily available in local supermarkets at the time. The avocados used to garnish the meal were shipped across the Atlantic, which together with tequila were the only ingredients that actually came from Mexico.[25]

On the Pacific Rim similar stories were told by Oshima Bari, chef and owner of La Bamba restaurant in Osaka, Japan. Like Estes, a member of the international counterculture, Bari studied Spanish at a university and spent two years backpacking in Peru and Mexico before returning home to open his restaurant in 1986. By this time it was possible to find packaged tortillas in Japan, but they arrived quite stale after the transoceanic voyage, and therefore he decided to make his own from imported masa. He obtained dried chiles and other ingredients through a personalized importing network that consisted of taking regular vacations to Mexico and Los Angeles, where he stuffed a hundred kilograms of kitchen supplies into checked luggage and the overhead compartment. Even with the airline's excess weight charges, he saved money on the import fees. Most of his provisions came in cans, but he also employed considerable ingenuity in re-creating Mexican ingredients at home. To make *chicharrones*, a popular snack of pork cracklings, he learned to shave a whole hog. Provisioning the restaurant grew easier as Japanese consumers gained interest in exotic commodities; for example, avocados were difficult to find in the mid-1980s but had become cheaply available in local supermarkets a decade later.[26]

In some locations high-priced ingredients were considered a normal cost of doing business, and customers did not object. In 1978 Fran Tate opened Pepe's North of the Border as the first Mexican restaurant inside the Arctic Circle. Then as now, Barrow, Alaska, was a remote, largely Inuit town dependent for income on seasonal fishing, oil drilling, and Cold War radar stations. After the sun set in mid-November, not to return again until late January, customers were willing to pay high prices for a bit of warmth, even if only a cup of guacamole made from avocados costing six dollars each. Canned guacamole was cheaper, but Tate ordered only one batch: "It was horrible." At least she did not have to make fresh tortillas since they could be flown in regularly from California and fried into taco shells and enchiladas. Finding Mexican cooks was the biggest problem before migrant laborers arrived in large numbers. José Gómez, an employee from Guadalajara, explained, "I thought the restaurant would be like a big igloo."[27]

Tacos benefited from a French infatuation with all things Texan in the late 1980s. The Tex-Mex historian Robb Walsh attributes this fad to Jean-Jacques Beineix's hugely popular film *Betty Blue* (1986), about a mentally unbalanced woman and her tequila-swigging, chili-con-carne-cooking lover, Zorg. When the film premiered, a struggling Tex-Mex restaurant called Le Studio, in the Marais neighborhood of Paris, founded a few years earlier by a French Jewish Texan named Frank Shera, became an overnight success and spawned a dozen imitators, including the Indiana Tex-Mex Café.[28] However, while the French fascination with outlaw cowboys certainly helped, it does not explain the wider European and global interest in Tex-Mex food. Timing was important in that moment between the Cold War and the millennial crusade, when Texans bearing jalapeños appeared less a threat to world peace than a pleasant anachronism. More general popular culture associations were also present. Nachos smothered in Velveeta cheese became a standard snack in movie theaters, and California avocado growers launched media campaigns to associate guacamole with the Super Bowl.[29]

The entrance of corporate chains and affluent investors into Western European markets in the 1990s transformed the nature of the business. When Texas oilman Russell Ramsland decided London needed a good place to get nachos and a margarita, there was no question that he would be making tortillas in the morning. After a long search, Ramsland found a suitable location for his grandiosely named Texas Embassy Cantina near London's Trafalgar

Square in the building that had once housed the ticket office of the Titanic. Unfortunately, when he attempted to close the deal wearing a snakeskin blazer and cowboy boots, the real estate agent decided he was an inappropriate tenant for the building. It took a full year to secure the lease, and even longer to renovate the site. Despite the assurances of local contractors, the kitchen was not ready by the time of the grand opening in 1994, and the staff had to hire caterers with salmon rolls and pizza bites instead of serving fajitas and chimichangas. Meanwhile, the mavericks moved east with the fall of the Iron Curtain. Hungarian American entrepreneur George Hemmingway opened the Acapulco Restaurant in Budapest, while the Cowboy Bar and Tequila House sought to capitalize on the trend in the former Soviet Union.[30]

Suddenly fashionable Tex-Mex foods also spread to grocery and department stores beyond the vicinity of army bases. Already in 1989 Jean-Pierre and Elaine Bourbeillon had opened The General Store in Paris's seventh arrondissement, selling taco kits and chili spices, mild for locals and extra hot for North American expatriates.[31] Old El Paso promoted overseas expansion aggressively, and the ease of marketing and preparation helped the company's distinctive yellow cans and boxes achieve global recognition. Nevertheless, local competitors began to challenge the company's hold on international markets; for example, in Sweden, where people have reported eating tacos once a month on average, the food-processing firm Nordfalks actually changed its name to Santa Maria after its best-selling brand of taco shells and salsas. Scandinavian tacos typically contain the usual mix of ground beef, lettuce, and cheese, but with a distinctive touch of canned corn.[32]

As the Swedish example illustrates, Mexican food has continued to undergo a process of localization to fit with the cultural expectations of consumers. At times this amounted to little more than dishes cooked in the fashion of the host country; one Parisian travel guide warned of "faux Mexican foods (fajita de pollo that tastes like coq au vin)."[33] Alternately, the cuisine has been pigeonholed within a particular market niche, such as the vegetarian burrito restaurants in Germany that appealed to ecotourists whose associations of Mexico ran toward backpacking at Palenque and to the artwork of Frida Kahlo. Indeed, a restaurant named after the feminist icon opened in the former East Berlin's Rosa Luxemburg Platz. Painted the exact shade of blue as her Coyoacán home, it catered mainly to university students squatting in nearby tenements. Both lifestyle and local preferences converged in British Mexican restaurants, where the frijoles often tasted like baked beans and the food was secondary to music and alcohol. A review of London's now-defunct Down Mexico Way observed: "It's billed as a restaurant for a quiet, romantic dinner, but I have to say that for most people, live, energetic Latin music punctuated by deafening taped music to accompany the floor show of Salsa dancing is not the ideal accompaniment to seduction over the Fajitas!"[34] Japanese versions of Mexican, by contrast, emphasized artful presentation of composed salads with seafood, greens, and avocado. Some restaurants even obtained plastic replicas of tacos and quesadillas for display windows to attract curious pedestrians.

At the risk of perpetuating national stereotypes, people seem to find themselves reflected in the global culture that they consume—including their Mexican food. This localization has occurred since the sixteenth century, when maize traveled the world under assumed identities, becoming known as the "Turkish" grain in Europe and "Mecca" corn in India. Contemporary globalization was stimulated in large part by the Cold War, although it has since taken on an industrial logic of its own. Nevertheless, the formative influences date back to the mass-market stereotypes established in the United States. The granddaddy of overseas Mexican restaurants, founded in 1967 by Californian Bill Chicote at Bondi Beach, the epicenter of Australian surf culture, is called Taco Bill. Even those who have acquired a Mexican food habit, such as the Stockholm food blogger Anne Skoogh, recognize this crucial point: "People here don't think of tacos as Mexican as much as they think they are American."[35]

Reclaiming Mexican

As long as their cuisine remained tied to the native soil, Mexicans took pleasure from their hidden gastronomic treasures, so the North American marketing of what they considered bastardized replicas aroused strong nationalist sentiments.[36] The foreign threat first galvanized the nation's culinary elite into recovering local foods, but most of these chefs had been trained abroad, and the *nueva cocina mexicana* consisted mainly of exotic ingredients prepared using the techniques of international haute cuisine. The Mexican food industry's efforts to promote national exports were likewise bedeviled by a dependent relationship with international capital. Beginning in the 1980s a succession of neoliberal presidents with Ivy League economics degrees sought to open the country to foreign investment. Under such circumstances, potential national champions found it profitable to follow Tex-Mex stereotypes, even while gradually introducing global consumers to the tastes of regional cuisines. As a result, these firms helped consolidate the burrito-and-nacho image of Mexican food as an inexpensive accompaniment to drunken revelry. Not surprisingly, alcohol became one the country's leading food exports.

Because elite dining had been dominated by foreign chefs, before culinary nationalists could respond to the Tex-Mex challenge, they had to decide just what constituted authentic Mexican cuisine. Regional specialties remained the ideal for many fine restaurants, particularly in the provinces, including Monterrey's El Rey del Cabrito, Mérida's Los Almendros, and Mexico City's Fonda el Refugio. But another, increasingly popular version of authenticity lay in the discovery of pre-Hispanic traditions, or rather, their reinvention by modern chefs. The founder of this tradition, Fortín Rojas Contreras, migrated to

Mexico City as a six-year-old orphan and worked selling tacos on the streets around the Merced market before opening a restaurant in the 1960s called Fonda Don Chon. His cuisine, based on childhood memories of rural festival foods and ingredients available in obscure corners of the popular market, became suddenly fashionable in the early 1980s, as Mexico's counterculture youth grew up and acquired expense accounts. Within a few years, however, his ideas had been taken over by restaurants in posh neighborhoods, which made pre-Hispanic foods such as agave worms and deer prohibitively expensive for the people who considered them as part of their culture rather than as the latest fad.[37]

For proponents of the *nueva cocina*, native ingredients provided both authenticity and distinction within the increasingly crowded world of international fine dining. Not all of these chefs came from privileged backgrounds; for example, Arnulfo Luengas Rosales, like Contreras, arrived in Mexico City as a young migrant from Oaxaca in 1951, but he found a patron in the expatriate French chef Emmanuel Decamp. In 1970 Luengas Rosales became the executive chef of the Banco Nacional de México, which provided him an opportunity for professional study in France. By the early 1980s he had begun to apply French techniques to local ingredients, developing recipes such as pork loin with *huauzontle* (an herb resembling broccoli rabe), puff pastry with *cabuches* (sort of like asparagus tips), and Beef Wellington with chiles.[38] While the Oaxacan chef avoided publicity, Patricia Quintana cultivated an international following as Mexico's culinary ambassador. Born to a French and Swiss émigré family, she traveled to Europe in her early twenties and worked with some of the luminaries of nouvelle cuisine, including Michel Guérard and Gaston Lenôtre. In a series of highly regarded cookbooks and Mexico City's most exclusive restaurant, Izote, she laid out a mestizo vision blending continental cuisine with Mexican traditions. Even while adapting to the latest trends, she grounded her work in a seemingly more authentic past: "The origins of much of what I do lie with the Mayans, whose grand civilizations rose and fell long before the Spanish conquistadors stepped foot in the New World."[39]

By the 1990s restaurateurs had carried these visions of Mexican cuisine, both regional and nouvelle, to global cities including New York, Paris, and Tokyo. While seeking fame and fortune, they also claimed the patriotic goal of countering the international debasement of Mexican fare. Stepping into Anahuacalli, a small Paris restaurant on the Left Bank not far from Notre Dame, is like entering an elegant Mexico City *fonda*, complete with blue-rimmed glasses on the tables and avant-garde art tastefully decorating the walls. Menu items, including *quesadillas de cuitlacoche* (fritters stuffed with corn fungus), pork and chicken tamales, and mole poblano, could likewise hold their own against those of any restaurant in Mexico. The owner, Cristina Prun, the Mexican wife of a French mathematician, felt an educational mission to inform Parisians about the foods of her native land. While gaining a following among Frenchmen who conquered initial fears of hot mole sauces, she still depended on a North American tourist clientele.[40] Prun deserves official recognition for her culinary diplomacy, and indeed she has begun catering receptions for the Mexican embassy, but such culinary apostles are the exception in the international restaurant industry. More common, perhaps, was the experience of two Mexican chefs on tour in India. Retained for a month in Delhi to train the staff of a Mexican restaurant, they quickly discovered that the local clientele was less interested in the food than in the alcohol, especially shots of tequila served up by bartenders wearing cowboy costumes.[41]

Influencing the mass market and even provisioning elite restaurants depended on Mexico's food industry and particularly its largest firm, Maseca. The tortilla flour giant had first entered the U.S. market in 1978, with the purchase of California-based Mission Foods. Los Angeles, with the second-largest Mexican community in the world, had an enormous potential market that was serviced by small, highly competitive neighborhood tortilla factories. Maseca bought out rivals, advertised heavily in Spanish-language media, and built an efficient distribution network to deliver tortillas to stores daily, and in some neighborhoods two or three times a day, to satisfy the Mexican community's desire for the freshest possible tortillas. Unlike some North American producers, intent on extending the supermarket shelf life—NASA reportedly requested a tortilla that would last for more than a year, presumably for future missions to Mars—a Maseca executive snorted: "We don't consider that product fresh."[42] However, by the 1990s the company had purchased tortilla factories across the country, following patterns of Mexican migration but also competing for nonethnic markets. At the same time it began building an international network of factories in South America, Europe, Australia, and most recently China. As the multinational reached beyond the Mexican community, it had to abandon a marketing strategy premised on just-in-time delivery. Without steady demand for fresh tortillas, the company expanded other product lines, including chips, wheat flour tortillas, and taco shells.[43]

The beer industry was another winner from the sudden interest in Mexican cuisine and may well have contributed to the larger trend. Corona, considered the Budweiser of Mexico, increased U.S. sales from 2.5 million cases to more than 14 million between 1982 and 1986. This surge in consumption brought Mexico almost level with Canada in beer imports to the United States, although both were still well behind Holland. The sudden demand apparently came as a surprise to the producer, Cervecería Modelo, and may have owed less to the quality of the beer than to the novelty of transparent glass bottles. Although darker bottles do a better job of preserving beer, the bright yellow struck the fancy of young men, who repeatedly told interviewers, no doubt grinning childishly: "It looks like another liquid."[44] As the company ramped up production for export, workers at the main plant in Mexico City demanded a share of the windfall profits. In 1990 Modelo broke the strike with government support in an action that was widely recognized as a foretaste of the local consequences of globalization. Neoliberal President Carlos Salinas de Gortari, in a speech before British Parliament, drew comparisons with the antiunion policies of Prime Minister Margaret Thatcher, although she was soon dumped by her own party. A few years later Modelo formed a strategic alliance with Anheuser Busch, and rivals Cuauhtémoc and Moctezuma hurried to find export representatives for North American and European markets. Promoting a youthful image, Corona advertised with popular musicians such as those with the Swedish "Rock Train" tour and became official sponsor of the German coed naked volleyball championship.[45]

Tequila likewise parlayed its associations with spring-break vacationers and border tourists into massive export sales. The political economy of production was more complicated than in the case of beer because revolutionary land reform of the early twentieth century had distributed agave fields among agricultural cooperatives, although they were organized to ensure votes for the ruling party rather than the interests of farmers. The manufacturers, including former hacienda owners, more recent entrepreneurs, and even a few factories run by growers, produced for two separate markets: high-quality bottles of pure blue agave aged in oak barrels; and a mass market of *mixto* (blended) with other alcohols. Advertisers sought to cultivate the top-shelf market using the language of wine connoisseurs: "One hundred percent blue agave tequila will smell of white pepper, pine needles and fresh herbs. Mixto tequila may exude an off aroma of burnt rubber."[46] The European Union granted legal recognition of tequila's "denomination of origin," ensuring the uniqueness of Mexican terroir, a French term for the mystique of local production. Nevertheless, such protection does not extend to the largest single market, the United States, and an agreement is unlikely because the industry leaders, José Cuervo and Sauza, profit from international alliances with Heublein and Allied Domecq to sell low-quality tequila in bulk for bottling north of the border.[47]

In the last two decades neoliberal governments have aggressively promoted international sales of other processed foods as well. The Foreign Trade Bank (Bancomext), founded in 1990, has helped build international marketing contacts for Mexican firms. It has also established a presence through trade fairs around the world, particularly Expo Comida Latina, with three annual events in New York, Los Angeles, and Houston. Meanwhile, the government has provided loans for food-processing technology to exporters such as Real Sazón from Tulancingo, Hidalgo, which uses vacuum sealing to prepare packets of traditional *barbacoa* (barbecue) along with consommé and salsa. Although these products are intended primarily for sale to migrant workers in the United States nostalgic for the foods of home, the potential for them to expand into mainstream markets helped motivate the initiative. Nevertheless, the industry has grown largely through strategic alliances with North American conglomerates. Heinz, for example, recently bought out the Monterrey-based Delimex frozen food company, while Hormel formed a joint venture with Herdez of Mexico City. In this way food-processing giants have been able to purchase a claim of authenticity without the trouble of developing their own brands.[48]

In the global struggle to represent Mexican cuisine, exemplified by the rivalry between the taco shell and the fresh corn tortilla, neoliberal governments have largely taken the attitude that if you cannot beat them, you might as well join them. North American manufacturers had already developed highly profitable versions of Mexican food with wide appeal, and national firms have relied on foreign partnerships to succeed in the global economy. The tourism industry, seemingly alone, has a significant stake in claims of authenticity. In a recent attempt to protect the uniqueness of Mexican culinary artistry from fast-food imitators, the country petitioned UNESCO for recognition of its cuisine as an intangible human patrimony, although the agency, which usually focuses on dance, music, and oral traditions, rejected the appeal.[49]

Conclusion

So what does it mean to eat Mexican in the contemporary era of globalization? Traditional recipes offer the most obvious answer, for cuisine is the shared cultural patrimony, if not of all humanity, then of particular ethnic groups. Nevertheless, as Meredith Abarca has insisted, the artistry of ordinary cooks is constantly evolving and not the unchanging product of ethnography.[50] By the same token, *terroir*, the unique produce of Mexican soil, can no longer be considered a limiting factor given the success of restaurants such as Anahuacalli and La Bamba, which rely largely on French and Japanese produce. Nor is nationality a necessary qualification, since dedicated home cooks of any background can make better tacos and mole than an absent-minded, corner-cutting chef from Mexico can. Still less can the contemporary regions of Mexico define the cuisine; the blanket dismissal of Tex-Mex resembles nothing so much as the colonial Spanish condescension toward Indian foods.

In this essay I have tried to examine the commercial interests behind rival attempts to define Mexican cuisine. On the one hand, efforts to regulate and codify the national cuisine along the lines of the UNESCO petition—with its claims of ethnographically documented recipes—stand to benefit a particular segment of tourist restaurants, although as the agency concluded, policing such boundaries seems a pointless exercise. The food-processing industry meanwhile has manufactured its own versions of authenticity through advertising. "Fire Roasted Zuni Zalza," for example, ironically evoked a mythical Mexican countryside: "The old patron walked down the mountainside overlooking the jalapeño field. He paused, turned to young Josélito (*sic*) and said, 'Make me a salsa, make me a salsa I can't refuse.'" The stakes in this contest are high, with global sales of tortillas alone estimated to be worth six billion dollars annually. Maseca can claim about half of that total, which is not such a strong showing against upstart foreign rivals, especially given the company's stranglehold on the Mexican market. The process of globalization, taking foods out of their ethnic context and adapting them to foreigners, has been standard practice for more than a century in the U.S. food-processing industry, as Donna Gabaccia has shown. Local knowledge may actually hinder such an enterprise, although Maseca never let authenticity stand in the way of a deal— the company has been supplying shells to Taco Bell for twenty years.[51]

Beyond the economic costs, international stereotypes of Mexico's sophisticated cuisines as cheap and easy party food may be as offensive to some as racial slurs such as "dog eater" are. For an example of how globalization has distorted Mexican voices, consider the story of María Dolores Torres Yzábal. Born to a prominent Sonoran family, she took a job as executive chef for an industrial group in Monterrey to pay the bills when she divorced her husband. After decades in the kitchen, she finally had the opportunity to publish her recipes through a book series by Weldon Russell, Ltd., of Australia. Although the deal was not particularly favorable, with a flat payment rather than royalties, at least she had the chance to reach an international audience. Unfortunately, because the book was assembled in Australia, the test kitchens had no idea of what the foods should actually look like. Glossy photos of chiles rellenos (stuffed chiles) looked decrepit because the cooks had not followed her directions to skin the peppers first. Worse still, the moles were prepared in a food processor, not a blender, which gave them an unspeakable chunky, brown appearance.[52]

Kitchen labor rather than ingredients defines the limits of ethnic cuisine in a global era. The arduous nature of preparing Mexican foods such as mole may lead even conscientious chefs to cut corners, especially when such changes fit with customer expectations. For precisely that reason, the best Mexican food is prepared at home, where the appreciation is not strictly monetary. The problem is compounded when cooks lack a connection to the ethnic community. Notwithstanding the current hysteria about migrant workers, Mexican restaurants have often been founded by outsiders, just as Italians historically opened French restaurants, Greeks took over Italian kitchens, and Chinese now dominate the Thai sector. In France the majority of Mexican restaurants are reportedly run by Lebanese migrants. Meanwhile, the Mexican restaurant Millie's, in Ulan Bator, apparently relied for its huevos rancheros on a Cuban chef who was studying in Tashkent when the Soviet Union dissolved.[53]

Anyone with an interest in Mexican food should certainly ponder the tensions between culinary innovation and colonial appropriation, but individual perspectives cannot be applied indiscriminately to a global phenomenon. The experiences of the fast-food mogul Glen Bell and the Swedish taco fanatic Anne Skoogh are as incommensurable as the Mexican cuisines of the celebrity chef Patricia Quintana and the Alaskan short-order cook José Gómez. While there will always be ill-mannered tourists to complain that Veracruz and Oaxaca restaurant fare cannot compare with the burritos they get at home, far more may find Tex-Mex to be an entrée to other regional specialties. Historically, the taco shell was welcomed as a more authentic alternative to chili con carne, and the contemporary expansion of Mexican food has benefited immigrant restaurants as well as corporate chains. With desire and enough tortillas, the whole world could become part of Greater Mexico.

Part IV
Sales

Chapter 12
The Aristocracy of the Market Basket: Self-Service Food Shopping in the New South

Lisa C. Tolbert

Eudora Welty was an avid grocery shopper. Whenever her mother's pantry failed to yield a necessary ingredient, Eudora was the first to volunteer for a trip to the neighborhood grocery store around the corner from her house in Jackson, Mississippi. Eudora remembered the neighborhood grocery store as her first taste of the world outside her home. For her, grocery shopping was never a chore; it was a fantasy experience. "The happiness of errands," Welty explained, "was in part that of running for the moment away from home, a free spirit." In contrast to the young Eudora, however, her mother, Chestina, avoided the grocery store like the plague. "As far as I can recall," Welty said, "she never set foot inside a grocery store." Chestina Welty did her regular grocery shopping by phone rather than in person. Eudora explained that her mother "stood at the telephone in our front hall and consulted with Mr. Lemly, of Lemly's Market and Grocery downtown, who took her order and sent it out on his next delivery." It was not that Chestina was averse to mundane chores; Welty remembered that her mother regularly milked the Jersey cow they kept in the backyard, for example.[1] No, Chestina, like other southern women of her class, was averse to the grocery store itself. Little did Chestina know it, but the days of grocery delivery service were numbered. Eudora Welty was seven years old when the first self-service Piggly Wiggly store opened in downtown Memphis.

In the summer of 1916 Clarence Saunders closed his Jefferson Street grocery store in downtown Memphis and hired a construction crew to gut the old-fashioned counters and re-create the interior. Housed in a commercial block on a busy downtown street at the center of the wholesale cotton trade, the first Piggly Wiggly store opened for business on Wednesday, September 6, 1916. Clarence Saunders, inventor of the Piggly Wiggly Self-Serving System, had reconfigured his 1,125-square-foot, traditional full-service store to compel his customers to serve themselves. By 1918 the Piggly Wiggly chain had stores in forty cities across the country, including fifteen in Memphis and five new stores in Chicago.

Piggly Wiggly has long been recognized by business historians as the most successful self-service chain of the early twentieth century. Though Piggly Wiggly stores were never as numerous as A&P outlets (with more than eleven thousand stores nationwide A&P was the largest grocery chain of the 1920s) the southern-based Piggly Wiggly certainly proved that self-service could be profitable. By 1926 sales at each Piggly Wiggly store were "worth well over twice that sold by the average A&P."[2] Self-service was an expanding phenomenon in a variety of retail settings, but the individual packaging and mass-marketing of food products made self-service particularly attractive to the grocery business. In his 1919 article in the *American Magazine*, Perry F. Nichols claimed, "There are hundreds, perhaps thousands, of these self-serve groceries scattered about the country, and new ones are springing up like dandelions in the spring."[3] Current scholarship emphasizes that grocers increasingly turned to self-service in the World War I era as a way to cut labor costs by hiring fewer clerks and eliminating delivery and credit, and explains the success of self-service as a first step toward the creation of the modern supermarket.[4] Some scholars have echoed the claims of store promoters during the World War I era that self-service enhanced consumer autonomy in an emerging mass market.[5] What has been overlooked, however, are the cultural and regional dimensions of self-service success. This chapter explores the particular appeal of self-service for grocers and customers in the segregated South, where paternalism outweighed consumer autonomy or financial considerations.

Despite the prominent role Piggly Wiggly plays in the history of self-service, the South has not been widely recognized as a region of self-service experimentation. This may be due to the prevailing concept of the South as primarily rural. While this is largely true, there was a great deal of commercial experimentation going on in southern urban centers. Most of the best-known innovations in self-service took place in the Midwest and West. In fact, Clarence Saunders was said to have been inspired to create Piggly Wiggly by a 1914 or 1915 visit to Lutey's Brothers Marketeria in Butte, Montana, where he observed the self-service grocery store the Lutey family had modeled on new cafeteria-style restaurants.[6] By 1919 there were ninety-five cities with Piggly Wiggly stores, some in nonsouthern locations, such as Bloomington, Illinois; Bridgeport, Connecticut; Cincinnati, Ohio; Denver, Colorado; and Grand Rapids, Michigan. However, although the Piggly Wiggly chain grew beyond the region, its strength remained in the South. The majority, sixty-eight stores, were in southern cities, more than a third of them in Texas.[7] Other urban southern grocers besides Saunders experimented with self-service store designs. Shoppers in Jackson, Mississippi, served themselves at the Jitney

Jungle. In Atlanta the self-service Nifty Jiffy store competed with Piggly Wiggly for consumer dollars. At least thirty-eight patents were issued for self-service stores or fixtures between 1917 and 1932—the vast majority during the 1920s. Patent applicants included merchants from fifteen different states, but there appears to have been a particular interest in self-service design among southern grocers; over 70 percent of these patents were issued to grocers living in the South.[8] What accounts for the particular appeal of self-service among southern grocers? This is an especially interesting question given the challenges they, more than grocers in other parts of the country, faced in attracting middle-class white female consumers to enter the stores and serve themselves. While merchants across the country worried about attracting the "new woman" consumer into their stores, northern merchants' complaints about female consumers were different from those of southern grocers. In the North, middle-class white women were already shoppers in groceries, and problems tended to revolve around haggling and other disruptive behavior. In the South, the chief problem was getting these middle-class white women into the groceries in the first place.[9]

That these women were white is as important as that they were middle-class. Working-class black and white women were already grocery shoppers, often in the same stores. In his study of the segregated urban South, Charles S. Johnson concludes that despite de jure segregation, day-to-day interracial consumer relations were defined by "constant uncertainty."[10] The notoriously small profit margin for selling food meant that grocers needed every customer they could attract. In practice the urban grocery store was a racially integrated commercial space where white and black, rich and poor, men and women interacted on a daily basis. Middle-class white women played a particularly strategic role, both practically and symbolically, as merchants reconfigured their store interiors and transformed the meanings of food shopping to reinforce white supremacy in the segregated New South city. In a practical sense, these women represented budget-wise consumers who would spend their dollars for cheaper brand-name products. Perhaps more importantly, defining the self-service grocery as a space of white middle-class female consumption symbolically recast what was in practice a racially integrated space. As household managers and "municipal housekeepers," "white southern 'ladies' exerted a powerful influence on an emerging culture of segregation and the meaning of whiteness in this new southern world" of urban consumption.[11] It was no accident then that Clarence Saunders's advertising strategies during the early days of his self-service experiment strategically targeted the "ladies"—members of what he called the "High Heel Society"—of Memphis. The symbolic reinterpretation of the self-service grocery through its new association with middle-class white women successfully segregated consumption in theory even as the spaces themselves remained open to and popular among diverse shoppers.

To many onlookers, including Clarence Saunders, middle-class white women's attitudes toward food shopping made the turn-of-the-century South seem an unlikely place for self-service success. "The North and the South— Is There a Difference?" asked the headline in a Piggly Wiggly advertisement as the self-service experiment got under way in Memphis, Tennessee. "Up North they said maybe a woman or a man would not be ashamed to go into the Piggly Wiggly and wait on themselves and then carry their purchases home with them, but not here in the South. Too much false pride, they said; too many folks who like to look and act like they imagine a millionaire ought to act. . . . They shook their heads and said it wouldn't work."[12] When asking whether southerners were ready to wait on themselves, the Piggly Wiggly chain echoed the concerns of other southern grocers that self-service might make good business sense but that it was fundamentally incompatible with southern culture. The idea that southerners, and particularly middle-class white women, would refuse to perform in public the menial labor of carrying their own market baskets was based on generations of consumer practice in the region. Perhaps more than their counterparts in any other region, southern grocers could not take female foot traffic for granted at the turn of the twentieth century.

Perceptions that the grocery store was an inappropriate site for ladies were widespread across the region in the early twentieth century. John Cutchins, who grew up in turn-of-the-century Richmond, Virginia, remembered that it was customary "in those days" that "the man—the head of the family—did the marketing."[13] Elizabeth O. Howse, whose father owned a grocery store in Murfreesboro, Tennessee, recalled that "all ladies called over the phone each morning for their order. It wouldn't have been considered 'nice' to get the groceries themselves."[14] William Holman explained that his family's early grocery store in Jackson, Mississippi, "was the hang-out for the males in the neighborhood. . . . Women rarely visited the store. They shopped by telephone, and groceries were delivered by wagon to their homes. At the end of the month, the husbands came to the store and paid, or were supposed to!"[15] It was a bold move, then, when Clarence Saunders banned telephones from Piggly Wiggly stores and eliminated all delivery service. "The Piggly Wiggly does not advocate telephoning, and neither does it allow telephoning. Look in any telephone directory and you will fail to find a single Piggly Wiggly store listed therein."[16] Piggly Wiggly customers would have to come inside the store and do their own shopping.

For all his bluster, Clarence Saunders was worried. His ads during Piggly Wiggly's first year of operation document his particular concerns about attracting affluent white female shoppers. At first he cast the "High Heel Society" of Memphis as snobs. Then he realized that cheaper prices alone would not convince southern ladies to serve themselves. Other chain stores also offered low prices as well as the convenience of home delivery. It would take nothing less than the reinvention of the grocery store to persuade the middle-class white women of Memphis to carry their own market baskets. Self-service grocers reinvented their stores in at least two interrelated ways, transforming the store interiors and the cultural context of food shopping.

The self-service transformation began inside the store with a complete re-organization of goods and an investment in new fixtures and finishes intended to attract middle-class white women. The neighborhood grocery store that Eudora Welty's mother avoided presented a completely different sensory experience from the self-service interior. Eudora's grocery store was dimly lit, and the nose rather than the eye made the initial assessment of its interior. The aromas arose from open packaging of bulk goods, which yielded the pungent mix of dill pickle brine, licorice, and freshly caught fish that lingered in her mind, and in the dimness she could see a jumble of mass-produced, brand-name products mingling on the shelves with locally produced items.[17] The modern housekeepers whom self-service grocers hoped to attract considered such pungent grocery odors to be unsanitary, and precarious towers of packaged goods were a liability in the self-service interior, where one wrong move by a customer might send the goods tumbling to the floor. In stark contrast to the disorganized sights and smells of old-fashioned grocery interiors, self-service interiors emphasized cleanliness and visual order.

Self-service store interiors appealed to the urban bourgeoisie because they were purposely designed for the efficient work of the modern housewife. Self-service grocers stressed themes of sanitation, order, and product quality. These themes echoed the advice of popular magazines and domestic scientists that promoted new standards of cleanliness and sanitation in the Progressive era. Once they entered the self-service store, shoppers encountered immaculate, bright, well-organized store interiors that successfully recast the cultural role of the grocery store as an emblem of modernity. For example, the perspective provided by Saunders's original patent presents the store as seen from the point of view of the customer entering the front door (see Figure 12.1).

The interior was revealed in layers as customers passed through the swinging door marked "entrance" and began to traverse the circuit created by double-sided cabinets arranged to form a winding path. Photographs of the Piggly Wiggly store, empty of shoppers, emphasize cleanliness and visual order. White tile floors gleam in the lobby. Canned goods containing like products grouped together are stacked in rigid uniformity on shelves. Modern refrigerators display perishables. Customers were attracted to the clean, orderly environment of the self-service grocery, but such an interior did not come cheaply for the grocer. Modern amenities such as electricity, refrigeration, and cash registers added substantially to merchants' overhead costs but increasingly were considered essential to attract middle-class white female trade.

The historian Edward Ayers estimates that opening a store in the turn-of-the-century South required between $500.00 and $2,000.00 of investment

Figure 12.1. Clarence Saunders filed his first patent for a "self-serving store" on October 9, 1917. Patent No. 1242872, United States Patent and Trademark Office, Washington, D.C.

capital. Independent grocery stores were probably at the lower end of that price range. In stark contrast, the Piggly Wiggly corporation created an expensive set of requirements for fixtures and finishes that would seem to have been a formula for complete corporate failure in the chronically cash-strapped South. Once Saunders patented the store interior in 1917 and began to sell Piggly Wiggly franchises to merchants in cities beyond Memphis, the company imposed standardization of building fixtures and finishes. The corporation required a whopping initial investment of $10,000.00 from any merchant who wanted to open a Piggly Wiggly store.[18] Costs might be higher if the selected store location needed upgrading. Merchants were required to heat the stores with modern steam systems rather than stove pipes, and stores had to be properly wired for lighting the lobby and display cabinets. The company was particular about the specifications for electrical work, providing detailed instructions about lighting the interior and requiring installation by professional electricians. The minimum cost for store equipment alone (not counting installation costs or the price of merchandise) in 1918 was $3470.78.[19] The cost of starting a Piggly Wiggly, then, would seem to have put self-service beyond the reach of most southern merchants. In addition, the stores did not include residential space, so there was no room for the grocer to house a family and thus combine the costs of home and business. Yet the chain spread quickly to southern cities beyond Memphis.

Beyond the improvements in store fixtures and finishes, self-service designs dramatically reconfigured the social relations of grocery stores in ways that appealed to middle-class white women customers. The openness of the interior spaces and the dependence of customers on full service by clerks made old-fashioned grocery stores spaces for social interaction. A visit to L. Christian & Company's Grocery Store on Main Street in downtown Richmond was "really a social event of considerable magnitude, as one always met many friends, not to mention the popular proprietors," John A. Cutchins fondly remembered.[20] However, southern grocery stores had long been distinguished as spaces of white male, not female, sociability. Elizabeth Howse remembered that "many of daddy's cronies spent a good deal of time in the store. This being before any local clubs were organized, the store proved an enjoyable place to spend a pleasant hour or two."[21] Memphis grocer Duke Bowers tried to broaden his clientele by removing the bar that made his grocery store a males-only space. Doing this was an effort to reassure mothers that it was safe for their children to run errands to his stores.[22] Patents for the new self-service stores of the 1920s removed bars, pot-bellied stoves, and cane-back chairs and reconfigured store interiors to encourage movement rather than conversation. The new store interiors were not simply cleaner and more modern; they also fundamentally reshaped the traditional social relations of the grocery store.

Quoted in a national trade magazine, one Piggly Wiggly manager explained that self-service appealed to middle-class white women because it reduced their interaction with male clerks. "A woman does not like to run a gauntlet of clerks looking her over when she enters a store. This is sometimes the case in stores where the clerks are not busy and loll over the counter sizing up the ladies." Emphasizing the particular advantages of his chain's store design, he explained that "in Piggly Wiggly stores, this cannot happen for no one but the checker is in front and his back is usually to the door." The historian Tracey Deutsch has argued that self-service chain stores were popular among Chicago consumers, particularly women, because they defused the social tensions of small neighborhood stores where interaction between grocer and customer could be contentious, based on disagreements over the price or quality of goods or the stress of hassles over credit.[23] Though Eudora Welty had fond memories of her interactions with the neighborhood grocer, Elizabeth Howse remembered her father telling her about grocers "who put sand in the sugar, who sold oats after the bugs were in, who got a man drunk before trying to trade with him. . . . 'You'd be surprised, daughter,' he would say, 'how many people cheat.'"[24] Saunders emphasized the idea that self-service liberated the customer from the tyranny of the grocer. Prices were clearly marked for each item, so there was no need to negotiate a deal. He observed, "Each customer is allowed to make his or her own selections of merchandise according to their own bent and inclination, without, by argument, persuasion or otherwise, being constrained to buy something that possibly he or she does not want to buy."[25]

Self-service store patents show that grocers had many practical concerns about how to make these stores work effectively. They were worried about how to avoid the potential confusion of women who entered the store to find specific items among all of the mass-produced possibilities on the shelves, how to make self-service work in the incredibly narrow store interiors of existing commercial blocks, and how to prevent shoplifting. All of the patents consisted of interior designs for creating pathways through stores that were small and narrow. Robert Tribble of Rolling Fork, Mississippi, explained that his path was devised "to keep the body of purchasers moving substantially continuously in the same direction in order to avoid confusion and congestion."[26] Merchants were especially concerned that customers not be confused about how to find particular products for fear that if they were, they would not return to the store. The patents tended to divide the valuable real estate of the store interior into similar sections: an entry lobby where shoppers could obtain market baskets for collecting their selections; single points of entry and exit (typically controlled by a turnstile or gate) just beyond the lobby; a small stockroom at the back of the store; and a checkout counter staffed by a single clerk. Some grocers experimented with track or rail systems that made it possible for customers to slide heavy baskets without lifting the full weight of merchandise. Different arrangements for price-tagging systems made it possible for customers to easily identify the cost of specific items. William McCarty of Jackson, Mississippi, wanted to overcome the disadvantage of self-service store designs that hid customers from the view of clerks. "Such a store is a standing invitation for the operations of professional shoplifters," he declared.[27]

The most common and striking feature of the patents, however, is their consistent experimentation with one-way path designs. Saunders was adamant that the path through Piggly Wiggly was a one-way street (see Figure 12.2). A Memphis newspaper ad declared to novice self-servers in advance of the store opening that "there will be no backward movements in the Piggly Wiggly—no turning around or back-stepping."[28] At first glance, the practicality of the one-way path seems central. Patents were designed to address the spatial constraints of existing commercial block buildings—small, deep, but narrow spaces on downtown lots. Creating an open path accessible from multiple directions in such confined spaces definitely presented some practical problems, and so the one-way path might be understood simply as a convenient design solution for refitting existing store spaces. The efficiency with which the one-way path enlisted the labor of customers to move goods through the store certainly appealed to merchants influenced by scientific management as a modern way of doing business. In fact, Saunders described his design for Piggly Wiggly as a scientific system, and company photographs documenting Piggly Wiggly store openings suggest that even in crowded stores, shopping in the Piggly Wiggly was an orderly experience (see Figure 12.3).

Beyond its practical appeal, the social aspect of the one-way path helps to explain its particular attraction for southern merchants. The one-way path meant that self-service shopping was a controlled process based on the authority of the merchant. It was a modernized urban method of imposing the traditional paternalism that had been practiced by the general-store merchant in more personalized rural contexts. Therefore, it is important to go beyond functional considerations of the problems merchants faced in retrofitting existing store spaces to consider the cultural meanings of the one-way path in the context of the segregated marketplace of the urban New South.

In her study of segregated consumption in the New South, the historian Grace Hale explains that in the rural general store, merchants helped to maintain white supremacy "by combining the old racial inferiority of plantations and paternalism with the new consuming world." In the general store, merchants controlled both what African Americans bought and how they experienced consumption. Rituals of deference through consumer negotiations reinforced racial hierarchies. However, the mingling of strangers in an urban context broke down traditional mechanisms for enforcing these racial hierarchies. "In an increasingly anonymous world where class status depended upon appearances, this uncertainty endangered the very meaning of white racial identity." Segregation was a modern, rational strategy for maintaining white supremacy in an increasingly mobile society based on cash relationships rather than locally maintained, traditional social hierarchies.[29] However, the secret to

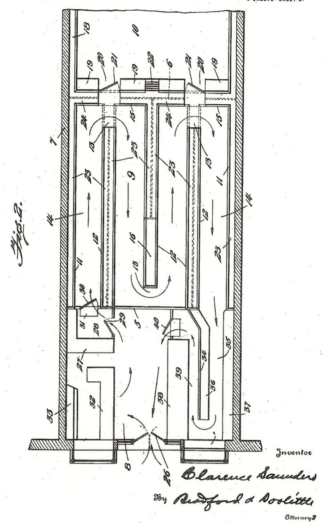

C. SAUNDERS.
SELF SERVING STORE.
APPLICATION FILED OCT. 21, 1916.

1,242,872.

Patented Oct. 9, 1917.
3 SHEETS—SHEET 2.

Inventor

Clarence Saunders

By Bradford & Doolittle

Attorneys

Figure 12.2. Saunders's first patent regulated the one-way path with a series of swinging doors. Within the first year Saunders perfected his design by replacing the swinging doors with turnstiles, befitting the machinelike efficiency of self-service. Adopting the turnstile as a corporate symbol, Piggly Wiggly published a monthly newsletter, *Turnstile*, whose masthead proclaimed that it was "devoted to the interest of scientific merchandising." Patent No. 1242872, United States Patent and Trademark Office, Washington, D.C.

Figure 12.3. In April 1920 the first Piggly Wiggly store in Lexington, Kentucky, opened downtown at the corner of Broadway and Short Streets. This photograph captures the integrated shopping experience of the self-service store. Two African American shoppers mingle with the store's white patrons. An African American shopper begins her one-way path, selecting onions in the first aisle, while another completes the self-service process in the check-out line. "1920 Interior of a Piggly Wiggly," Selected Images of Lexington (1930–50), 96PA101, Audio-Visual Archives, University of Kentucky Libraries, Lexington.

self-service success was in high foot traffic and volume sales. Because food shopping was a daily necessity for everybody, grocery stores were among the most racially integrated shopping spaces.

Self-service stores appealed to a variety of southern consumers because they depersonalized the act of shopping. Middle-class white women liked not having to negotiate the traditional male culture of the grocery store. For African Americans, the sociologist Charles S. Johnson found in his study of the segregated marketplace that "Negroes report that stores in which customers serve themselves offer fewer discriminatory practices than those in which customers must await the personal attention of a white clerk. The question of precedence of whites over Negroes does not intrude in self-service; it escapes another practice which Negroes find obnoxious—that of being offered inferior goods laid aside especially for the purpose."[30] However, it was not necessarily the white store designers' goal to create less discriminatory shopping environments.

To understand the cultural transformation at work in the self-service grocery store, we must look beyond the interior spaces of the grocery store to the very public act of food shopping and its long-established cultural role. If grocery stores had traditionally been the hangouts of idle males, food shopping had always been a daily necessity and a chore often performed by black domestic servants.[31] According to Elizabeth Howse, for example, Kank, the family's African American cook, regularly performed the marketing early every morning. "In the spring, before she came to work; she had been all over town to see where the best greens were to be found, or, if the berries were ripe enough for a pie, or if anyone had a fat rabbit or chicken for sale."[32] In practical terms, food shopping was time-consuming work at the turn of the century, and one had to get up early to get the best choices. Along with the problem of actually entering a grocery store, a middle-class white woman carrying a market basket brimming over with the raw materials of a meal directly conflicted with social construction of race, class, and gender in the segregated New South. It was appropriate work for a domestic servant but not for a white lady. Yet it is also clear that though southern ladies eschewed carrying their own market baskets, they were responsible for food purchases in the urban consumer household. The telephone made it possible to do the regular chore of food shopping without the necessity of going into a grocery store or carrying a market basket home through the public thoroughfare.

It is useful here to think in terms of the scholar James Carrier's argument that shopping, even something as mundane and seemingly methodical as food shopping, is a cultural activity as much as it is an economic one. Shoppers in a mass industrial context personalize undifferentiated mass-produced products by choosing particular commodities to buy. This can be understood as the cultural work of "appropriation—the work of making a personal possession of the anonymous commodity." Grocery shoppers transform the undifferentiated mass of commodities stacked on the shelves by choosing the particular products they desire. Carrier evaluates two different types of food shoppers to illustrate the varied meanings of shopping in a mass industrial context. The "Wise Shopper" devotes considerable time and resources to studying the marketplace in order to make the most informed selection of goods. The "Personal Shopper" selects goods by establishing a quasi-personal relationship with the seller, transforming commodities into personal possessions by associating shopping with sociability. In the 1920s sociability was eliminated in the self-service store, as grocers recast the act of shopping. Practically speaking, of course, the daily chore of food shopping continued to function as an economic exchange directly tied to the family budget. However, self-service grocers presented shopping in a stylish and modern self-service environment as a new kind of cultural work.[33]

The particular meanings of self-service food shopping in the culture of segregation are best illustrated by a 1920 ad for Piggly Wiggly stores in Atlanta. The ad offered a familiar list of reasons why "hundreds of thousands" of housewives in Atlanta preferred to buy their groceries at Piggly Wiggly every day:

They know they get full value in quality and quantity.

They know they can select exactly what they want, not what somebody wants to hand them. No one to persuade, no one to suggest, no one to recommend what they shall or shall not buy.

They know that at Piggly Wiggly they will not have to wait until Mrs. Extra Fussy, or Mrs. Can't Quit Talking, or Mrs. Perpetual Grouch have been waited on.

They know that they save money. They know that they save time.

They know that they get clean goods from a clean store.[34]

Getting quality merchandise at a good value, saving time and money, shopping in a clean store—these were typical expectations of middle-class white women consumers by the 1920s. However, what makes this ad particularly distinctive in a southern context is the idea proclaimed in its title: "The Aristocracy of the Piggly Wiggly Basket." A nicely dressed, though rather old-fashioned-looking, white woman carries a market basket brimming with her purchases. The concept of aristocracy echoed an antebellum past associating new forms of middle-class consumption with the affluence of a romanticized planter elite. The new urban middle class built its cultural authority on a fiction of continuity between the antebellum plantation household and the new consumer-oriented domesticity.[35] In the culture of segregation, the aristocracy of the market basket construed self-service as at once modern and traditional, democratic and paternalistic. The act of shopping itself became a marketing tool, and Piggly Wiggly, with its emphasis on the pleasures of choice in the marketplace, transformed the mundane and everyday practice of food shopping into a stylish and liberating activity of middle-class white women. The new aristocracy of the market basket redefined the cultural work of food shopping from a menial chore appropriately performed by black domestics to a respectable activity for bourgeois white women.

Surviving sources make it easier to evaluate merchants' desires and attitudes than to understand what women thought about self-service. Saunders especially blamed the arrogance of middle-class southerners unwilling to serve themselves, but there were good reasons why women shoppers might find disadvantages in self-service besides the inconvenience of no delivery. The cash-and-carry policy probably discouraged shoppers who depended on credit at the neighborhood grocery to get them through to the next paycheck. Piggly Wiggly's policy of carrying only name-brand, nationally advertised products may have provided the customer products of reliable quality and "protection against substitution," but it also denied access to locally produced products that had been familiar to many customers.[36] Store policies also prohibited selling parts of packages. "In other words, if an item is to be sold at 8c per pound you will not be able to buy a dime's worth or 25c worth," a rule that some shoppers may have found challenging to the limits of their food budgets.[37]

Despite the difficulty of locating actual consumers in the surviving sources, evidence suggests that merchants did not dictate policies or design their stores in a social vacuum. Interaction between grocer and customer in the vernacular design process that marked the early years of tinkering to make self-service work suggests some of the ways that women may have influenced store design before corporate standards were solidified. In the early stages of operation, the design process allowed for relatively rapid response to consumer demand. During the first week of operation Saunders announced store rules that required customers to purchase market baskets for three cents apiece at the entrance to the store or to bring their own baskets.[38] A few weeks later a Piggly Wiggly ad explained that market baskets are "furnished FREE in which you may collect the different articles you desire to purchase." Initial ads had emphasized that only customers who meant business should visit the store—no sightseers allowed. Curious crowds made this rule impossible to enforce, so Saunders relented: "If you want to visit the Piggly Wiggly just to look through and see the system without buying anything, you will be welcome to call, and nobody will ask you why you didn't buy anything." Traffic flow had been a problem, so "[a] change in the checking system will be in effect Monday morning which will relieve the congestion that has sometimes resulted in the last aisle."

About a year after the Piggly Wiggly opened, Saunders explicitly requested the assistance of his customers in perfecting the way the store worked, offering cash prizes for the winning ideas in two categories, best suggestion for store improvement and responses to the theme "Why the Piggly Wiggly Is All Right."[39] In addition to the four top winners in each category, fifty-seven other participants were each awarded one dollar for their helpful suggestions. Interestingly, the majority of award winners were female shoppers. Sixty-seven percent (thirty-eight) of the prizewinners were women, and 33 percent (nineteen) were men. Of the eight top prizewinners, six were women and two were men. Mrs. G. Greif won the ten-dollar first prize for best suggestion in store improvement for her idea that a list of alphabetized items be placed "at the beginning of every aisle." She explained, "I know from my own experience that it is hard to find every item one wants in such a large stock as you handle." This problem was echoed by Miss Jeanette Kemp, who won five dollars for her second-place suggestion requesting that customers be supplied with a store directory "so that the goods could be found promptly," because "it is a little inconvenient to find the articles which I want." Frederick Mayo was the first-prize winner for his explanation of "Why the Piggly Wiggly Is All Right." His response actually assumed that his wife was the primary grocery shopper and presented the point of view of a male head of household. He particularly liked the fact that self-service had shifted the food-shopping responsibility from domestic servant to housewife, believing that the wife had greater incentive to pay attention to the family budget. He said, "The prime advantage of PIGGLY WIGGLY is that it makes the women market for themselves. Before the PIGGLY WIGGLY the servant did the buying and the knocking down, without regard to price or quality she bought in jumbo quantities and 'toated' in proportion. It is no wonder banks prohibited overdrafts. Friend Husband could'nt [*sic*] stand the pressure." In addition to presenting shopping as economic work, his response signaled his attitudes about shopping as cultural work. Self-service was preferable to full service because his wife would not have to wait her turn. According to Mayo, "She can reflect and select without interruption or embarrassment or waste or time. No first come first served here. It is the only place in the world where everybody is waited on at once."[40] Regardless of her actual status, every shopper could envision herself a member of the aristocracy of the market basket when she was not compelled to wait for service.

Evidence suggests that responses of some women defied the expectations and goals of store designers. Store patents document a variety of experiments at controlling the traffic flow of customers who stopped to chat or came to the store with specific items in mind and refused to complete the full circuit. In 1934 Jitney Jungle in Jackson, Mississippi (archrival of Piggly Wiggly), opened the first of a "new generation of stores" as the company experimented with a new supermarket concept. The store provided a measure of how successful self-service grocers had been in reconfiguring not only their grocery interiors but also the cultural role of food shopping. Like the first generation of self-service stores patented by southern grocers in the 1920s, the new supermarket displayed the newest technological innovations. However, unlike the earliest experiments in self-service devoted to machinelike efficiency, the new Jitney Jungle catered to the comfort of its middle-class white women customers. Company founders claimed that "it was the second of its type in the country to be air-conditioned." In addition, "[t]here were also other fringe benefits, including the first rest room for women customers in any of our stores; and there were chairs for youngsters, assuming the kids could sit still while their mothers shopped!" In a striking transformation of the once male-dominated grocery space, the new store was fully feminized. "Of course the store became a super social institution, where ladies made appointments with each other to visit, drink a 'Coke,' and buy their bags of groceries." Women considered the self-service Jitney Jungle to be a social gathering place rather than an efficient selling apparatus. Their goal seemed to be to linger rather than to move through the store. "Jitney shopping became a social ritual, for which ladies bought cotton frocks, which they actually called 'jitney dresses.' No longer was the grocery store the haven of the idle male. It had become the hangout of the women!"[41] Most of the self-service store patents had emphasized the importance of moving large volumes of people efficiently through the self-service store, and this new emphasis on the leisurely choice as an advantage of self-service may actually reflect the impact of middle-class white female consumers. Certainly the women who wore "jitney dresses" signaled a new attitude among white middle-class women about serving themselves at the grocery store.

The Piggly Wiggly corporate newsletter featured a story in 1923 that suggests some of the ways that southern women internalized a message of self-service food shopping as a new kind of fantasy experience—a new kind of cultural work. This story shows that the idea of the aristocracy of the market basket appealed to white women who were not necessarily members of the new middle class but who identified with the concept: "Last week a shower was given by the nurses of St. Thomas' Hospital, Nashville, Tennessee, in honor of Miss Ella Belle Tucker, a graduate nurse who is to be married to Mr. G. B. Greer, manager of Piggly Wiggly Store No. 12, on January 24, 1923. On arrival Miss Tucker found that a complete Piggly Wiggly store had been arranged with a turnstile, counters, etc. She was presented with a basket upon entering the turnstile and was told to help herself to the beautiful gifts placed on the counters by her workers and friends. Just over the door a sign which read: The Road to Happiness Through Piggly Wiggly."[42] These professional, wage-earning women acted out the fantasy of self-service shopping in the workplace. The St. Thomas nurses represented a new generation of wage-earning southern women who did not fit traditional definitions of southern femininity. In the first three decades of the twentieth century, for example, rural "white women showed the highest migration rates to Nashville while black women showed the second highest rates."[43] Some of these rural migrants attended new business colleges and acquired jobs as clerical workers. Others went to work as teachers in expanding public school systems or became factory workers. These new wage-earning women offered both challenge and opportunity for southern merchants. Self-service grocers worked particularly hard to cast these women as a new, more modern generation of sensible shoppers compared to their old-fashioned mothers, bound to the phone at home. However, this fantasy of self-service also domesticated the new professional woman. It is interesting to note that the context of the nurses' shopping fantasy was a bridal shower. In national advertising campaigns of the 1920s, Piggly Wiggly particularly emphasized the wedding as a turning point in the responsibilities of new young wives just setting out to learn the business of housekeeping. In this context, self-service food shopping was portrayed as an educational tool for budgeting and meal planning. The bridal-shower narrative helped to contain the professional women within the context of domesticity.

To understand the attraction of self-service for middle-class white women in the South, we must go beyond historical explanations that focus primarily on the business practices of merchants to consider the historically specific cultural context in which the self-service grocery first appeared. Piggly Wiggly's experiments in store design and its distinctive business strategies reflect the chain's origins in the segregated New South. Clarence Saunders and other self-service grocers spent large sums to remake the commercial landscape with new attention to the concerns of middle-class white female shoppers. Self-service store owners reinvented the grocery store in both material and symbolic ways. They created new store interiors that transformed the social relations of the old-fashioned, male-dominated grocery and successfully recast the cultural role of the grocery store as an emblem of modernity for the stylish and businesslike white woman of the New South. While the depersonalization of food shopping appealed to African American consumers and store spaces remained integrated in practice, local and national advertising campaigns created new meanings for food shopping as a consumer fantasy and an appropriate activity for southern ladies. One did not actually have to be a wealthy woman to participate in the fantasy. By making their stores appeal to middle-class white women, southern self-service grocers symbolically feminized grocery shopping through the invention of a new aristocracy of the market basket.

Chapter 13
Making Markets Marxist? The East European Grocery Store from Rationing to Rationality to Rationalizations

Patrick Hyder Patterson

As revealed in the new historiography of modern business and agricultural production, the food chains that linked farms, factories, stores, and shoppers in Western Europe and North America became increasingly intricate during the twentieth century: farming was industrialized, commodities optimized, processing Taylorized, products specialized, distribution rationalized, advertising customized, retailing standardized. In addition, with the growing movement of capital, corporations, commodities, and technologies across state borders, the system as a whole was, at least in some respects, globalized. Plenty of local variety remained, to be sure, as such innovations were introduced to different degrees at different times and in different places. Despite their widening reach, these systematized features of the modern food trade have been linked in both the popular and the historical imagination with businesses in the classic sites of market economics, and especially with the United States, an association that has fueled numerous controversies about the costs of Americanization. The linkage has been so strong and so definitive, in fact, that such organizational practices are often taken to *constitute* the "free-market" food system, and vice versa.[1] All this encourages us to think of what has happened to the production and consumption of food over the course of the past hundred years or so as a consummate product of liberal economics.

So far, so capitalist. But the association is deceptively incomplete. In fact, there were little-noticed socialist analogues to these developments, as systems of food provisioning in the socialist societies of Eastern Europe underwent a spectacular transition during the period from 1945 to 1975. After an initial phase of extreme scarcity and persistent rationing following World War II, the governments of the new communist states were able to achieve, albeit with difficulty and with many setbacks, what must be acknowledged as a dramatic transformation in living standards, agricultural production, food distribution, and commercial practice. By the 1970s some of the more prosperous East European countries had created systems of retail food distribution that (at least in larger urban areas) emphasized the establishment of inviting, consumer-oriented, and well-stocked supermarkets and large self-service grocery stores. The new theories, styles, and practices of grocery sales thus bore more than a passing resemblance to the confidently and enthusiastically "modern" systems that had come to characterize the Affluent Society of the postwar West.[2]

This outcome was, in some respects, quite surprising. In their effort to distinguish socialist society from its ideological competitors in the capitalist world, communist party officials and government administrators routinely articulated the idea that they were pioneering a new, distinctive form of "socialist commerce." Grocery retailing was a key part of that enterprise. Despite its seemingly banal and quotidian nature—or more accurately, I argue, precisely *because* of that everyday significance—grocery sales implicated critical aspects of economic policy at the highest levels: socialism had shifted ultimate responsibility for provisioning to the state, and the ongoing (and not always successful) effort to keep food and other necessities on the shelves was a government activity that connected most directly and most frequently with the lived experience of ordinary citizens. What was happening in the stores can thus tell us a great deal about what happened to communism: its initial fixation on the difficult task of securing even a bare subsistence standard, its frustrated attempts to move beyond that modest level to match or even outpace the Good Life of the postwar West, its occasional dalliances with the pleasures of Western-style "consumer society," and its eventual collapse in the face of ongoing difficulties in the economic contest with capitalism.

The historical record of Hungary, Yugoslavia, and the German Democratic Republic, countries that led the way toward a more consumer-friendly socialism, shows that the architects of socialist commerce and food policy welcomed the new forms of self-service shopping, and later the supermarket, as a way of constructing what they saw from a Marxist-Leninist perspective as a highly rational, modern, and efficient food distribution network, one appealingly amenable to technocratic management and planning.[3] What was called rationalization or modernization in state-socialist parlance often meant, in fact, Westernization, as the methods of capitalist retailing were studied, analyzed, and imported. Given the power of U.S. business models, this in turn often implied no small degree of Americanization. Not at issue here, however, is globalization in its strictest sense, that is, expanding multinational coordination of business ownership and governance (a sense that helpfully keeps the term from scooping up almost anything that involves a border crossing). Indeed, the communist interlude represented a tremendous disruption in that dynamic. Rather, what we see in these cases is a less formal process: the transnational transfer of culture and practice.

Though the self-service system built in the socialist East never managed to mirror the phenomenal spread and elaboration of the American supermarket model (indeed, even capitalist Western Europe lagged well behind that), it did take root to a remarkable extent. These successes in delivering an impressive (and expanding) range of food and grocery items in convenient, appealing retail settings served in some ways to strengthen communist authority and build public support. With time, however, the self-service store and the supermarket also fed the growth of a lively consumer culture, one cultivated by socialist businesses and marketing specialists and, in turn, embraced and given new forms by ordinary consumers. The further this culture moved away from the levers of government and party power—and it did move in that direction— the more it proved hard to control and, ultimately, subversive of the socialist system. Enterprise managers and government officials in the communist states thus found themselves shifting, as it were, from rationing to rationality to rationalizations: first battling real deprivation and hardship in the early postwar years, then attempting to optimize outcomes in conditions of both rapid economic growth and enduring scarcity, and finally struggling to justify the prevalence of dubious, seemingly capitalist forms on the grounds that these business practices were in essence system-neutral, and not the carriers of undesirable behaviors and values from the West.

Contrary to such protestations, the new ways of shopping and spending and eating did indeed make socialist consumers resemble their counterparts abroad in important ways. When institutions and techniques were borrowed from the West, as the supermarket and the self-service grocery undeniably were, it proved impossible to strip off entirely the cultural accretions that came with them. The process was not a matter of straightforward transplantation, of course, and it would be a mistake to deny the many local particularities that were at work. While there is little evidence of any distinctively and genuinely "socialist supermarket," the economic constraints and policy preferences of communist governance clearly did shape and limit the use of self-service in the various settings in which it was deployed. The aim of this essay, however, is instead to call attention to the critical international and comparative dimensions of the problems at hand.[4] And for that larger history of food, business, and the food business, the experience of socialist Europe proves extraordinarily important: it allows us to discover and trace the spread of what I identify here as a common, transnational "culture of the supermarket," one marked by characteristic elements and values that were by no means exclusive to the capitalist system, although they were certainly present in and hospitable to it.[5]

From Rationality to Rationalizations: Making Sense of the Supermarket in Marxist Society

The theoretical approaches of state socialism conceived of commerce as a practical application of Marxism's economic "science," grounded in an ideology of rationality and empiricism. Accordingly, business and trade were understood as something to be planned, measured, controlled, and adjusted as required to serve the overarching aims of the socialist society. The ends of commerce included not just strictly economic matters but the broader concerns of party ideology and social policy as well. Retail sales came at the end of a long chain of planning choices, and thus the interests of the retailing sector had to compete with a host of other planning desiderata, including, for example, a long-range agenda to shift production from agriculture to the communists' preferred industrial orientation; support of underdeveloped towns and regions through the build-up of manufacturing capacity; preservation of full employment; maintenance of an egalitarian wage policy; elimination of class distinctions and other forms of "social differentiation"; provision of goods at prices manageable for the vast majority of the population; and other similar considerations. Accordingly, communist formulations tended, especially in their more orthodox variants, to relegate sales and distribution to a secondary status as tools for the implementation of communist decisions about other, ostensibly more important, economic matters. In good Marxist fashion, those first-order decisions typically arose from a focus on production rather than consumption. Encountered in this context, retailing received a decidedly instrumentalist treatment, as a sphere of activity through which the aims of the planners could be realized.

What could stores and sellers and ads do for the national economy and the effort to "build socialism"? As a matter of both theory and practice, this was the question that often lay behind the state-socialist approach to retail commerce. Although distribution and sales functions did come to be regarded as integral parts of larger economic processes, and although they did, with time, receive ample and often quite sophisticated attention from state officials and business-enterprise leaders, the world of commerce never had pride of place. It remained distinctly subordinate, and often somewhat suspect. With some notable (though partial) exceptions in Yugoslavia and to a lesser extent in Hungary after those two countries' market-oriented reforms in the mid-to-late 1960s, retailers in socialist states did not enjoy the autonomy that would have been required to raise consumption to a more prominent position in the organization of national economic life. Even when they did attempt to react to consumers' wishes and preferences, they typically lacked the economic and political leverage to make producers and manufacturers respond in turn. The potential for sales did not drive the system; instead, the system governed the potential for sales.

It is therefore surprising, given the prevailing image of communist hostility to the iniquities of Western liberal economics, that the historical record of state socialism and its commercial enterprises reveals an increasingly keen interest in the acquisition of skills and practices that had traditionally been associated with "business," that quintessentially capitalist enterprise. There was, it turned out, plenty of common ground: because Marxist-Leninist economic management showed such a pronounced preference for the rational, the quantifiable, and the scientific, those retailing techniques and methods of sales and promotion that held the prospect of increased efficiency and the further "rationalization" of the economy could and did spark the interest of administrators and enterprise leaders. With their impressive record of success abroad,[6] the self-service grocery store and the supermarket seemed to offer precisely that. The Yugoslav trade journal *Supermarket* thus noted admiringly that "when [Clarence] Saunders, from Memphis in the United States, opened the Piggly Wiggly Store in 1916—the first grocery store with self-service—he did not even have an inkling of what that sales method would mean for modern commerce."[7] Reflecting on Yugoslavia's two decades of self-service sales in 1976, the journal concluded that these techniques had been nothing less than a "revolution" in shopkeeping, offering

the shortest stay in the store, the greatest selection of products on display, the maximum opportunity to get close to the products, complete information about the product, the possibility to get products according to the shopper's wishes and needs, excellent presentation of products in the sales place, a good orientation to opportunities for purchase of products because they are arranged by groups and displayed so as to be maximally visible on the shelves, packaging in the role of the sales-clerk, a great reduction of the cost of doing business, simpler sales, better utilization of space in the store, etc.—all of which has a positive influence on the cost of the products.[8]

Though they originated in the disreputable capitalist West, these commercial technologies promised so much potential economic gain—with so little apparent political threat—that they could be eagerly adopted and adapted as welcome innovations in "socialist commerce." Verging on the hagiographic, *Supermarket* concluded that Saunders "deserves to be recognized" for his trailblazing role in all this: "He changed what was *known* into what was a *reality*, without which today we could not even imagine the modern distribution that has already become a part of ourselves."[9]

Those most deeply involved in socialist retailing promoted the self-service grocery store and the supermarket as, above all, breakthroughs in the pursuit of economic efficiency, both at the level of the individual store and business enterprise and, more broadly, at the level of the national economy. Specifically, the self-service grocery store and the supermarket appeared to offer a way to sell off more quickly and completely the products of socialist planning in agriculture and manufacturing, and to lower substantially the cost of sales.

Another frequently cited advantage of the self-service store and the supermarket was the prospect of marked productivity gains through labor savings. There was, however, a potential (if largely unacknowledged) problem with the labor-saving aspects of the new retail forms, since they could, in theory at least, cut against the interests of the working class by eliminating positions in the retail sector. While the pursuit of efficiency was a point on which specialists in both capitalist and socialist commerce could agree to some extent, the overlap ended when it came to handling (or even being willing to incur in the first place) the social costs of mechanization, standardization, and other forms of cost-cutting "rationality." In practice, despite the enticements of higher productivity and economies of scale, socialist retailing tended to sacrifice efficiency to the continuity of the tried-and-seemingly-true, to workplace stability, and to the maintenance of networks of broadly distributed, small-sized (and low-productivity) local outlets that were very near shoppers' homes. The supermarket could therefore seem a rather daring novelty, and one that did not immediately appeal to all suppliers or their customers.

Yet the new food-store systems did promise to deliver big benefits for the wider public. A chief advantage of the new forms of grocery sales, and one cited frequently in the literature of socialist grocery retailing, was the apparent savings in time for shoppers. (Here again, there were clear points of correspondence with Western representations of these business forms.) East European proponents of the self-service store and the supermarket continually portrayed the introduction of these new methods as a great boon to socialist worker-consumers, and especially to working-class women, who were entering the labor force in increasing numbers and who found themselves with tremendous demands on their time as they struggled to balance the responsibilities of both the job site and the home.

Socialist commercial specialists also stressed that the new retail forms could and should be part of an integrated planning approach to meeting the needs of ordinary citizens. In this respect, the socialist experience differed significantly from that of the West, and particularly of the United States, where the rise of the supermarket in its classic form—a vast, free-standing building surrounded by parking areas—was driven by the triumph of the automobile and suburban sprawl over patterns of more concentrated residential building along public transportation lines.[10] In contrast to this *laissez-faire* and *laissez-construire* model, socialist planners had the power to put the people in dense block developments with populations large enough to justify (if not always to sustain in purely economic terms) the construction of a supermarket. The urbanism of the supermarket in Eastern Europe thus advanced along lines quite unlike its classic American antecedents.

Government officials could treat the new retail system as a way to achieve other social goals as well. Organized in large, multi-store chains and run by enterprise managers in a centralized fashion (with ample input from state and party authorities), the new self-service stores and supermarkets also functioned as venues for the explicit propaganda of government policies and to communicate with the public with regard to the state's broader aims in the realms of health, education, culture, and economic development. They could be, in effect, arms of the state and the party.[11] Here again, the new retail forms were conceived of as a tool of the further rationalization of the country's social and economic structure.

In much the same way, the modern grocery store also served as an important site for reaching customers with messages designed to introduce, explain, and promote the use of the new products of socialist industry. Here, too, administrators could conceive of the supermarket as the final link in a continuous chain of carefully planned, managed, and integrated agricultural and industrial operations.

To a remarkable extent, the thoroughgoing changes that accompanied the introduction of the large self-service grocery and the supermarket were understood (or arguably, rationalized away) as being fundamentally in harmony with socialist values. Nothing that was tainted as inherently capitalist, the business specialists suggested, would have to be borrowed in these transactions. Rather, from this perspective, the adoption of the supermarket and self-service models entailed only the transfer of technical, transparent, and system-neutral features—ideologically all quite safe, it was implied—that could be readily implemented in socialist commerce with no threat to the principles and goals of socialism.

Values! Values! Values! Toward a Transnational Culture of the Supermarket

The dominant tendency in contemporary academic analyses of consumption and shopping has been to approach modern retailing methods not just as manifestations but as instruments of an aggressively expansive capitalist world-system. Yet with regard to the fundamental issues of ownership and governance, the supermarket and the self-service grocery actually proved, in practice, to be institutions that could make the jump to the socialist setting with little difficulty. In this respect—which is, from the point of view of political economy at least, the most critical—there was nothing inherently "capitalist" about them. But were these, in fact, system-neutral forms when it came to the *culture* and *values* of the broader society, as the socialist planners and business experts also seemed to assume?

The addition of new inquiries that reach beyond the high-capitalist core now makes it possible to speak, if perhaps tentatively in some respects, of a late twentieth-century "culture of the supermarket," one that arose in the conditions of mature capitalism but proved able to cross borders to less developed societies and even, in many respects, to span the formidable East-West divide. As the evidence from Eastern Europe demonstrates, this transnational culture was not specific to capitalism, although in important ways it was, I conclude, more readily reconciled with capitalist economics and production relations. Especially for that reason, the culture of the supermarket would prove fateful for the history of socialism.

At the outset, it is useful to distinguish popular culture from business culture in a more narrow sense, though the two were certainly interdependent. Not all aspects of grocery sales have had a substantial relationship to the experience of shopper-consumers; some have, in fact, little connection with popular culture. Our concern here is with those practices of large-scale grocery sales that tended to generate and reinforce among consumers a set of *commonly held* and *collectively expressed* values, attitudes, beliefs, images, and ideas about themselves, their lives, their society, and their government. It is this shared, expressive quality of grocery consumption that can endow everyday acts such as browsing the aisles, choosing from alternative offerings, and discovering new products with a social and historical significance well beyond what a casual and superficial glance at the phenomenon might suggest. This communicative potential is, in other words, what made modern grocery shopping part of a genuine public *culture* of consumption.

The supermarket is a retail form with just this sort of power. It is not culturally "empty." More than a mere design for selling goods, it has the capacity to shape experiences and to create values—the capacity, that is, to contribute to the construction of a popular culture.[12] To a remarkable extent it has succeeded. Even where it has proven difficult or unprofitable to introduce "true" supermarkets—enormous structures with hundreds of square meters of sales area, carrying thousands of items—the supermarket *style* has, in effect, filtered downward and outward, shaping the world of self-service stores more generally. Thus the culture of the supermarket can be present even when the stores in question are more modest—a fact with major implications for Eastern (and Western) Europe, where the proliferation of the supermarket in its classic, grand-scale form has lagged behind the American pattern. There is, of course, always considerable slippage between the culture that advertisers and retailers hope to create and the one that shoppers make for themselves. Nevertheless, we can profit enormously from examining the values, ideas, attitudes, and behaviors that the supermarket generally *seeks* and *tends* to produce.

What, then, were the elements of this culture of the supermarket? What common understandings have been expressed by consumers—and promoted by retailers and advertisers—through their engagement with the new world of modern food shopping?

The Transformation of the Feminine Domain

Grocery shopping remained a strongly gendered activity in the early decades of the supermarket era, and elaboration of this linkage was itself an important element of the transnational cultural pattern identified here. Some of this was a matter of business strategy. As Tracey Deutsch has shown, for example, the classic American supermarket imagery that had emerged by 1950 resulted from "grocers' desire to build a new gendered order," an aim fulfilled "by converging on the notion that food shopping could be pleasant, even relaxing, for upper middle-class women shoppers."[13] In some respects, of course, this association of food with the woman's world represented a continuation of previously existing attitudes and practices, which frequently tended to treat both shopping for groceries and the preparation and service of meals as distinctly feminine pursuits.

But this was a gender culture with a twist: while it honored certain traditions and shored up customary gender roles in some ways, the relationship to society through food that the supermarket model reinforced as it spread was anything but static. Quite to the contrary, the supermarket posited a modernizing refinement of the expression of the feminine, acknowledging and even celebrating the far-reaching changes that were taking place in women's lives in the industrialized and industrializing societies of the twentieth century. With longer store hours, product promotions framed as helpful "hints," "tips," and "advice" for the busy wife, and a profound emphasis on labor-saving convenience, modern food retailing and grocery operations recognized and catered to the new responsibilities of women who now not only maintained their traditional domestic and maternal duties but also held down full-time jobs in increasing numbers. In its classic phase from the 1950s through the 1970s, the supermarket thus functioned as a place where the modern woman who faced the burdens of "*doing* it all" could enjoy the rewards of "*having* it all."

In the postcommunist era, the supermarket continues to facilitate the revision and updating of gender roles. Perhaps paradoxically, this domain may end up much less strongly marked as feminine (and indeed, there is evidence that important changes along these lines have already taken place, as grocery shopping has, in some locales at least, become men's work, too). The all-encompassing scale, homogeneity, and universality of this particular retail form may, in effect, serve to promote a culture that opens up a kind of shopping for Everyman (and Everywoman): if not a thoroughgoing de-gendering of grocery shopping, then at least a remarkable pluralization of the gender roles that can be expressed and maintained in the consumer's encounter with food.

The Joy of Shopping

The culture of the supermarket has relied heavily on the notion of shopping as a pleasure. Those who have guided the modern grocery store have continually exploited its design, organization, and day-to-day presentation for opportunities to encourage customers to think of their shopping time as a happy diversion, as something exciting, entertaining, fun, and ultimately beneficial.

Historians and cultural analysts who stress the liberative and ludic aspects of consumption are, in this respect, onto something: the supermarket style did indeed offer new, pleasurable experiences and refreshing departures from older ways of encountering the world of goods.

In the state-socialist context as well, this notion of shopping-as-fun surfaced surprisingly often during the good years of comparative prosperity and rapid economic expansion in the 1960s and 1970s. The professional literature of socialist grocery retailing is saturated with the idea that shopping should be made into an appealing activity, with an eye both to satisfying and rewarding customers and, not least, to boosting sales. As one reviewer of an East German handbook on supermarket operations observed, the expansive new self-service forms were not without their own challenges when it came to making shopping exciting: "The bigger the building is, the more urgent it becomes that the design does not work in a monotonous and uniform way."[14] But these new settings also presented opportunities—expectations, even—to make time spent in the store more consistently engaging and attractive for shoppers. In the supermarkets (*Kaufhallen*) of the German Democratic Republic, the reviewer noted, "the border between display window and sales floor completely disappears. The sales floor becomes the display window, and in that way becomes increasingly more interesting for advertising. The customer expects, moreover, a pleasurable atmosphere."[15] The influence of Western practice here was both obvious and profound. In one very positive Yugoslav report, for example, an industry commentator marveled at the success of Switzerland's Merkur supermarkets in "turning shopping into an adventure for the consumer," offering a rich set of in-store photographs to show just how it was done.[16]

The Promise of Spontaneity and Discovery

Another key element of the culture of the supermarket was the understanding that shopping was not just a means of quickly executing a set of consciously chosen and previously scheduled purchases; it was also a time for indulging in unplanned "extra" consumption. The importance of impulse buying was, in fact, built into the very architecture of the supermarket, with its accent on open and inviting spaces, grabby visual techniques, and the intentionally sequenced flow of shopping opportunities—a programmed spontaneity, as it were. To amplify the appeal of the unplanned purchase, sellers tried to pump up the volume with vivid displays, end-of-row specials, and alluring last-minute finds at the checkout.

Industry specialists treated this sort of continuous visual relationship with the customer as indispensable to modern store operations. Reviewing the prevailing designs of American stores at the end of the 1950s, one retail consulting firm's report to the Super Market Institute thus insisted that still more needed to be done to make the supermarket into an attractive, engaging, varied, and consumer-friendly site of "visual impact" rather than a mere "distribution center." To that end, the advisers said, store design and interior layout would always have to be carefully thought out, with ample opportunities for "dramatic display" and well-planned locations selected for likely "impulse items."[17]

Socialist shop managers and commercial experts eagerly embraced these principles, and they looked carefully to Western experience and Western designs for models that could be pressed into service at home. Perhaps because it was a far more flexible and less capital-intensive way of creating "supermarket feel" than store construction and design (and could bring that supermarket style even to smaller stores), in-store advertising proved particularly attractive among socialist retail specialists, especially for its value in helping customers discover unfamiliar products. By the early 1970s point-of-sale advertising was becoming a standard practice in Eastern Europe's self-service stores, and commentary on this technique appears again and again in the trade literature. Along these lines, a leading Hungarian handbook stressed that the cultivation of spontaneous impulse buying and the deliberate guidance of shoppers' choices were nothing short of essential:

To take an example from our own Hungarian experience, consider how many brands of coffee are on the shelves of our stores: Omnia, Kolumbia, Rió, Orient, Mokka, Ali Baba, Amigó, Cafe do Brasil, etc. How is the buyer to choose between them, especially if she doesn't know about their qualities? It is obvious that, lacking any information or advertising beforehand, she will choose the one that appears in the most conspicuous, the most vivid, and yet attractive and tasteful presentation on the shops' counters. Indeed, truly effective point-of-sale advertising already begins in the display window, and it is also in this way that the kind of advertising that drives them into the stores [*a beterelő propaganda*] comes to life.[18]

Though such techniques for stimulating the impulse purchase had been developed in capitalist conditions, they were accepted in a rapid and ready way in socialist commerce. Here again, the supermarket style and the culture it promoted proved transnational, as customers were continually trained to expect shopping to offer the pleasures of the unfamiliar, the unexpected, and the unplanned.[19]

The Virtue of Novelty

Along with spontaneity, supermarket culture hammered home a message about the great value of the novel: it was not without reason that the phrase "new and improved" came to be seen as a hackneyed trope of American grocery advertising. In this respect as well, socialist practice proved remarkably open to cultural patterns refined in the West. Novelty was treated in socialist business and commercial discourse as a highly desirable end, and it was marketed to retail customers as such in the media and, importantly, in the stores themselves.[20]

Though this aspect of supermarket culture managed to leap the borders between capitalism and communism with little difficulty, it carried a very real threat to the ultimate stability of the communist system. In both East and West, store promotions repeatedly sent the message to consumers that a good store was one well stocked with novel items, with frequent additions to the product assortment. By implication, these practices also reinforced the idea that a properly functioning manufacturing economy was one that could continually produce innovations and offer up new consumer goods. The logic of modern retail culture thereby established terms on which state socialism, with its comparatively limited flexibility, was ill-equipped to compete.

The Security of Satisfaction Guaranteed

The large, modern self-service store and the supermarket fostered a public culture that favored the uniformity and consistency of product offerings across both time and space. The new model communicated the idea that goods for sale in a store yesterday were likely to be available next week and next month, and they would also probably be on hand in any grocery chain's other outlets as well. Systematized business practices sought wherever possible to eliminate shortages and minimize undesirable variability in supply. Uniformity came to be taken as a marker not just of reliable and consistent quality but of high quality itself, and standard packaging and production procedures meant that buyers could treat goods from a given source as essentially fungible, with little or no need for inspection and selection. Under the older cultural model of the local market square, buyers had the opportunity—and, in many cases, a perceived duty—to check the offerings of many different sellers, to seek out the best goods available on any given day, and to negotiate the best possible deals. With modern grocery retailing, those aspects of the former mode of shopping were greatly diminished, if not eliminated entirely. The culture of the supermarket thus offered simultaneously a heightened sense of shopping adventure with a reduced sense of risk.

Guaranteeing customer satisfaction was no easy task for socialist enterprises. Because of structural economic problems that plagued the agricultural and manufacturing sectors through the period of communist rule, East European grocery companies had difficulty maintaining reliable supplies of high-quality merchandise. Still, such consistency and certainty were among the chief aims of the distribution system, and planners and enterprise leaders regularly spoke of the self-service store and the supermarket as key instruments in realizing this goal. This feature of the supermarket culture was one that socialist businesspeople themselves internalized, seeing it as a matter of professional pride. As the manager of Zagreb's Slavija supermarket put it, "Is there anything harder for a true businessman than to have to say 'we don't have it' to a customer?"[21]

The Restructuring of Shopping Sociability

Writing about his experience "shopping for images" in 1950s California, Allen Ginsberg described the supermarket as an uncertain mixture of shiny new consumerist pleasures with a sense of isolation and alienation that was itself profoundly modern. Summoning up the decidedly pre-modern figure of Walt Whitman to play Virgil to his Dante, Ginsberg told of a late-evening "odyssey in the supermarket," a place where community and social relations had been refocused and reconstituted in an odd, spectacular, unsettling new way: "What peaches and what penumbras! Whole families shopping at night! Aisles full of husbands! Wives in the avocados, babies in the tomatoes!" While the new form undeniably had its joys, it could also lay bare a feeling of emptiness and disconnection: after all the encounters among the "brilliant stacks of cans" in the store, Ginsberg and his fellow shoppers seemed likely to end up disappointed, left to "stroll dreaming of the lost America of love past blue automobiles in driveways."[22] Was this, then, the hollow new way of social interaction that the supermarket left wherever it arrived?

Ginsberg's anxieties probably overstate the case, but the culture of the supermarket did radically reconfigure the social relations of provisioning. Shopping became more a mass experience and, at the same time, less social in important ways. The greater scale of the self-service grocery and the supermarket meant that customers would typically encounter many more people during the time spent in a store, but there were fewer opportunities for significant interaction with most of them, and the encounters themselves were often less intimate. The old counter-service, corner-store model had tended to bring together people who lived near one another within a single neighborhood, with a higher chance that customers and employees would have or develop social relationships beyond the shop. Under the traditional system, time spent waiting in line offered a patron the chance to chat with familiar customers, neighbors, and acquaintances, while the slower pace of a less crowded day might allow her a longer conversation with the store's employees. By contrast, the social ways of the supermarket fostered, and at the same time expressed, the development of a more atomized, anonymous mass culture, one in which the impersonal (or pseudo-personal) techniques of commercial promotion, display, and advertising displaced human interactions. Emotional connections to the items on sale counted for more; affective bonds to sellers and other buyers mattered less. The self-service store could be social, certainly, but it did not have to be.

These changes also came to socialist Europe with the culture of the supermarket. For societies founded on explicitly communitarian ideology, they posed particular problems. Noting that some countries in Western Europe were, by 1976, experiencing something of a backlash against the newer, impersonal styles, the Yugoslav industrial psychologist Marko Goluža suggested that the fervor for all things modern had come at some cost. The hunger for a return to older, more intimate ways, he speculated, "is probably caused by people having had enough of the offerings on an enormous scale in which, with regard to service, there is a lack of precisely that which 'my' neighborhood shop [*dućan*] offers: a personal approach, a way of doing business in the course of which they greet me by name, a salesperson with whom I can exchange thoughts and converse about something that doesn't have anything to do with the purchase, or even share some of my worries." Because of that, Goluža said, the more thoroughly modernized commercial cultures were now seeing a longing "to get back to 'the good old neighborhood shop,' to the kind which, let's say, we went to when we were kids and in which the sales clerk sometimes even knew that we had forgotten to ask for one of the things that our mother had sent us for."[23]

The Celebration of Abundance

The culture of the supermarket was, emphatically and unapologetically, a culture of plenty. In its form, its operations, and its content, the modern mode of grocery retailing telegraphed continuous messages about the joys of material abundance, about the wondrous new possibility of enjoying that abundance on a day-to-day basis, and about its centrality to both social and individual well-being. From this standpoint, success meant material wealth and sensory pleasure. The Good Society was a prosperous society.

In the domain of everyday consumption, the supermarket was the primary symbol, the primary site, and the primary source of this new engagement with abundance. As Emanuela Scarpellini has observed of the spread of American styles to Italy (a capitalist polity that faced many of the same problems of underdevelopment as the socialist states), the large-scale, self-service retail model was not only transnational but also remarkably powerful, and the adoption of new, "imported" modes of grocery sales could have dramatic cultural effects. Central to that power was the supermarket's promise of the Good Life: "Twentieth-century supermarkets," Scarpellini concludes, "proposed an image of feasting, where the great abundance and variety of commodities negated feelings of shortage and poverty for everybody."[24]

The spectacular achievements of the postwar capitalist economies fixed this image of previously unimaginable abundance as a dominant cultural model. This happened not just in the West but in the socialist East as well, establishing the terms of an ideological and economic competition that played an important role in the larger geopolitical conflict of the Cold War.[25] In the logic of the supermarket, bigger meant better. This was an idea that found a receptive audience in socialist Eastern Europe. Thus one columnist for the Hungarian mass-market news and features magazine *Tükör* (Mirror) noted, a little wistfully, just how strong this bias in favor of the big stores had become by the early 1970s: the further proliferation of small-scale shops with limited selection, he observed, was being held in check by "serious opponents" among the country's city managers, builders, and transportation planners, who "increasingly insist [that] the future belongs to the supermarkets that cover a large area, to the shopping centers that satisfy every demand."[26]

Having jettisoned the heavy-industry fantasies of Stalinism in favor of a more consumer-oriented approach, many of those who held political and economic power in the socialist states of Eastern Europe were eager to provide the same sort of material satisfaction for their own citizens, and to demonstrate that socialism could deliver on its promises and effectively compete with, or even surpass, the capacities of capitalism. Seen from this perspective, the effort to rival the success of the West in food and grocery provisioning became an essential part of state policy. The abundance of the supermarket was no longer merely desirable; it was politically imperative as well.

The Promotion of Variety and Choice

Complementing the celebration of abundance in the culture of the supermarket was a profound emphasis on the value of product diversity and consumer choice. Variety was made a virtue, and the customer's freedom to select products that suited her precise needs and tastes became a recurring theme in commercial promotion and, increasingly, a constant expectation on the part of consumers themselves. Large-scale grocery retailing repeatedly advanced this idea of the superiority of variety, and with time, the notion that choice was desirable gave way to an understanding that choice was, in fact, necessary. In this new cultural constellation, rising expectations changed the very definition of success. Abundance came to mean more than just satisfying basic needs adequately; material plenty also meant having plenty of options. "Enough" was no longer enough.

A similar dynamic emerged in socialist Eastern Europe as well. As part of their introduction of supermarkets and large self-service stores, business enterprises in Yugoslavia, Hungary, and East Germany endorsed and actively promoted a vision of the advantages of variety and choice. But these values proved problematic for the struggling socialist societies. Holding up variety and choice as positive ends also sent messages about their absence: rather than something familiar that represented "just the way things have always been," relative scarcity and a restricted product assortment could now be seen as more serious defects and failings in a political and economic system that had promised more. And despite the dramatic progress of the postwar decades, agricultural and industrial production and distribution quite frequently could not deliver the desired or promised level of consumer satisfaction. In this respect, socialist economies found themselves ill-equipped to compete on the terms that the logic of the supermarket established and reinforced. Reflecting on the state of the stores in the mid-1970s, one interviewee for Yugoslavia's *Supermarket* admitted that even his country's shining example of socialist consumerism left something to be desired: "With regard to the variety of goods, what is on offer to us is still not anything special, apart from some occasional exceptions. In other words: either we still don't have enough of the goods that most people are looking for, or perhaps too much of the kind of goods nobody at all needs."[27] Much the same judgment, he observed, had been expressed in the Hungarian press about shortages in Budapest stores. This was a pattern that emerged in each of these more prosperous, consumer-oriented socialist societies: the celebratory public culture of socialist consumption had, in effect, run too far ahead of real economic capacities.

The Affirmation of Competition

Modern supermarket operations have tended to place a heightened value on competitive business relationships and, in the process, have contributed to the development of a mass culture that endorses and welcomes direct competition as a public virtue. This has taken place in a variety of ways, some explicit, some less so. Traditionally, and most obviously, it has appeared in the fierce price competition seen among American grocery stores: this is a business in which much of the day-to-day advertising is designed to highlight differences of just a few pennies. In addition to these outright battles over price, retailers and manufacturers have attempted to outdo their rivals by reaching the grocery consumer with many other forms of product and store promotion. The industry is relentlessly competitive, and stores constantly remind consumers that this struggle works to their ultimate benefit.

The culture of the supermarket affirms the virtue of competition in much more subtle ways as well. The very abundance and diversity of the product offerings that typify the modern, large-scale grocery store reinforce the logic of the marketplace. By seeing to it that customers find many alternatives on the shelves, grocery sellers communicate not just the value of choice as such, but also the value of the underlying competitive relationships that are calculated to influence that choice. In choosing a store to patronize and in making selections from among contending products, consumers find themselves with the opportunity to experience competition as something satisfying and valuable, and perhaps even necessary.

All this competition, however, sits uneasily with the values of Marxism, or at least with the more orthodox varieties of state-socialist political thought, which tended to dismiss capitalist markets as either mired in anti-competitive monopoly or disintegrating into wild, hyper-competitive "anarchy." In encouraging the use of a grocery sales format that inherently promoted a deeper appreciation for economic competition, policy-makers, enterprise managers, and retail specialists had introduced a set of business practices that carried with them the potential to subvert a number of the fundamental principles on which socialist society was supposed to be organized. In this respect as well the supermarket model could itself serve as an instrument of important social and political change.

The Pursuit of Modernity

While it has affirmed the traditional in certain ways, supermarket culture reflected, in the main, a thoroughgoing embrace of the new. Steeped in their own culture of revolutionary modernity, communist societies were fertile ground for this sort of appeal. For example, in the self-styled (and self-consciously) "young" society of the German Democratic Republic, where after Nazism so much of what was "old" and "traditional" in German life had to be rejected as threatening and wrong, the shapers of public culture held up a confident, even bold vision of modernity as the social ideal. In this spirit, one mass-circulation women's magazine advertisement for the GDR's HO-Kaufhalle supermarket chain courted potential grocery customers with the message "Modern people buy the modern way," using the image of a well-supplied self-service store where the shopping was easy, reliable, and satisfying. Showing three generations of female shoppers—a young girl, her mother, and her grandmother, filling their baskets and introduced to readers as "Young–Younger–Youngest"—the Kaufhalle supermarkets presented the new mode of large-scale self-service as something that active, modern working people and even customers rooted in traditional ways could immediately appreciate: "Whether young or older, people like shopping here. HO-Kaufhalle supermarkets offer a wide assortment of goods and in that way shorten your shopping trips."[28] In the communist context, however, this sort of appeal also involved a less obvious double message: it amounted to an advertisement for East German socialism itself, reminding readers of the state's achievements in delivering "the modern way," that is, the convenience and abundance of the supermarket, to its citizen-consumers.

Although consumption scholarship has thus far tended to see this advocacy of high modernity as a distinctive trope of capitalist consumerism, the experience of the socialist societies suggests the need for a rather different conceptualization. As it happened, the emphasis on progressive, modern living that was associated with the culture of the supermarket played well in the larger ideological context of the socialist experiment, and in the specific setting of grocery retailing (though not only in that setting) the eager pursuit of the modern appears again and again.

The Ascent of Leisure and the Eclipse of Labor

A love of ease and convenience characterized the popular culture that the twentieth-century supermarket engendered. Food preparation, home life, shopping—in all these areas the world of the supermarket drove home the message that leisure was to be prized, free time maximized, and unnecessary work avoided. The idea was a catchy one, and it traveled well. Noting the dramatic rise in the consumption of ready-to-eat foods and highly processed items such as powdered soups, tinned meats, and easy-to-prepare "quick" dishes, one writer for Hungary's leading women's magazine thus challenged those who balked at the higher cost of these supermarket items:

Isn't our time expensive? Let's look around the world a bit. In the industrially developed [that is, capitalist] countries they are already outpacing us by a lot in this respect. And the same path stands before us: to simplify and modernize our household work. Let "cooking a feast" remain a holiday passion! If a woman can save enough time from her cooking to be able to read a novel, to have a conversation with her children, to take a walk or go to the movies with her husband, then she hasn't lost anything by paying more. And if she is better rested, with a more cheerful spirit, the next day's work will also be easier.[29]

A new attitude toward work emerged in other ways as well. In its physical design and its methods of operation, the new form of grocery retailing emphasized commodities and downplayed labor. The layout of the self-service store and the supermarket showcased the products on offer, continually seeking to bring them to the shopper's eye. This feature combined with the reduction of personal service to limit the extent to which customers had occasion to deal in any direct way with the individual workers who were responsible for bringing all these goods to market.

Traditional methods of food provision—the peddler's cart, the market stall, the counter-service store, the grocery-delivery service—had often entailed what was essentially a blended economic activity, mixing services and commodities. The supermarket style shifted that balance dramatically in favor of more thoroughly commoditized transactions, rendering labor more anonymous and impersonal, and considerably less visible (with the most obvious exception of the cashier). Socialism did not immunize Eastern Europe against such changes. Alarmed by them, one writer for the leading East German women's weekly *Für Dich* (For You) tried to call attention to what was happening: "Who among us customers ever thinks about what the women working in the grocery store have to deal with in order to make shopping pleasant?" In a profile of one Progress (*Fortschritt*) supermarket in the East German territory of Brandenburg, she reminded her readers that the store's staff had to labor during the day—and overnight, out of sight and out of mind—to ensure that the shelves in the store were arranged "with personal care" and fully stocked: "they put their entire reputation on the line, so that everything is tip-top. They are always putting the food items back in the proper order on the shelves, seeing to it that everything is in place—even when a customer has preferred to take a package of noodles from all the way in the back of the shelves."[30] The self-service experience obscured that hard work.

There were, to be sure, some variations from this pattern, places in which modern supermarket culture, as it evolved, actually worked to elevate (or re-store) certain service aspects of the grocery-shopping experience. Where strong sales might depend on the suggestion of a reliable personal connection, a place for it could be found in the large-scale food store. Along these lines, for example, the 1960 *Loewy Report* to the U.S.-based Super Market Institute rec-ommended that future supermarket meat counters be redesigned "in a 'U' shape inside which meat personnel will be visible and available for customer questions." In this way, the consultants suggested, "the potent image of 'my butcher' returns to the meat department."[31]

In the main, however, the culture of the supermarket encouraged and ex-pressed new attitudes toward the prominence and significance of work. For a socialist economy, of course, this re-imagining of the position of labor was a particularly meaningful development. On one hand, as long as ownership rested in the proper place, that is, with the working class and its state, Marxist theory and Marxist-Leninist practice could accept rather comfortably the transformation of grocery sales away from the old shopkeeper-entrepreneur model and toward an ambitious new retail scheme that relied more heavily on technology, that made grocery sales more "industrial," and that seemed to be a fitting match for the bigger scale of state socialism's collectivized agriculture and expanding manufacturing economy. But the way in which the supermar-ket made labor less visible, and workers' service less appreciated, was another matter entirely. Here, too, the new retail model functioned in a manner that was potentially subversive of socialist values. In the main, however, this threat appeared to go unrecognized by the communist authorities.

The Exaltation of Consumption

The culture of the supermarket expressed a view of consumption as a positive end in itself. Through advertising, in-store promotion, and the physical design of the large self-service store, the message disseminated in modern grocery retailing was that to consume more, and more richly, was to live better.

Sentiments such as these, obviously, could not easily be welcomed in any ex-plicit or unadulterated form in socialist Europe. Indeed, as domestic social crit-ics and communist politicians detected a creeping tendency toward the rise of "consumer society" under socialism, the idea of consumption-as-virtue came in for scathing, repeated attacks. Advertising practice was an easy target, and a frequent one, yet the critics typically did not view the adoption of the large-scale grocery store as involving such dangers of corruption and "infection."

Unlike advertising, the supermarket as an institutional form did not communicate any obviously and immediately suspicious "message" to citizens. (Therein lay the problem: there were plenty of implicit and unrecognized messages.) Even the most bitter and vocal opponents of rampant consumerism therefore tended to leave this particular manifestation of modern consumer culture untouched, failing to alert to the possibility that the supermarket model might itself undermine the principles on which socialist society was based.

There was, to be sure, some reason to worry that the public had forsaken socialist values in favor of the allure of spending. The pursuit of plenty in the aisles of the big stores had become, in effect, disarmingly ordinary: accepted, expected, and for many if not most, respected. One Hungarian commentator thus remarked on the public's keen attention to, and demonstrable fondness for, all the new shopping opportunities: "It is certain that if, for example, a new supermarket opens in Budapest, or a department store for manufactured goods in one of the city's outlying districts, the inhabitants of the smallest village will hear about it immediately. The modern forms of sales, the self-service store and the supermarket, *have become a natural mode of our life.*"[32]

The Acknowledgment of the Sovereign Consumer

Finally, the culture of the supermarket has involved powerful and repeated affirmations—some obvious, some not—of the much-vaunted principle of consumer sovereignty. This staple of Western marketing theory has found a natural home in modern grocery retailing. In the world of the supermarket, both the external commercial promotion designed to attract customers and encourage spending and the in-store experience have communicated a paramount concern for making customers happy. If the ultimate goal is to serve the interests of sellers by turning a profit, it has been pursued through what is promised to be a constant effort to identify and satisfy the needs and desires of the public.

The most severe critics of modern consumer culture have been inclined to see the claim of consumer sovereignty as a sham. In this view, the techniques of retailing and commercial promotion are, first and foremost, exercises in manipulation. Among committed communists there was a lingering tendency to reject the notion of consumer sovereignty as a capitalist rationalization, or in the words of one East German critic, "nothing other than bourgeois apologetic and charlatanry" that gave only an illusory "freedom," so that "workers can only buy the essential necessities of life, [while] those who belong to the dominant classes acquire the luxury goods."[33]

Yet in actual practice, the principle of consumer sovereignty did not depend on the profit motive. It could take root in the absence of capitalism, and with time, socialist commerce did indeed tend to yield to the idea that "His Majesty the Consumer," as one Yugoslav source put it, should come first.[34] These developments were especially pronounced in the "revolutionized" retail culture of large-scale, choice-centered abundance that emerged in the more prosperous parts of Eastern Europe in the 1960s and 1970s and that was embodied in the supermarket model.

Here, then, was yet another danger for socialism: telling customers that they are in charge could lead them to think of themselves as in charge, and to act accordingly. All the insistence on the primacy of customer satisfaction may have served, in fact, to create and reinforce a corresponding set of expectations—a claim of sovereignty, as it were—on the part of consumers themselves.

To the extent that dynamics such as these were inherent in the transnational culture of large-scale, modern grocery sales, they posed serious threats to the foundational principles of state socialism. The culture of the supermarket was not an intrinsically capitalist culture, but in important respects it proved inhospitable to communist rule. As consumption eclipsed production as the raison d'être of the economy in the public mind, and as government administrators, planners, and party leaders acceded to the accumulated demand for greater consumer satisfaction, many of the old, reliable tenets of Marxist-Leninist governance were questioned, and some were turned upside down. When the supermarket came to Eastern Europe, socialism itself was forced to change.

Chapter 14
Tools and Spaces: Food and Cooking in Working-Class Neighborhoods, 1880–1930

Katherine Leonard Turner

Three women of immigrant families who lived in Pittsburgh between 1900 and 1930 had very different experiences with home cooking. One, born in 1901 in what is now Serbia, emigrated with her parents in 1905. In America her mother helped run the family confectionery store, cooked for her boarders, and put up enormous quantities of food for her family. Her daughter remembered, "In the fall [her mother] would make her own sauerkraut, make her own wine and butcher a 300-400 pound hog. Then she would have that smoked and some meat, it would be fresh. She would salt it down and garlic it and everything. She would buy two, three sacks of potatoes and cabbage and kidney beans [to preserve]. . . . Every year."[1] The second woman, also born in 1901 but to Italian parents in Pittsburgh, remembered her mother's cooking. The mother made all her own bread and pasta and took the children foraging for wild dandelion greens. The daughter also had vivid childhood memories of a woman who lived across the street; who had had a stroke and so could not cook. That woman bought day-old bread from the bakers rather than baking for herself.[2] The third woman, an Italian, born in Termini in 1892, emigrated in 1922 around the age of thirty. Her husband sold fruits and vegetables, and they lived above their store near Pittsburgh. She baked no bread because she was too busy helping her husband run the store. Family meals were mainly sandwiches and almost never featured the traditional Italian festival dishes.[3]

These women, like other working-class women of the time, made different trade-offs between expending effort and spending cash when they provided food for their families. Some threw themselves into home production, buying nothing if they could make it for themselves. Some were too busy with businesses and wage work to cook much. Others, like the woman with the stroke, simply did not have the luxury of cooking.

Studies of working-class foodways during this period often privilege ethnicity, since the working class was largely composed of recent immigrants and their children.[4] For these Pittsburgh women, access to resources such as stoves, barrels, open land, and baker's bread was as critical as cultural heritage when they made everyday food decisions. Despite immense cultural differences, working-class people shared many characteristics of their material culture. Tools and spaces—the sorts of kitchens, cooking tools, houses, and yards people had—mattered as much as their ethnic heritage when it came to day-to-day, practical food decisions. Further, their houses, yards, and utilities were directly related to the size and density of their neighborhoods and cities. The cooking and eating habits of working-class people in Pittsburgh, Chicago, and New York demonstrate that although ethnic differences suggested *what* to eat, class and material culture decided *how* to get it.

How did working-class people cook in American cities in the years 1880 to 1930? Who did most of their cooking at home, and who bought prepared food? Food straddles production and consumption: it is (and was) commonly produced at home, but it is also purchased ready to eat. The decision about whether to make food or buy purchased food is really about the allocation of resources (cash and labor). The Pittsburgh working-class women could have spent a few hours baking bread or they could have spent a few nickels to buy baker's bread. Susan Porter Benson argues that for working-class people, consumption was not an individual decision but part of a complicated family economy that included earning wages, producing food and other items at home, and buying, selling, trading, and sharing goods and services with neighbors. The family economy was both complex and contested: contributions and benefits were unequal, and a constant lack of financial security sharpened the conflicts around money that arose in families.[5]

Stereotypically, women made the decisions about buying and serving food. In Benson's evidence (which echoes the work of Progressive-era social workers such as Margaret Byington), working-class women constantly faced the difficult task of stretching the food dollar—combining home food production, shopping, and trading in order to serve appetizing, satisfying meals on a limited budget.[6] In actuality, the responsibility for food buying probably did lie most often with wives and mothers. However, one can easily imagine other situations: wives who worked outside the home too much to do any "managing" at all; husbands who demanded certain dishes, no matter their price or convenience; teenaged children who bought some of their meals outside the home with their wages; single men and women who found it impractical if not impossible to cook for one. Working-class men's role in home food production is well documented: men made wine, butchered hogs, and laid down root vegetables. In other words, wives and mothers were not the only ones making these decisions.

How did families decide whether to buy bread or butcher hogs or to do both? It is difficult to study the family dynamic of food buying and cooking due to the lack of direct evidence about who made the food decisions. These were tough, everyday, unglamorous decisions made in the opacity of the household or family circle. The evidence available is about the material world: the kitchens, neighborhoods, and businesses of the working class. From the material evidence we can reconstruct something about the decision-making process.

It makes sense to start with the kitchen. Working-class people in the late nineteenth and early twentieth centuries defined a kitchen very differently from middle-class people. In the middle class the kitchen was a separate, clearly defined room. Well-designed modern homes had kitchens whose activities would not be seen, heard, or smelled by anyone else in the house, especially guests; they were places for servants to work unobtrusively. The clearly defined kitchen went hand in hand with the formal dining room to separate the acts of cooking and eating.[7] After the turn of the twentieth century, architects and "domestic feminists" designed kitchens that used new technologies to lighten household work. Middle-class women wanted rationalized, efficient kitchens in which to supervise their cooks, in the same way that middle-class men supervised other workers in efficient workplaces.[8] In the early twentieth century it became more socially acceptable for middle-class women to "do their own work" with fewer or no servants, partly because their kitchens were now clean, light, and well designed. In contrast, working-class kitchens were usually not specialized spaces; they were not clearly defined, and they were not particularly efficient. The area for cooking and food preparation was simply that room—or part of a room—with the stove, sink, and table.

Evidence about the size and shape of urban working-class kitchens can be gleaned from the writings and legislation of the tenement-reform movement of the late nineteenth and early twentieth centuries. New York State's Tenement House Act of 1867 legally defined a tenement as "Any house, building, or portion thereof, which is rented, leased, let or hired out to be occupied or is occupied, as the home or residence of more than three families living independently of one another and doing their own cooking upon the premises, or by more than two families upon a floor, so living and cooking and having a common right in the halls, stairways, yards, water closets, or privies, or some of them."[9] Here cooking was considered the primary defining characteristic of a household. Three families cooking separately under one roof could not be considered one household. Despite the centrality of cooking to this definition, the 1867 act said little about the provision of kitchen spaces or utilities in city housing. Subsequent legislation in 1879, 1887, and 1901 was mostly concerned with "air and light" and dealt with minimum-square-footage requirements, windows, ventilation, toilets, and sanitary issues.[10] The only legislation that referred at all to cooking was the requirement for ash chutes. The many drawings and plans for "improved" or "scientific" tenement housing showed the floor plans of the individual apartments. These drawings named a dedicated kitchen room only about half the time: rooms were usually titled "Room" or "Living Room," and only the indication of a sink or a plate on which to place a stove showed that cooking would be done there.[11] Dining rooms were not clearly marked either. Photographic evidence suggests that people ate wherever it was convenient, usually at a table, the same place where they worked. In 1912 the photojournalist Lewis Hine photographed the Cardinale home to demonstrate home piecework for the National Child Labor Committee. (See Figure 14.1.) In the photo Mrs. Cardinale and her son are doing piecework in their apartment on New York's Carmine Street. The work table is pressed right up against the stove, either for warmth or because there was no other place for it. The Hine photos, of course, are not simply unmediated images; like other photographers, Hine composed his images carefully and may have moved furniture and people to get a better shot. The furniture placement in his photos is therefore suggestive, not conclusive.

The Cardinales' use of space was partly, but not entirely, due to a lack of resources. Working-class homes were small and were usually designed to maximize revenue for the builder or landlord, not for the tenant's comfort or efficiency. The Cardinale home was typical of New York City's tenement apartments.[12] In cities such as Chicago and Pittsburgh, which were less dense than New York, older, single-family houses were often subdivided into multiple apartments, with improvised kitchen facilities in each. There was simply not room for spacious kitchens with large work spaces and storage, and most families could not afford to rent larger apartments or houses with more rooms. Builders and designers assumed that working-class families could not afford the luxury of a separate or well-defined kitchen space. In fact, workers moving into this type of housing—with no differentiated kitchen—did not usually take steps to create one. They did not necessarily want an isolated kitchen. The kitchen was the center of the home, not physically separated from other activities such as eating, socializing, and working.

Working people in general did not try to effect a genteel separation between cooking and eating. Lizabeth Cohen explains that there were both material and cultural reasons that working people simply were not interested in clearly defined, differentiated home spaces. Materially, they could not afford to light and heat several rooms of the home at once; activities were huddled around the source of heat or light. Culturally, the middle-class ideal of separate spaces seemed isolated and unhomelike; working-class people were accustomed to sharing their living and working spaces closely with others. While middle-class women believed that their homes should be refuges from the economic world, working-class women constantly performed wage-earning work there, keeping boarders, doing piecework, or working in the adjoining family business. As a result, "the reformer ideal of the kitchen as an efficient laboratory servicing other parts of the house found little acceptance among workers."[13] Instead, working-class people preferred to socialize in their kitchens even if they had

Figure 14.1. The Cardinale family, New York City, 1912. Photograph by Lewis Hine for the National Child Labor Committee, January 29, 1912. Library of Congress, Prints & Photographs Division, National Child Labor Committee Collection, Lot 7481, no. 2815.

other rooms. If there was a separate parlor or dining room in the home—and these were rare—it was kept for formal socializing, not generally used to dine.[14] Margaret Byington reported that among steelworkers' families in Homestead (near Pittsburgh), "though a full set of dining room furniture, side-board, table, and dining chair, are usually in evidence, they are rarely used at meals. The family sewing is done there . . . but rarely is the room used for breakfast, dinner, or supper."[15]

Although working-class people were constrained by small and cramped living spaces and lack of storage, they still sought to arrange and decorate their living spaces according to their own ideas, and they often refused to rearrange their lives according to middle-class ideas of propriety.[16] Families that had steady incomes bought the largest, grandest furniture they could afford, and they were particularly fond of luxurious-looking items such as plush furniture, drapes, lace curtains, and mirrors. Kitchens and dining rooms were decorated with extensive lace, fabric, or paper drapes or valences on every shelf, some-times covering up sinks and stoves. Sideboards and cupboards displayed stacks of ceramics and rows of glassware. Walls were adorned with colorful chromolithographs, advertisements, religious images, and calendars.[17] In the Cardinale family kitchen, pictured above, every possible surface is decorated with lace trim, statues, china, and fringe. Working people in cities clearly intended to live in their kitchens, not to isolate the space from their families and social life.

The lack of separation did mean, however, that working-class people were living right on top of the cooking area. A 1913 picture by Lewis Hine, also taken in New York City for the National Child Labor Committee, shows a young boy, Jimmy Chinquanana, with his family in their lodgings behind their store (see Figure 14.2). There is very little space between the bed and the stove; although this would have been comforting in cold weather, it would have been uncomfortable in hot, and certainly inconvenient for housekeeping. In the Chinquananas' home, and in countless other working-class homes, heat from cooking (and from washing and ironing) was unbearable in warm months, and there was no cooler place in the house to which the family could escape.[18] The photo also shows the lack of room, which constrained food preparation. The kitchen was used for many activities, and space was provisional: extra room in which to knead dough, cut up large pieces of meat, or roll out noodles had to be constructed by moving aside other furniture and objects. Working-class kitchens may have been sociable, but they were certainly inconvenient for all but the simplest cooking tasks.

Tools, as well as spaces, marked the difference between working-class and middle-class kitchens. Working-class kitchens generally had older tools and equipment. The cast-iron stove remained essentially the same tool from the Civil War until the widespread adoption of gas stoves around 1900. Most stoves could burn wood or coal interchangeably, and it was the fuel that made the difference, both in money and in comfort. In the late nineteenth century more working-class people probably burned wood, even though coal burned hotter and longer and was less bulky to store. (In the photo the Chinquananas have a hatchet on their stove, suggesting the use of wood.) Hard (anthracite) coal was more expensive but burned cleaner and hotter than the cheaper soft coal. The only real advantage to wood over coal was that in some rural and semirural areas it was still possible to forage for wood. A woman who emigrated from Austro-Hungary in 1909 at the age of eight recalled that in her parents' home near Pittsburgh they used a woodstove since they could not afford coal: "Of course you could have bought coal if you had the money, but if you didn't have the money you had to substitute the wood."[19] Urban dwellers could sometimes pick up coal in the streets, dropped by coal haulers. In the early twentieth century working-class people with coal stoves lagged technologically behind those in the middle class who were acquiring new gas ranges.[20]

A stove was an absolute necessity for any kind of cooking. When working-class families moved into rental housing, stoves were sometimes provided as

Figure 14.2. Jimmy Chinquanana and his family, New York City, 1913. Photograph by Lewis Hine for the National Child Labor Committee, September 16, 1913. Library of Congress, Prints & Photographs Division, National Child Labor Committee Collection, Lot 7483, vol. 2, no. 3532.

part of the furnishings. Other times families had to bring their own stoves. In 1897 the cheapest kitchen stove from the Sears, Roebuck catalog cost $7.20; in that year the average weekly wages of a man working in industry were about $8.48.[21] Used stoves could be purchased for less. In 1911 Mabel Hyde Kittredge, who wrote a book advising tenement dwellers how to furnish their apartments, assumed that a stove would have to be purchased and gave the price as $9.00 for a tenement apartment with five people.[22]

Stoves were difficult and time-consuming to operate and maintain, requiring constant supervision and care. A wood or coal stove had to be constantly fueled. If the ashes were not removed each day, the fire would not light; and if the stove was not cleaned regularly, it would not draw properly, smoking up the room. Inexpensive stoves were more or less simple boxes, whose heat was hard to control; complicated systems of dampers controlled the heat in more expensive stoves, requiring time and attention to learn. Stoves—even coal burning— could emit noxious gas if used improperly. In addition, any stove would rust into uselessness if not "blacked" with stove polish as often as every few days.[23] Susan Strasser makes an important point about these stoves: "Wood and coal stoves were never 'turned on'; they were used only when economical in time, in labor, and in fuel. This made them less flexible than modern gas and electric stoves, which cooks can use one burner at a time."[24] In other words, stoves were either entirely off or on for long periods of time. Wood and coal stoves were impractical for "cooking for one." They were more suited to the housekeeper whose other tasks kept her in the house, where she could maintain the fire, than to the wageworker who returned home only to eat.

Burning coal was more efficient than burning wood, but using either a wood or a coal cookstove still required fuel hauling, constant fire building, and standing uncomfortably close to the source of heat in order to cook. The experience of cooking began to change only with different types of fuels, which could be turned on and off more easily and did not emit so much radiant heat. Stoves using different kinds of fuel were patented beginning in the 1860s. These new stoves used coal oil, gas, kerosene, gasoline, or petroleum. They were inexpensive and relatively easy to use, but the burning oil smelled bad, and there was great risk of fire and explosion.[25] Most working-class people did not have gas lines hooked up to their homes, or found the fuel too expensive, until the 1910s or later. Many homes pictured in the Hine photographs and other working-class interiors had small portable stoves with two burners (essentially hot plates), which were designed to burn either gas or gasoline (but not both) and were usually placed on top of their old coal stoves. These could be used for heating a pot but not for the more time-consuming baking. Another New York City family was photographed by Lewis Hine crocheting caps in their East Side apartment in 1912 (see figure 14.3). They have a gasoline hot plate on top of their coal stove that could be used without heating the apartment as much as the coal stove would. Working people who could not afford gas ranges could afford small, transitional appliances such as this one. The 1897 Sears, Roebuck catalog offered one-burner oil stoves for as little as 85¢ and gasoline stoves for $2.63, with the statement "*There is positively no danger in using the Acme Gasoline Stove. It cannot explode,*" suggesting that consumers were aware of the possible dangers of gasoline stoves.[26] In 1902 a two-hole portable gas stove cost $1.50, or less if secondhand. It was connected to a gas meter fed with quarters.[27] Other families used oil stoves for small cooking tasks, to save on gas or coal. The social reformer and home economist Helen Campbell wrote of the struggles of two formerly genteel women who were reduced to sewing to make a meager living. Campbell was surprised that they used only 12¢ worth of coal per week and asked, "How could twelve cents' worth of coal do a week's cooking?" One woman responded, "It couldn't. It didn't. I've a little oil stove that just boils the kettle, and tea and bread and butter are what we have mostly. A gallon of oil goes a long way, and I can cook small things over it, too."[28] Well into the twentieth century manufacturers produced hybrid stove models, combining two or more different types of fuels, for consumers who were not willing to make a

Figure 14.3. Crocheting caps, New York City, 1912. Photograph by Lewis Hine for the National Child Labor Committee, November 1912. Library of Congress, Prints & Photographs Division, National Child Labor Committee Collection, Lot 7481, no. 3123.

complete switch. These stoves could burn coal and wood on one side and gas or oil on the other at the same time.[29]

By the 1920s gas was becoming commonplace in working-class homes. About two-thirds of the families in Muncie, Indiana, in the 1920s cooked with gas; most of the remainder used gasoline or coal, and a few cooked with electricity.[30] A woman who grew up in Pittsburgh recalled that when her family moved into a new house around 1922, they "had big pot belly stoves. When we moved in that house, my dad bought a combination stove, a great big one with four burners of gas and four coal. We used to burn coal."[31]

Most working-class kitchens consistently lacked an important utility for cooking—convenient running hot water—and this made cooking more difficult than it was for more comfortable households. Susan Strasser writes, "Well into the twentieth century, indoor plumbing remained a matter of class: the rich had it, the poor did not."[32] In the late nineteenth century most working-class people had to haul water, either from a single sink in their apartment building or from a pump in the backyard or on the corner. Hallway sinks were common in city apartment buildings well into the twentieth century. This water was rarely hot; cold water drawn from the sink or pump usually had to be carried to the stove to be heated.

Plumbing was expensive to install, and landlords who rented to working-class people avoided doing so until required by law. In Chicago a 1902 city ordinance required that every new tenement have one sink with running water on each floor of the building. Older buildings were required to have a sink with running water "easily accessible" to each apartment, which probably meant one sink on the ground floor.[33] The laws, however, were often flouted; Polish families living in industrial Chicago had to involve social workers in their demands for sewer connections. As Dominic Pacyga reports, "Houses without sewer connections existed because the city claimed that not enough buildings stood on the streets to allow a connection with the water system," but when social workers investigated, they found that "the population of the block equaled that of many other blocks with more dwellings on them."[34] The city's hesitation to install adequate sewer connections was based solely on the ethnic, working-class nature of the neighborhood. People who lived on the outskirts of cities and in rural areas fared the worst. In Homestead in 1907 only forty-seven of ninety families (52 percent) lived in buildings with running water. This included thirteen families who owned their homes, of whom nine had running water (69 percent).[35] In the 1920s the authors of *Middletown* estimated that one of four residents of Muncie, Indiana, lacked running water.[36] By the 1930s most working-class housing, even the most dilapidated, had running water. Until then, water had to be carried in from a faucet in the hallway, on the bottom floor of the building, or from a pump in the yard. All the water used for boiling food and for washing dishes, clothes, and bodies had to be carried back out again.

When every drop of water used for cooking, cleaning, and bathing had to be carried in and heated on the stove, women adjusted their patterns of work around that fact. In 1899 a group of social reformers and home economists created the New England Kitchen, a public kitchen in Boston that offered nutritious cooked food at low prices, in an attempt both to feed the hungry and to demonstrate by example how to cook wholesome food and keep clean kitchens. The organizers began offering hot water to neighborhood people who could not (or would not) carry and heat water in their own kitchens. According to Mary Hinman Abel, "We have started a sort of hot-water mission, or rather the people started it by first asking for what we should never have thought to offer, and now the whole neighborhood draws on our supply of hot water, and this means a great deal for health and cleanliness, especially in the summer months."[37] Imagine the logistics of a home kitchen in which acquiring hot water was such an onerous hassle that people would rather walk down the street, or even several blocks, to carry hot water back with them. The New England Kitchen, fitted with restaurant-style cooking capacity, most likely had running water that was piped directly into a basin in the stove to heat. The large cookstoves of middle-class houses had hot-water reservoirs—large, covered metal basins attached to the stoves, with faucets for access—which could produce constant supplies of hot water if the stoves were kept permanently lit and the reservoirs refilled as they were used (which still required carrying water). The people who took advantage of the New England Kitchen's hot water may not have had reservoirs on their stoves, may not have wanted to heat the stoves in the summer, or may have been boarders or lodgers with no cooking facilities at all. In these kitchens working-class women avoided cleaning tasks in the summer, and their families bathed less frequently. If they avoided heating their stoves for hot water, they must have avoided cooking on them as well.

In Pittsburgh working-class neighborhoods suffered from noticeably inadequate utilities. The mills on the river flats used so much water that those living in the surrounding hills had no water pressure. As Susan J. Kleinberg writes, "During the summer, many neighborhoods in the largest industrial section of the city (the South Side) had no water from seven in the morning until six at night when the mills operated."[38] Women had to carefully plan their working days around the mills' schedules, with the heavy work of laundry and cleaning reserved for the early morning or evening hours. Kleinberg argues that this directly affected the efficiency of the working-class woman's work: "Her washing and cleaning chores, made difficult by Pittsburgh's heavy particle pollution and the grime and sweat on her family's clothes, were made more arduous by the city decision to provide decent [municipal] services only to those who could pay for them."[39]

Working-class women "could not afford the rents in houses which had indoor water, they could not afford to install the plumbing, nor did they always live near the necessary sewer and water lines. . . . As a result, working class women carried indoors 'every drop of water they would use.'"[40] Because of the constraints of outdated utilities and tools, the work that poorer women did in their kitchens was less efficient than work done by women with more resources.[41] The same amount of effort produced smaller results when utilities and tools were inferior or less convenient. Of course, this is not to suggest that working-class women (or any women other than home economists) thought explicitly in these terms. However, women who worked constantly with limited resources must have been aware of the costs and benefits of their labor. Some tasks must have been considered, under the circumstances, just too much work.

Kleinberg's point about the lack of water in poor neighborhoods suggests a larger truth about working-class housework. Next to the material culture of kitchens, another set of factors influenced home cooks' decisions: the neighborhood. The utilities, services, density, and markets in the surrounding neighborhoods had unavoidable effects on the work done inside working-class kitchens.

The density of the neighborhood affected a family's decisions about whether and how much food to produce at home. Crowded city neighbor-hoods and scattered rural ones had different housing options available: were there affordable houses with yards or apartments with access to yards or only tiny, cramped apartments? Families that had access to yards or other outdoor spaces had a distinct advantage in their housework. First, in good weather a yard meant an expansion of living and working space: space to do laundry, to prepare food, and for children to play. Second, the yard offered the opportu-nity to grow vegetables or fruit and to raise poultry or other small livestock.

Chicago's unevenly dense working-class neighborhoods, a combination of family-owned homes and overcrowded rented homes, offered some opportuni-ties for home food production in yards and empty lots.[42] A photograph from the *Chicago Daily News* shows a woman in an urbanized area keeping several chickens in 1928 (see Figure 14.4). She might have kept the eggs, meat, and feathers for her own use, sold them, or traded them locally. In any case, keep-ing chickens could benefit a full-time housewife, as well as a wage earner who happened to have the advantage of a yard. A United States Bureau of Labor Statistics study in 1918 found that in Chicago almost 30 percent of the fami-lies surveyed made some profit from produce, chickens, or small livestock. Many more families must have had yards that provided food for the family but not enough for profit. In contrast, in much denser New York City a scant 3 per-cent of families (17 of 518) had income from gardens, poultry, and so forth.[43] (Those New Yorkers who kept chickens probably did so in much smaller spaces: a small pen in a courtyard or even in the apartment.) In Pittsburgh, which was less dense than either New York or Chicago, the keeping of small livestock was quite common. An 1890 U.S. commissioner of labor report on pig-iron workers in Pennsylvania indicated that about 64 percent of the work-ers kept pigs, and most kept chickens or at least small vegetable gardens.[44]

Keeping small livestock and raising vegetables were somewhat luxuries that could be indulged only when a family had abundant space and did not require constant wage work of all members. In the Department of Labor study, most of the families with garden income were about in the middle of the working classes: not destitute but not able to depend on a single income as more well-to-do working-class families were. Unfortunately, earlier Department of Labor and other budget studies generally did not record information about garden income, so it is hard to compare over time. However, it suggests that home food production was something of a privilege; working-class people with the lowest incomes might not have been able to rent houses with yards and so could not take advantage of those spaces. Especially in cities such as Chicago and Pittsburgh, women's labor at home, caring for boarders, was more lucrative than working for wages at a job.[45] But caring for boarders included the ex-hausting work of cooking, cleaning, and doing laundry, and it left little time for the more involved forms of home food production.

Not everyone could grow or raise some of their own food, but almost every-

Figure 14.4. Women in yard with chickens, Chicago, 1928. *Chicago Daily News* negative collection, call number DN-0085452, Chicago History Museum.

one could buy some of it ready-made, if they chose. On at least one category of food—bread—the record is fairly clear: working-class people were more likely to buy bread than to bake it themselves, compared with people in other classes. Bakeries sold everyday bread as well as a wide assortment of rolls, cakes, and pastries for snacks and desserts. Commercial bakeries expanded tremendously during this period. In 1879 there were 6,396 bakeries in the United States, roughly 1 for every 7,800 Americans. In 1899 there were 14,836; that amounted to 1 bakery for every 5,100 Americans. By 1909 there were 23,926 bakeries in the United States, or 1 for every 3,800 people.[46] In short, there were twice as many bakeries per capita in 1910 as there had been in 1880. Population density per square mile nearly doubled in the same years, meaning that more people lived close to bakeries.[47] It became convenient for urban working-class people to walk to nearby bakers and buy bread, rather than spend the time and labor baking it at home. The neighborhood offered the possibility to "opt out" of at least one part of home food production.

Quick, easy, and requiring no fuel or materials, baker's bread was the choice of many urban working-class families. Baker's bread was associated with the working class because it required little or no space or time at home for preparing bread, and it suggested a mother who worked for wages, inside or outside the home. As Susan Porter Benson writes of the interwar years, "For a woman, to purchase a dress was not just to buy the thing, but to buy the labor that went into it instead of supplying it herself; buying a loaf of bread bought her way out of the long and delicate process of producing it herself. The three most frequent services purchased were baking, sewing, and laundry, in that order."[48] A Pittsburgh dietary study of the 1890s compared families of different income levels: those of a professional man, a skilled artisan, a skilled laborer, an average day laborer, and an unskilled mill workman. Only in the household of the professional (a lawyer) was bread regularly baked at home, and there was most likely at least one maid or cook to help. The other families all used baker's bread and cake; each family also bought crackers, pies, and other bakery goods.[49]

Middle-class women regarded baker's bread as cheap and of low quality. The moral imperative of housekeeping meant that women were supposed to bake bread for their families, to keep their health and the family integrity intact. To buy baker's bread was to allow commerce to pollute the family sphere.[50] Yet for many of the new industrial workers of the turn of the century, baker's bread might never have had a negative stigma.

The prevalence of European immigrants and American rural migrants in turn-of-the-century cities meant that the American "tradition" of home bread baking was not as widespread as middle-class reformers liked to believe. Most urban Europeans had bought baker's bread at least since the Middle Ages. The historian Ken Albala notes that in European cities from the Middle Ages onward, "baking was only generally done by those who could afford an oven and the fuel to heat it"—a category that left out much of the urban laboring poor.[51] Tracy N. Poe notes that southern Italians who migrated to Chicago around the turn of the century had been accustomed to baking bread once or twice a week in communal ovens. No one was expected to have the space for a large oven or the fuel to heat it to bake bread for just one family. Southern Italians who migrated to Chicago were therefore unlikely to attempt home bread baking in their cramped new industrial homes and bought high-status white baker's bread instead.[52]

European immigrants were not alone in lacking a home bread-baking tradition. Americans who migrated from rural areas to cities and towns had been accustomed to traditional nonyeast quick breads such as biscuits and cornbread. Elizabeth S. D. Engelhardt's study of bread making among turn-of-the-century Appalachian women supports the argument about the importance of material requirements for different types of home cooking. Appalachian women made beaten biscuits for special occasions and cornbread for everyday use and were generally uninterested in the yeast-risen bread recipes taught them by Progressive community leaders. Engelhardt notes that "biscuits work better with marble rolling boards, rolling pins, biscuit cutters, mallets or cleavers, and ovens with consistent and steady temperatures. Corn bread needs only a bowl, a spoon (although fingers will do), a skillet of some kind, and a heat source."[53] Women who migrated to the cities from rural areas such as Appalachia were more likely to continue making simple quick breads at home or to begin buying baker's yeast bread; they were unlikely to begin baking yeast-risen bread at home.

At least in the case of bread, urban working-class people commonly opted to purchase the product—to purchase the labor rather than producing it in their small, inefficient kitchens. Single people, who may have had only rudimentary kitchens or no kitchens at all, clearly bought many meals from saloons and other small food businesses. How often did families buy ready-to-eat food, apart from bread? Robert Coit Chapin, who carried out budget studies in New York in 1908, calculated that 42 percent of the 318 workers' families studied took some meals away from home.[54] In the 1918 Department of Labor study, one-third of workers in Pittsburgh ate some meals away from home each year. Half of Chicago workers ate out at least occasionally, and almost two-thirds of New York families ate some meals out. The average price of meals eaten out was about twenty-seven cents. In 1918 twenty-seven cents could buy a steak entrée, soup, coffee, and pie from a lunchroom or a hot sandwich from a pushcart or a few beers and a meal at any saloons not yet closed by Prohibition. Especially in dense areas, meals and snacks out were an important part of the family budget. Although it is harder to trace, working-class people must have eaten some of this food for meals at home—either to replace or to supplement home-cooked food. A few items from the bakery or delicatessen could greatly reduce the amount of cooking done at home; or workday lunches at the saloon or cafeteria could be followed by more elaborate and traditional home-cooked meals on Sundays.

Working-class life was a balancing act: juggling cash earnings and home production to try to keep all members of the household fed, safe, employed, educated, and healthy. In the case of food, people had to balance their time, resources, and energy for cooking against the cash required to buy ready-to-eat food. Ultimately, this balancing act was based on the family's material circumstances: what kind of tools and living space they had and the neighborhood in which they lived. Working-class cooking was done in cramped, difficult circumstances and with an abundance of options to eliminate it in the neighborhood nearby. Of course, there were still plenty of times when home food production made sense. There is lots of clear evidence of home food production, but there is also lots of evidence of ready-to-eat food in working-class neighborhoods, if one knows where to look. Most families combined these strategies according to their own circumstances. The Serbian woman living in Pittsburgh could not have butchered hogs and made wine if she lived in a tenement in New York City. The woman who had a stroke could not make her own bread, whether she wanted to or not; luckily, there were neighborhood bakeries ready to sell bread to her, and to any others who simply did not want to bake it. Their decisions may have been conditioned by their heritage and their personal preferences, but the deal was sealed by their physical environment. These simple, daily decisions about food together added up to an important feature of life for urban working-class Americans. As we learn more about the material culture of working-class lives, more will be revealed about the complicated role of cooking and food production in that culture.

Chapter 15
Wheeling One's Groceries around the Store: The Invention of the Shopping Cart, 1936–1953

Catherine Grandclément

Introduction

The shopping cart is undoubtedly a crucial linkage in the food-supply chain of the mass-consumption era.[1] It allows consumer goods to be freed from their weight and to travel easily from the store shelves to the cashier and then to the trunk of the customer's car. However, for a time this seemingly simple device had a hesitant career, failing to meet a stable shape. And yet, this innovation was to confront a central "reverse salient" (to adopt Thomas Hughes's formulation)[2] of the expansion of the supermarket, that is, a localized but acute problem that hampered the growth of the "system" as a whole. This "reverse salient" was primarily in this case a problem of weight: an inadequate adjustment between the capacity of customers' market baskets and the general increase of self-service foodstuff array. As American supermarkets expanded in the 1930s—in terms of retail space, proliferation of merchandise, economies of scale, and expansion of automobile access[3]—the carriage of groceries within and out of the store became an issue. How did the shopping cart emerge as a solution? How did this device find its path to the supermarket?

The history of this "vehicle" of the mass-consumption economy is one of innovation. As is usual in innovation stories, the "first" shopping cart carries a bundle of great men and great ideas together with paternity disputes and property quarrels. The sociology of innovation has taught us to be cautious with simplistic narratives of innovation, and this includes in particular too heroic plots that overemphasize the role of singular individuals along with too tragic plots that overstress the part played by unmanageable social forces or historical trends. I draw here on a perspective grounded in science and technology studies that innovation is always a collective endeavor that only rarely consists of a linear path from idea to application. The imputation of causes and responsibilities is an issue not only for the historian but also for actors at stake in the innovation process.[4]

The story of the invention of the shopping cart already has a hero. When one searches for information on the shopping cart's origins, the name Sylvan N. Goldman immediately appears. An authorized biography, many citations in the press and in academic sources, and the presence of Goldman's "first shopping cart" in the collection of the Smithsonian Institution's department of artifacts attest to his importance. His claim, though, is not undisputable. In 2001 the Smithsonian Institution's archive department acquired the personal files of Orla E. Watson, the inventor of "another" first shopping cart. In this chapter, I reconstruct the early episodes of this innovation in the light of this recently available archival material.

This chapter clarifies some factual aspects of the invention of the shopping cart, but its main objective is not to dispute who invented it and when. I am more interested in the object as such: its vacillating shape, its evolving functioning, and its emerging use. Several "scripts"[5] were embedded into its early design, that is, several ways in which the technical device was to reconfigure the very act of shopping and getting food out of the store. The shopping cart was a crucial ingredient of the self-service revolution that characterized mass consumption in the 1930s in the United States of America and then in the rest of the world. A detailed examination of its early features (for example, the functioning of the wheels, the configuration of the basket, the system of storage) is of use for understanding some aspects of the "how" of this revolution. Early difficulties and design alternatives in the invention of the shopping cart make explicit the different problems and solutions that intermingled together in the nascent supermarket architecture, eventually tracing the path for an irreversible evolution.[6] To configure the shopping cart meant, at least in part, to reconfigure the market.

The chapter thus traces the early history of this market-enabling device, with close attention to the initial ideas of what the shopping cart was meant to do or "make do"—to the store, to shoppers, and to groceries. It is also a contribution to the comprehension of what constituted innovation in the twentieth-century mass-consumption business. The case of the shopping cart confirms that innovation is not a matter of pure technological insight or of pure economic entrepreneurship, but rather a compound ensemble created by heterogeneous actors that try to "interest" each other in the face of material contingency and radical uncertainty.[7]

The chapter opens with Sylvan N. Goldman's story, followed first through Terry P. Wilson's hagiographic account.[8] It describes Goldman's entrepreneurial venture and the meanders of his inventiveness in the face of what I call the supermarket "reverse salient": the burden of carrying a market basket. Of particular interest are the way in which the shopping cart emerged first as a "basket carriage" device (literally, a folding chair with wheels), the crucial problem of cart storage, and the emergence of the "telescoping" shopping cart. The second part of the chapter turns attention to Orla E. Watson, the actual inventor of the telescoping solution: a key element for the framing of a stable shape and path for the shopping cart. I analyze Watson's strategies, his commercial and legal battle against Goldman, and the fate of the device and the "trials" it went through.

From Market Baskets to Basket Carriers, 1936–1947

Goldman's History of the First Shopping Cart

More than just an authorized biography, Terry P. Wilson's *The Cart That Changed the World: The Career of Sylvan N. Goldman* is truly a hagiography and has actually been severely criticized in this respect, for instance by Richard Tedlow.[9] However, Wilson's account provides a useful point of departure for our travel along the cart's trail. In the mid-1930s, Wilson tells us, Sylvan N. Goldman was the owner of ten self-service stores in Oklahoma City. Compared to over-the-counter selling, self-service involved an extensive redistribution of trade identities and skills. Familiarity with the products, for instance, was no longer the prerogative of salespersons; in the new configuration salespersons moved backstage, off the selling scene. Information was communicated via the product itself, through artifacts such as packaging and branding. With the elimination of the counter, the free movement of customers among the shelves, and the widening of choice, the transportation of products was also reconfigured and retail sales logistics shifted over to the customer. From the mid-1910s some shops made wicker baskets available for their customers.[10] Goldman, observing his customers in the mid-1930s, noted how the size and weight of the shopping basket limited the volume of purchases.

One evening in 1936 Goldman had a brilliant idea. Noticing two folding chairs in his office, he "found the solution," Wilson says, to the problem of carrying shopping: "[I]f the seat of a folding chair was raised several inches and another similar seat added below, a basket could be placed on each of them. Wheels attached to each leg would make the chair mobile, and the back of the chair could be adapted as a handle to push the cart."[11] Goldman instructed Fred Young, a handyman employed in one of his shops, to work on that idea. There were problems: for instance, the cart tended to return to the state of a folding chair and to fold up when the wheels bumped into something, or it tipped over when going around corners. After a few months of work, the shopping cart, equipped with two wire mesh baskets, was ready (see Figure 15.1).

On June 4, 1937, Goldman placed an advertisement in the Oklahoma City press showing a woman harassed by the weight of her shopping basket. "It's

Figure 15.1. Sylvan N. Goldman's folding cart, c. 1937. National Museum of American History, Smithsonian Institution, Washington, D.C.

new—It's sensational. No more baskets to carry" promised the advertisement—without any information as to how this extraordinary result would be achieved. Goldman was expecting that curiosity would bring customers to the stores and make them readily adopt the basket carriers. Unfortunately, this did not work out as he had hoped. Customers came in as they were used to, probably having forgotten the advertisement they saw in the newspapers, and they were loath to use the basket carriers. While men protested that they were strong enough to carry baskets, women argued that they had pushed around enough baby carriages in their lives not to want the same yoke in the grocery store. The launch plan was a flop, concluded a bitter Goldman.

Yet, Goldman would not give up. He placed another advertisement the following week, as mysterious as the first one, emphatically—and wrongly—announcing that the " 'No Basket Carrying plan' met with instant approval last week-end." Then in his main store he employed shills, men and women of various ages, with whom everyone could identify, to perform their shopping with the basket carriers. Seeing other shoppers using this new system, the customers accepted the carts offered to them by a hostess. Within weeks all of Goldman's stores were using the folding carts.[12]

On a national scale, the story of the diffusion of the folding cart presented by Wilson follows the same pattern. Nationally, the customers were not the end users but the managers of supermarkets who had to decide to buy the basket carriers. Goldman took advantage of the first Super Market Convention in September 1937 to launch his product and met a favorable response. However, when Goldman's sales representatives went to visit supermarket managers, they encountered some resistance. Managers worried, for example, about the damage that their customers' children could cause by playing with shopping carts. To educate potential clients, Goldman used his employees as actors in a movie that showed how smoothly stores equipped with carts functioned. Pleased and reassured by what they saw, supermarket managers ended up adopting Goldman's folding cart. At least according to Wilson's account, that was how the folding cart invaded the world of mass consumption and Goldman's new firm, the Folding Basket Carrier Company (later renamed Folding Carrier Corp.), became outstandingly prosperous.

Wilson's (and Goldman's) tale of innovation adoption suggests that the innovation of the basket carrier typically encountered the problem of social acceptability. End users and supermarket managers showed reluctance to employ the carrier because using it would have meant a loss of dignity (end users) and of civility (managers). Only after seeing members of their social group—or representatives of their customers, in the case of managers—shopping with carts would they accept the innovation. So goes the implicit explanatory model embedded in Wilson's and Goldman's tale. This model posits irrational users incapable of sensing the innovation's benefits, with their only motive for action, and hence motive for adopting an innovation, being conforming to a social norm.

Although such a vision may please innovators—a matter of good technique in the hands of users socially reluctant toward novelty—it is rather at odds with a perspective that would consider how social and technical elements are mutually shaped in innovation stories. I would argue against Wilson that the fake users—at the store entrance or in the movie—were less instrumental in spreading a new social norm than in demonstrating the new use that could be performed with the cart. Their role as demonstrators, rather than as models for imitation, was crucial.[13] Demonstrators are there, in particular, to unfold the "script" of the technical object; they help the user throughout the process of what Madeleine Akrich calls "de-scription": the ideal scenario of use imagined by the designer ("script") needs to be deployed so that conceived use transforms into actual use ("de-scription").[14] Within this perspective, a user in front of a new technical object cannot be reduced to a follower in front of a new, potentially collective practice. The user, perhaps a bit of an innovator herself, needs to make sense of the object's functioning. She needs to bridge the gap between the ideal use (whose rules are embedded into the design) and what is actually going on in the real situation of use. However, in order to engage in this process of "de-scription," users would rather not be alone. The first shoppers in Wilson's story did not properly engage in this process. The fake users then moved to act as proper demonstrators of a new use: wheel one's groceries around the store. They put into motion the "script" that was inscribed into the new device.

Regarding the design of the folding basket carrier, the choice of a chair was less of a coincidence than it seems. The innovation started with what imagination mobilizes most readily, which happens to be there, is available, and constitutes the material of opportunity. In his study of the objects that populate our daily lives, Henry Petroski claims that the development of these objects starts less with abstract ideas or laboratory studies than with situated adjustments, trial and error, tinkering with the objects.[15] An intellectual genealogy of the development of the shopping cart would lead us to dozens of objects, similar to the shopping cart, from the industrial cart to the dinner wagon in bourgeois homes, via all sorts of agricultural carts, bag trucks, pushcarts, and baby carriages. Goldman's (through Wilson's) account shows, by contrast, a situational genetics of the object: it was the chair as an available resource that generated the form of the invention.

The choice of a *folding* chair is nevertheless worth considering. Why did Goldman invest in complex design work—which Wilson says lasted several months—to ensure that the basket carrier would not unexpectedly collapse, when it was possible to use an ordinary stable chair? Design specialists often comment ironically on the survival of objects with completely obsolete functions or elements, simply due to the weight of things, because the element in question opened a way that no one had thought of closing. An example is the "R" key on fixed phones, which is still there even though no one knows its purpose.[16] However, this explanation is not valid here, for Goldman deliberately tried to manufacture a folding cart. His biography indicates that the small amount of space occupied in the store by the folded basket carrier and piled-up baskets was one of his strongest selling points.[17]

At this point Wilson's account arouses doubt as to its reliability. The basket-carrier-cum-folding-chair is an answer to two problems: first, the weight of shopping, and, second, the perverse effects of the solution to the first problem, that is, the space taken in the store by the system for carrying goods. In other words, the folding element of the shopping cart was a response to a problem that had not yet arisen. The problem may have been apparent beforehand to space-conscious managers. But it seems worthwhile wondering whether the basket carrier was really all that new.

Goldman's Precursors and Predecessors

Wilson does mention the existence of precursors, which he situates in the 1920s but whose relevance he is quick to disqualify. An example is Henke & Pillot, a Houston store that was laid out in the shape of an "M" for reshelving from the rear. According to Wilson, the store had a fifteen-inch wide track, raised about thirty inches from the floor and fitted with low side rails that ran along the shelves and carried baskets equipped with tiny wheels grooved to slide inside the rails. "While this system eliminated the burden of carrying overladen baskets, it was not adaptable to stores with different floor plans. In addition, shoppers were forced to follow the entire track. This discouraged people who came in to buy a few items and had to wait behind slower customers."[18] This example, which was not the only one of its kind, highlights the superior fluidity of clientele movements that could be obtained with a cart, as opposed to a wagon on rails.[19]

Closer examination of the advertisements and patents for basket carriers during that period gives us yet another picture. In 1937 no fewer than four cart manufacturers (United Steel and Wire, American Wire Form, Roll'er Basket, and Folding Basket Carrier) advertised in the trade journal *Super Market Merchandising* (*SMM*). What is more, basket carriers were used in many stores at least from 1936; some had only three wheels, others could bear only one single basket, and on others, baskets of specified size had to be hooked to the frame instead of placing any container on a platform.[20] Thus, Goldman was not the only one to be concerned about what appeared to be a thorny problem for the entire profession in the late 1930s: the carrying of one's shopping choices within large self-service stores. Looking at these instances, the genealogy of the shopping cart appears with far more continuity than in the one reported by Wilson. Months before the first Goldman advertisement in an Oklahoman newspaper in June 1937, a solution to the weight of merchandise had already emerged in the form of a frame on wheels, on which one or two baskets were placed.

With this context we can better understand why Goldman was so interested in the fact that the chair folded. These carriers took up space, whereas Goldman's invention saved space. He provided a clever answer to the real problem of storing shopping carts.[21] But is this really so? Knowing Goldman, it is wise to check twice. A careful examination of the available sources leads to two additional findings. First, there was at least one folding basket carrier before Goldman's. The Roll'er Basket Company indeed advertised a folding carrier in May 1937.[22] Second, there was another "first" folding carrier by Goldman before Goldman's official first folding carrier. The earliest illustrated advertisement of the Folding Basket Carrier Company, published in *SMM*, in October 1937 shows a cart bearing a strong resemblance to a folding chair and which, when unfolded, formed not a seat but a sort of folding basket integrated into the structure. This corresponded to Goldman's first patent and what was probably the first real *shopping cart* with the basket permanently attached to the frame, not simply a basket carrier (see Figure 15.2).[23]

This episode requires us to reassess Goldman's contribution to the invention of the shopping cart. In 1937 Goldman proposed a solution not to the first problem of carrying goods while shopping nor to the second problem of storing devices for carrying shopping, but to a third problem, that of the effort required to set up and dismantle the basket carrier. This solution consisted of a system in which the basket was part of the structure and yet could be compacted. In other words, Goldman was even more of a precursor than he claimed to be. But he was also a great storyteller. Why, indeed, further complicate a story, already nicely packed with obstacles (recalcitrant users and obstructive buyers) that the hero had ingeniously overcome, with details irrelevant to the progression of the tale? Goldman never seemed to mention this first cart anywhere. He simplified the cart, and this early, more sophisticated version purely disappeared from his official story. Gone (from the story) also were the competitors and the remarkable and relatively quick convergence in the second half of the 1930s of shopping carts designed as two-basket carriers. After all, Goldman's company, Folding Carrier Corp., was by far the largest cart manufacturer in the United States from the late 1930s to the early 1960s, which may have naturally led Goldman to neglect competitors in a retrospective account.

From the Telescoping Cart to the Nest-Kart, 1946–1953

Ten years were needed to definitely find a solution to storing the carts and then open the path to the development and diffusion of the modern shopping cart. In 1947, Wilson says, Goldman's Folding Carrier Corp. introduced the "Nest-Baskart" (later renamed "Nest-Kart"), a new cart that "enabled grocers to store one-piece carriers in a smaller area than that required by the older models with their removable baskets. The back section of the carrier basket, now an integral part of the frame, swung forward when the front of a second carrier was pushed against it, allowing any number of carts to nest, each partly enclosing the one behind it."[24]

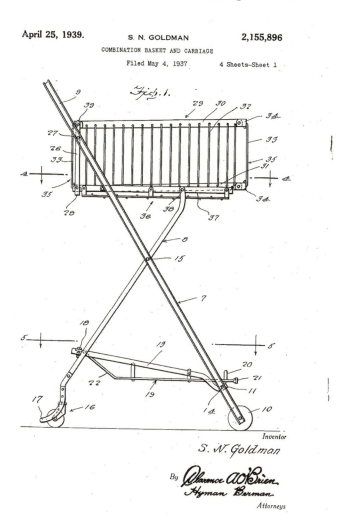

April 25, 1939.   S. N. GOLDMAN   2,155,896
COMBINATION BASKET AND CARRIAGE
Filed May 4, 1937   4 Sheets-Sheet 1

Fig. 1.

Inventor
S. N. Goldman
By Clarence A. O'Brien
Hyman Berman
Attorneys

Figure 15.2. Goldman's first folding cart, May 1937. United States Patent and Trademark Office, Washington, D.C.

The lack of specifics in Wilson's book concerning such an important alteration is particularly surprising, especially in an account that is otherwise so quick to praise the slightest details of its subject's ingenuity. Between the folding cart carrying two baskets, designed in 1936, and the "Nest-Baskart" of 1950, which resembled much more today's shopping carts, there was a real breakthrough in design. How was the step taken from one to the other?

Orla Watson's Telescoping Invention

At the beginning of 1946, fifty-year-old Orla E. Watson left his job as drafts-man at the Crafting and Processing Engineering Company in Kansas City to establish himself as a free-lance inventor.[25] In 1944 he had filed patent applications for inventions such as a pump, a valve, and an injection device. In 1946 he started focusing attention on the "problem" of shopping carts when he noticed the important amount of space they occupied in front of stores. Thinking about a way of improving existing carts, he started toying with the idea of horizontally telescoping frames rather than vertically stacked baskets. Watson initially followed the design mode of the day. The idea that he described to his wife Edith in April applied to separate elements: the structure on wheels and, separately, the baskets. In the initial design and the first prototypes produced in July 1946, the telescoping applied only to the structure (like the luggage trolleys now found currently in railway stations and airports), to which two baskets were added once they had been extracted from their lodging.

In the summer of 1946 Watson built two prototypes, which he showed to about ten individuals likely to start commercializing them. Among the people watching his demonstrations was Fred E. Taylor, a retired Kansas City grocer, who would go into financial partnership with Watson. At the end of August, Watson hired a lawyer to patent his carts. In early September the telescoping frames were lent for a ten-day trial period to one of the Milgram's Store outlets in Kansas City, situated close to Watson's workshop. The test was carried out with ordinary baskets. At the same time Watson was working on improving the telescoping frames by adding baskets that could also fit into one another. By mid-September he had designed new prototypes and modified the patent application to reflect these improvements (see Figure 15.3).

Watson's 1946 telescoping carts differed from their predecessors in two ways. They not only fitted into one another, owing to the swinging gate at the rear end of the baskets, but also were attached to the baskets so that they were permanently *shopping carts* and no longer basket carriers with distinct, separable elements. This was far from self-evident: Watson first conceived of telescoping frames before thinking of adding telescoping baskets as well and attaching them to the frames. Yet the strength of the system was clearly its combination of the two: telescoping and attachment. The "parking problem" that the telescoping carts claimed to solve was less the one and only problem of parking—the saving of space was the folding cart's advantage over its predecessors—than the double-sided one of parking *and* unparking, that is, the conversion of stock into flows.

Watson's cart made compatible two contradictory commands of the folding cart system: storage and use. The small and ingenious device of the tilting of the rear end of the basket absorbed alone those two injunctions by maintain-

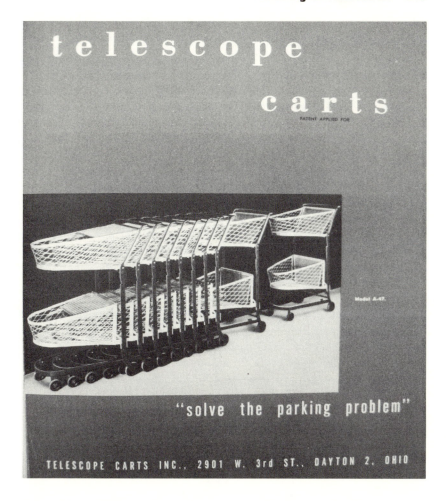

telescope

c a r t s

PATENT APPLIED FOR

Model A-47.

"solve the parking problem"

TELESCOPE CARTS INC., 2901 W. 3rd ST., DAYTON 2, OHIO

Figure 15.3. "Telescope Carts" brochure, c. 1947. Telescoping Shopping Cart Collection, Box 2, Folder 3, Archives Center, National Museum of American History, Smithsonian Institution, Washington, D.C.

ing the form of the cart in each state: stored or ready for use. Consequently, the effort required to accomplish that conversion was reduced, from the long sequence of setting up/dismantling to the easy movement of pulling and pushing. From the self-service development logic, this simplification is particularly interesting insofar as it allows for a transfer of the effort of putting the cart into use from the store employees to the customers. This, in addition, permits a quasi-perfect adjustment of the rate of stock-flow conversion to the customers' flows. Thus, both the availability of shopping carts and storage space are not only increased but permanently optimized.[26]

Yet, despite its superiority over the basket carrier, Watson's shopping cart was still close to its origins. Just as the folding chair was discernible in the folding cart, so the folding cart appeared in the telescoping cart. Economists often describe the irreversibility of an initial technological choice as a "path-dependence" phenomenon.[27] Watson indeed remained faithful to the principle of superimposing two baskets; the idea of a single, bigger basket like the one typical of today's shopping carts did not seem to occur to him. However, Watson was not so much a prisoner of the two-basket carrier silhouette as of the well-established organization of customer checkout in the late 1940s supermarket.

At that time the cashier stand was a long counter firmly dividing the space into two sides, one for the cashier and one for the customer. Its general shape was similar to our contemporary checkout stands, except that there was no conveyor belt and, most importantly, customers were usually not required to unload their baskets themselves. To gain access to the customer's purchase, the cashier had to bend toward the counter to pick up the upper basket while the sacker went around the counter to lift the lower basket and pass it to the cashier. This mode of doing was incompatible with a cart whose baskets were no longer removable. There was an improved checkout counter design available in the mid-1940s that was less common. Referred to as the "cut-out check-stand," it had a space between the till and the counter to lodge the cart in order for the cashier to check the products directly from the upper basket. After having proceeded with the first basket, she would place the lower basket on the upper platform.[28]

Wilson anticipated either expanded use of the cut-out check-stand or improvements that still depended on the two-basket system. He improved his original design by making the top basket of his cart able to tilt back and the bottom one to be raised to the upper position—the integration of the baskets to the frame analyzed above was thus only partial. In 1946 Watson filed a patent for the "Power Lift," a motorized check-out stand that was of the "cut-out" type. When the customer checked out, access to the bottom basket was further improved by a motorized platform incorporated into the counter. The cashier would press a pedal, and the basket, sliding vertically, was lifted to the level of the counter.

I believe that in so designing his cart and quasi-simultaneously the "Power Lift," Watson followed not only the design path of basket carriers but also the more global design of the "technical ensemble"[29] of the shopping cart and the checkout counter. However, he was probably less a passive prisoner of the existing path than an active compromiser, fully aware of the gesture organizing the checkout station. By sticking to the double-basket design and making them partially removable from the frame, he fostered a sort of a compromise: combining the telescoping cart with the supermarket with cut-out check-stand while respecting the current distribution of tasks between the customer and the cashier. All this ingenuity, effort, and care, though, seemed to have been in vain once the new ensemble of the long counter, single-basket shopping cart and the self-unloading customer were generalized. The patent application for the Power Lift was eventually withdrawn.

The Market for Telescoping Carts

In autumn 1946 Watson, like any good innovator, tried to create a network for his invention. He went into partnership with Fred E. Taylor, a man who was more enterprising than himself and better at business, especially retail trade. Thanks to Taylor, Watson's carts and counters benefited from an experimental site and showroom from the end of 1946. Floyd Day's market in Kansas City served as a "guinea pig store," as Watson and Taylor called it. Taylor also put Watson in touch with George O'Donnell, a salesman for Hill, a company that manufactured refrigerator equipment for stores. In constant contact with supermarket managers and wholesalers specializing in point-of-sale furniture, O'Donnell was familiar with the market and aware of the potential of Watson's inventions.[30]

Telescope Carts, Inc. was officially founded in April 1947. Under the partnership, Watson handled design and production, O'Donnell managed sales, and Taylor held overall managerial duties. By the end of the summer of 1947, O'Donnell had orders from his regular business clients for over one hundred carts. After their first participation in a trade fair in October in Peoria, Illinois, they decided to present the telescoping cart at the Super Market Convention, a crucial meeting point for the self-service industry, which opened on November 2, 1947. It was at the inaugural convention ten years earlier that Sylvan N. Goldman had presented his folding shopping cart.

Initial orders were strong, but the situation became tense on the production side. The switch to industrial production entailed many problems that Watson had to solve ad hoc: defects in the telescoping, problems with wheels and handles, risks related to sharp angles, for example. Throughout 1947 he constantly revised the telescoping shopping cart model. In autumn 1947 nothing had left the Dayton factory yet. Only two Kansas City stores (Floyd Day's and Chas Ball Supermarkets) had telescoping carts, produced one by one by Watson. At this stage the market, which Watson's team believed to be large and seemingly easy to monopolize, suddenly became highly competitive due to a new entrant.

At the chain store operators' trade fair in October 1947, Goldman's firm, the Folding Carrier Corp., preannounced the launch of the "New Triple-Plus Capacity Nest-Baskart," a shopping cart that tripled the quantity of shopping a customer could transport, saved parking space, and speeded up the checking-out process. This triple performance stemmed from a twofold innovation: a large, single basket and a telescoping system that was surprisingly similar to Watson's.

George O'Donnell panicked: was it possible that others had invented the system of telescoping carts before Watson? On visiting the Folding Carrier stand at the Food Chain Operators Convention incognito, O'Donnell learned that the unexpected competitor was selling its shopping carts for nearly three dollars less per unit than those of Telescope Carts and that it had already received orders for three thousand. Goldman's firm moreover announced that it would be present at the Super Market Convention in November and that it had already launched an advertising campaign. The announcement of the Nest-Baskart launch appeared in the October and November issues of *Super Market Merchandising*[31] (see Figure 15.4). To Watson's, Taylor's, and O'Donnell's dismay, everything pointed to the fact that Goldman had copied their innovation and that Telescope Carts was about to be overtaken in the race for the commercialization of telescoping carts. Watson's invention was public and available for examination by competitors—at the guinea-pig store in Kansas City, for instance. However, for Watson, this publicity was backed with a patent. The preliminary investigations carried out with a view to filing a patent application had shown that no other device of a "telescopic nature" for shopping carts or similar instruments existed. Once the initial anxiety had subsided, the three men felt confident that the patent problem would be sorted out easily.

Turning Universal Too Quickly: The Contest over the Watson Patent

Watson and Taylor assumed that Goldman, having gotten wind of their innovation, had gone to Kansas City in June 1947 to visit stores equipped by Watson and then worked on a shopping cart with the same telescoping system—for which he filed a patent application registered on May 5, 1948.[32] On October 25 of that year, following Watson's various claims, an interference procedure concerning Watson's and Goldman's patent applications was officially opened by the patent office. In 1949, however, production setbacks and commercial difficulties competing with Goldman led Watson and his partners to favor an out-of-court settlement—to salvage something from the wreckage.

On June 3, 1949, Goldman and Watson signed an agreement that put an end to the interference procedure. Goldman recognized Watson's invention and paid one dollar in damages for the counterfeit product. In exchange Watson granted Goldman an exclusive operating license (apart from three licenses that had already been granted to other cart manufacturers: Binkley, Chatillon, and Campbell-French). Watson officially received the telescoping shopping cart patent but gave up the idea of producing and commercializing them. On December 31, 1949, Telescope Carts ceased manufacturing carts and became a holding company entirely devoted to the management of its patent operating licenses.

Figure 15.4. Folding Carrier's advance announcement. Telescoping Shopping Cart Collection, Archives Center, National Museum of American History, Smithsonian Institution, Washington, D.C.

Watson's invention survived. Its proliferation was the result not of aggressive marketing but rather of its connection to a competitor with industrial know-how in the emerging market for shopping carts. By hitching Goldman's network to his innovation, albeit reluctantly, Watson was nevertheless able to "conquer the world" as he had intended to. The single-basket telescoping shopping cart, the fruit of unexpected and forced collaboration between Goldman and Watson, swiftly became a universal object of mass distribution. However, being "universal" is not without risks.

Watson's solution to the "problem" of shopping carts (and to the "reverse salient" of the self-service system as a whole) was more than ingenious: it turned unavoidable. Manufacturers of shopping carts excluded from Watson's operating license commercialized telescoping carts anyway. In 1950 a legal battle broke out between Telescope Carts and one of those manufacturers, United Steel and Wire Co. Telescope Carts sued United Steel and Wire for patent infringement, and the latter company defended itself on the grounds that the patent was invalid.[33] Again Watson was confronted with the uncomfortable situation of gaining back the paternity on an invention that had quickly become a generic pattern for shopping carts.

The commercial success of Watson's cart was eventually due to its reprise and reinterpretation by competitors. Others created a hybrid cart based on Watson's initial innovation, thereby making it difficult for Watson to reassert his initial contribution to the modern shopping cart. The 1950 shopping cart was quite different in appearance and design from the 1947 Telescope Cart and even from the 1947 Nest-Baskart (compare Figures 15.3 and 15.4 to Figure 15.5). Furthermore, it was even more different than the object featured in the 1946 patent. In fact, this patent was not particularly detailed. Some of the claims forgot to mention the "hinged swinging gate at the rear end of the basket," which form the essential part of Watson's invention. Of course, all those arguments were put forward by United Steel and Wire to differentiate its cart from Watson's patent. In addition, United Steel and Wire argued that the Watson patent relied on generic—and then not patentable—elements such as the hinge. At that time Watson sensed also the fragility of the partnership with his former rival. In 1951 and 1952 Goldman challenged the payment of royalties to Telescope Carts, contending that many manufacturers were infringing a patent that in addition was possibly invalid.

Fortunately for Watson, the courts eventually upheld his patent, the trial being ultimately terminated in July 1953. It is quite interesting to note here that in the judge's opinion, the main evidence of the patentability of Watson's shopping cart was its commercial success—precisely the phenomenon that twice almost expropriated Watson from his invention. The judge did recognize the competitors' contributions to the improvement of Watson's cart and thereby to its commercial success but nevertheless noted that Watson was clearly the inventor of the telescoping cart, which, within a few

UNITED NESTING CARRIERS LOOK BETTER LONGER

STYLED RIGHT

Bright as a dollar and as smart as your new car, United Nesting Carriers are right for the modern store. They stay new looking for years without any upkeep expense. The rich brilliant chrome finish is permanently plated on, will not chip, scratch, or flake off.

BUILT RIGHT

You can't beat that Tubular Steel Frame for strength with light weight. (It's the same construction as used in big airplanes). Basket is made from extra heavy gauge steel wire to stand the abuse of constant nesting and maximum loads (it's replaceable in case of accidental damage). Full 4″ wheels and ball bearing swivel castors assure smooth easy operation.

SELL RIGHT

United Nesting Carriers sell more goods because the single basket is at the top where it is easy to load. It will hold all the purchases the average customer wants to buy. In addition, the lower shelf provides a place for case goods and bulky bags. And, of course, they nest, leaving you more space for store displays.

PROMPT SHIPMENTS

 UNITED STEEL AND WIRE CO.

140 FONDA AVENUE, BATTLE CREEK, MICHIGAN

Figure 15.5. United Steel and Wire Co. advertisement, October 1949. Used with permission from Rehrig-United, successor to United Steel and Wire Co.

years, had replaced all the other types. After 1953 new cases of infringement sporadically arose, and Telescope Carts systematically sued offenders. Owing to the fact that the court had upheld the validity of the patent, this was more or less a matter of routine, with no risk for the interests secured by Telescope Carts.

Conclusion

What does a shopping cart do? An analysis of mundane artifacts in the line of Bruno Latour[34] allows making sense of the "programs" that are inscribed into them, that is, in the sort of action they help institute. The shopping cart's early programs came out of the experiences of innovators confronting what I have called, following Hughes, the supermarket's "reverse salient" in the 1930s: a breach of fluidity in food chain and mass retail distribution caused by the trouble of carrying groceries around the store. I use the plural for "programs" because the early shopping cart evolved in shape and purpose, as did the sorts of problems the cart was meant to solve.

The idea of a rolling basket carrier first emerged as a direct response to the weight of market baskets in self-service stores that grew larger and larger from the 1930s onward. After much effort, the innovation started to fit the supermarket environment smoothly. However, the very existence of this new, potentially cumbersome object called forth another sequence of "problematizing" in regard to its storage. Using a folding structure was indeed a solution to the storage problem, but not to the (newly emergent) need of having the carts both out of the way and readily available. The telescoping method translated this requirement into the cart's new program. The swinging gate at the rear of the basket was the "crux" of the device, the feature around which the innovation stabilized.

The sources used in this chapter help an understanding of the way the shopping cart grew literally—but slowly—from the market basket. They also point to a multitude of actors and factors that intervened in the innovation process. There were neither one nor two inventors of *the* shopping cart but rather a collective and distributed endeavor, sometimes collaborative but also fiercely competitive and conflictive at some other points. Inventiveness (always inspired by available materials and constraints) intermingled together with industrial opportunities in the constitution of the shopping cart's innovation network. This network, a "techno-economic network" in the sense developed by Michel Callon,[35] included both Sylvan N. Goldman and Orla E. Watson, along with their associates and providers, retailers willing to turn their stores into testing sites, particular legal devices aimed at instituting and protecting intellectual property rights, professional meetings and publications, networks for the provision of manufacturing materials, and others. This compound and continuous dimension of innovation contributed towards the establishment of an increasingly robust object whose form was progressively set and composed. That is how the shopping cart adhered to (and also enhanced) the larger "programs" of self-service supermarkets in the 1930s, which included dimensions such as boosting the continuity of food-provision flow; shifting as many operations as possible over to the technical devices and customers themselves; and, last but not least, encouraging people to grab whatever they wished from the shelves, so that they could carry more and buy more.

Notes

Chapter 2. How Much Depends on Dinner?

1. Robert Heinlein, *The Moon Is a Harsh Mistress* (New York: Putnam, 1966). Barry Commoner's "Four Laws of Ecology" were found in his *Closing Circle* (New York: Knopf, 1971):

Everything is connected to everything else.
Everything must go somewhere.
Nature knows best.
There's no such thing as a free lunch. (16–24)

2. Joseph M. Carlin, "Saloons," in the *Oxford Encyclopedia of Food and Drink in America*, ed. Andrew F. Smith (New York: Oxford, 2004), 387–89.

3. Nick Fiddes, *Meat: A Natural Symbol* (London: Routledge, 1991), 115; Percy Bysshe Shelley, "A Vindication of Natural Diet" (1813), in *Ethical Vegetarianism: From Pythagoras to Peter Singer*, ed. Kerry S. Walters and Lisa Portmess (Albany: State University of New York Press, 1999), 73; Frances Moore Lappe, *Diet for a Small Planet* (New York: Ballantine, 1971).

4. Claude Fischler, "The 'Mad Cow' Crisis: A Global Perspective," in *Food in Global History*, ed. Raymond Grew (Boulder, Colo.: Westview, 1999), 213.

5. William Vogt, *The Road to Survival* (New York: William Sloane Associates, 1948), 285, 63.

6. J. Russell Smith, *The World's Food Resources* (New York: Henry Holt, 1919), 7.

7. The concept of "delocalization" is developed in Gretel H. Pelto and Pertti J. Pelto, "Diet and Delocalization: Dietary Changes Since 1750," in *Hunger and History: The Impact of Changing Food Production and Consumption Patterns on Society*, ed. Robert I. Rotberg and Theodore K. Rabb (Cambridge: Cambridge University Press, 1983), 309–30.

8. William Jevons, 1865, quoted in Garrett Hardin, *Living within Limits: Ecology, Economics, and Population Taboos* (New York: Oxford University Press, 1993), 134.

9. Jeffrey M. Pilcher, *Food in World History* (New York: Routledge, 2006), 71–78.

10. Edward M. East, *Mankind at the Crossroads* (New York: Charles Scribner's Sons, 1924), 64.

11. Henry Martyn, *Considerations on the East India Trade* (London, 1701); Pilcher, *Food in World History*, 27–33; Andrew Dalby, *Dangerous Tastes: The Story of Spices* (Berkeley: University of California Press, 2000), 11.

12. David Orr, *Earth in Mind: On Education, Environment, and the Human Prospect* (Washington, D.C.: Island Press, 1994), 172.

13. Whole Foods "Declaration of Interdependence," http://www.wholefoods market.com/company/declaration.html, accessed August 10, 2007.

14. Alan Meng and Hui Meng, "Food Chains and Webs," http://www.vtaide.com/png/foodchains.htm, accessed November 14, 2007.

15. Brower quoted by John McPhee, *Encounters with the Archdruid: Narratives about a Conservationist and Three of His Natural Enemies* (New York: Farrar, Straus and Giroux, 1971), 82.

16. Joseph F. Coates, John B. Mahaffie, and Andy Hines, *2025: Scenarios of US and Global Society Reshaped by Science and Technology* (Greensboro, N.C.: Oakhill Press, 1997), 380–81.

17. Octavia E. Butler, *Parable of the Sower* (New York: Four Walls Eight Windows, 1993); Starhawk, *The Fifth Sacred Thing* (New York: Bantam Books, 1993); T. C. Boyle, *A Friend of the Earth* (New York: Viking Books, 2002).

Chapter 3. Analyzing Commodity Chains

1. Wendell Berry, *What Are People For?* (San Francisco: North Point Press, 1990), 145, 146.

2. Michael Pollan, *The Omnivore's Dilemma: A Natural History of Four Meals* (New York: Penguin Books, 2006). Claude Fischler coined the similar phrase "omnivore's paradox" in "Food, Self, and Identity," *Social Science Information* 27, no. 2 (1988): 275–93.

3. William Friedland and Amy Barton, "Tomato Technology," *Society*, (September/October 1976): 34–42; William H. Friedland, Amy Barton, and Robert J. Thomas, *Manufacturing Green Gold: Capital, Labor, and Technology in the Lettuce Industry* (Cambridge: Cambridge University Press, 1981); William H. Friedland, "Commodity Systems Analysis: An Approach to the Sociology of Agriculture," *Research in Rural Sociology and Development* 1 (1984): 221–35.

4. William H. Friedland, "The End of Rural Society and the Future of Rural Sociology," *Rural Sociology* 47, no. 4 (1982): 598–608.

5. Friedland reviewed much of this literature in "Reprise on Commodity Systems Methodology," *International Journal of Sociology of Agriculture and Food* 9, no. 1 (2001): 82-103. Another useful overview is Peter Jackson, Neil Ward, and Polly Russell, "Mobilising the Commodity Chain Concept in the Politics of Food and Farming," *Journal of Rural Studies* 22 (April 2006): 129–41.

6. The key primary works on the "agrarian question" include Friedrich Engels, "The Agricultural Proletariat," in *The Condition of the Working Class in England* (1845); Karl Marx, "The Eighteenth Brumaire of Louis Napoleon" (1852); Karl Kautsky, *The Agrarian Question* (1899); and Vladimir Lenin, *The Development of Capitalism in Russia* (1899). Recent analyses of the "agrarian question" include Susan Mann, *Agrarian Capitalism in Theory and Practice* (Chapel Hill: University of North Carolina Press, 1990); William H. Friedland, "Shaping the New Political Economy of Advanced Capitalist Agriculture," in *Towards a New Political Economy of Agriculture*, ed. Friedland, Frederick H. Buttel, and Alan P. Rudy (Boulder, Colo.: Westview Press, 1991), 1–34; and Michael Watts, "Development III: The Global Agrofood System in Late-Twentieth Century Development (or Kautsky Redux)," *Progress in Human Geography* 20, no. 2 (1996): 230–45.

7. See, for good examples, Miriam J. Wells, *Strawberry Fields: Politics, Class, and Work in California Agriculture* (Ithaca, N.Y.: Cornell University Press, 1996); George L. Henderson, *California and the Fictions of Capital* (New York: Oxford University Press, 1999); David Goodman and Michael Redclift, *Refashioning Nature: Food, Ecology, and Culture* (London: Routledge, 1991); and Lawrence Busch, William B. Lacy, and Jeffry Burkhardt, *Plants, Power and Profit: Social, Economic, and Ethical Consequences of the New Plant Biotechnology* (Cambridge: Blackwell, 1991).

8. Margaret FitzSimmons, "The New Industrial Agriculture: The Regional Integration of Specialty Crop Production," *Economic Geography* 62 (October 1986): 334–53; Sidney Mintz, *Sweetness and Power: The Place of Sugar in Modern History* (New York: Penguin Books, 1985); Brian Page and Richard Walker, "From Settlement to Fordism: The Agro-Industrial Revolution in the American Midwest," *Economic Geography* 67 (1991): 281–315; Brian Page, "Across the Great Divide: Agriculture and Industrial Geography," *Economic Geography* 72 (October 1996): 376–97; Ron Tobey and Charles Weatherell, "The Citrus Industry and the Revolution of Corporate Capitalism in Southern California, 1887-1944," *California History* 74 (Spring 1995): 6–21.

9. Ben Fine, "Toward a Political Economy of Food," *Review of International Political Economy* 1, no. 3 (1994): 519–45, quotes on 526, 520. One strongly worded critique of Fine's article came from Friedland, "Reprise on Commodity Systems Methodology," 87–89.

10. Philip McMichael, ed., *The Global Restructuring of Agro-Food Systems* (Ithaca, N.Y.: Cornell University Press, 1994), vii.

11. Peter Coclanis, "Food Chains: The Burdens of the (Re)past," *Agricultural History* 72 (Fall 1998): 661–74; Peter Coclanis, "Breaking New Ground: From the History of Agriculture to the History of Food Systems," *Historical Methods* 38 (Winter 2005): 5–15.

12. James C. Scott, *Seeing Like a State: How Certain Schemes to Improve the Human Condition Have Failed* (New Haven, Conn.: Yale University Press, 1998); James Scott and Nina Bhatt, eds., *Agrarian Studies: Synthetic Work at the Cutting Edge* (New Haven, Conn.: Yale University Press, 2001); Akhil Gupta, *Postcolonial Developments: Agriculture in the Making of Modern India* (Durham, N.C.: Duke University Press, 1998); Deborah K. Fitzgerald, *Every Farm a Factory: The Industrial Ideal in American Agriculture* (New Haven, Conn.: Yale University Press, 2003); Richard A. Walker, *The Conquest of Bread: 150 Years of Agribusiness in California* (New York: New Press, 2004).

13. William Boyd, "Making Meat: Science, Technology, and American Poultry Production," *Technology and Culture* 42 (October 2001): 631–64; Roger Horowitz, "Making the Chicken of Tomorrow: Reworking Poultry as Commodities and as Creatures, 1945–1990," in *Industrializing Organisms*, ed. Susan R. Schrepfer and Philip Scranton (New York: Routledge, 2004), 215–35; Steve Striffler, *Chicken: The Dangerous Transformation of America's Favorite Food* (New Haven, Conn.: Yale University Press, 2005).

14. Daniel R. Block, "The Development of Regional Institutions in Agriculture: The Chicago Milk Marketing Order" (Ph.D. diss., University of California–Los Angeles, 1997); Shane Hamilton, "Cold Capitalism: The Political Ecology of Frozen Concentrated Orange Juice," *Agricultural History* 77 (Fall 2003): 557–81; John Soluri, *Banana Cultures: Agriculture, Consumption, and Environmental Change in Honduras and the United States* (Austin: University of Texas Press, 2005); Ian MacLachlan, *Kill and Chill: Restructuring Canada's Beef Commodity Chain* (Toronto: University of Toronto Press, 2001); Julie Guthman, *Agrarian Dreams: The Paradox of Organic Farming in California* (Berkeley: University of California Press, 2004).

15. Jack R. Kloppenburg, Jr., *First the Seed: The Political Economy of Plant Biotechnology, 1492–2000*, 2d ed. (Cambridge: Cambridge University Press, 2004); Busch et al., *Plants, Power and Profit*; Jeremy Rifkin, *The Biotech Century: Harnessing the Gene and Remaking the World* (New York: Tarcher, 1998).

16. Hugh Gusterson, "Decoding the Debate on Frankenfoods," in *Making Threats: Biofears and Environmental Anxieties*, ed. Betsy Hartmann, Banu Subramaniam, and Charles Zerner (Lanham, Md.: Rowman and Littlefield, 2005), 152–87.

17. Michel Callon, "Society in the Making," in *The Social Construction of Technological Systems*, ed. Wiebe Bijker, Thomas P. Hughes, and Trevor Pinch (Cambridge, Mass.: MIT Press, 1987), 85–103; Bruno Latour, *Science in Action: How to Follow Scientists and Engineers through Society* (Cambridge, Mass.: Harvard University Press, 1987).

18. Michel Callon, "Some Elements of a Sociology of Translation: Domestication of the Scallops and the Fishermen of St. Brieuc Bay," in *Power, Action & Belief*, ed. John Law (London: Routledge, 1986), 196–229.

19. Keiko Tanaka, Arunas Juska, and Lawrence Busch, "Globalization of Agricultural Production and Research: The Case of the Rapeseed Subsector," *Sociologia Ruralis* 39, no. 1 (1999): 54–77.

20. John Soluri, "People, Plants, and Pathogens: The Eco-Social Dynamics of Export Banana Production in Honduras, 1875–1950," *Hispanic American Historical Review* 80 (August 2000): 463–501.

21. Ronald C. Wimberley and Libby V. Morris, "The Poor Rural Areas That Must Support the 'Cities of the Future,'" *Sociation Today* 4 (Fall 2006), available online at http://www.ncsociology.org/sociationtoday/v42/wim.htm.

22. Terence K. Hopkins and Immanuel Wallerstein, "Commodity Chains in the World Economy prior to 1800," *Review, the Journal of the Fernand Braudel Center* 10, no. 1 (1986): 157–70.

23. One of the best summaries and critiques of world-systems theory is Lauren Benton, "From the World-Systems Perspective to Institutional World History: Culture and Economy in Global Theory," *Journal of World History* 7 (Fall 1996): 261–95. The best introduction to global commodity chains analysis is Gary Gereffi and Miguel Korzeniewicz, eds., *Commodity Chains and Global Capitalism* (Westport, Conn.: Praeger, 1994).

24. William H. Friedland, Frederick H. Buttel, and Alan P. Rudy, eds., *Towards a New Political Economy of Agriculture* (Boulder, Colo.: Westview Press, 1991), 18–19.

25. Harriet Friedmann, "The Political Economy of Food: The Rise and Fall of the Postwar International Food Order," *American Journal of Sociology* 88 (1982): S248–S286. This analysis has been revised multiple times in response to critiques; see Harriet Friedmann, "The Political Economy of Food: A Global Crisis," *New Left Review* 197 (1993): 29–57.

26. Scholars who maintain that nation-states continue to matter include David Vail and Laura T. Raynolds; see Vail, "Sweden's 1990 Food Policy Reform: From Democratic Corporatism to Neoliberalism," in *Global Restructuring of Agro-Food Systems*, ed. McMichael, 53–75; and Raynolds, "The Restructuring of Third World Agro-Exports: Changing Production Relations in the Dominican Republic," ibid., 214–38. Key works in the literature on globalization of food and agriculture are included in the following collections: Alessandro Bonanno, Lawrence Busch, William H. Friedland, Lourdes Gouveia, and Enzo Mingione, *From Columbus to ConAgra: The Globalization of Agriculture and Food* (Lawrence: University Press of Kansas, 1994); David Goodman and Michael Watts, eds., *Globalising Food: Agrarian Questions and Global Restructuring* (London: Routledge, 1997).

27. James Watson, ed., *Golden Arches East: McDonald's in East Asia* (Stanford: Stanford, Calif.: University Press, 1997). See also James Watson and Melissa Caldwell, eds., *The Cultural Politics of Food and Eating: A Reader* (Malden, Mass.: Blackwell, 2005); and Warren Belasco and Philip Scranton, eds., *Food Nations: Selling Taste in Consumer Societies* (New York: Routledge, 2002).

28. Susanne Freidberg, *French Beans and Food Scares: Culture and Commerce in an Anxious Age* (New York: Oxford University Press, 2004).

29. John H. Davis, "Business Responsibility and the Market for Farm Products" address before Boston Conference on Distribution, October 17, 1955, John H. Davis Papers, National Agricultural Library, Special Collections, Beltsville, Md., Box 1, Folder 2, p. 4

30. Coclanis, "Breaking New Ground," 5–6; Shane Hamilton, "The Political Etymology of *Agribusiness*" (presentation at the Agricultural History Society Conference, Ames, Iowa, June 23, 2007).

31. David Goodman and Michael Redclift, *Refashioning Nature: Food, Ecology, and Culture* (London: Routledge, 1991); Jane Dixon, "A Cultural Economy Model for Studying Food Systems," *Agriculture and Human Values* 16, no. 2 (1999): 151–60; Lawrence Busch, "How to Study Agricultural Commodity Chains: A Methodological Proposal," in *Economie des Filieres en Regions Chaude*, ed. Michel Griffon (Paris: CIRAD, 1990), 13–24.

32. Jackson, Ward, and Russell, "Mobilising the Commodity Chain Concept," 130.

33. Philip McMichael and Chul-Kyoo Kim, "Japanese and South Korean Agricultural Restructuring in Comparative and Global Perspective," in *Global Restructuring of Agro-Food Systems*, ed. McMichael, 46; Bonanno et al., "Introduction," in *From Columbus to ConAgra*, 15.

34. Roger Horowitz, *Putting Meat on the American Table: Taste, Technology, Transformation* (Baltimore: Johns Hopkins University Press, 2005); E. Melanie DuPuis, *Nature's Perfect Food: How Milk Became America's Drink* (New York: New York University Press, 2002); Deborah K. Fitzgerald, "Eating and Remembering," *Agricultural History* 79 (Fall 2005): 393–408.

Chapter 4. Lard to Lean

The author is grateful for the assistance and advice of Roger Horowitz, Phil Scranton, Katherine Grier, Jenny Barker-Devine, William C. Page, Roger Hunsley, Dawn Liverman, Tony Crawford (Kansas State University Special Collections), Bertha Ihnat (Ohio State University Archives), and the entire Special Collections staff at Iowa State University.

1. Elizabeth Weise, "The New Pork: It's Now the Other 'Lite' Meat," *USA Today*, July 5, 2006, D7; Amy Lorentzen, "Hog 'Diet' Said to Chop Pork Fat to Chicken Level," *Des Moines Sunday Register*, July 2, 2006.

2. For a brief overview of the transformation in the pork industry and especially the process of swine testing to make lean pork, see William Colgan Page, *Leaner Pork for a Healthier America: Looking Back on the Northeast Iowa Swine Testing Station* (Iowa Department of Transportation in cooperation with the Federal Highway Administration, and the State Historical Society of Iowa, 2000). See also Roger Horowitz, *Putting Meat on the American Table: Taste, Technology, Transformation* (Baltimore: Johns Hopkins University Press, 2006); Edmund Russell, "Introduction: The Garden in the Machine," in *Industrializing Organisms: Introducing Evolutionary History*, ed. Susan R. Schrepfer and Philip Scranton (New York and London: Routledge, 2004), 6–8.

3. Paul W. Gates, *The Farmer's Age, 1815–1860* (New York: Holt, Rinehart, and Winston, 1960), 214–21; Clarence H. Danhof, *Change in Agriculture: The Northern United States, 1820-1870* (Cambridge, Mass.: Harvard University Press, 1969), 175–78.

4. USDA, "1972 Handbook of Agricultural Charts," in *Agriculture Handbook No.*

439 (Washington, D.C.: U.S. Government Printing Office, 1972), 71; Stewart H. Fowler, *The Marketing of Livestock and Meat* (Danville, Ill.: Interstate Printers and Publishers, Inc., 1961), 71, 73–75.

5. Geoffrey Shepherd, "Why Is the Demand for Pork Dropping?," *Iowa Farm Science* (June 1956): 7–8.

6. Ibid.; Bernard Ebbing, "Importance of Muscling in Meat Type Hogs," Booklet 4, *The Provisioner Little Library* (The National Provisioner, 1954), Rath Packing Company Collection, Section F, Box 3, Folder 8, Iowa State University Special Collections; Al Bull, "Consumers Want Lean Meat," *Wallaces' Farmer and Iowa Homestead*, May 4, 1957 (hereafter cited as *Wallaces' Farmer*); Gil Vander Kolk, "Retailer's View on Fresh Products," in *The Pork Industry: Problems and Progress*, ed. David G. Topel (Ames: Iowa State University Press, 1968), 14.

7. W. H. Bruner, "Meat-Type Hog," in *The Hog Annual, 1952* (Cincinnati: *The Farm Quarterly*, 1952), 246; Walter A. Wilcox, *The Farmer in the Second World War* (Ames: Iowa State College Press, 1947), 184–88, 196–98.

8. Glenn E. Conatser, Gordon Jones, and Ken Stalder, "Performance Testing," http://aniamalscience.ag.utk.edu/swine/performance_testing.htm (accessed September 14, 2006), 3, 5; Bruner, "Meat-Type Hog," 246–48.

9. Richard Dougherty, *In Quest of Quality: Hormel's First 75 Years* (Austin, Tex.: George A. Hormel Company, 1966), 228–31; Homer Hush, "Judge Hogs by Meat Cuts," *Wallaces' Farmer*, October 1, 1949, 1126; "Lean Hogs Worth Most," *Wallaces' Farmer*, October 7, 1950, 63.

10. W. H. Bruner, "The Ohio Pork Improvement Program," in *Summary of Reports: Fourth Annual Swine Day Special Report 137*, Agricultural Experiment Station, Oregon State University, Corvallis, September 1962, 3–7.

11. Bruner, "Meat-Type Hog," 250–52; Bernard Ebbing, "Can We Afford the Meat-Type Hog," in proceedings, Iowa Feed Conference, September 22–23, 1961, Factors Affecting the Performance of Livestock, Project III, Agricultural Production, Management, and Natural Resource Use, Cooperative Extension, *Annual Report, Entomology and Wildlife*, October 1, 1960–September 30, 1961, Special Collections, Parks Library, Iowa State University.

12. *Iowa Book of Agriculture, 1954–1955* (Des Moines: State of Iowa, 1956), 227–28; *Iowa Swine Breeders Directory* (Des Moines: Iowa Department of Agriculture, 1955), 45, 53, Box 1, Folder 23, Records of the Iowa Pork Producers Association, Special Collections, Iowa State University; "Michigan Joins the Search for the Meat-Type Hog," *Successful Farming* (September 1955): 33; Conatser et al., "Performance Testing," 5; "At National Duroc Show, Meat-Type Gets Spotlight," *Wallaces' Farmer*, July 16, 1955, 63.

13. D. Howard Doane, "Is It Feeding or Breeding That Gives Us the Meat-Type Hog?," *Successful Farming* (September 1952): 108, 110, 112–13; "Leaner Hogs from Ladino Found in Georgia Study," *National Provisioner*, April 2, 1955, 53; D. E. Becker, "Limited Feeding for Hogs," *Illinois Research* (Summer 1962): 3–4.

14. "Where Are We Going with the Meat-Type Hog?," *Agricultural Research* (September 1953): 8–9; Al Bull, "Here's How to Raise Meat Type Hogs" *Wallaces' Farmer*, July 16, 1955, 14; W. A. Craft, "Swine Breeding Research at the Regional Swine Breeding Laboratory," U.S. Department of Agriculture *Miscellaneous Publication No. 523* (Washington, D.C.: U.S. Government Printing Office, July 1943), 1–2, 12.

15. Conatser et al., "Performance Testing"; Ruth Steyn, "Streamlining the Hog, an Abused Individual," in *That We May Eat: The 1975 Yearbook of Agriculture*, ed. Jack Hayes (Washington, D.C.: U.S. Government Printing Office, 1975), 135;

Gilbert C. Fite, *Farm to Factory: A History of the Consumers Cooperative Association* (Columbia: University of Missouri Press, 1965), 260; Dougherty, *In Quest of Quality*, 279; "Swine Testing Station Planned for Missouri," *Cooperative Consumer*, July 31, 1958, 2; "Kansans Hustle Hog Station into Use," *Cooperative Consumer*, January 15, 1959, 7; "Nebraska Will Have Co-Op Feed Mill and Testing Station," *Cooperative Consumer*, May 15, 1959, 1; "Wahoo Is Swine Test Site," *Cooperative Consumer*, February 29, 1960, 1; "New Nebraska CCA Testing Station Opened," *National Hog Farmer* (March 1966): 59.

16. "Iowa's Swine Testing Stations and the Pork Producer," Iowa State University Cooperative Extension Service, *Pamphlet 291*, Ames, Iowa, June 1962, 8–13; "Iowa's Two New Swine Test Stations Open for Business," *Cooperative Consumer*, October 15, 1958, 11.

17. "Measure Fat and Muscle in Live Animal Carcass," in *Agricultural Research in Indiana*, Sixty-Eighth Annual Report of the Director for the Year Ending June 30, 1955 (Lafayette, Ind.: Purdue University Agricultural Experiment Station, 1955), 27–29; "Measure Fat and Lean on Live Hogs with Electronic Instrument," *National Provisioner*, June 11, 1955, 48.

18. L. N. Hazel and E. A. Kline, "Mechanical Measurement of Fatness and Carcass Value on Live Hogs," *Journal of Animal Science* (May 1952): 313–18; Al Bull, "Testing Station Helps Find Better Boars," *Wallaces' Farmer*, August 4, 1956, 11.

19. R. Alan Williams, "A Special Breed of People," in *Iowa Pork and People: A History of Iowa's Pork Producers*, ed. and chief writer Don Muhm (Clive: Iowa Pork Foundation, 1995), 187–89.

20. *Iowa Book of Agriculture, 1952–1953* (Des Moines: State of Iowa, 1954), 281; Wilbur Plager to Bernard Ebbing, May 10, 1955, Rath Packing Company Collection, Section F, Box 3, Folder 8, Special Collections, Iowa State University; "Washington Producers Told to Raise Meat Type Hogs and Stick with the Business," *National Provisioner*, October 1, 1955, 28; Dougherty, *In Quest of Quality*, 279.

21. "Sell Farmers on Meaty Hog," *National Provisioner*, February 19, 1955, 23–24.

22. "Buy a Meat Type Boar," *Wallaces' Farmer*, September 3, 1955, 60; "Meat-Type Boar for You?," *Wallaces' Farmer*, August 15, 1953, 16.

23. "Swine Testing Stations Put Better Hams on Dinner Table," *Cooperative Consumer*, October 15, 1958, 5; Jack Everly, "More Money in Certified Meat-Type Hogs," *Successful Farming* (September 1955): 24.

24. Everly, "More Money in Certified Meat-Type hogs"; "Pay More for Meat Hogs," *Wallaces' Farmer*, June 20, 1953, 20.

25. "They're After Meat Type," *Wallaces' Farmer*, November 3, 1956, 11; Jim Rutter, "Are Your Hogs Meat Type?," *Wallaces' Farmer*, September 6, 1958, 70; Neal Black, "Boar Testing Stations Rising on Breeders' Farms," *National Hog Farmer* (September 1972): 36–37; Neal Black, "Check Boars for Commercial Herd in Testing Station," *National Hog Farmer* (April 1972): 46.

26. Emmett J. Stevermer and Palmer Holden, "Campus Specialists Ready to Serve," in *Iowa Pork and People*, ed. Muhm, 119; Steyn, "Streamlining the Hog," 138; Wendell A. Moyer, "On the Move with Moyer," *Kansas Farmer*, September 19, 1970, 12–13; John C. Phillips, "Today's Hogs Neither as Bad, Nor as Good, as Some Think," *National Hog Farmer* (April 1978): 48; "51.24% New Ham-Loin Record," *National Hog Farmer* (March 1972): 74.

27. Ron Lutz, "They Have a 'New Look,'" *Wallaces' Farmer*, July 26, 1969, 22; Jimmy M. Skaggs, *Prime Cut: Livestock Raising and Meatpacking in the United States,*

1607–1983 (College Station: Texas A&M University Press, 1986), 184; National Research Council, *Designing Foods: Animal Product Options in the Marketplace* (Washington, D.C.: National Academy Press, 1988), 34–35.

28. *American Heirloom Pork Cookbook from Checkerboard Kitchens* (New York: McGraw-Hill Book Company, 1971); Margaret Landin, "New Pork Cook Book Valuable Reference," *National Hog Farmer* (March 1972): 21; Ralston Purina advertisement, *National Hog Farmer* (September 1972): 57.

29. Page Lowry to Joyce Oberman, July 14, 1975, Joyce Oberman to Page Lowry, July 22, 1975, Donna Keppy Scrapbook, Box 19, Iowa Porkettes Records, Iowa Women's Archive, University of Iowa Libraries.

30. Lee Housewright, "Packer's View on Cured and Processed Products," in *The Pork Industry*, ed. Topel, 20; Irvin T. Omtvedt, "Some Heritability Characteristics and Their Importance in a Selection Program," in *The Pork Industry*, ed. Topel, 128; Lauren T. Christian, "Limits for Rapidity of Genetic Improvement for Fat, Muscle, and Quantitative Traits," in *The Pork Industry*, ed. Topel, 160.

31. Harvey Levenstein, *Paradox of Plenty: A Social History of Eating in Modern America* (Berkeley and Los Angeles: University of California Press, 2003), 136, 242; National Research Council, *Designing Foods*, 63.

32. "Stop TV Attacks on Lard," *National Hog Farmer* (August 1966): 4.

33. *Iowa Book of Agriculture, 1968–1969*, 231; "The Story of the Husker Chop," *National Hog Farmer* (September 1966): 14; *Iowa Book of Agriculture, 1975–1977*, 200–201; "Wilson Introducing Specially Trimmed, Fresh Pork with Brand Name Label," *National Hog Farmer* (January 1978): 45.

34. Karen Brown, "Pork Needs a New Image," *Hog Farm Management* (February 1980): 20; Helen Nichols, "Old Pork Ideas Warp Consumer Attitudes," *Hog Farm Management* (March 1980): 135–36.

35. Bernard Collins, "One Man's Decision," *National Hog Farmer* (May 1966): 42; Rolland "Pig" Paul, J. Marvin Garner, and Orville K. Sweet, *The Pork Story: Legend and Legacy* (Kansas City, Mo.: National Pork Producers Council, 1991), 52–66; *Iowa Book of Agriculture, 1968–1969*, 230–31; *Iowa Book of Agriculture, 1970–1971*, 218–19; *Iowa Book of Agriculture, 1975–1977*, 203.

36. "Pork Trimmings Become 'Chops,'" *National Hog Farmer* (April 1972): 26–27, quoting Mandingo; Stephen Striffler, *Chicken: The Dangerous Transformation of America's Favorite Food* (New Haven, Conn.: Yale University Press, 2007), 17–19, 26–29.

37. Paul et al., *The Pork Story*, 180–81.

38. Ibid., 183–84.

39. "New York Press Conference Introduces Other White Meat," *National Hog Farmer*, February 15, 1987; "'White Meat' Foodservice Ads Generate Awareness, Recipe Requests," *National Hog Farmer*, December 15, 1987, 83; "White Meat Campaign Changes Consumer Attitudes about Pork," *National Hog Farmer*, December 15, 1987, 83; "Checkup on the Checkoff," *National Hog Farmer* (September 1987): 34–35.

40. David Huinker, "Thoughts about Hogs . . . and Change," in *Iowa Pork and People*, ed. Muhm, 180; Nathanael Johnson, "Swine of the Times: The Making of the Modern Pig," *Harper's Magazine* (May 2006): 47–56.

41. Johnson, "Swine of the Times"; Elizabeth Lee, "Hog Heaven," *Atlanta Journal-Constitution*, September 20, 2006, E1, E8; Tom Perry, "Top Chefs Requesting Fattier Pork," *Des Moines Register*, July 9, 2007.

42. Johnson, "Swine of the Times."

43. Dorothy Mayes, "Fat from Pork, Beef in U.S. Diets Drops 26% in 10 Years," *National Hog Farmer*, March 15, 1987, 41–42; Striffler, *Chicken*, 30–31.

Chapter 5. The Chicken, the Factory Farm, and the Supermarket

This essay has benefited from the generous funding of the Museum of English Rural Life (MERL), University of Reading, and privileged access to the wealth of MERL's archival collections. We have also received generous assistance from the Sainsbury Archive. Our thanks go to both organizations.

1. For an overview of the Jewish immigrant population in New York, see Andrew C. Godley, *Jewish Immigrant Entrepreneurship in London and New York: Enterprise and Culture* (Basingstoke and New York: Palgrave Macmillan, 2001), chap. 4.

2. Roger Horowitz, *Putting Meat on the American Table: Taste, Technology, Transformation* (Baltimore: Johns Hopkins University Press, 2006), chap. 5. Delmarva is an acronym for the three states of Delaware, Maryland, and Virginia, across which borders the peninsula carries.

3. Horowitz, *Putting Meat on the American Table*, 105, on broiling, and 102–16; Ross Talbot, *The Chicken War: An International Trade Conflict between the United States and the EEC, 1961–1964* (Des Moines: Iowa State University Press, 1978), 2–5, on Delmarva origins. Denby Wilkinson was secretary of the official British National Broiler Tests, on breed selection, from 1959 to 1964. His correspondence is held at the archive of the Museum of English Rural Life (MERL) and contains copious notes on the origins of the American industry (reference MERL DW/ AD8/4).

4. Talbot, *Chicken War*, 3; Geoffrey Sykes, *Poultry—A Modern Agribusiness* (London: Sykes, Crosby, Lockwood and Sons, 1963), chap. 5.

5. Talbot, *Chicken War*, 4.

6. Horowitz, *Putting Meat on the American Table*, 111.

7. Lou Galambos, *Networks of Innovation: Vaccine Development at Merck, Sharp & Dohme, and Mulford, 1895–1995* (Cambridge: Cambridge University Press, 1999), 126–32, on poultry medicines; Talbot, *Chicken War*, 5, on the importance of Merck's discovery of synthetic vitamin B_{12} for poultry rearing.

8. Talbot, *Chicken War*, 5; Sykes, *Poultry*, 7. Partly because U.S. maize growers were unable to reach their export markets after 1942, they switched to supplying the poultry feedstuff producers, thus boosting the industry's productivity.

9. They were also known as Cornish Rocks. See Horowitz, *Putting Meat on the American Table*, 113. The figures refer to sales of Vantress birds at auction, which accounted for the overwhelming majority of transactions in the U.S. See Denby Wilkinson correspondence (MERL DW AD8/4), on the Vantress hatchery in Georgia.

10. Sykes, *Poultry*, 74, 77–78; Talbot, *Chicken War*, 5–8; Horowitz, *Putting Meat on the American Table*, 118–20; Denby Wilkinson correspondence (MERL DW AD8/4), on the development of the U.S. system.

11. The best source for a comparative analysis of British and U.S. manufacturing is S. N. Broadberry, *The Productivity Race* (Cambridge: Cambridge University Press, 1997).

12. B. R. Mitchell, *Abstract of British Historical Statistics* (Cambridge: Cambridge University Press, 1962), 83, shows that poultry numbers rose from forty-nine million to seventy-three million from 1927 to 1935 before falling to sixty-four million by 1939.

13. P. Mathias, *Retailing Revolution: A History of Multiple Retailing in the Food Trades Based upon the Allied Suppliers Group of Companies* (London: Longmans, 1967), 16–34, esp. 25–28, on middle-class family consumption of twenty to thirty fresh eggs per week and poor-family consumption of fewer than twelve eggs per week.

14. Mathias, *Retailing Revolution*, 27–28, says that over 3 billion out of an annual

British egg consumption of 3.9 billion (or around three-quarters) were imported before 1914. See Bridget Williams, *The Best Butter in the World: A History of Sainsbury's* (London: Ebury Press, 1994), 35–36, 93 (imports), on eggs; and James B. Jefferys, *The Distribution of Consumer Goods* (Cambridge: Cambridge University Press, 1950), chart I. On eggs from China and Russia, see Ning Jennifer Chang, "Vertical Integration, Business Diversification, and Firm Architecture: The Case of the China Egg Produce Company in Shanghai, 1923–1950," *Enterprise and Society* 6 (2005): 419–51; and Stuart Thompstone, "'Bab'ye Khozyaystvo': Poultry-Keeping and Its Contribution to Peasant Income in Pre-1914 Russia," *Agricultural History Review* 40 (1992): 52–63.

15. "Packing Stations," *Poultry Farmer*, March 28, 1953. The packing station network was expanded as a mechanism for wartime food distribution.

16. Williams, *Best Butter*, 50, on seasonality; Sykes, *Poultry*, 7, on "sideline." See Lady Denman, *The Practical Education of Women for Rural Life: Report of a Sub-Committee of the Inter-Departmental Ccommittee of the Ministry of Agriculture and Board of Education* (London: HMSO, 1928), for her endorsement of the "pocket money" activity.

17. Henry Clarke and Hilary Binding, *The History of Lloyd Maunder, 1898–1998, a West Country Family Business* (Halsgrove: Tiverton, 1998), 85, on slaughtering "spent" hens.

18. *Poultry Farmer*, January 16, 1954. This was the poultry industry's trade journal and reflected the transition from an egg- to a meat-producing industry with its title change to *Poultry Farmer and Packer* in 1959 (hereafter *PF* and *PF&P*). See Thompstone, "Bab'ye Khozyaystvo"; and Brian Short, ""The Art and Craft of Chicken Cramming': Poultry in the Weald of Sussex 1850–1950," *Agricultural History Review* 30 (1982): 17–30, on imports.

19. One exception to this direction is photographic evidence of a Japanese firm exhibiting its plucking machinery at Agricultural Shows in Britain in 1950. See the outstanding *Farmer's Weekly* photographic archive at Museum for English Rural Life.

20. Gerald Frost, *Antony Fishers: Champion of Liberty* (London: Profile Books, 2002), 49; Sykes, *Poultry*, 7. It was not until 1959 that the first National Broiler (Random Sample) tests were instigated at the Ministry of Agriculture's test ground near Godalming, Surrey. U.S. producers tried hard to get access to the British market, repeatedly disparaging the government's "so-called protective health measures" (*PF* July 2, 1955, 1). Talbot, *Chicken War*, 10–12, tells of the enormous exports of chicken meat from the United States to Germany from 1960, thwarting the development of any poultry industry there, which suggests that the protection offered to British farmers was in fact genuine.

21. National Farmer's Union (NFU), "Report on Marketing," February 6, 1957, 6, "During the war . . . table poultry disappeared from the market" (NFU Archive, Ref. 6340 P.63: 381, MERL).

22. Williams, *Best Butter*, 135; "Mr Alan discusses," *JS Journal* (April 1947): 13; Giles Emerson, *Sainsbury's: The Record Years, 1950–1992* (London: Haggerston Press, 2006), 49–50. MacFisheries began as a personal indulgence of Lord Leverhulme but was amalgamated into Unilever after his death. Its history is nevertheless a neglected part of that empire. See Charles Wilson, *The History of Unilever*, 2 vols. (London: Cassell, 1954), 1:261–63. Despite its initial embarrassment to the parent company, with 360 stores it went on to become an important source of profits for Unilever (311). Charles Wilson, *Unilever 1945–1965: Challenge and Response in the Post-War Industrial Revolution* (London: Cassell, 1968), gives a very occasional reference to postwar developments. See J. B. Jeffreys, *Retail Trading in Britain,*

1850–1950 (Cambridge: Cambridge University Press, 1954), 244–52, esp. 248, on MacFisheries; and Jeffreys, *Distribution of Consumer Goods*, 179–89 (there were over fifty thousand independents in the egg and poultry trade in 1938 [188]). For the company's late 1950s development, see *PF&P*, September 19, 1959, 19, on MacFisheries' new Manchester store.

23. Clarke and Binding, *History of Maunder*, 43, 46–47, 52 on Frank Sainsbury's turkey farm. Also see Williams, *Best Butter*, 35–37; and Emerson, *Sainsbury's*, 49–50, on the company's egg-collecting operations that preceded its forays into poultry farming. Jeffreys, *Retail Trading*, 195, confirms that Sainsbury's closeness with suppliers differentiated it from other British provisions merchants.

24. Horowitz, *Putting Meat on the American Table*, 103, and 111; Richard Tedlow, *New and Improved: The Story of Mass Marketing in America* (New York: Basic Books, 1990), chap. 4, covers the history of A&P, but without referring to any role in the poultry industry.

25. Jim Woods, Sainsbury's merchandising and marketing manager, claimed that Sainsbury did 12–15 percent of all available trade in the regions where the company's shops were present, which mapped onto those locations where poultry demand was disproportionately high (London and the home counties). Given that Sainsbury was particularly competitive in poultry, it seems not unreasonable to assume that the company's share of the nascent broiler-chicken market was around this figure. (See letter from Jim Woods to Anthony Tennant of Mather & Crowther advertising agency, January 20, 1960, Sainsbury Archive MERL.) For the other regional grocers, see Emerson, *Sainsbury's*, 66, 156; and *PF*, October 2, 1954, for information on David Greig, another leading regional grocer. Sykes, *Poultry*, 30, states that with "8 to 12 [chains] dominating Britain's food retailing," it was far more concentrated than retailing in the United States was.

26. *PF*, September 10, 1955, 5.

27. *PF*, September 10, 1954, on Sainsbury; *PF*, September 18, 1954, on equivalent attempts at grading in the Midlands and Scotland; *PF*, October 2, 1954, on grading attempts at David Greig.

28. *PF*, October 30, 1954, 15. Also see Sykes's comment in *PF*, October 27, 1956, on how "retailers are finding that the nation's demand is for a smaller bird (3lb to 3¼lb)."

29. See *PF*, November 22, 1958, 21, for Alan Sainsbury. Contrast with Horowitz, *Putting Meat on the American Table*, 120, on Perdue's attempts to market yellow-fleshed chickens that attracted a price premium in the United States. Sainsbury's buyers were also used for grading at the tests. The company sponsored two of the cups awarded annually for poultry production, the only retailer to participate in this way (MERL DW AD2/6).

30. *PF*, January 16, 1954, and *PF*, September 11, 1954 on Sainsbury dropping the term; *PF*, October 2, 1954, for similar moves at Greig. It retained some currency although was never again the prevailing descriptor.

31. See Clarke and Binding, *History of Maunder*, 85; John Maunder interview with Andrew Godley and Bridget Williams, Tiverton, Devon, U.K., August 30, 2006.

32. Emerson, *Sainsbury's* 43–57; Williams, *Best Butter*, 124–217; Clarke and Binding, *History of Maunder*, 79, 85. Horowitz, *Putting Meat on the American Table*, chap. 6, discusses the slow progress of self-service in American meat retailing.

33. Ralph G. Towsey, *Self-Service Retailing: Its Profitable Application to All Trades* (London: Iliffe Books, 1964), 84. On U.S. practice, see Tedlow, *New and Improved*, chap. 4.

34. See Sykes in *PF*, November 14, 1953; and Sykes, *Poultry*, 197. The Vestey retail empire did not retail chicken, for example. See Richard Perren, *Taste, Trade and Technology: The Development of the International Meat Industry since 1840* (Ashgate: Aldershot, 2006), esp. 205–8.

35. Harold Temperton speaking at the inaugural National Association of Poultry Packers' Annual Conference, reported in *PF*, May 15, 1954.

36. Emerson, *Sainsbury's*, 49–50.

37. *PF*, October 16, 1954, reporting a speech by Hugh Finn, chairman of Stonegate Poultry of Canterbury.

38. Tony Pendry in *PF&P*, October 31, 1959, 30. See also *PF&P*, November 21, 1959: "56% of all eviscerate poultry is packed in just four stations."

39. Horowitz, *Putting Meat on the American Table*, 114–15, cites examples of processing plants in the United States with a much lower capacity. Adding evisceration increased labor demands, and new equipment needs were minimal. The adoption of new wrapping materials that replaced cellophane (pioneered by the Cryovac company) were beginning in the red-meat industry (ibid., chap. 6). Our thanks go to Roger Horowitz for drawing this important observation.

40. *PF*, September 19, 1958, 9; *PF&P*, September 19, 1959, and *PF*, September 12, 1959, 19, on shrink-wrapping extensive discussion passim. Factory evisceration "still had its problems" and was still labor intensive (Pendry in *PF&P*, October 31, 1959).

41. PF, October 25, 1958.

42. Buxted, for example, was using refrigerated vehicles to deliver frozen chickens to Sainsbury's London depot five years before the company began to operate similar vehicles out of its new Basingstoke depot in 1964 (*JS Journal* [April/May 1964]: 11–15).

43. *PF&P*, October 25, 1958. In consequence, Hugh Finn (of Stonegate Poultry) castigated retailers, hotels, and restaurants with insufficient refrigeration capacity: "the wastage of birds going through their hands was appalling" (*PF*, October 16, 1954, 1). Also see *PF*, November 29, 1959, 19, on equipment manufacturers at the Northern Poultry Show, where prices ranged from £369 to "approx £500." According to *Self-Service Retailing*, Towsey, 84, "the cost of refrigerators can vary as much as from £30 to £110 per foot run."

44. In *JS Journal* (January 1956), on engineering at Lewisham, Alan Rickman (Sainsbury's engineer) discusses twenty-four refrigerated wall cabinets in total in the store. Also see *JS Journal* (December 1955), interview with F. G. Fry, the electrical engineer responsible for development of Sainsbury's refrigerated cabinets.

45. Mathias, *Retailing Revolution*.

46. MERL DW A/8/4. Sykes, *Poultry*, 12, emphasises that overall U.K., self-service was behind that in the United States.

47. Sykes in *PF*, April 10, 1954, on three per annum; Sykes, *Poultry*, 103, on five per annum; *PF&P*, July 17, 1963, on ten-week season (with a two-to-three week resting period in between crops for disease control).

48. Talbot, *Chicken War*, 9; Sykes, *Poultry*, 74.

49. Speech reported in *PF*, September 10, 1955, 5.

50. One leading poultry entrepreneur claimed in his speech at the inaugural broiler industry conference that "it was useless to produce on a speculative basis. It was also necessary . . . to co-operate fully with the chick supplier, feed merchant, and final market" (*PF*, September 10, 1955, 5).

51. *PF&P*, October 25, 1958, 21.

52. Maunder interview. Alan Sainsbury was chairman of the Ministry of Food's

import committees for the supply and distribution of poultry and rabbits and also chief representative of the multiple grocers on the Ministry of Food's retail advisory committees during the war. See James Boswell, ed., *JS 100* (London: J. Sainsbury Ltd., 1969), 54–55.

53. Maunder interview.

54. "Ready to Cook," *JS Journal* (September 1957): 10–13. See Frost, *Fisher*, 50; and Emerson, *Sainsbury's*, 49–50.

55. Maunder interview.

56. See Sykes, *Poultry*, 12, on retailer incentives for collaboration, and 30–34, on the rise of long-term contracts and coordination. Sykes contrasts the role of retailers driving up quality with the role of marketing boards, 34 (in direct contrast to his earlier view that the Fatstock Marketing Board ought to regulate prices in the chicken industry; see *PF*, July 30, 1955).

57. Ed Covell, interview by Roger Horowitz, February 1, 1995. We thank Roger Horowitz for making a transcript of the interview available to us. See Maunder interview on the "arms-length contracts" and U.S. processors buying meat at auction.

58. Citation from *Economist*, February 15, 1964; also see February 22, 1964 (copies held at National Union of Agricultural Workers' archives, MERL). Frost, *Fisher*, 55–58 mentions that Allied Foods then took over the business. Buxted was acquired by Ross, which in turn was acquired by David Thompson's and Harry Solomon's Hillsdown Holdings. This was eventually acquired by Hicks Muse, an American private equity group (now renamed Lion Capital), in 1999, whereupon the original poultry businesses were all shut down. Lloyd Maunder acquired its own feed producing capacity and has remained privately controlled and independent.

59. Sykes, *Poultry*, 47; see his chart for the breakdown.

60. *PF&P*, October 25, 1958, 21, reports data from growth trials in both countries. On U.S. processing, see Talbot, *Chicken War*, 8–9, for 1963 data showing that U.S. plants processed 6.5 million to 7.0 million chickens per year. The Buxted and Maunder processing plants easily equaled such throughput.

61. Maunder interview.

62. Sykes comments in *PF*, October 29, 1956, on one million in 1950 and ten million in 1956 and forecasts one hundred million by 1960. A c. 1961 National Union of Agricultural Workers leaflet on the broiler industry, stated that the 1953 total was five million, rising to one hundred million by 1960 (the NUAW archive is held at MERL). National Farmer's Union, "Report on Marketing," February 6, 1957, 6 on 1955, and 1961 forecast one hundred million. K. Hunt and K. Clark, *Poultry and Eggs in Britain, 1966–1967* (Oxford: Agricultural Economics Research Institute, University of Oxford, 1967), 34, lists British hatchery chick placings for table poultry from 1964–65 to 1966–67.

63. Hunt and Clark, *Poultry and Eggs*, 7.

64. Sainsbury's sales were 4.7 million birds in 1957–58, rising to 11.9 million in 1959 and 13.4 million in 1960 (out of a total market rapidly approaching 100 million; see note 63). See J. Sainsbury, "Financial Reviews," 1960 and 1961 (Sainsbury Archive, MERL). The poultry department was the lead performer at that time. "Once again a large part of the additional trade was due to the poultry department" (ibid., 1960). Fisher and Pendry had captured almost one-fifth of the total British broiler market for Buxted. Frost, *Fisher*, 51, states that the company output was around 25 million per annum in 1964, when total output can be inferred from Hunt and Clark, *Poultry and Eggs*, 34, on chick placings. This lists 157 million chicks placed with table-poultry farms in 1964–65, rising to 182

million and then 202 million in 1965–66 and 1966–67 respectively. Backward extrapolation would imply perhaps 130 million to 135 million broilers reared in 1963–64.

65. According to Hunt and Clark, *Poultry and Eggs*, 7, the industry was "very efficient" by 1963.

66. *PF*, September 11, 1954.

67. Hunt and Clark, *Poultry and Eggs*, 83. Also see *PF&P*, October 31, 1959.

68. See Andrew C. Godley and Bridget Williams, "Democratizing Luxury and the Contentious 'Invention of the Technological Chicken' in Britain," *University of Reading Discussion Paper in Management and Economics*, 2007.

69. Frost, *Fisher*, 51.

Chapter 6. Trading Quality, Producing Value

1. National Marine Fisheries Service, *U.S. Annual Per Capita Consumption of Commercial Fish and Shellfish, 1910–2005* (Silver Spring, Md.: National Oceanic and Atmospheric Administration, Department of Commerce, 2005).

2. Harvest increases calculated from National Marine Fisheries Service data. See National Marine Fisheries Service, "Personal Communication from the National Marine Fisheries Service, Fisheries Statistics Division, Silver Spring, Md," to the author (Silver Spring, Md.: 2007).

3. Akin, Gump, Strauss, Hauer and Feld, L.L.P. *Investigation No. Ta-201-71 Crabmeat from Swimming Crabs: Prehearing Brief on Behalf of the Coalition for Free Trade of Crabmeat*, United States International Trade Commission (Washington, D.C., 2000), 47.

4. Panisuan Chamnaanwet, interview by the author, Bangkok, 2006.

5. Steven Jaffee and P. Gordon, *Exporting High Value Food Commodities: Success Stories from Developing Countries*, Discussion Paper 198 (Washington, D.C.: World Bank, 1993).

6. Hillary French, *Costly Trade Offs: Reconciling Trade and the Environment*, Worldwatch Paper 113 (Washington, D.C.: Worldwatch Institute, 1993); John Kurien, *Fish Trade for the People: Toward Understanding the Relationship between International Fish Trade and Food Security* (Rome: Food and Agriculture Organization, 2004).

7. Food and Agricultural Organization (FAO), *The State of the World Fisheries and Aquaculture 2000* (Rome: Food and Agriculture Organization, 2000); Lahsen Abadouch, *Fish Top Traded Commodity* (Food and Agriculture Organization, 2004), accessed May 23, 2005, available at http://www.fao.org/documents/show _cdr.asp?url_file=/docrep/007/y4722e/y4722e00.htm.

8. Lynne Phillips, "Food and Globalization," *Annual Review of Anthropology* 35 (2006): 37–57.

9. Michael Power, *The Audit Society: Rituals of Verification* (Oxford: Oxford University Press, 1997).

10. Marion Nestle, *Safe Food: Bacteria, Biotechnology, and Bioterrorism* (Berkeley: University of California Press, 2004).

11. Power, *Audit Society*.

12. Kris Olds and Henry Wai-Chung Yeung, "(Re)Shaping 'Chinese' Business Networks in a Globalising Era," *Environment and Planning D: Society and Space* 17, no. 5 (1999): 539.

13. Peter Dicken et al., "Chains and Networks, Territories and Scales: Towards a Relational Framework for Analysing the Global Economy," *Global Networks* 1, no. 2 (2001): 94–95.

14. Keiko Tanaka and Lawrence Busch, "Standardization as a Means for Globalizing a Commodity: The Case of Rapeseed in China," *Rural Sociology* 68, no. 1 (2003): 25–45.

15. Becky Mansfield, "Spatializing Globalization: A 'Geography of Quality' in the Seafood Industry," *Economic Geography* 79, no. 1 (2003): 1–16.

16. Terry Marsden, "Creating Space for Food: The Distinctiveness of Recent Agrarian Development," in *Globalizing Food: Agrarian Questions and Global Restructuring*, ed. David Goodman and Michael J. Watts (London: Routledge, 1997), 169–91; Tanaka and Busch "Standardization."

17. Becky Mansfield, "Fish, Factory Trawlers, and Imitation Crab: The Nature of Quality in the Seafood Industry," *Journal of Rural Studies* 19 (2003): 9–21.

18. Mansfield, "Spatializing Globalization."

19. This observation was also noted during a 1957 survey of the crabmeat industry. See Robert Littleford, *Third Annual Report, 1956-57 of the Seafood Processing Laboratory, Crisfield Maryland* (College Park: University of Maryland, 1957).

20. Becky Mansfield, "Rules of Privatization: Contradictions in Neoliberal Regulation of North Pacific Fisheries," *Annals of the Association of American Geographers* 94, no. 3 (2004): 565–84.

21. Jack Brooks, Bill Brooks, and Joe Brooks, interview by the author, Cambridge, Md.: 2006.

22. *United States International Trade Commission Hearing before the U.S. International Trade Commission on Investigation No. Ta-201-71: Crabmeat from Swimming Crabs* (Washington, D.C.: U.S. International Trade Commission, 2000), 273.

23. Specifically this was section 202(b)(1)(A) of the Trade Act of 1974.

24. United States International Trade Commission, *Crabmeat from Swimming Crabs: Investigation No. Ta-201-71, Determination and Views of the Commission* (Washington, D.C.: USITC Publications, 2000), 2.

25. Ibid., 3.

26. Richard Dodds, "Black Pioneers of Seafood Packing," *Weather Gauge* 22, no. 1 (1994): 4–9.

27. Ibid.

28. Ibid.

29. David Dressel and Donald Whitaker, *The U.S. Blue Crab Industry: An Economic Profile for Policy and Regulatory Analysts* (Washington, D.C.: National Marine Fisheries Service for the National Fisheries Institute, 1983); F. B. Thomas and S. D. Thomas, *Technical Operations Manual for the Blue Crab Industry* (1974; Chapel Hill: Sea Grant Program, University of North Carolina, 1983).

30. "Threat Prompts Crab Parley," *Baltimore Sun*, December 27, 1952; "Crabmeat Packers, Health Unit to Discuss Sanitary Measures," *Baltimore Sun*, December 12, 1952.

31. The lab was supported by a Saltonstall-Kennedy grant, which supported research, development, and marketing for the seafood industry, but the grant program was cut in 1969.

32. Calvert Tolley, *Paper by Calvert Tolley on Mechanizing Crab Picking* (1967), available at http://www.cfast.vt.edu/downloads/bluecrabpubs/Calvert%20Tolley%20 Paper.pdf (accessed April 11, 2007).

33. Charles Lee, George Knobl, and Emmett Deady, "Mechanizing the Blue Crab Industry Part 3: Strengthening the Industry's Economic Position," *Commercial Fisheries Review* 26, no. 1 (1964): 1–7.

34. Tom Rippen, telephone interview by the author, 2005.

35. Dressel and Whitaker, *The U.S. Blue Crab Industry*; Akin et al., *Investigation No.*

Ta-201-71 Crabmeat from Swimming Crabs; Lee et al., "Mechanizing the Blue Crab Industry Part 3."

36. Mrs. Paul's frozen deviled crab cakes were one of the earliest versions. See U.S. Food and Drug Administration, *Section 540.285 Crabmeat Products 1973: Labeling, Crabmeat Products with Added Fish or Other Seafood Ingredients, Revised 1980* (Washington, D.C.: Food and Drug Administration, 1980); Lloyd Byrd, interview by the author, Berlin, Md., 2005); Brooks et al. interview.

37. Paul Wall, interview by the author, Ocean City, Md., 2005.

38. Caroline Mayer, "Phillips Restaurants Grow Fat on Seafood," *Washington Post*, August 12, 1985.

39. Ibid.

40. Dungeness crabs are caught on the Pacific coast. See *Hearing before the U.S. International Trade Commission on Investigation No. Ta-201-71.*

41. Jon Goldstein, "King Crab: An Interview with Mark Sneed of Phillips Foods," Baltimore Sun *Sunspot News*, July 2, 2001; Wall interview.

42. *Hearing before the U.S. International Trade Commission on Investigation No. Ta-201-71.*

43. Harvest trends were produced from National Marine Fisheries Service, "Personal Communication." MSY data are from Lee et al., "Mechanizing the Blue Crab Industry Part 3."

44. Norman Whittington III and Gary Foxwell, interview by the author, Berlin, Md., 2005.

45. For example, Joe's Crab Shack and Legal Seafoods both expanded outside of their home bases to become regional chains.

46. Byrd interview; Neil Wrigley, "The Consolidation Wave in U.S. Food Retailing: A European Perspective," *Agribusiness* 7, no. 4 (2001): 489–513; "1995: The Year in Review: Acquisitions," *Nation's Restaurant News* 29, no. 50 (1995): 80–83.

47. The United States started this process much later than U.K. and European food retailers. See Wrigley, "Consolidation Wave." See also Norman Whittington III, interview by the author, Berlin, Md., 2005.

48. *Hearing before the U.S. International Trade Commission on Investigation No. Ta-201-71.*

49. U.S. Food Service and Super Giant testified. By 2000 both were owned by Royal Ahold, a Belgian company and the world's fourth-largest food retail and service group, giving Ahold control over most of the U.S. food distribution system, especially along the Atlantic seaboard. See "Ahold Anticipates Revival through US Split," *Food and Drink Europe Newsletter*, November 11, 2005; Wrigley, "Consolidation Wave," 489–513. *Hearing before the U.S. International Trade Commission on Investigation No. Ta-201-71*, 173.

50. *Hearing before the U.S. International Trade Commission on Investigation No. Ta-201-71.*

51. Ibid., 168.

52. Lawrence Busch, "Grades and Standards in the Social Construction of Safe Food," in *The Politics of Food*, ed. Marianne Elisabeth Lien and Brigitte Nerlich (New York: Berg, 2004), 163–78.

53. E. S. Garrett, M. Hudak-Roos, and D. R. Ward, "Implementation of the HACCP Program by the Fresh and Processed Seafood Industry," in *HACCP in Meat, Poultry and Fish Processing: Advances in Meat Research Series*, ed. A. M. Pearson and T. R. Dutson (London: Blackie Academic Professional, 1996), 109–30.

54. *S. 2538, the Consumer Seafood Safety Act: Hearing before the National Ocean Policy Study*, U.S. Senate, Committee on Commerce, Science, and Transportation (Washington, D.C.: U.S. Government Printing Office, 1992).

55. Ibid.

56. Ulrich Beck, *Risk Society: Towards a New Modernity* (London: Sage, 1992).

57. Nestle, *Safe Food*.

58. Ibid.

59. National Oceanic and Atmospheric Administration (NOAA), *Fisheries of the United States 1987, Current Fishery Statistics* (Washington, D.C.: U.S. Department of Commerce, NOAA, National Marine Fisheries Service, 1988), 8700; E. Spencer Garrett and Martha Hudak-Roos, "Developing an HACCP-Based Inspection System for the Seafood Industry," *Food Technology* 45 (1991): 53–57.

60. Ahmed Farid, ed., *Seafood Safety: Committee on the Evaluation of Fishery Products* (Washington, D.C.: National Academy Press, Food and Nutrition Board, 1991).

61. *S. 2538, the Consumer Seafood Safety Act: Hearing before the National Ocean Policy Study*.

62. Ibid.

63. H. E. Bauman, "The Origin and Concept of HACCP," in *HACCP in Meat, Poultry and Fish Processing*, ed. Pearson and Dutson, 1–7.

64. William Sperber, "HACCP Does Not Work from Farm to Table," *Food Control* 16, no. 6 (2005): 505–9.

65. Julie Caswell and Neal Hooker, "HACCP as an International Trade Standard," *American Journal of Agricultural Economics* 78, no. 3 (1996): 775–80. Nestle, *Safe Food*.

66. Power, *Audit Society*; Terry Marsden, Andrew Flynn, and Michelle Harrison, *Consuming Interests: The Social Provision of Foods* (London: UCL Press, 2000).

67. Bauman, "Origin and Concept of HACCP."

68. Susanne Freidberg, *French Beans and Food Scares: Culture and Commerce in an Anxious Age* (Oxford: Oxford University Press, 2004).

69. Caswell and Hooker, "HACCP."

70. Ibid.

71. Garrett et al., "Implementation of the HACCP Program."

72. Chamnaanwet interview.

73. Olli-Pekka Ruohmaki, *Fishermen No More?: Livelihood and Environment in Southern Thai Maritime Villages* (Bangkok: White Lotus Press, 1999).

74. Board of Investment, *Boi Investment Policies since 2000* (Ministry of Commerce, Royal Thai Government, 2000), available at http://www.boi.go.th/english/about/boi_policies.asp (accessed March 20, 2006); Orapin Siripanich, *Report on the Study of the Canned Seafood Industry of Thailand* (Bangkok: Development and Planning Section, Board of Investment, Ministry of Industry, Royal Thai Government, 1995).

75. Pakphanang Coldstorage Public Company, *Annual Report for 1998* (Bangkok: Pakphanang Coldstorage Company Limited, 1999).

76. Commercial Economic Department, "Guidelines and Targets for Fishery Products and Value Added Exports 1988, Group 5: Fisheries Products" (Bangkok: Ministry of Commerce, Royal Thai Government, 1987).

77. For example, Spain banned squid because of cadmium levels, while Italy banned squid because it contained the food additive EDTA (ethylenediaminetetraacetic acid), which is approved by the U.S. FDA at 300 ppm, while some EU countries banned it or allowed only 250 ppm. See the Center for Science in the Public Interest Web site, Food Additives, http://www.cspinet.org/reports/chem cuisine.htm#Alphabetical. See also Clinic Marketing Co., *Report from the Study on the Canned Seafood Industry in Thailand* (Bangkok: Board of Investment, Ministry of Commerce, Royal Thai Government, 1991).

78. Siripanich, *Report*.

79. Ibid.

80. Other global quality standards were part of this development effort,

including ISO 9000, GMP certificates, and certification by the British Retail Consortium (BRC), in order to meet the specific and more stringent requirements of the EU.

81. Thai Frozen Foods Association, *Thirty-Six Years of the Thai Frozen Foods Association* (Bangkok: Thammada Press, 2004).

82. Ibid.

83. Ibid.; Fishery Inspection Auditor, interview by the author, Phunphim, Thailand, Department of Fisheries Inspection Office, 2006.

84. Thomas Fraser, *Fishermen of South Thailand: The Malay Villagers* (New York: Rinehart and Winston Co., 1966); Suwanee Tipmad, interview by the author, Phumriang, Thailand, 2006.

85. Suwanee Tipmad interview.

86. Kanjana Maniwan, interview by the author, Hat Yai, Thailand, 2006.

87. Rippen interview; Kanjana Maniwan interview.

88. Director of National Food and Agricultural Product Standards Office, *Memo to Provincial Fisheries Offices: Draft of the National Food and Agricultural Product Standards for Blue Swimming Crab* (Bangkok: Agricultural Commodities and Food Standards Office, Ministry of Agriculture and Cooperatives, Royal Thai Government, 2004).

89. Kanjana Maniwan interview.

90. Pakfoods HACCP manager and crabmeat buyer, interview by the author, Phakpanang, Thailand, 2006.

91. Suwanee Tipmad interview.

92. Kanjana Maniwan interview.

93. Ibid.

94. Pakfoods quality-control technicians, interview by the author, Phakpanang, Thailand, 2006.

95. Byrd interview.

96. Ibid.

97. United States International Trade Commission, *Crabmeat from Swimming Crabs*.

98. Ibid.

Chapter 7. Anchovy Sauce and Pickled Tripe

This chapter owes a great deal to the diligent work of Sarah Marion, who acted as my research assistant and whose interest in the project led to useful conversations during which some of the ideas in this essay emerged in the kind of mutual intellectual process that cannot be done justice with simple concepts of authorship. I appreciate her generosity and contribution, especially given that her own research interests lie in the twenty-first century. I would also like to thank Warren Belasco and Roger Horowitz for organizing and the Hagley Museum and Library for hosting what was one of the most intellectually stimulating and engaging conferences I have ever attended. I also thank Frank Trentmann and the Cultures of Consumption Program, funded by the ESRC of the United Kingdom, which provided a fellowship during which I started the research for this essay.

1. Mathis Wackernagel and William Rees, *Our Ecological Footprint: Reducing Human Impact on the Earth* (Gabriola Island, B.C.: New Society Publishers, 1996).

2. Igor Kopytoff, "The Cultural Biography of Things: Commoditization as Process," in *The Social-Life of Things*, ed. Arjun Appadurai (Cambridge: Cambridge

University Press, 1986), 64–94. See also Grant McCracken, *Culture and Consumption* (Bloomington: Indiana University Press, 1988), on the way commodities become cultural valuables through the process of "patination."

3. Thomas Princen, "Distancing: Consumption and the Severing of Feedback," in *Confronting Consumption*, ed. T. Princen, Michael Maniates, and Ken Conca (Cambridge, Mass.: MIT Press, 2002), 103–32.

4. Steve Striffler and Mark Moberg, eds., *Banana Wars: Power, Production, and History in the Americas* (Durham, N.C.: Duke University Press, 2003). See also the Belizean case study by Mark Moberg, *Myths of Ethnicity and Nation: Immigration, Work, and Identity in the Belize Banana Industry* (Knoxville: University of Tennessee Press, 1997).

5. This complex topic is largely the domain of the relatively new field of eco-logical economics. Princen summarizes this approach in "Distancing" (103–14), but a more complete discussion on the ecological effects of normal capitalist business practices can be found in an excellent text, Joshua Farley and Herman E. Daly, *Ecological Economics: Principles and Applications* (Washington, D.C.: Island Press, 2003).

6. See Richard Wilk, *Home Cooking in the Global Village* (Oxford: Berg, 2006), 1.

7. For general history of branding in the United States and the United Kingdom, see Jackson Lears, *Fables of Abundance: A Cultural History of Advertising in America* (New York: Basic Books, 1995); Susan Strasser, *Satisfaction Guaranteed: The Making of the American Mass Market* (Washington, D.C.: Smithsonian Institution Press, 1989), 29–57; and Thomas Richards, *The Commodity Culture of Victorian Britain: Advertising and Spectacle, 1851–1914* (Stanford, Calif.: Stanford University Press, 1991).

8. The Chinese example is from Gary Lai and Chi-Kong Lai, "Consumerism without Capitalism: Consumption and Brand Names in Late Imperial China," in *The Social Economy of Consumption*, ed. Henry Rutz and Benjamin Orlove (Lanham, Md.: University Press of America, 1989), 253–80. While an early brand is identi-fied with a place, individual, family, or factory of origin, contemporary branding depends instead on entirely imaginary discorporate entities. "Sony," for exam-ple, has no place or person as a referent, beyond being vaguely Japanese.

9. I discuss this history at greater length in my *Home Cooking*. On the history of branding in the United States see Strasser, *Satisfaction Guaranteed*, 29–57, and for contemporary brand theories, see Jonathan Schroeder and Miriam Salzer-Mörling, *Brand Cultures* (New York: Routledge, 2006).

10. Erika Diane Rappaport, "Packaging China: Foreign Articles and Dangerous Tastes in the Mid-Victorian Tea Party," in *The Making of the Consumer: Knowledge, Power and Identity in the Modern World*, ed. Frank Trentmann (Oxford: Berg, 2006), 125–46. On food adulteration in Victorian England, see Sarah Freeman, *Mutton and Oysters: The Victorians and Their Food* (London: Victor Gollancz, 1989).

11. Real women were sometimes hired to publicly play the parts of imaginary brand characters; the case of Betty Crocker is discussed in Laura Shapiro, *Something from the Oven: Reinventing Dinner in 1950s America* (New York and London: Viking, 2004).

12. On the ability of brands to evoke romantic images of the rural, historical, and exotic, see Heather Paxson, "Artisanal Cheese and Economies of Sentiment in New England," in *Fast Food/Slow Food: The Cultural Economy of the Global Food System*, ed. Richard Wilk (Walnut Creek, Calif.: Altamira, 2006); and Maria Gaytán, "Globalizing Resistance: Slow Food and New Local Imaginaries," *Food, Culture and Society* 7, no. 2 (2005): 97–116.

13. For examples of how complex it is to do a full life-cycle analysis of the

environmental costs of modern consumer goods, see J. Ryan and A. Durning, *Stuff: The Secret Lives of Everyday Things* (Seattle: Northwest Environment Watch, 1997).

14. For excellent assessments of "displaced" environmental effects in the past, see essays in Alf Hornborg and Carole L. Crumley, eds., *The World System and the Earth System: Global Socioenvironmental Change and Sustainability since the Neolithic* (Walnut Creek, Calif.: Left Coast Press, 2006).

15. Recent historical ecology in the Caribbean demonstrates the huge impact of removing millions of sea turtles, the top grazers in the ecosystem. See Jeremy Jackson, "Reefs since Columbus," *Coral Reefs* 16 (1997): S23–S32; and Jeremy Jackson, "What Was Natural in Coastal Oceans?," *Proceedings of the National Academy of Sciences* 98, no. 10 (2001): 5411–518.

16. On the important role of food in triggering nostalgia, national identity, and memory, see David Sutton, *Remembrance of Repasts* (Oxford: Berg, 2001).

17. Crosse & Blackwell was established as a maker of preserved fruits in 1706 and retained a British aura even after being bought by Nestle in 1950, though it is now owned by the British food-processing giant Premier Foods.

18. Unfortunately the series of surviving newspapers published in Belize City is incomplete; scattered issues survive from the 1820s, 1840s, and 1860s, but continuous series do not begin until the late 1870s.

19. Anne McCants, *Exotic Good, Popular Consumption and the Standard of Living: Thinking about Globalization in the Early Modern World*, http://web.mit.edu/kayla/Public/ToPrint/globaltrade.pdf (accessed August 16, 2007).

20. On early trade, see Elizabeth Schumpeter, *English Overseas Trade Statistics 1697–1808* (Oxford: Clarendon Books, 1960); and yet earlier, T. S. Willan, *Studies in Elizabethan Foreign Trade* (Manchester: Manchester University Press, 1959).

21. Niels Steensgaard, "The Growth and Composition of the Long-Distance Trade of England and the Dutch Republic before 1750," in *The Rise of Merchant Empires*, ed. J. Tracy (Cambridge: Cambridge University Press, 1990), 102–52.

22. Michael Pawson and David Buissert, *Port Royal, Jamaica* (Mona: University of the West Indies Press, 2000). The archaeological literature is highly regionalized, typically dealing with a single site or a single kind of package or trade. A typical source would be Olive Jones, *Cylindrical English Wine and Beer Bottles, 1735-1850* (Ottawa, Ontario: National Historic Parks and Sites Branch, Parks Canada, 1984). There are also many collectors' publications that illustrate many bottles without adequate provenance.

23. Jacob Price, "What Did Merchants Do? Reflections on British Overseas Trade, 1660–1790," *Journal of Economic History* 49, no. 2 (1989): 277.

24. Schumpeter, *English Overseas Trade*, 13.

25. S. B. Saul, *Studies in British Overseas Trade 1870–1914* (Liverpool: Liverpool University Press, 1960).

26. A good contemporary source on the complexities of trade policy is W. S. Lindsay, *History of Merchant Shipping and Ancient Commerce* (London: Sampson Low, Marston, Low, and Searle, 1874).

27. Olive R. Jones, "Commercial Foods, 1740–1820," *Historical Archaeology* 27, no. 2 (1993): 27.

28. Alec Davis, *Package and Print: The Development of Container and Label Design* (New York: Clarkson N. Potter, Inc., 1968), 50–52. Sago is a starch made from the trunks of palm trees that grow in Malaysia and Melanesia; it was widely adopted in England for making puddings that were reputedly easy for children and in-

valids to digest. Like many exotic food products, its original use was medicinal, in treating dysentery. By the late 1700s a counterfeit product was being produced in the southern United States from sweet potatoes.

29. Price, "What Did Merchants Do?," 273.

30. Soren Mentz, *The English Gentleman Merchant at Work: Madras and the City of London 1660–1740* (Copenhagen: Museum Tusculanum Press, 2005), 53–55; Price, "What Did Merchants Do?," 279–83.

31. Many nineteenth-century legal cases concerning cargoes and trade are recounted in great detail in Robert Stevens, *On the Stowage of Ships and Their Cargoes, with Information Regarding Freights, Charter-Parties, etc., etc.*, 6th ed. (London: Longmans, Green, Reader, and Dyer, 1873).

32. Ronald Zupko, *A Dictionary of English Weights and Measures from Anglo-Saxon Times to the Nineteenth Century* (Madison: University of Wisconsin Press, 1968), 61–62.

33. Alec Davis, *Package and Print: The Development of Container and Label Design* (New York: Clarkson N. Potter, Inc., 1968); Jones, "Commercial Foods."

34. Denys Forrest, *Tea for the British: The Social and Economic History of a Famous Trade* (London: Chatto and Windus, 1973).

35. Stevens, *On the Stowage of Ships*, 574.

36. Hoh-cheung Mui and Loma H. Mui, *The Management of Monopoly: A Study of the East India Company's Conduct of Its Tea Trade 1784–1833* (Vancouver: University of British Columbia Press, 1984), 13, 32.

37. Richards, *Commodity Culture*, chap 1.

38. Jones, "Commercial Foods." By 1823 canned meats were arriving in the port of Belize for retail sale.

39. George Elkington, *The Coopers: Company and Craft* (London: Sampson Low, Marston and Co., 1933).

40. The elaboration of packaging in Britain is thoroughly examined by Davis, *Package and Print*. Processing machinery in the United States is discussed briefly by Joy Santlofer, "Hard as the Hubs of Hell," *Food, Culture & Society* 10, no. 2 (2007): 191–209.

41. Wilk, *Home Cooking*.

42. Jones, "Commercial Foods," 35.

43. On the early forms of preservation, see Sue Shephard, *Pickled, Potted, and Canned* (New York: Simon & Schuster, 2000). The example of portable soup is from Jones, "Commercial Foods," 30.

44. William Falconer gives an early account of manufacturing ship's biscuits in *A New Universal Dictionary of the Marine* (London: T. Cadell, 1815).

45. Santlofer, "Hard as the Hubs of Hell."

46. All of these examples come from Stevens, *On the Stowage of Ships*, though I have filled in missing details from various food encyclopedias and herbaria.

47. Jones, "Commercial Foods," 28–29.

48. Forrest, *Tea for the British*, 166–67.

49. Historically only a few vertically integrated companies ever had their own retail outlets, even in the United States, where the process of integration was more complete than in Britain. Only in the last few decades has retailing once again become part of a single corporate supply chain, through the agency of large retailing chains such as Wal-Mart, which now extend their power back to some basic producers.

Chapter 8. What's Left at the Bottom of the Glass

1. The Stilwell-Bierce & Smith-Vaile Co., "The 'Victor' Ice and Refrigerating Machines," 1899, National Museum of American History (NMAH), Washington, D.C.

2. *Ice and Refrigeration* 22 (February 1902): 54.

3. Henry Hall, "The Ice Industry of the United States with a Brief Sketch of Its History and Estimates of Production in Different States" (Washington, D.C., 1883), 2.

4. On Tudor's life and career, see Gavin Weightman, *The Frozen Water Trade* (New York: Hyperion, 2003).

5. Clipping in the Frederic Tudor Diaries, near April 22, 1817, Frederic Tudor Papers, Historical Collections, Baker Library, Boston.

6. Frederic Tudor to Robert Hooper, January 22, 1849, in *Massachusetts Historical Society Proceedings, 1855–1858* (Boston: John Wilson and Son, 1859), 53.

7. Frederic Tudor to John Barnard, February 1, 1821, Frederic Tudor Papers (II), Box 11.

8. Tudor to Hooper, 56.

9. Frederic Tudor Diaries, January 17, 1828, Microfilm Reel #1.

10. Colin Woodward, *The Lobster Coast* (New York: Penguin Books, 2004), 166.

11. *Kennebec Journal*, July 29, 1961.

12. Tudor Diaries, February 10, 1830.

13. Maine Bureau of Industrial and Labor Statistics, *Fifth Annual Report* (Augusta: Burleigh and Flint, 1892), 171.

14. *Ice Trade Journal* 3 (November 1879): 3.

15. Henry David Thoreau, *Walden* (1854; Princeton, N.J.: Princeton University Press, 2004), 296.

16. *Ice Trade Journal* 5 (December 1881): 2.

17. Thoreau, *Walden*, 296.

18. Hollis Godfrey, "The City's Ice," *Atlantic Monthly* 104 (July 1909): 121.

19. Julius Adams, "On the Pollution of Rivers . . . ," in *Report of the Commission of Engineers on the Water Supply of Philadelphia* (Philadelphia: E. C. Markley and Son, 1875), 65.

20. Booth and Garrett, "Report of Messrs. Booth and Garrett . . . ," in *Report of the Commission of Engineers*, c. 1880, 111. The report does not include Booth's or Garrett's first names.

21. Adams, *Report of the Commission of Engineers*, 51.

22. "C.M.C.," *Philadelphia Public Ledger Supplement*, January 13, 1883.

23. *Ice Trade Journal* 7 (March 1884): 2.

24. Joseph C. Jones, *American Ice Boxes* (Humble, Tex.: Jobeco Books, 1981), 29.

25. Jonathan M. Zenilman, "Typhoid Fever," *Journal of the American Medical Association* 278 (September 10, 1997): 848.

26. Leslie L. Lumsden, "The Causation and Prevention of Typhoid Fever," 4th ed., Public Health Bulletin No. 51 (1911; Washington, D.C.: U.S. Government Printing Office, 1914).

27. Nelson Manford Blake, *Water for the Cities* (Syracuse, N.Y.: Syracuse University Press, 1956), 260–61.

28. Michael McCarthy, *Typhoid and the Politics of Public Health in Nineteenth-Century Philadelphia* (Philadelphia: American Philosophical Society, 1987), 11.

29. *Scientific American* 56 (1887): 179.

30. William R. D. Blackwood, "Ice—How to Obtain It Pure," *Ice and Refrigeration* 5 (December 1893): 390.

31. R. H. Hutchings and A. W. Wheeler, "An Epidemic of Typhoid Fever Due to Impure Ice," *American Journal of the Medical Sciences* 126 (October 1903): 680-84. Modern research has confirmed these findings. For example, a 1985 study (conducted in order to test the safety of ordering cocktails in underdeveloped countries) found that 20 percent of typhoid bacteria survived in ice cubes after a week. See Lynn Dickens, Herbert L. DuPont, and Philip C. Johnson, "Survival of Bacteria Enteropathogens in the Ice of Popular Drinks," *Journal of the American Medical Association* 253 (June 7, 1985): 3141–43.

32. *New York Times*, May 31, 1903.

33. Thomas M. Drown, "The Purification of Water by Freezing," *Engineering News* 29 (June 29, 1893): n.p.

34. *Ice and Refrigeration* 3 (July 1892): 29.

35. Natural Ice Association of America, "'The Handwriting on the Wall': A Warning with Stereoptican Views and a Call to Arms!" n.p., c. 1915, Mohonk Mountain House Collection, Box 13, Hagley Museum and Library, Wilmington, Del.

36. Hans-Liudger Dienel, *Linde: History of a Technology Corporation, 1879–2004* (Hampshire, U.K.: Palgrave Macmillan, 2004), 24–28.

37. *Cold Storage and Ice Trades Review* 15 (March 21, 1912): 59.

38. The De La Vergne Refrigerating Machine Company, "Souvenir from the De La Vergne Refrigerating Machine Company" (New York, 1893), Refrigerating Catalogues and Miscellaneous, NMAH, n.p.

39. *Ice Trade Journal* 7 (March 1884) 2.

40. Ibid. (May 1884): 2.

41. Mary Yeager, *Competition and Regulation: The Development of Oligopoly in the Meat Packing Industry* (Greenwich, Conn.: JAI Press, 1981), 51–55, 58–60.

42. William Cronon, *Nature's Metropolis: Chicago and the Great West* (New York: Norton, 1991), 235.

43. *Ice and Refrigeration* 10 (April 1896): 262.

44. Anthony W. Thompson, Robert J. Church, and Bruce H. Jones, *PFE: Pacific Fruit Express* (Wilton, Calif.: Central Valley Road Publications, 1992), 8, 338–39.

45. *Scientific American* 78 (1914): 172, clipping from the Roy Eillers Collection, NMAH.

46. The Stilwell-Bierce & Smith-Vaile Co., "Victor Ice Machine," 6.

47. *Ice and Refrigeration* 16 (April 1899): 304.

48. *Cold Storage and Ice Trades Review* 14 (August 17, 1911): 233.

49. *Cold Storage* 1 (April 1899): 3.

50. *Ice* 1 (January 1908): 24.

51. *Ice and Refrigeration* 4 (April 1893): 295.

52. *Bangor Daily News*, January 19, 1953.

53. The De La Vergne Refrigerating Machine Company, "Ice Manufacture," 13, Refrigerating Catalogues and Miscellaneous, NMAH.

54. *New York Times*, May 31, 1903.

55. *Ice* 2 (May 1908): 30.

56. *Ice Trade Journal* 20 (August 1896): 6.

57. Ibid., 10.

58. Ibid., 1.

59. *Cold Storage* 1 (April 1899): 3.

60. H. W. Bahrenburg, "What the Dealer in Natural Ice Must Do to Retain His Position in the Industry," *Ice and Refrigeration* 37 (December 1909): 241.

61. *Ice and Refrigeration* 37 (October 1909): 123.

62. Ralph Potter, "How It Works If a Lamp Socket Is Your Omnipresent Iceman," *New York Tribune*, July 23, 1922.

63. *Ice and Refrigeration* 47 (July 1914): 12.

Chapter 9. Provisioning Man's Best Friend

1. American Pet Products Manufacturers Association, "Industry Statistics and Trends," http://www.appma.org/press_industrytrends.asp. (accessed September 1, 2007).

2. For the most current overview of the operations of the packing industry, see Roger Horowitz, *Putting Meat on the American Table: Taste, Technology, Transformation* (Baltimore, Md.: Johns Hopkins University Press, 2005).

3. For a discussion of the roles that dogs played in communities, see Katherine C. Grier, *Pets in America: A History* (Chapel Hill: University of North Carolina Press, 2006), esp. chaps. 1 and 4.

4. Mary Elizabeth Thurnston, *The Lost History of the Canine Race: Our 15,000-Year Love Affair with Dogs* (Kansas City, Mo.: Andrews and McMeel, 1996), 235; J. P. Crowdy, "The Science of the Soldier's Food," *Army Quarterly and Defence Journal (Great Britain)* 110, no. 3 (1980): 266–79.

5. A 1928 advertisement for Spratt's Patent Limited stated that the firm had been in business for seventy-five years. *Pet Dealer* (May 1928): 17. Advertisement for Spratts, *American Kennel Gazette*, January 1889, cover. On its dominance of "benching and feeding," see James A. Watson, *The Dog Book: A Popular History of the Dog, with Practical Information on the Care and Management of House, Kennel, and Exhibition Dogs; and a Description of All Important Breeds* (Garden City, N.Y.: Doubleday & Company, 1916), 64.

6. The advertisements for Fibrine Dog Cakes include a patent date of 1881, although the nature of this patent remains unknown at present. See *Spratt's Patent Limited, Catalogue and Short Treatise on Dog Diseases, Poultry Feeding, Etc., 1895 Edition (3), 105th Thousand* (New York: Spratts Patent Limited, 1895), 28, 33. For a discussion of this language in reference to the diet of Victorian humans, see Harvey Green, *Fit for America: Health, Fitness, Sport, and American Society* (New York: Pantheon Books, 1985).

7. Sears, Roebuck and Company, *Consumer's Guide, Catalogue No. 104* (1897; repr., New York: Chelsea House Publishers, 1976), n.p.

8. Potter and Wrightington, *Your Dog* (Charlestown, Mass.: by the company, [ca. 1910], 3–5.

9. For a time line of Ralston-Purina, see http://purina.com/company/pro file/timeline.

10. Advertisement for Kennel Food Supply Company, *American Kennel Gazette*, June 30, 1916, back cover.

11. National Industrial Recovery Administration (NIRA), *Hearing on Code of Fair Practices and Competition Presented by the Dog Food Industry February 16, 1934, Vol. 3*, Jesse Ward of Ward & Paul, official reporter, Earle Building, Washington, D.C., 112–16.

12. "Horse Flesh for Europe," *New York Times* (hereafter *NYT*), December 22, 1891, 6; "Horse-Meat," *NYT*, July 23, 1895, 4; "Work of Canning Horse Meat Begun," *NYT*, July 20, 1895, 1; "Horse Meat in New Jersey," *NYT*, December 15,

1897, 1; "Horse Meat for Beef," *NYT*, January 17, 1901, 1. See also Clay McShane and Joel Tarr, *The Horse in the City: Living Machines in the Nineteenth Century* (Baltimore, Md.: Johns Hopkins University Press, 2007).

13. Leroy Judson Daniels, as told to Helen S. Herrick, *Tales of an Old Horsetrader* (Iowa City: University of Iowa Press, 1987), 140–44.

14. NIRA, *Hearing*, 67–68.

15. "Output of Dog Food and Animal Feeds," *National Provisioner* 99 (November 20–26, 1938): 28.

16. Noting that "edibility is a relative term," the *Encyclopedia of Meat Sciences* points out that approximately 50 percent of live weight in cattle, 40 percent in pigs, and 30 percent in broiler chickens is considered "inedible." These percentages may be somewhat larger than in the past because "as further processing, pre-packaging, and table-ready meat products are brought to the marketplace, the inedible portions have increased in relation to the original weight of the animal." In 2002 the United States meat-processing industry processed 139 million head of livestock and 16 billion kilograms of live poultry, resulting in 234.4 to 24.3 billion kilograms of inedible by-products. See G. G. Pearl, "By-Products, Inedible," *Encyclopedia of Meat Sciences*, v. 1 (Oxford: Elsevier Academic Press, 2004).

17. Rudolph A. Clemen, *By-Products in the Packing Industry* (Chicago: University of Chicago Press, 1927), vii.

18. Ibid., 1.

19. Ibid., 10.

20. Pearl, "By-Products, Inedible," 112.

21. Clemen, *By-Products*, 311, 325.

22. Ibid., 258, 259.

23. "Advice on Feeding a Dog Including a Report on Canned Dog Food," *Consumers' Research Bulletin* 9, no. 2 (November 1941): 5.

24. "Meat Packers Show Interest in Profit Possibilities in Related Lines," *National Provisioner* 90, April 21, 1934): 15.

25. "Processing Dog Food," *National Provisioner* 91 (October 28–November 3, 1934): 40.

26. Hugh B. Killough, "The Amplitude of the Marketing Task," *Annals of the American Academy of Political and Social Science* 209, *Marketing in Our American Economy* (May 1940): 25.

27. NIRA, *Hearing*, 96–98.

28. H. A. Halverson, H. J. Witteveen, and Ragna Bergman, *The Composition of Commercial Dog Foods* (Minneapolis: State of Minnesota Department of Agriculture and Dairy and Food, 1942).

29. Jimmy M. Skaggs, *Prime Cut: Livestock Raising and Meatpacking in the United States 1607–1983* (College Station: Texas A&M University Press, 1986), 153.

30. Steven Katz, grandson of Irving Katz, the founder of Rival dog food, interview by the author, September 28, 2006.

31. "Dog Food Trade to Act," *NYT*, July 2, 1933, N13; NIRA, *Hearing*, 37–38.

32. NIRA, *Hearing*, 99, 101.

33. "Practical Points for the Trade: Dog Food Formulas," *National Provisioner* 93 (December, 15–23, 1935): 13.

34. "Dog Food Diet Is Forced on U.S., Says Dickinson," *Chicago Daily Tribune*, April 28, 1936, 4.

35. NIRA, *Hearing*, 107.

36. "Dog Food as Human Food," *National Provisioner* 94 (April 26–May 2, 1936): 13.

37. "New Dog Food Regulation," *National Provisioner* 94 (May 3–9, 1936): 38.

38. "New Dog Food Inspection Bill Is Offered," *National Provisioner* 94 (May 17–23, 1936): 17; Susan A. Jones, *Valuing Animals: Veterinarians and Their Patients in Modern America* (Baltimore, Md.: Johns Hopkins University Press, 2002), 119.

39. "Heads Dog Food Work," *National Provisioner* 96 (March 27–April 3, 1937): 40.

40. General Mills, Inc., *So You Own a Dog!* (Minneapolis: Washburn Crosby Company [div. General Mills]), 1941), 29.

41. Albers Brothers Milling Company, *A New Day Dawns for the Dog: How to Train Your Dog; How to Keep Your Dog Healthy. Tested. Eighteen Months of Study in the Albers Laboratory* (Seattle: by the company, 1935). The booklet describes tests with dogs and with white rats and includes illustrations of the facility. See also Albers Milling Company, *How to Keep Your Dog Frisky* (Hollywood, Calif.: by the company, 1952), 14. By then Friskies offered a canned food with a "meaty" texture but emphasized its kibbled foods.

42. Bob Becker, "Mostly about Dogs: Dog Foods to Get Expert Tests," *Chicago Daily Tribune*, June 6, 1937, G4.

43. L. A. Horswell, quoted in ibid. Horswell apparently printed a table of costs on a can of dog food, showing that cost for production, labeling, shipping, and selling was 5.17 cents a can.

44. Carl J. Koehn, "Preparing Samples of Canned Dog Food for Proximate Chemical Analysis," *Industrial and Engineering Chemistry* 10, no. 6 (1938): 326–27.

45. "Advice on Feeding Dogs," *Consumers' Research Bulletin*, 7.

46. "Feeding Your Dog in Wartime and After," *Consumers' Research Bulletin* 15, no. 1 (January 1945):16.

47. "Dog Food Crisis," *Business Week*, March 7, 1942, 34.

48. "Swift's War Work Vastly Expanded," *New York Times*, January 22, 1943, 29.

49. "Wickard Curtains Protein Content of Pet Animal Food," *Wall Street Journal*, January 29, 1943, 3.

50. "Feeding Your Dog in Wartime and After," 15–17. The research was developed and sponsored by the American Humane Association in collaboration with the Committee on Foods of the American Veterinary Medical Association and the American Animal Hospital Association.

51. James J. Nagle, "Pet Food Market Big—and Growing," *New York Times*, April 18, 1954, F1, F7.

Chapter 10. Empire of Ice Cream

1. Katherine Verdery, *What Was Socialism, and What Comes Next?* (Princeton, N.J.: Princeton University Press, 1996).

2. "Toward an Even Higher Output of Ice Cream," *Molochnaia Promyshlennost'* (July 1961): 18–21.

3. As early as 1947 (a year of famine in the U.S.S.R.) a dairy plant in Baku reported that one-sixth of its daily output was in ice cream. See Russian State Economic Archive, "Materials, Protocols and Reports of the Bureau of Technical Expertise for MinMiasProm (Ministry of Meat Production)," fond 8295, opis 4, delo 198, list 197.

4. Yu. A Olenev and N. D. Zubova, *Kak Proizvodstvo Morozhenoe* (How to Manufacture Ice Cream: A Manual for the Professional Cadre) (Moscow: Pishchevai Promyshlennost' Izdat, 1977), 3.

5. "Resolutions of the First All-Union Industrial Conference of the Workers of

Public Nutrition," *Voprosy Pitaniia*, no. 6 (1933): 2. For an overview of communal feeding projects, see Susan Reid, "Cold War in the Kitchen: Gender and De-Stalinization of Consumer Taste in the Soviet Union under Khrushchev," *Slavic Review*, no. 2 (2002): 211–52.

6. J. A. Newth, "Soviet Agriculture: The Private Sector 1950-1959; Animal Husbandry," *Soviet Studies*, no. 4 (1962).

7. Elena Zubkova, *Russia after the War: Hopes, Illusions, and Disappointments, 1945–1957*, trans. Hugh Ragsdale (Armonk, N.Y.: M. E. Sharpe, 1998); Julie Hessler, *A Social History of Soviet Trade: Trade Policy, Retail Practice, and Consumption, 1917–1953* (Princeton, N.J.: Princeton University Press, 2004).

8. Harison E. Salisbury, "Nixon in Wrangle with Khrushchev," *New York Times*, July 25, 1959.

9. Hessler, *Social History of Soviet Trade*.

10. Paul Minneman to USDA, Washington, D.C., September 1961, National Archives, "Soviet Sugar Policy," RG 166 (Records of the Foreign Agricultural Service Narrative Reports, 1955–61), Box 883. The statement on imports is made for 1955 onward but is true for the earlier period as well.

11. "Development of Industrial Ice Cream Processing," *Kholodil'naia Tekhnika*, no. 5 (1970): 1–3. As late as 1969 the Soviet Union had only three hundred small-capacity freezer trucks and two hundred "reefer" large-capacity trucks in its entire fleet.

12. "Dairy Product Distribution in Kharkov," *Molochnaia Promyshlennost'*, no. 3 (1956): n.p.

13. Lewis H. Siegelbaum, "Cars, Cars and More Cars, the Faustian Bargain of the Brezhnev Era," in *Borders of Socialism: Private Spheres of Soviet Russia* (New York: Palgrave Macmillan, 2006).

14. "New Developments in Cooling Railroad Cars," *Kholodil'naia Tekhnika*, no. 3 (1960): 46–47.

15. For one Leningrad municipal cold locker, the cost of purchasing a new freezer in 1954 was almost half the annual operating cost of the facility: 1044.8 rubles of 2621.2 total. See "Annual Report of the Leningrad Trust for 1954: *MinMiasMolProm* (Ministry of Meat and Dairy Production)," Russian State Economic Archive, fond 9355, opis 4, delo 4, list 8.

16. "About Dry Ice," *Kholodil'naia Tekhnika*, no. 3 (1960): 43–45.

17. "Work on Home Refrigerators: A Report by Mechanic M. Badzhi," *Kholodil'naia Tekhnika*, no. 5 (1960): 51–52.

18. Ibid.

19. N. Lyubimov and A. Burmakin, "New Equipment for a Mechanization of Ice Cream Production at RosMiasorybtorg Plants," *Kholodil'naia Tekhnika*, no. 3 (1960): 32.

20. "Increasing the Output of High Quality Ice Cream," *Pishchevaia Promyshlennost' (Molochnaia)*, no. 3 (1961): 11.

21. "Development of Industrial Ice Cream Processing," 1–3.

22. *Proizvodstvo Masla I Morozhenog: Uchebnye Posobie* (The Production of Fats and Frozen Goods: Educational Materials) (Leningrad: Leningrad Technological Institute of Refrigerated Products, 1976), 31.

23. "New Varieties of Ice Cream, by G. Azov," *Kholdil'naia Tekhnika*, no. 1 (1960): 39–41. Recipes are given for tomato, carrot, and prune ice cream.

24. Consumer preferences are notoriously hard to identify in the Soviet Union, as marketing research was scarce. However, at least one publication is specific about the *plombir* preference, "Increasing the Output of High Quality Ice

Cream," 11. The crème brûlée preference is my own conclusion based on informal discussions with Russians who remember this period rather than on archival evidence.

25. "Development of Industrial Ice Cream Processing," 1–3.

26. Ibid.

27. Andy Carvin, home page, http://www.andycarvin.com/archives/2006/05/belarus_flash_mobs_a.html (accessed October 2007).

Chapter 11. Eating Mexican in a Global Age

1. I thank my colleague and international population expert Bob McCaa for his regular taco reports from IPUMS conferences around the world. For Mexican food in outer space, listen to the Kitchen Sisters, Davia Nelson and Nikki Silva, "Beyond Tang: Food in Space," a segment of their NPR series, *Hidden Kitchens*, http://www.npr.org/templates/story/story.php?storyId=10792763 (aired and accessed June 7, 2007). See also Kim Severson, "Taking Humdrum Astronaut Food, and Kicking It Up a Notch," *New York Times*, August 29, 2006.

2. Frederik Barth, ed., *Ethnic Groups and Boundaries: The Social Organization of Cultural Difference* (Boston: Little Brown, 1969); Arlene Dávila, *Latinos, Inc.: The Marketing and Making of a People* (Berkeley: University of California Press, 2001).

3. Anne Goldman, "'I Yam What I Yam': Cooking, Culture, and Colonialism," in *De/Colonizing the Subject*, ed. Sidonie Smith and Julia Watson (Minneapolis: University of Minnesota Press, 1992), 169–95.

4. Uma Narayan, "Eating Cultures: Incorporation, Identity, and Indian Food," *Social Identities* 1, no. 1 (1995): 63–86; Lisa Heldke, *Exotic Appetites: Ruminations of a Food Adventurer* (New York: Routledge, 2003).

5. Meredith E. Abarca, "Authentic or Not, It's Original," *Food and Foodways* 12 (2004): 1–25.

6. Jeffrey M. Pilcher, *¡Que vivan los tamales! Food and the Making of Mexican Identity* (Albuquerque: University of New Mexico Press, 1998).

7. Arnold J. Bauer, *Goods, Power, History: Latin America's Material Culture* (Cambridge: Cambridge University Press, 2001); Lynn Stephen, *Zapotec Women* (Austin: University of Texas Press, 1990).

8. Pilcher, *¡Que vivan los tamales!*, chaps. 3 and 4.

9. Felipe Torres et al., eds., *La industria de la masa y la tortilla: Desarrollo y tecnología* (Mexico City: Universidad Nacional Autónoma de México, 1996); Jaime Aboites A., *Breve historia de un invento olvidado: Las máquinas tortilladoras en México* (Mexico City: Universidad Autónoma Metropolitana, 1989); Enrique C. Ochoa, *Feeding Mexico: The Politics of Food since 1910* (Wilmington, Del.: Scholarly Resources, Inc., 2000); Jeffrey M. Pilcher, "Industrial Tortillas and Folkloric Pepsi: The Nutritional Consequences of Hybrid Cuisines in Mexico," in *Food Nations: Selling Taste in Consumer Societies*, ed. Warren Belasco and Philip Scranton (New York: Routledge, 2002), 222–39.

10. William W. Dunmire, *Gardens of New Spain: How Mediterranean Plants and Foods Changed America* (Austin: University of Texas Press, 2004); Marilyn Tausend, *Cocina de la Familia* (New York: Simon and Schuster, 1997).

11. Arnoldo de León, *They Called Them Greasers: Anglo Attitudes toward Mexicans in Texas, 1821–1900* (Austin: University of Texas Press, 1983), 67; David Montejano, *Anglos and Mexicans in the Making of Texas, 1836–1986* (Austin: University of Texas Press, 1987), 181–86, 199.

12. Quoted in Donna R. Gabaccia, *We Are What We Eat: Ethnic Food and the Making of Americans* (Cambridge, Mass.: Harvard University Press, 1998), 108–9.

13. Victor M. Valle and Rodolfo D. Torres, *Latino Metropolis* (Minneapolis: University of Minnesota Press, 2000), 74; "A 'Fence' Located in a Tamale Stand," *Los Angeles Times*, April 14, 1895; "Half-Demented Tamale Vender," *Los Angeles Times*, September 6, 1904; "Dry Squad Nabs Eighteen," *Los Angeles Times*, March 2, 1925.

14. Francisco J. Santamaria, *Diccionario de Mejicanismos*, 5th ed. (Mexico City: Editorial Porrúa, 1992), 385.

15. Quote from Mrs. E. G. Myers, ed., *The Capitol Cook Book* (1899; Austin: Brick Row Book Shop, 1966), 56. See also Gabaccia, *We Are What We Eat*, 159–60; Keith J. Guenther, "The Development of the Mexican-American Cuisine," in *National and Regional Styles of Cookery: Proceedings of the Oxford Symposium on Food and Cookery*, ed. Alan Davidson (London: Prospect Books, 1981), 278; "Miscellaneous Items," *Los Angeles Times*, November 19, 1899; and "E. C. Ortega Taken by Death," *Los Angeles Times*, February 21, 1942.

16. Patricia Preciado Martin, *Songs My Mother Sang to Me: An Oral History of Mexican American Women* (Tucson: University of Arizona Press, 1992), 116; Mary E. Livingston, *San Antonio in the 1920s and 1930s* (Charleston, S.C.: Arcadia Publishing, 2000), 41–42; Jeffrey Steele, "Mexican Goes Mainstream," *Restaurante Mexicano* 1, no. 1 (January/February 1997): 6–15; Marrill Shindler, *El Cholo Cookbook: Recipes and Lore from California's Best-Loved Mexican Kitchen* (Santa Monica, Calif.: Angel City Press, 1998), 15; "News of Food," *New York Times*, May 3, 1952.

17. Vicki L. Ruiz, *From Out of the Shadows: Mexican Women in Twentieth-Century America* (New York: Oxford University Press, 1998), 51–67, 72–75; Vanessa Fonseca, "Fractal Capitalism and the Latinization of the U.S. Market" (Ph.D. diss., University of Texas, Austin, 2003); "'Tamalina' 70 Years Old," *San Antonio News*, June 16, 1966; Gilberto Hinojosa, "Story of the Corn Chip," *San Antonio Express News*, August 24, 1997; Jeffrey M. Pilcher, "Was the Taco Invented in Southern California?," *Gastronomica: The Journal of Food and Culture* (forthcoming).

18. Elizabeth Webb Herrick, *Curious California Customs* (Los Angeles: Pacific Carbon & Printing Company, 1935), 109.

19. Pilcher, "Was the Taco Invented in Southern California?"; George Ritzer, *The McDonaldization of Society* (Thousand Oaks, Calif.: Pine Forge Press, 1993).

20. Gabaccia, "We Are What We Eat," 165, 219–20; Fonseca, "Fractal Capitalism," 42, 52–57. See also the ads in *Los Angeles Times*, November 6, 1952, February 10, 1955; and *Chicago Tribune*, September 16, 1960.

21. Art Buchwald, "The Tourist Is Welcome Here," *Los Angeles Times*, August 4, 1959.

22. Phyllis Pooler, *Hon-Dah a la Fiesta Cook Book* (Phoenix: Arizona Messenger Printing Co, 1968), 21.

23. Ella K. Daggett Stumpf, "Cheers for Chili Con Carne!," *San Antonio Magazine* (March 1978): 47.

24. Tom Estes, interview by author, Paris, France, June 1, 1999.

25. Earlene Ridge, "Cook Who Makes Mexican Food in Paris Has to Go by Way of the Arab Market," *Arizona Daily Star* (Tucson), December 18, 1996.

26. Oshima Bari, Author's interview, Osaka, Japan, September 10, 2000.

27. Lyn Kidder, *Tacos on the Tundra: The Story of Pepe's North of the Border* (Anchorage: Bonapart Books, 1996), 98–101, 112, 141–42.

28. Robb Walsh, *The Tex-Mex Cookbook: A History in Recipes and Photos* (New York: Broadway Books, 2004), 247.

29. Jeffrey Charles, "Searching for Gold in Guacamole: California Growers

Market the Avocado, 1910–1994," in *Food Nations: Selling Taste in Consumer Societies*, ed. Warren Belasco and Philip Scranton (New York: Routledge, 2002), 149.

30. Tara Parker-Pope, "Texans Bite Off All They Can Chew in U.K. Restaurant," *Wall Street Journal* (Europe), December 2, 1994; *Budapest Sun*, October 19, 1995; "Wild, Wild, East," *Economist*, August 31, 1996.

31. Anne Bogart, "Western Europe: The Tex-Mex Invasion," *Harper's Bazaar* (February 1989): 48.

32. Gregory Rodriguez, "Swedish Mexican Food, Straight from the U.S.," *Los Angeles Times*, September 24, 2006.

33. *The Berkeley Guides: Paris '96* (New York: Fodor's Travel Publications, 1995), 153.

34. Lisa Teoh, "Dine-online," http://www.dine-online.co.uk/downmex.htm (accessed July 3, 2007).

35. Rodriguez, "Swedish Mexican Food."

36. See, for example, a description of the first encounter of the emperors Maximilian and Carlota with mole poblano by Concepción Lombardo de Miramón, *Memorias* (Mexico City: Editorial Porrúa, 1980), 473. An early nationalist statement came from Judith Van Bueren: "Quality in all ingredients makes for high costs and the temptation is mostly not resisted to grind old chile into powder and hop it up hot enough so that the falsification cannot be detected— nor any other taste," quoted in Richard Condon and Wendy Condon, *Great Recipes in the Classic Mexican Tradition* (Dallas: Taylor Publishing Company, 1988), 16.

37. Fortín Rojas Contreras, interview by author, Mexico City, July 4, 2006.

38. *El universo de la cocina mexicana: Recetario* (Mexico City: Fomento Cultural Banamex, 1988), 18, 40, 48.

39. "Alta Cocina Patricia Quintana," http://www.jamesbeard.org/old/events/1999/10/029.html (accessed September 28, 2006).

40. Cristin Prun, interview by author, Paris, June 3, 1999.

41. "A Slice of Mexico on Your Platter," *Hindustan Times* (New Delhi), February 4, 2005.

42. José Galán, "Señala investigación de la UAM sobre el alimento," *Reforma*, April 14, 2001; Jenalia Moreno, "A Fresh Tortilla That Will Endure," *Houston Chronicle*, November 27, 2004.

43. John Norton, "Candy's Stock Jumps," *Pueblo (Colorado) Chieftain*, April 12, 1994; "Wrapping the Globe in Tortillas," *Business Week*, February 26, 2007; "Food Manufacture," *Processing News* 75, no. 1 (January 2000): 7.

44. "Impresionante, la demanda que tiene la cerveza Corona en EU," *El Universal*, September 11, 1986; "Corona se coloca como la cerveza Mexicana de mayor venta en EU," *Excelsior*, September 8, 1986.

45. Antonio Vázquez, "Rechazan obreros de Modelo el convenio," *Uno Más Uno*, April 3, 1990; Carlos Galguera Roiz, "Una oportunidad de definición," *Uno Más Uno*, April 4, 1990; Alejandro Claps, "Se logro la aperture del mercado Sueco," *Excelsior*, April 17, 1992; "Cervezas mexicanas conquistan Europa," *El Financiero*, August 25, 1992; "Se asoció la Modelo con la Anheuser Busch," *La Jornada*, March 23, 1993.

46. Matthew Debord, "Más Tequila!," *Wine Spectator* 28, no. 2 (May 15, 2003). See also José Orozco, "Gabriel Espíndola Martínez: Tequila Master," in *The Human Tradition in Mexico*, ed. Jeffrey M. Pilcher (Wilmington, Del.: Scholarly Resources, Inc., 2003).

47. Gabriel Torres, "The Agave War: Toward an Agenda for the Post-NAFTA Ejido," in *The Future Role of the Ejido in Rural Mexico*, ed. Richard Snyder and Gabriel

Torres (La Jolla: Center for U.S.-Mexico Studies, University of California, San Diego, 1998), 73–100.

48. Alejandro Ascencio, "Envían a paisanos menudo y barbacoa," *Reforma*, July 4, 2006; Oscar Gonzalez, "The Latino Way for Frozen Food," *InfoAmericas Tendencias Latin American Market Report* 39 (March 27, 2003); "Celebrating Mexican," *Frozen Food Age* 54, no. 3 (October 2005).

49. Arturo Cruz Barcenas, "Fallo en contra de la comida mexicana," *La Jornada*, November 26, 2005.

50. Meredith E. Abarca, *Voices in the Kitchen: Views of Food and the World from Working-Class Mexican and Mexican American Women* (College Station: Texas A&M University Press, 2006), 78–108; Abarca, "Authentic or Not," 4, 18–20. See also Hermann Bausinger, *Folk Culture in a World of Technology*, trans. Elke Dettmer (Bloomington: Indiana University Press, 1990).

51. Dan Malovany, "Tortilla Trends," *Snack Food and Wholesale Bakery* (August 2006); "Wrapping the Globe in Tortillas," *Business Week*, February 26, 2007; Gabaccia, *We Are What We Eat*, 149–74.

52. María Dolores Torres Yzábal and Shelton Wiseman, *The Mexican Gourmet: Authentic Ingredients and Traditional Recipes from the Kitchens of Mexico* (Sydney: Gold Street Press, 1995).

53. "Marie's World Tour 2001," http://www.mariesworldtour.com/entries/0504.html (accessed October 16, 2006); Prun interview.

Chapter 12. The Aristocracy of the Market Basket

I am very grateful to the participants in the April 2006 Hagley Seminar Series, members of the audience at the Hagley Library "Food Chains" conference, November 2006, for their challenging questions and helpful insights on earlier drafts of this chapter. Earlier versions of this essay were also presented at the Southern Historical Association, November 2006, and the Organization of American Historians, March 2007. I would especially like to thank Catherine Grier, Tracey Deutsch, Warren Belasco, Robin Bachin, Ted Ownby, Patrick Lucas, and Roslyn Holdzkom for their careful readings and constructive criticism.

1. Eudora Welty, "The Little Store," in *Mississippi Writers: Reflections of Childhood and Youth, Volume II: Nonfiction*, ed. Dorothy Abbott (Jackson: University Press of Mississippi, 1985), 644, 639.

2. Susan Strasser, *Satisfaction Guaranteed: The Making of the American Mass Market* (New York: Pantheon Books, 1989), 248.

3. Perry F. Nichols, "How about Waiting on Yourself? A New Development in Stores—Hastened by the War," *American Magazine* (April 1919): 31.

4. Chester H. Liebs, *Main Street to Miracle Mile: American Roadside Architecture* (Baltimore: Johns Hopkins University Press, 1985); James M. Mayo, *The American Grocery Store: The Business Evolution of an Architectural Space* (Westport, Conn.: Greenwood Press, 1993).

5. Eric Foner, *The Story of American Freedom* (New York: W. W. Norton & Company, 1998), 147–48. Tracey Deutsch offers a more rigorous and nuanced analysis of the grocery stores in the 1920s. She argues that chain stores succeeded by depersonalizing the often tense social relations of traditional independent grocery stores, but she emphasizes, "Self-service and the independence it promised were seen as especially important advantages in attracting women customers." See

Tracey Deutsch, "Untangling Alliances: Social Tensions Surrounding Independent Grocery Stores and the Rise of Mass Retailing," in *Food Nations: Selling Taste in Consumer Societies*, ed. Warren Belasco and Philip Scranton (New York: Routledge, 2002), 156–74, quote on 168.

6. Kent Lutey, "Lutey Brothers Marketeria: America's First Self-Service Grocers," *Montana* 28, no. 2 (1978): 50–57.

7. Piggly Wiggly Contract Requirements Etc., Piggly Wiggly Home Office, Memphis, Tenn., May 1919, p. 5.

8. Twenty-seven of thirty-eight self-service store patents were submitted by southern grocers. This includes patents from Texas as part of the southern region.

9. Tracey Ann Deutsch, "Making Change at the Grocery Store: Government, Grocers, and the Problem of Women's Autonomy in the Creation of Chicago's Supermarkets, 1920–1950" (Ph.D. diss., University of Wisconsin-Madison, 2001).

10. Charles S. Johnson, *Patterns of Negro Segregation* (New York: Harper & Brothers, 1943), 64.

11. Grace Elizabeth Hale, *Making Whiteness: The Culture of Segregation in the South, 1890–1940* (New York: Vintage Books, 1998), 88.

12. *Memphis Commercial Appeal*, September 24, 1916 (Sunday morning), 13.

13. John A Cutchins, *Memories of Old Richmond* (Verona, Va.: McClure Press, 1973), 28.

14. Elizabeth O. Howse, *Falling Stars*, copyright by Mrs. G. S. Ridley, Jr., 1960, 6.

15. William Henry Holman, Jr., *"Save a Nickel on a Quarter": The Story of Jitney-Jungle Stores of America* (New York: Newcomen Society in North America, 1974), 12.

16. *Memphis Commercial Appeal*, September 7, 1917 (Friday morning), 2.

17. Welty, "Little Store," 642. It is useful to note that mass production of brand-name products occurred before the modernization of store interiors. Prepackaged merchandise made self-service store design possible.

18. Edward L. Ayers, *The Promise of the New South: Life After Reconstruction* (New York: Oxford University Press, 1992), 92. Clarence Saunders, *Piggly Wiggly Store Investment Requirements* (Memphis: Linotype Printing Co., 1918).

19. Price List, Piggly Wiggly Store Equipment, Piggly Wiggly Home Office, Memphis, Tenn., June 1, 1918.

20. Cutchins, *Memories*, 28.

21. Howse, 65.

22. *Memphis Commercial Appeal*, 19 August, 1916, [Saturday morning], p.4.

23. Piggly Wiggly clerk, quoted in Deutsch, "Untangling Alliances," 166.

24. Howse, *Falling Stars*, 21–22.

25. *Eligibility to Piggly Wiggly*, Piggly Wiggly Home Office, Memphis, Tenn., June 1, 1918, 6. Memphis Public Library Special Collections.

26. Patent 1,305,033, R. A. Tribble, Vending Apparatus, patented May 27, 1919.

27. Patent 1,348,024, William B. McCarty, Self-Serving Store, patented July 27, 1920.

28. *Memphis Commercial Appeal*, September 4, 1916 (Monday morning), 5.

29. Grace Elizabeth Hale, "'For Colored' and 'For White': Segregating Consumption in the South," in *Jumpin' Jim Crow: Southern Politics from Civil War to Civil Rights*, ed. Jane Dailey, Glenda Elizabeth Gilmore, and Bryant Simon (Princeton, N.J.: Princeton University Press, 2000), 170, 164, 166.

30. Charles S. Johnson, *Patterns of Negro Segregation* (New York: Harper & Brothers, 1943), 64.

31. Although southern white women of all classes continued to benefit from the underpaid domestic labor of African American women, the historian Tera Hunter estimates that "between 1910 and 1920, the proportion of wage-earning black women in household work dropped from 84 to 75 percent." See Tera W. Hunter, "'The Women Are Asking for BREAD, Why Give Them STONE': Women, Work, and Protests in Atlanta and Norfolk during World War I," in *Labor in the Modern South*, ed. Glenn T. Eskew (Athens: University of Georgia Press, 2001), 62–82, quote on 74.

32. Howse, *Falling Stars*, 161.

33. James Carrier, "Reconciling Personal Commodities and Personal Relations in Industrial Society," *Theory and Society* 19, no. 5 (October 1990): 587, 583. My understanding of food shopping as cultural work is also based on the work of Susan Porter Benson, *Counter Cultures: Saleswomen, Managers, and Customers in American Department Stores, 1890–1940* (Urbana: University of Illinois Press, 1987).

34. *Atlanta Constitution*, July 31, 1920, 2.

35. Hale, *Making Whiteness*, 87–93.

36. *Memphis News Scimitar*, June 17, 1919.

37. *Memphis Commercial Appeal*, August 27, 1916 (Sunday morning), 11.

38. Ibid., September 10, 1916 (Sunday morning), 9.

39. Ibid., June 3, 1917, 2.

40. *Memphis News Scimitar*, June 19, 1917.

41. Holman, *"Save a Nickel,"* 21–22, 15. Holman estimates that by 1946, 90 percent of Jutney customers were women.

42. *Turnstile* 5, no. 8 (January 25, 1923).

43. Louis M. Kyriakoudes, *The Social Origins of the Urban South: Race, Gender, and Migration in Nashville and Middle Tennessee, 1890–1930* (Chapel Hill: University of North Carolina Press, 2003), 102.

Chapter 13. Making Markets Marxist?

For their valuable comments and suggestions, I would like to thank my editors Warren Belasco and Roger Horowitz, Tracey Deutsch, Paulina Bren, Brigitte LeNormand, Nicole Münnich, Shane Hamilton, Lisa Tolbert, Catherine Grandclément, and the other participants in the Hagley Museum and Library's "Food Chains" conference. Vital funding for the research was provided by the American Council for Learned Societies, the International Research and Exchanges Board, the National Council for Eurasian and East European Research, and the Hagley Museum and Library.

1. Of course, with its history of massive subsidies, cultivation restrictions, and protective tariffs, the "free-market" system of agricultural production and sales in the capitalist West has really been anything but a pure arena for unrestricted market forces.

2. On the history of grocery sales and supermarkets in their classic Western settings, see, e.g., Kim Humphery, *Shelf Life: Supermarkets and the Changing Cultures of Consumption* (Cambridge: Cambridge University Press, 1998); and James M. Mayo, *The American Grocery Store: The Business Evolution of an Architectural Space* (Westport, Conn.: Greenwood Press, 1993).

3. My more limited review of sources relevant to other cases suggests a similar conclusion. On the introduction of the self-service model in communist Czechoslovakia, see, e.g., Dr. Rulf-Šafařik, "Az önkiszolgáló boltok fejlődése és

eredményei a Csehslovák Szocialista Köztársaságban," *Kereskedelmi Szemle: A Belkereskedelmi Kutatóintézet folyóirata* 2, no. 1 (1961): 33–36. Little scholarship has been published in Western languages on any of these cases, but see, e.g., Dennison Rusinow, "Yugoslavia's Supermarket Revolution: The Self-Service Shopping Cart as a Vehicle of Modernization," *American Universities Field Staff Reports, Southeast Europe Series* 16, no. 1 (1969): 1–18; Shane Hamilton, "Supermarket USA Confronts State Socialism: Airlifting the Technopolitics of Industrial Food Distribution into Cold-War Yugoslavia," in *Cold War Kitchen: Americanization, Technology, and European Users*, ed. Ruth Oldenziel and Karin Zachmann (Cambridge, Mass.: MIT Press, forthcoming 2009); Nicole Münnich, "Öffentlicher Stadtraum zwischen Herrschaftsanspruch und gesellschaftlichem Eigensinn: Urbanität im sozialistischen Belgrad der 1960er Jahre" (Ph.D. diss., Center for Metropolitan Studies, Berlin, in progress).

4. My effort here to understand the nature and function of self-service and supermarkets in communist states is an outgrowth of a broader project on the history of market culture and consumerism in socialist society. See Patrick Hyder Patterson, "Truth Half Told: Finding the Perfect Pitch for Advertising and Marketing in Socialist Yugoslavia, 1950–1991," *Enterprise & Society: The International Journal of Business History* 4, no. 2 (June 2003): 179–225; and Patrick Hyder Patterson, "The New Class: Consumer Culture under Socialism and the Unmaking of the Yugoslav Dream, 1945–1991" (Ph.D. diss., University of Michigan, 2001).

5. My conclusions here derive substantially from a review of what turns out to be a vast professional literature on retailing in the socialist societies under consideration. These sources are too numerous to list comprehensively, but see, e.g., Gerd Baron, Harri Gerold, Herbert Karsten, and Werner Schmidt, *Warenhäuser: Entwicklung, Leitung, Organisation* (Berlin: Verlag die Wirtschaft, 1966); Imre Horváth and István Kázsmér, *Az önkiszolgáló bolt* (Budapest: Közgazdasági és jogi könyvkiadó, 1962); György Hollai et al., *Az ABC Áruházak (Super-Marketek) létesítése és üzemeltetése*, Belkereskedelmi Kutató Intézet Közleményei no. 84 (Budapest: Belkereskedelmi Kutató Intézet, [1963]); and István Szabó, Ferencné Kurucz, and Rudolf Rajnai, *A szupermarketek (ABC Áruházak) fejlesztésének főbb tendenciái* (Budapest: Kereskedelmi Munka- és Üzemszervezési Intézet, 1980). An indispensable source for analysis of the Yugoslav case is the retail trade journal *Supermarket*.

6. For a representative Western treatment of the nature of grocery and supermarket sales, see, e.g., Edward A. Brand, *Modern Supermarket Operation* (New York: Fairchild Publications, 1963).

7. Ante Rodin, "'Magnet' za Kupce," *Supermarket* 1, no. 5 (September 1976): 8–9, at 8. Unless otherwise noted, all translations from foreign languages are my own.

8. "Revolucija u trgovini," *Supermarket* 1, no. 6 (October 1976): 8-9. The first self-service store in Yugoslavia had been opened in Ivanec in 1956, followed by a Zagreb store in 1957; the country's first supermarket opened in Belgrade in 1958 (Ibid., at 9).

9. Ibid. (emphasis in original).

10. On the connections between automobile culture and the rise of the supermarket, see Richard Longstreth, *The Drive-In, the Supermarket, and the Transformation of Commercial Space in Los Angeles, 1914–1941* (Cambridge, Mass.: MIT Press, 1999).

11. This was more the case in Hungary and, especially, the GDR, and less so in reformist Yugoslavia, where central control was abandoned in the 1950s in

favor of decentralized "worker self-management," in which enterprises were theoretically responsible for their own market decisions.

12. As Emanuela Scarpellini has observed in connection with the transfer of the American supermarket style to less-developed Italy, "modern forms of mass distribution were at the same time subject and object of the evolution of consumption, a powerful vehicle of new models of penetration of consumer culture." (Scarpellini, "Shopping American-Style: The Arrival of the Supermarket in Postwar Italy," *Enterprise & Society* 5, no. 4 [December 2004]: 625–68, at 665). Much the same sort of reciprocal relationships arose in socialist Eastern Europe as well.

13. Tracey Deutsch, "From 'Wild Animal Stores' to Women's Sphere: Supermarkets and the Politics of Mass Consumption, 1930–1950," *Business & Economic History* 28, no. 2 (Fall 1999): 143–53, at 151 and 143.

14. R. Krause, review of Herbert Karsten and Harri Peters, *Die Kaufhalle: Entwicklung, Leitung, Organisation, Technologie* (Berlin: Verlag Die Wirtschaft, 1972), in *Neue Werbung* 20, no. 2 (March 1973): 49.

15. Ibid.

16. F. S., "Švicarski supermarket: Mnoštvo usluga," *Supermarket* 1, no. 1 (May 1976): 15–17, at 15.

17. Loewy [Raymond] Associates, *Super Markets of the Sixties: The Loewy Report to SMI* (Chicago: Super Market Institute, 1960).

18. Károly Ravasz and György Kaminski, *A reklám kézikönyve* [Handbook of Advertising] (Budapest: Közgazdasági és Jogi Könyvkiadó, 1973), 222. Similarly, a commentator in East Germany's trade journal *Neue Werbung* (New Advertising) praised stores in which "special offers were accentuated in an imaginative (*phantasievoll*) way," at the same time cautioning that with this approach "there always exists the danger of a forest of signs" (Ria Liermann, "Das Haus, in dem man kauft," *Neue Werbung* 11, no. 12 (December 1964): 22–26, at 25).

19. See, e.g., *Neue Werbung* 23, no. 5 (September 1976): 34 (in-store displays for cheese products). In-store advertising and checkout displays in Budapest from the late 1970s and early 1980s document the use of foreign display materials, with the signs in German promoting the Coca-Cola "Refreshment Center" and the Vileda products slogan "This Is Modern Housekeeping" (Budapest City Archives [Budapest Főváros Levéltára, BFL]), BFL XXIX.1021, Kelenföldi Közért Vállalat, Box 26, envelopes labeled "Andrikó et 11064" and "11510 Boltnyitás 83 XX 13").

20. See, e.g., photographs documenting the in-store promotion, with tasting of free samples, for Mirelite-brand fruit cream products at one of the Közért chain's grocery shops in Budapest's Kelenföld district (store no. 11503, April 12, 1983). (Budapest City Archives, BFL XXIX.1021, Kelenföldi Közért Vállalat, Box 26, envelope marked "11503 Mirelite gyümölcskrém kóstoló '83 IV 2").

21. Stjepan Kempfel, quoted in D. B. K., "Pravome trgovcu najteze je reći 'nema'," *Supermarket* 1, no. 6 (October 1976): 13–15, at 14.

22. Allen Ginsberg, "A Supermarket in California" (1955), in *West of the West: Imagining California* ed. Leonard Michaels, David Reid, and Raquel Sherr (San Francisco: North Point Press, 1989), 181–82.

23. "Prodavači ili čuvari robe?" (interview with Marko Goluža), *Supermarket* 1, nos. 7/9 (November/December 1976): 20–22, at 22.

24. Scarpellini, "Shopping American-Style," 665.

25. See, e.g., Susan Reid, "Cold War in the Kitchen: Gender and De-

Stalinization of Consumer Taste in the Soviet Union under Khrushchev," *Slavic Review* 61 (Summer 2002): 211–52.

26. László Siklós, "Üzlet az árkádok alatt," *Tükör* 9, no. 5 (February 1, 1972): 15.

27. Marko Goluža, quoted in "Prodavači ili čuvari robe?," 22.

28. Advertisement for HO-Kaufhalle stores, *Für Dich*, no. 11 (March 1967): 41.

29. E. Sz., "Korszerűsödik-e a háztartási munka?," *Nők lapja* 24, no. 33 (August 12, 1972): 4.

30. Ines Tews, "Zwischen Rampe und Ladentisch," *Für Dich*, no. 7 (1984): 12–15, at 14.

31. Loewy [Raymond] Associates, *Super Markets of the Sixties: The Loewy Report to SMI*, vol. 2 (Chicago: Super Market Institute, 1960), plan Meat B-3.

32. K. O., "Régi boltok—mai üzletek," *Nők lapja* 19, no. 31 (August 5, 1967): 24–25 (emphasis added).

33. Günter Manz, "Wo gibt es Freiheit des Konsumenten?," *Neue Werbung* 7, no. 7 (July 1960): 4–5, at 5.

34. D. B. K., "Njegovo veličanstvo potrošač," *Supermarket* 1, no. 2 (June 1976): 11–13. For evidence of the socialist commercial specialists' attention to consumer desire, see, e.g., Gy. F., "És mit szól a vásárló?," *Kirakat* 7, no. 4 (April 1963): 8–9.

Chapter 14. Tools and Spaces

1. Oral history respondent number S-20-A, pps. 3–7 of transcript, in "Women, Ethnicity, and Mental Health: A Comparative Oral History Project, 1975–1977," Archives of Industrial Society, Hillman Library, University of Pittsburgh, call number AIS 78:11.

2. Oral history respondent number I-3-A, pps. 3–45 of transcript, in "Women, Ethnicity, and Mental Health."

3. Oral history respondents numbers I-23-A and I-23-B, in "Women, Ethnicity, and Mental Health.

4. Some recent, excellent examples of ethnic food scholarship are Tracy Poe, "Food, Culture, and Entrepreneurship among African-Americans, Italians, and Swedes in Chicago" (Ph.D. diss., Harvard University, 1999); Donna Gabaccia, *We Are What We Eat: Ethnic Food and the Making of Americans* (Cambridge, Mass.: Harvard University Press, 1998); and Hasia Diner, *Hungering for America: Italian, Irish, and Jewish Foodways in the Age of Migration* (Cambridge, Mass.: Harvard University Press, 2001). Poe and Gabaccia study the business history of food; Diner is more interested in cultural continuity between the Old and New Worlds.

5. Susan Porter Benson, *Household Accounts: Working-Class Family Economies in the Interwar United States* (Ithaca and London: Cornell University Press, 2007), 7–10.

6. Margaret F. Byington wrote *Homestead: The Households of a Mill Town* (1910; repr., Pittsburgh: University of Pittsburgh Press, 1974), a detailed and sympathetic account of steel-mill workers outside Pittsburgh, as part of the Pittsburgh Survey, a sociological analysis performed in the 1910s.

7. Katherine C. Grier, *Culture and Comfort: Parlor Making and Middle-Class Identity, 1850–1930* (Washington and London: Smithsonian Institution Press, 1988), 71.

8. See Ellen M. Plante, *The American Kitchen 1700 to the Present* (New York: Facts on File, 1995), for an account of the evolution of nineteenth- and twentieth-century middle-class kitchens.

9. Richard Plunz, *A History of Housing in New York City: Dwelling Type and Social Change in the American Metropolis* (New York: Columbia University Press, 1990), 22.

10. New York City had the most comprehensive housing legislation of any U.S. city at the time, due to its greater density. Housing legislation in other cities was even less likely to mention kitchens. An exception is the New Jersey Tenement House Acts of 1915 and 1925, which laid down detailed requirements for the installation of stoves, for the prevention of fire. See Lawrence Veiller, *Housing Conditions and Tenement Laws in Leading American Cities* (prepared for the Tenement House Commission) (New York: Evening Post Job Printing House, 1900).

11. Plunz, *History of Housing in New York City*, 21–29.

12. See ibid.; and Gwendolyn Wright, *Building the Dream: A Social History of Housing in America* (New York: Pantheon Books, 1981).

13. Lizabeth A. Cohen, "Embellishing a Life of Labor: An Interpretation of the Material Culture of American Working-Class Homes, 1885-1915," *Journal of American Culture* 3, no. 4 (Winter 1980) 752–75, quote at 763.

14. Susan Williams, *Savory Suppers and Fashionable Feasts: Dining in Victorian America* (New York: Pantheon Books, 1985), 56–57.

15. Byington, *Homestead*, 56.

16. Cohen, "Embellishing a Life of Labor," 763.

17. See Louise Bolard More, *Wage-Earners' Budgets* (New York: Henry Holt and Co., 1907), 132–34; Byington, *Homestead*; Grier, *Culture and Comfort*, 85–86.

18. According to Hine's notes, the Chinquananas had suffered many hardships—"[Jimmy] is the ninth child, six of whom are dead. Father abused the wife; drinks. Boy below grade; is bad at times"—that may have belied the stability of small business ownership.

19. Oral history respondent number S-1-A, p. 15 of transcript, in "Women, Ethnicity, and Mental Health.

20. See Priscilla J. Brewer, *From Fireplace to Cookstove: Technology and the Domestic Ideal in America* (Syracuse, N.Y.: Syracuse University Press, 2000), for an account of cookstoves. Gas became commonly available in urban working-class homes after 1900. Most often the gas was available only for lighting. Some homes had gas "meters" by which gas for lighting or cooking could be purchased by inserting quarters. See Susan Strasser, *Never Done: A History of American Housework* (New York: Pantheon Books, 1982), 71.

21. Stove price from *1897 Sears, Roebuck Catalogue* (1897; repr., Philadelphia: Chelsea House Publishers, 1968), 119. Wages from Paul H. Douglas, *Real Wages in the United States, 1890–1926* (Boston and New York: Houghton Mifflin Company, 1930): wages calculated from Table 73, p. 205; hourly earnings for all industry extrapolated to yearly and then to weekly by assuming full employment, 2,080 hours per year.

22. Mabel Hyde Kittredge, *Housekeeping Notes: How to Furnish and Keep House in a Tenement Flat* (Boston: Whitcomb and Barrows, 1911), 1.

23. Brewer, *From Fireplace to Cookstove*, 170.

24. Strasser, *Never Done*, 41.

25. Brewer, *From Fireplace to Cookstove*, 229.

26. *1985 Sears, Roebuck Catalogue*, 115, emphasis in original.

27. Abraham Cahan, "Woman of Valor," June 29, 1902, in Moses Rischin, *Grandma Never Lived in America: The New Journalism of Abraham Cahan* (Bloomington: Indiana University Press), 406. The (fictional) family who owns this stove earns two dollars per day by the combined work of the father and children.

28. Helen Campbell, *Prisoners of Poverty: Women Wage-Workers, Their Trades and Their Lives* (1887; repr., Westport, Conn.: Greenwood Press, 1970), 119.

29. Brewer, *From Fireplace to Cookstove*, 238.

30. Robert S. Lynd and Helen Merrell Lynd, *Middletown: A Study in Modern American Culture* (1929; San Diego, New York, and London: A Harvest Book, Harcourt Brace & Co., 1957), 98.

31. Oral history respondent number I-5-A, in "Women, Ethnicity, and Mental Health."

32. Strasser, *Never Done*, 100.

33. Edith Abbot, *The Tenements of Chicago, 1908–1935* (Chicago: University of Chicago Press, 1936), 59–61.

34. Dominic A. Pacyga, *Polish Immigrants and Industrial Chicago: Workers on the South Side, 1880–1922* (Columbus: Ohio State University Press, 1991), 70–71.

35. Byington, *Homestead*, 54.

36. Lynd and Lynd, *Middletown*, 97.

37. Mary Hinman Abel, "A Study in Social Economics: The Story of the New England Kitchen," in Ellen Henrietta Richards, *Plain Words about Food: The Rumford Kitchen Leaflets* (Boston: Home Science Publishing Co., 1899), 137–38. The account did not describe how, exactly, the people got the hot water back to their homes, but it was probably carried in buckets. Customers of the New England Kitchen had to bring their own containers to buy cooked food by the pound or gallon (commonly buckets, basins, and jars), and most working-class families would have had metal buckets in which to carry water, lunches, or beer.

38. S. J. Kleinberg, "Technology and Women's Work: The Lives of Working-Class Women in Pittsburgh, 1870–1900," *Labor History* 17, no. 1 (Winter 19): 58–72, quote at 62.

39. Ibid., 63.

40. Ibid.

41. Jeanne Boydston makes a similar point for women in American cities in the early nineteenth century in *Home and Work: Housework, Wages, and the Ideology of Labor in the Early Republic* (New York and Oxford: Oxford University Press, 1990).

42. James R. Barrett, *Work and Community in the Jungle: Chicago's Packinghouse Workers, 1894–1922* (Urbana and Chicago: University of Illinois Press, 1987). Barrett notes that neighborhoods such as Packingtown were unevenly dense, with areas of high density around packinghouses and less density in the areas between (72–74).

43. *Cost of Living in the United States*, Bulletin No. 357 (May 1924), U.S. Department of Labor and the Bureau of Labor Statistics (Washington, D.C.: U.S. Government Printing Office, 1924).

44. *Sixth Annual Report of the Commissioner of Labor, 1890: Cost of Production: Iron, Steel, Coal, et cetera* (Washington, D.C.: U.S. Government Printing Office, 1891), 806–10. The report was organized by industry and did not specify a town or region of Pennsylvania. Pig-iron production took place mostly in the southern central part of the state, probably in small towns or semirural areas similar in nature to the outskirts of Pittsburgh. The report indicated that 36 percent of pig-iron workers in Illinois kept pigs and that 53 percent of those in New York did so.

45. Barrett, *Work and Community in the Jungle*, 97.

46. Data from the *Abstract of Census of Manufactures, 1919*, in Hazel Kyrk and Joseph Stancliffe Davis, *The American Baking Industry, 1849–1923, As Shown in the Census Reports* (Stanford, Calif.: Stanford University Press, 1925), 82. See population figures from the U.S. Census Bureau at www.census.gov: http://www.census.gov/population/censusdata/table-2.pdf, accessed April 15, 2008.

47. Population density figures at http://www.census.gov/population/census data/table-2.pdf, accessed April 15, 2008.

48. Benson, *Household Accounts*, 141.

49. Isabel Bevier, "Nutrition Investigations in Pittsburg, Pennsylvania 1894–1896," USDA Office of Experiment Stations, Bulletin No. 52 (Washington, D.C.: U.S. Government Printing Office, 1898).

50. For a discussion of the home and commerce, see Wendy Gamber, *The Boardinghouse in Nineteenth-Century America* (Baltimore: Johns Hopkins University Press, 2007).

51. Ken Albala, *Food in Early Modern Europe* (Westport, Conn.: Greenwood Press, 2003), 96.

52. Tracy N. Poe, "The Labour and Leisure of Food Production as a Mode of Ethnic Identity Building among Italians in Chicago, 1890–1940," *Rethinking History* 51, no. 1 (2001): 131–48.

53. Elizabeth S. D. Engelhardt, "Beating the Biscuits in Appalachia: Race, Class, and Gender Politics of Women Baking Bread," in *Cooking Lessons: The Politics of Gender and Food*, ed. Sherrie A. Innes (Lanham, Md.: Rowman and Littlefield Publishers, Inc., 2001), 160.

54. Robert Coit Chapin, *The Standard of Living among Workingmen's Families in New York City* (New York: Charities Publication Committee, 1909), 145.

Chapter 15. Wheeling One's Groceries around the Store

This research was supported by a Fulbright grant in 2004. I wish to thank the French-American Commission, David Stark and Monique Girard at Columbia University, Deborra Richardson and the members of the Archives Center of the Smithsonian Institution, and David Shayt, also at the Smithsonian Institution, for their invaluable help in this research. I feel especially indebted to Madeleine Akrich and Fabian Muniesa at the Ecole des Mines de Paris for their support while writing this essay. I also want to warmly thank Liz Libbrecht for her translation of the first version of this chapter, and Phillip Scranton and Roger Horowitz, whose detailed readings and comments helped improve the text. Some elements of this research have been used in Catherine Grandclément and Franck Cochoy, "Histoires du chariot de supermarché: Ou comment emboîter le pas de la consommation de masse," *Vingtième Siècle* 91 (2006): 77–93.

1. This chapter draws on the following three main sources: the Telescoping Shopping Cart Collection at the Smithsonian Institution Archives Center, hereafter referred to as TSCC; the trade journal *Super Market Merchandising*, which began to appear in November 1936, hereafter referred to as *SMM*; and U.S. patent records.

2. See Thomas P. Hughes, *Networks of Power: Electrification in Western Society, 1880–1930* (Baltimore: Johns Hopkins University Press, 1983), 79–80.

3. See Max M. Zimmerman, *The Super Market: A Revolution in Distribution* (New York: McGraw-Hill Book Company, 1955); Susan Strasser, *Satisfaction Guaranteed: The Making of the American Mass Market* (Washington, D.C.: Smithsonian Institution Press, 1989); Richard S. Tedlow, *New and Improved: The Story of Mass Marketing in America* (New York: Basic Books, 1990); James M. Mayo, *The American Grocery Store: The Business Evolution of an Architectural Space* (Westport, Conn.: Greenwood Press, 1993); and Richard Longstreth, *The Drive-In, the Supermarket, and the Transformation of Commercial Space in Los Angeles, 1914–1941* (Cambridge, Mass.: MIT Press, 1999).

4. See, for instance, Wiebe Bijker and John Law, eds., *Shaping Technology / Building Society: Studies in Sociotechnical Change* (Cambridge, Mass.: MIT Press, 1992); Wiebe Bijker, Thomas P. Hughes, and Trevor Pinch, eds., *The Social Construction of Technological Systems: New Directions in the Sociology and History of Technology* (Cambridge, Mass.: MIT Press, 1989); and Michel Callon, John Law, and Arie Rip, eds., *Mapping the Dynamics of Science and Technology: Sociology of Science in the Real World* (London: Macmillan, 1986).

5. Madeleine Akrich, "The De-Scription of Technical Objects," in *Shaping Technology / Building Society*, ed. Bijker and Law, 205–24.

6. Michel Callon, "Techno-Economic Networks and Irreversibility," in *A Sociology of Monsters: Essays on Power, Technology and Domination*, ed. John Law (London: Routledge, 1991), 132–64.

7. Madeleine Akrich, Michel Callon, and Bruno Latour, "The Key to Success in Innovation, Part I: The Art of Interessement, Part II: The Art of Choosing Good Spokespersons," *International Journal of Innovation Management* 6, no. 2 (2002): 187–206, 207–25.

8. Terry P. Wilson, *The Cart That Changed the World: The Career of Sylvan N. Goldman* (Norman: University of Oklahoma Press, 1978).

9. Richard S. Tedlow, review of Wilson, *Cart That Changed the World*, *Business History Review* 54, no. 1 (1980): 135–36.

10. Lisa Tolbert, "The Aristocracy of the Market Basket: Self-Service Food Shopping in the New South," this volume.

11. Wilson, *Cart That Changed the World*, 78.

12. Ibid., 87, 88.

13. As confirmation, Goldman's early account of his carts' launch does not include the shills episode. No "mediators" were present the first week to initiate the carts' use. It was only during the second week that a hostess presented the carts and showed customers how to use them. See Zimmerman, *Super Market*, 59.

14. Akrich, "De-Scription of Technical Objects"; Madeleine Akrich and Bruno Latour, "A Summary of a Convenient Vocabulary for the Semiotics of Human and Nonhuman Assemblies," in *Shaping Technology / Building Society*, ed. Bijker and Law, 259–63.

15. Henry Petroski, *The Evolution of Useful Things* (New York: Knopf, 1992); Henry Petroski, *Small Things Considered: Why There Is No Perfect Design* (New York: Knopf, 2003).

16. Donald A. Norman, *The Design of Everyday Things* (New York: Doubleday/ Currency, 1990).

17. Wilson, *Cart That Changed the World*, 82.

18. Ibid., 83.

19. I am very grateful to Lisa Tolbert for pointing me to a patent for a similar 1919 store layout, in Louisiana (patent no. 1,337,050 filed on September 6, 1919). Another system equipping the store rather than the customer was briefly in use at Upham's Corner Market in Boston. Clerks at various counters put the customers' shopping on basins that were brought to a central cashier point through "an overhead conveyor belt kept moving by electrically operated rollers beneath it." See William H. Marnell, *Once upon a Store: A Biography of the World's First Supermarket* (New York: Herder and Herder, 1971), 33.

20. See, for instance, Max M. Zimmerman, "Building History's Greatest Food Market," *SMM* 1, no. 1 (1936): 4–5, 20–21; "Getting the Most Out of the Super Market," *SMM* 1, no. 2 (1936): 4–5, 12–13; "Eba's Introduce 2 Supers at Seattle," *SMM* 1, no. 19 (1937): 19; and "Shopping Made Easy in Bohack Market," *SMM*

2, no. 3 (1937): 18. See also Zimmerman, *Super Market*, 26–28. Advertisements for basket carriers were published in *SMM* 2, no. 2 (1937): 5; 2, no. 3 (1937): 16; 2, no. 4 (1937): 9, 15; 2, no. 5 (1937): 12, 27, 28; and elsewhere.

21. It is interesting to note that, according to Zimmerman's descriptions in 1936, basket carriers were offered to customers at any place on the selling floor; therefore, the assigned park area for carts was still to be invented, and customers still had to get accustomed to it. The problem of saving parking space had not yet been identified. See Zimmerman's account in "Building History's Greatest Food Market."

22. *SMM* 2, no. 5 (1937): 28.

23. The corresponding object was first advertised in *SMM* 2, no. 10 (1937): 36. Two months later the Folding Basket Carrier Corp. began to go backward and advertised, along with the first cart, a standard basket carrier with both baskets removable (2, no. 12 (1937): 27). The two types of Goldman's cart were, however, displayed at the first Super Market Convention in September 1937 (photograph in *SMM* 2, no. 10 (1937): 28). Goldman filed a patent for the second cart on March 14, 1938 (patent no. 2,196,914), which does not mention the first one, as if Goldman had already conceived of erasing his first cart from historical records. The second cart and patent correspond to the simplified, "historical" cart given to the Smithsonian Institution.

24. Wilson, *Cart That Changed the World*, 103.

25. Here I draw on material from the TSCC, in particular: "A Brief History of the Telescoping Grocery Carts," document signed by Leslie S. Simmons, personal representative, Edith Watson Estate, Box 1, Folder 1; private correspondence of Watson and Taylor spouses, Box 1, Folder 5; documents related to a preliminary search of patent for Telescoping Grocery Carts, August 28 and 31, 1946, Box 1, Folder 6; "Letters Patent no. 2 479 530," Box 2, Folder 1; "Supplemental Statement with Law Brief Annexed of Orla E. and Edith Watson in Support of Their Claim on Form 843 for a Refund of Federal Income Taxes Paid for the Calendar Year 1950, Containing 33 Pages," June 15, 1953, Box 2, Folder 8; "Summary of Orla E. Watson's Activity with Respect to Application Serial No. 699 777, Filed September 27, 1946, Issued as Patent no. 2 479 530 August 16, 1949," November 13, 1950, Box 2, Folder 9; accounting documents of the Western Machine Company, July and August 1946, Box 2, Folder 10; witnesses' sworn statements for the interference procedure, 1949, Box 2, Folder 11; Watson's drawing of June 3, 1946, "Oversize Platters."

26. It is worthwhile noting here that Watson was a man of the flux industry (he worked in the oil sector and in air-conditioning systems and was used to pumps, valves, fluids, and circulation) and thus may have had a potentially different approach to shopping carts than the one developed in the retail sector. Sylvan N. Goldman, a grocer, and American Wire Form and United Steel and Wire, two basket manufacturers, based their invention on the market basket. However, a market basket implies a neat difference between stock and flow: when not in use, market baskets are piled up, out of use. Orla E. Watson approached the issue primarily as a problem of fluidity. With the back flap, he devised a kind of "valve principle" for baskets, which maintains a horizontal continuity between the cart in use and the cart out of use.

27. W. Brian Arthur, "Competing Technologies, Increasing Returns, and Lock-In by Historical Events," *Economic Journal* 99, no. 394 (1989): 116–31; Paul A. David, "Clio and the Economics of QWERTY," *American Economic Review* 75, no. 2 (1985): 332–37.

28. See, for instance L. L. Shoemaker, "Checking Out the Customer," *SMM* 2, no. 10 (1937): 44–45, 47; "The Architect's Board—The Checkout Stand," *SMM* 11, no. 8 (1946): 124–25; S. Goldman, "Achieving an Efficient Checkout System," *SMM* 11, no. 10 (1946): 89–93; National Cash Register Company brochure, c. 1947, TSCC, Box 2, Folder 5.

29. Hughes, *Networks of Power*.

30. Relevant sources from the TSCC for this episode, in addition to the above-mentioned, are: business correspondence between Watson, Taylor, and O'Donnell, Box 1, Folder 4 (especially O'Donnell's letters to Taylor, December 7, 8, and 22, 1947; O'Donnell's letter to Watson, November 5, 1946; and Watson's letter to O'Donnell, Hanson, and Taylor, October 18, 1947); "O'Donnell & Watson Agreement," October 5, 1946, and "Partnership Agreement," November 30, 1946, Box 2, Folder 10.

31. *SMM* 12, no. 10 (1947): 126, and 12, no. 11 (1947): 209.

32. Goldman filed two patents applications, respectively, in May 1948 and January 1949. This story is reported from the following TSCC documents: "A Brief History of the Telescoping Grocery Carts," Box 1, Folder 1; "Declaration of Interference," Box 2, Folder 2; "License Agreements," Box 2, Folder 7; "Brief for Plaintiffs on Rehearing," *Orla E. Watson and Telescope Carts, Inc. v. Henry Heil and J. Henry Heil*, civil action no. 4946, United States District Court, District of Maryland, October 3, 1953, document submitted to the judge by Watson's attorneys in the 1952–53 patent contest, Box 2, Folder 9.

33. Main documents from the TSCC for this episode are: letter from F. E. Taylor to N. W. Mailman at John Chatillon & Son, March 27, 1952, Box 1, Folder 3; agreement and license agreement between Telescope Carts, Inc., Orla E. Watson, and Folding Carrier Corp, January 1, 1952; supplemental agreement (same parties), January 7, 1952; assignment of royalties between Telescope Carts, Inc., Orla E. Watson, and Charles E. Frances, trustee under the Morris Dreyfus Trusts, January 8, 1952; agreement and assignment of royalties between Telescope Carts, Inc., Orla E. Watson, and W. A. Colement, trustee under the Morris Dreyfus Trusts, September 12, 1953, Box 2, Folder 7; opinion filed on October 23, 1952, Chesnut, District Judge, in civil action no. 4946, district court for the District of Maryland, *Orla E. Watson and Telescope Carts, Inc. v. Henry Heil and J. Henry Heil*, Box 2, Folder 9.

34. Bruno Latour, "Where Are the Missing Masses? The Sociology of a Few Mundane Artifacts," in *Shaping Technology/Building Society*, ed. Bijker and Law, 225–58.

35. Callon, "Techno-Economic Networks and Irreversibility."

Contributors

J. L. Anderson earned his Ph.D. at Iowa State University in agricultural history and rural studies and teaches history at Mount Royal College. He is the author of *Industrializing the Corn Belt: Agriculture, Technology, and the Environment* (2009).

Warren Belasco teaches American studies at the University of Maryland, Baltimore County. He is the author of *Appetite for Change: How the Counterculture Took on the Food Industry* (2006), *Meals to Come: A History of the Future of Food* (2006), and *Food: The Key Concepts* (2008). He is the coeditor of *Food Nations: Selling Taste in Consumer Societies* (2002) and senior editor of *The Oxford Encyclopedia of Food and Drink in America* (2004). He is also chief editor of *Food, Culture and Society: An International Journal of Multidisciplinary Research*.

Kelly Feltault is a doctoral candidate in anthropology at American University. She holds a master's degree in folklore and oral history from the University of North Carolina, and has worked in applied anthropology and international development. Her dissertation examines HACCP as a global governance standard to understand how companies and states coordinate and sustain global crabmeat networks and the creation of competing quality conventions.

Andrew C. Godley is Professor of Business History at the Centre for International Business History, University of Reading. He has published widely in the area of retailing and marketing history, including *Jewish Immigrant Entrepreneurship in London and New York, 1880–1914: Enterprise and Culture* (2001), a study of cultural assimilation among Jewish immigrants in the garment trade.

Catherine Grandclément has a doctorate in sociology from the Ecole des Mines de Paris (France). She investigates the construction of contemporary shopping through a material, historical anthropology of the supermarket. She has published (with F. Cochoy) "Publicizing Goldilocks' Choice at the Supermarket: The Political Work of Shopping Packs, Carts and Talk," in Bruno Latour and Peter Weibel, eds., *Making Things Public: Atmospheres of Democracy* (2005).

Katherine C. Grier is Professor in the Department of History, University of Delaware, and Director of the Museum Studies Program. She is the author of *Pets in America: A History* (2007) and executive editor of *Winterthur Portfolio*, the journal of American material culture studies.

Shane Hamilton is Assistant Professor of History at the University of Georgia. His work on the political economy of industrial agriculture has appeared in *Agricultural History* and *Business History Review* and in the forthcoming book, *Trucking Country: The Road to America's Wal-Mart Economy*.

Roger Horowitz is Associate Director of the Center for the History of Business, Technology, and Society at the Hagley Museum and Library and Secretary-Treasurer of the Business History Conference. His most recent book is *Putting Meat on the American Table: Taste, Technology, Transformation* (2005).

Patrick Hyder Patterson is an assistant professor in the Department of History at the University of California, San Diego. A specialist in the history of popular culture and everyday life in Eastern Europe and the Balkans, he is currently working on a book-length study of consumption and market culture in socialist Hungary, Yugoslavia, and the German Democratic Republic.

Jeffrey M. Pilcher is Professor of History at the University of Minnesota. His books include, *¡Que vivan los tamales! Food and the Making of Mexican Identity* (1998), *The Sausage Rebellion: Public Health, Private Enterprise, and Meat in Mexico City, 1890–1917* (2006), and *Food in World History* (2006). He is currently writing a book entitled *Planet Taco: The Global Borderlands of Mexican Cuisine.*

Jonathan Rees is Associate Professor of History at Colorado State University–Pueblo. His article on the safety of early ice manufacturing plants appears in the July 2005 issue of *Technology and Culture.* He is working on a book about the American ice and refrigeration industries from 1805 to 1930.

Jenny Leigh Smith is an assistant professor in the School of History, Technology, and Society at the Georgia Institute of Technology. Broadly interested in issues of food, farming, and the environmental impact of industrial activity, she is currently completing a manuscript provisionally entitled "Animal Farms," about the industrialization of Soviet farm animals.

Lisa C. Tolbert is Associate Professor of History at the University of North Carolina at Greensboro and the author of *Constructing Townscapes: Space and Society in Antebellum Tennessee* (1999).

Katherine Leonard Turner received her Ph.D. in 2008 from the University of Delaware. Her dissertation, "Good Food for Little Money: Food and Cooking among Working-Class Urban Americans, 1875–1930," is about the ways working-class families met the challenges of preparing food in cramped apartments, combining home food production with ready-to-eat food prepared and sold in the neighborhood.

Richard R. Wilk is Professor of Anthropology and Gender Studies at Indiana University. He has conducted field research on energy use in households in California, on western consumer goods in West African markets, and on household decision making, migration, development, and consumer culture in the Central American country of Belize. He is the author of *Economies and Cultures: Foundations of Economic Anthropology.*

Bridget Williams is Visiting Research Fellow at the Centre for International Business History, University of Reading, and was for many years the archivist at J. Sainsbury PLC and was instrumental in establishing the Sainsbury Archive. She is the author of *The Best Butter in the World: A History of Sainsbury's* (1994, reprinted 2008).